RELIGION AND THE AMERICAN CONSTITUTIONAL EXPERIMENT

ESSENTIAL RIGHTS AND LIBERTIES

JOHN WITTE JR.
EMORY UNIVERSITY

A Member of the Perseus Books Group

Copyright © 2000 by Westview Press, A Member of the Perseus Books Group

Published in 2000 in the United States of America by Westview Press, 5500 Central Avenue, Boulder, Colorado 80301-2877, and in the United Kingdom by Westview Press, 12 Hid's Copse Road, Cumnor Hill, Oxford OX2 9JJ

Find us on the World Wide Web at www.westviewpress.com

Library of Congress Cataloging-in-Publication Data
Witte, John, 1959–
  Religion and the American constitutional experiment : essential
rights and liberties / John Witte Jr.
    p. cm.
  Includes bibliographical references and index.
  ISBN 0-8133-3305-9 (hc).—ISBN 0-8133-3306-7 (pb)
    1. Freedom of religion—United States—History.   2. Church and
State—United States—History.   3. Freedom of religion—United
States.   4. Church and State—United States.   5. United States
Constitution.   1st Amendment.   I. Title.
KF4783.Z9.W58   1999
342.73'0852—dc21   99-34552
                                                                                                                              CIP

The paper used in this publication meets the requirements of the American National Standard for Permanence of Paper for Printed Library Materials Z39.48-1984.

PERSEUS
POD
ON DEMAND   10   9   8   7   6   5   4   3

RELIGION AND THE AMERICAN CONSTITUTIONAL EXPERIMENT

For Eliza Ellison,
my angel

CONTENTS

TABLES AND FIGURES

Tables

Figures

PREFACE

This volume is at once an introduction for students, a provocation for specialists, and an invitation for the public to view afresh the American experiment in religious rights and liberties. Historical, doctrinal, and comparative methods are combined to tell the unique American story of religious freedom—from the formation of the First Amendment in 1789 to the Supreme Court's most recent interpretations of its guarantees of disestablishment and free exercise of religion.

This volume is calibrated to press uninitiated readers beyond simple incantation of Jefferson's wall of separation as the source and summary of the First Amendment. It is also calculated to lift seasoned readers above simple lamentation over the Supreme Court's recent First Amendment cases. I have sought to provide just enough historical, case law, and comparative analysis for readers to appreciate the ingenuity of the American founders and the intricacies of the experiment that they unleashed. I have also sought to provide just enough of an argument for the principled integration of religious liberty for readers to see the robust promise that the American experiment still holds.

This volume, however, deliberately sidesteps most of the thickets of casuistry in which First Amendment scholarship has become heavily entangled of late. Casuistry, of course, is essential for the constant reformation of the First Amendment. And Summae Jurisprudentiae are essential for the careful preservation of the best reforms to come from the same. But accessible condensation of this specialized material is also essential lest we become tempted to academic condescension. And a summary of our jurisprudence is essential lest we lose sight of the vigor and vitality of the American story of religious freedom. Such is the task of this volume.

I would like to express my appreciation to Spencer Carr, former Executive Editor at Westview Press, and his successor, Leo Wiegman at Westview Press, now an imprint of the Perseus Books Group, who commissioned this volume and worked so assiduously to bring it into print.

Several friends and colleagues lent liberally of their advice and criticisms. I would like especially to thank Thomas C. Arthur, Thomas C. Berg, Harold J. Berman, A. Morgan Cloud, Daniel L. Dreisbach, Frederick Mark Gedicks, T. Jeremy Gunn, and Douglas Laycock, who each read large portions of this volume and made numerous edifying suggestions and criticisms. I hope that the quality of this volume begins to approximate the quality of their advice.

A number of students at Emory Law School provided me with able and ample assistance in teaching my course on "American Constitutional Law: Church and State" over the past decade and in preparing this volume over the past few months. The names that come to mind are Scott Blevins, Blaine Bortnick, Bruce Frohnen, M. Christian Green, Jay Todd Hahn, Jeffrey Hammond, Heidi Hansan, David Hilts, Henry Kimmel, Tamara McCracken, Joel Nichols, Woodruff Polk, Audra Pontes, Stuart Poppel, Jeri Nazary Sute, Elizabeth Swinton, Jason Waite, and Gordon Young, all of whom I wish to thank. I owe a special word of thanks to Joel Nichols for his efforts in preparing the tables that appear in Appendices 2 and 3. Given my porous gray matter, I may well have forgotten the names of one or two other student assistants over the years and ask their indulgence in being thanked anonymously rather than personally.

I would like to thank my friend and colleague, Dean Howard O. Hunter, for his unstinting support of me throughout my time at Emory and for his generosity in granting me a sabbatical leave this year to complete this volume, among other projects. I would also like to thank Will Haines, Holliday Osborne, and Rosalie Sanderson of the Emory Law Library for their impeccable library support, and Louise Jackson for her faithful secretarial services.

Prototypes of some of the material presented in this volume have appeared in print elsewhere. I express my gratitude to the publishers for permission to include revised excerpts from the following:

"Church and State," in *Encyclopedia of Religion,* ed. Mircea Eliade (New York: MacMillan and Free Press, 1987), 3:489–505 (coauthored with Harold J. Berman);

"How to Govern a City on the Hill: The Early Puritan Contribution to American Constitutionalism," *Emory Law Journal* 39 (1990): 41–64;

"Law, Religion, and Human Rights," *Columbia Human Rights Law Review* 28 (1996): 1–31;

"Tax Exemption of Church Property: Historical Anomaly or Valid Constitutional Practice?" *Southern California Law Review* 64 (1991): 363–415;

"The Essential Rights and Liberties of Religion in the American Constitutional Experiment," *Notre Dame Law Review* 71 (1996): 371–445;

"The Integration of Religious Liberty," *Michigan Law Review* 90 (1992): 1363–1383.

John Witte Jr.

INTRODUCTION

Thomas Jefferson once described the new religious liberty clauses of 1776–1789 as a "fair" and "novel experiment."[1] These new state and federal guarantees defied the millennium-old assumptions inherited from Western Europe—that one form of Christianity must be established in a community and that the state must protect and support it against other religions. America would no longer suffer such prescriptions and proscriptions of religion by government, Jefferson declared. All forms of Christianity must now stand on their own feet and on an equal footing with all other faiths. Their survival and growth must turn on the cogency of their word, not the coercion of the sword, on the faith of their members, not the force of the law.

This bold constitutional experiment in granting religious liberty to all remains in place, and in progress, in the United States. From 1776 to 1940, principal governance of the experiment lay with the states. The First Amendment applied by its terms only to the federal government—"*Congress* shall make no law respecting an establishment of religion, or prohibiting the free exercise thereof." And these guarantees were only superficially enforced in the federal courts. Most questions of religious liberty were left to the states to resolve, each in accordance with its own state constitution. After 1940, principal control of the experiment shifted abruptly to the federal courts. In *Cantwell v. Connecticut* (1940) and *Everson v. Board of Education* (1947), the United States Supreme Court applied the First Amendment religion clauses to the states, reading its guarantees into the general liberty guarantee of the Fourteenth Amendment—"No state shall deprive any person of . . . liberty . . . without due process of law."[2] In more than 150 cases since 1940, the Court has sought to create a national law on religious liberty binding on all federal, state, and local officials.

The American experiment in religious liberty initially inspired exuberant rhetoric throughout the young republic and beyond. Preacher Elhanan Winchester declared proudly to a London audience in 1788:

> There is but one country in the world where liberty, and especially religious liberty, is so much enjoyed as in these kingdoms, and that is the United States

1

of America: there religious liberty is in the highest perfection. All stand there on equal ground. There are no religious establishments, no preference of one denomination of Christians above another. The constitution knows no difference between one good man, and another. A man may be chosen there to the highest civil offices, without being obliged to give any account of his faith, subscribe [to] any religious test, or go to the communion-table of any church.[3]

Yale President Ezra Stiles predicted robustly in 1783:

> The United States will embosom all the religious sects or denominations in christendom. Here they may all enjoy their whole respective systems of worship and church government, complete. . . . All religious denominations will be independent of one another . . . and having, on account of religion, no superiority as to secular powers and civil immunities, they will cohabit together in harmony, and I hope, with a most generous catholicism and benevolence.[4]

Dozens of such enthusiastic endorsements of the American experiment can be found among the founders' writings of the later eighteenth century.

Today, the American experiment inspires far more criticism than praise. The United States does "embosom" all religious sects and denominations, not only from Christendom but from around the world—more than 1,000 religious denominations, in which more than two-thirds of the American population claims membership.[5] American citizens and groups do enjoy remarkable freedom of religion—too much freedom, according to some commentators. But the laboratory of the United States Supreme Court, which has directed the American experiment for the past half century, no longer inspires confidence. The Court's recent holdings against Jews, Muslims, and Native Americans have evoked withering attacks in the popular and professional media.[6] Indeed, the Court's entire record on religious rights and liberties has become vilified for its lack of consistent and coherent principles and its uncritical use of mechanical tests and misleading metaphors. "Religion Clause jurisprudence," writes one leading commentator, "has been described on all sides, and even by Justices themselves, as unprincipled, incoherent, and unworkable. . . . [T]he Court must now grapple seriously with the formidable interpretive problems that were overlooked or given short shrift in the past. The task is an urgent one, for it concerns nothing less than the cultural foundations of our experiment in ordered liberty."[7]

The United States Supreme Court is not the only body that is now "grappling" with the experiment. In the past few years, the testing ground seems to be shifting away from the federal government to the states and away from the courts to the legislatures—a trend encouraged by the generous nods toward federalism and separation of powers in several recent Supreme Court opinions. State legislatures and courts of late have become bolder in conducting their own experiments in religious liberty, which seem calculated to revisit, if not rechallenge, prevailing Supreme Court interpretations of the disestablishment and free exercise clauses. At the same time, Congress has issued a number of laws to defend the free exercise rights of particular claimants—Native Americans, religious employers, religious school groups, and religious military personnel, among others. With the passage of the Religious Freedom Restoration Act of 1993, Congress took the further bold step of defining the appropriate free exercise analysis to be used in future cases—only to have the Supreme Court overturn the statute on the same principles of federalism and separation of powers that it had held out to Congress in earlier cases.[8]

These recent developments have bred not only frustration about the vast inconsistencies of the American experiment but doubts about its very efficacy. Leading constitutional scholars now write openly that "the entire body of modern constitutional discourse on the subject of religious freedom" is "idolatrous," "founded on empty premises and false assumptions," and ensnared in "an irresolvable rhetorical dialectic between secular individualism and religious communitarianism."[9] Urgent talk of a comprehensive new constitutional amendment on religious freedom is again upon us.[10]

When an experiment becomes a "kind of wandering inquiry, without any regular system of operations," wrote Francis Bacon, the seventeenth-century "father" of the experimental method, "prudence commends three correctives."[11] First, said Bacon, we must "return to first principles and axioms," reassess them in light of our experience, and "if necessary refine them." Second, we must assess "our experience with the experiment" in light of these first principles, to determine where "the experiment should be adjusted." Third, we must "compare our experiments" and experiences with those of fellow scientists, and where we see in that comparison "superior techniques," we must "amend our experiments" and even our first principles accordingly.[12] Although Bacon offered these prudential instructions principally to correct scientific experiments that had gone awry, his instructions commend themselves to legal and political experiments as well—as he himself sought to demonstrate in seventeenth-century England.[13]

This volume applies Bacon's prudential instructions to the American constitutional experiment in religious rights and liberties—an experiment that today is indeed, as Bacon put it, "wandering, without any regular system of operations."

Applying Bacon's first instruction, Chapters 1–4 return to the "first principles" that inspired and informed the original American experiment. Looking backward from 1789, these chapters survey the theological and political movements that were most critical to the formation of the new constitutional laws on religious liberty—the Puritan, Evangelical, Enlightenment, and Republican movements, each viewed in broader European context. These four groups of founders, I argue, while often independent and wide-ranging in their efforts, helped to forge the "first principles" of the American experiment in religious liberty.

Six principles stand out in these founders' writings: (1) liberty of conscience; (2) free exercise of religion; (3) religious pluralism; (4) religious equality; (5) separation of church and state; and (6) disestablishment of religion. These six principles were, in effect, "incorporated" into the First Amendment religion clauses as well as a number of the other state constitutional bills of rights. They remain the guiding principles of the American experiment today—in their original form, and in provocative new constructions and combinations such as "religious accommodationism," "equal access," and "substantive neutrality."

Applying Bacon's second instruction, Chapters 5–9 analyze the American constitutional experience in light of these first principles. I first review the plight of these principles in the state constitutions before 1940 and in the 32 cases on religious liberty that reached United States Supreme Court before 1940. I then analyze the more than 150 free exercise and disestablishment cases issued since 1940. These modern cases have served both to enhance and to frustrate the American experiment, I argue—in part because these two lines of cases have not been effectively merged, in part because the Court has often dealt inconsistently with the first principles of the experiment.

In its free exercise cases from 1940 to 1980, the Court sought to incorporate the full range of first principles into its analysis—catalyzing great advances in the protection of religious rights and liberties. Since the mid-1980s, however, the Court has reduced the free exercise clause to a single principle of "neutrality," which has effectively neutralized the free exercise clause's protection of religious liberty. It is no small irony that today the free speech clause of the First Amendment affords considerably more protection to religion than the free exercise clause.

The trend in disestablishment law has been exactly the opposite. In its disestablishment cases from 1947 to 1982, the Court was almost single-minded in its devotion to the principle of separation of church and state—sometimes yielding secularist dicta and decisions that seemed anomalous to a nation so widely devoted to a public religion and a religious public. Since the mid-1980s, however, the Court has opened its disestablishment calculus to a wider range of first principles, which the Court is now struggling mightily to integrate. To illustrate these trends in First Amendment analysis and to demonstrate the possibilities for a more multiprincipled understanding of religious liberty, Chapter 9 offers a close study of the history and constitutional conundrums of tax exemption of religious property.

Applying Bacon's third instruction, Chapter 10 compares the principles and practices of the American experiment with prevailing international norms of religious rights and liberties. International human rights norms, I argue, are no panacea to the current constitutional confusion, but they do open promising new pathways toward a more integrated approach to the First Amendment religion clauses. The priority given to liberty of conscience, free exercise, and equality principles at international law might well serve as a prototype for the integration of the guarantees of free exercise and disestablishment. The firm insistence of international human rights instruments that state abridgments of religious rights be both "necessary" and "proportionate" encourages a stricter free exercise test than currently in vogue. The growing emphasis at international law on the rights of religious groups and on the need for affirmative state action toward them encourages greater protection of religious minorities in America and greater cooperation of religious and political officials on vital social tasks. The international doctrine of "a margin of appreciation" for local religious and political practices could be put to good use in our federalist system of government. The international debate over the "universalism versus relativism" of human rights has profound implications for the American debate concerning federal and state jurisdiction over religious rights.

The methodology at work in this volume is more expansionist than revisionist in intention. The argument that the First Amendment religion clauses reflect both the theology and the politics of the eighteenth century is not new. But I do give voice to some religious groups and theological sources that have not been conventionally included among the founders. Moreover, I argue that a more candid acknowledgment of the theological pedigree of the First Amendment is an instance of constitutional correction, not "religious correctness."[14] We cannot hold up as normative those eighteenth-century texts that happen to anticipate contemporary secular fashions and deprecate others that do not have modern forms. We cannot pretend that the First Amendment is a purely secular trope, or just another category of liberty and autonomy, and expect citizens to believe in it.[15] It is better, in my view, to acknowledge the explicitly religious sources that helped to form the First Amendment and then seek to include more religious and nonreligious voices and values in the modern constitutional dialogue.[16] It is better, in Judge John Noonan's words, for judges not "to pretend that they are neutrals somehow free from all prejudice when they decide intrachurch disputes, determine who has a religious claim, or balance the State's interest in relation to the First Amendment."[17]

The First Amendment, in both its formation and its enforcement, is predicated in part on theological visions and values. It has to be. To insist that it is merely a neutral instrument, bleached of all religious qualities, only invites secular prejudices to become constitutional prerogatives. If we have learned anything from "postmodernism," it is that each narrative has its own nomos—its own beliefs, values, and ideals.[18] If we have learned anything from "legal realism," it is that judges in constitutional cases do not operate with mechanical logic but with feelings, passions, and prejudices. A more candid acknowledgment of these religious metasources of the First Amendment law on the books and in action enriches more than endangers our understanding.[19]

The six principles of religious liberty analyzed and advocated herein are not new creations. But I have grounded these principles in several European legal traditions, eighteenth-century American texts, and twentieth-century human rights instruments that have not been part of the conventional literature. I have labeled and grouped them in a way that was more conventional in the eighteenth century than in the twentieth. And I have stripped them of some of the thick accretions of casuistry, which have tended to obscure their essential value and vigor in informing and integrating the twin religion clauses of the First Amendment.

The free exercise clause, I argue, outlawed government proscriptions of religion—actions that unduly burdened the conscience, restricted religious expression, discriminated against religion, or invaded the autonomy of churches and other religious bodies. The disestablishment clause outlawed government prescriptions of religion—actions that coerced the conscience, mandated forms of religious expression, discriminated in favor of religion, or improperly allied the state with churches or other religious bodies. Both the free exercise and the disestablishment clauses thereby provided complementary protections to the first principles of the American experiment—liberty of conscience, freedom of religious expression, equality of plural faiths before the law, and separation of church and state.

The call for a more integrated framework of religious liberty in America, built on these first principles, is also not new. But I warn against efforts to reduce the religion clause guarantees to one or two principles alone—even to such vaunted principles as coercion, neutrality, or accommodationism, currently in vogue. Religion is simply too vital and valuable a source of individual flourishing and social cohesion to be left to one or two legal defenses. As both the eighteenth-century American founders and twentieth-century international jurists have repeatedly argued, a variety of principles must be integrated into an interlocking and interdependent shield of religious liberties and rights for all. The principles of liberty of conscience, free exercise, pluralism, equality, separation, and disestablishment form the essential amalgam of the American shield.

1

THE AMERICAN
EXPERIMENT IN
HISTORICAL CONTEXT

The American founders did not create their experiment on religious liberty out of whole cloth. They had more than a century and a half of colonial experience and more than a millennium and a half of European experience from which they could draw both examples and counterexamples.

Historical examples and exemplars of religious liberty were amply at hand. Foremost among these sources was the Christian Bible, with its bracing aphorisms on freedom: "For freedom, Christ has set us free." "You were called to freedom." "Where the Spirit of the Lord is, there is freedom." "You will know the truth, and the truth will make you free." "You will be free indeed." You have been given "the glorious liberty of the children of God."[1] Such biblical passages inspired hundreds of impassioned sermons in defense of spiritual and civil liberty; indeed, political sermons constituted some 80 percent of all the American political literature published in the 1770s and 1780s.[2] Beyond the Bible, the American founders also turned for inspiration to the martyred prophets of religious liberty in the West—Thomas Becket, John Wycliff, John Hus, and an ample number of early modern Continental Anabaptists and English Levellers. They turned for instruction to a host of European theologians and philosophers, from the early Protestant reformers, Martin Luther and John Calvin, to later European voices of liberty, such as John Locke, Baron Montesquieu, William Blackstone, and a host of others. A recent statistical study of the American founders' political writings from 1760 to 1805 shows that well over half of all their citations were to the Bible, Montesquieu, Blackstone, and Locke—in that order of priority.[3]

Historical counterexamples also came readily to mind, particularly as the founders prepared sermons, speeches, and pamphlets denouncing traditional religious establishments. In defending the novelty of the American experiment, the founders often dismissed their Western inheritance as a veritable "career of intolerance," in James Madison's apt phrase.[4] "No doubt," one pamphleteer wrote,

> Constantine the Great, who first established christianity [in the fourth century], had a good intention in the same; but all the darkness that has since overspread the Christian church, the exorbitant power of the popes and church of Rome, all the oceans of blood that have been shed in the contests about religion, between different sects of Christians, the almost total cessation of the progress of christianity, the rise of Mahometanism, the rise and spread of deism, the general contempt in which christianity is fallen; all may fairly be laid at the door of that establishment.[5]

Thomas Jefferson concurred: "Millions of innocent men, women, and children, since the introduction of Christianity, have been burnt, tortured, fined, imprisoned; yet we have not advanced one inch towards uniformity."[6]

Madison wrote similarly:

> During almost fifteen centuries has the legal establishment of Christianity been on trial. What has been its fruits? More or less in all places, pride and indolence in the Clergy, ignorance or servility in the laity, in both, superstition, bigotry and persecution. . . . Torrents of blood have been spilt in the old world, by vain attempts of the secular arm, to extinguish Religious discord, by proscribing all differences in Religious opinion. Time has at length revealed the True Remedy. . . . The American Theatre has exhibited proofs that equal and compleat liberty, if it does not wholly eradicate it, sufficiently destroys its malignant influence on the health and prosperity of the state.[7]

Anyone who was still not convinced could turn to John Adams's massive three-volume *A Defense of the Constitutions of Government in the United States of America (1788)* for an exhaustive account of the "gory ecclesiastical or civil tyranny" of the Western tradition and the "glorious new experiment" of the American republic.[8]

To set the American experiment in historical relief and context, it is worth recounting briefly the main events and figures in the Western tradition of religious liberty. This story, even briefly told, bears out not only the genius of the eighteenth-century American experiment but also its genesis in texts and beliefs that antedate the American founding, sometimes by many centuries.

The American founders revolutionized the Western tradition of religious liberty. But they also remained within this Western tradition, dependent on its enduring and evolving postulates about God and humanity, authority and liberty, church and state. This Western pedigree of the American experiment in religious liberty might be a source of comfort to modern skeptics, who see in it a betrayal of the classic ideals of Western Christendom. This Western pedigree of the American experiment might also be a source of warning to modern enthusiasts, who see in it a universal formula of the good life and good society to be enforced throughout the world.

The First Millennium

In the first three centuries of its existence, the Christian church was largely isolated from official Roman society. It received virtually no support from the Roman political authorities and virtually no protection against oppression by them. Christians refused to acknowledge the divinity of the emperor, as required by Roman law, or to swear the oaths or to join the pagan rituals necessary for participation in the government or the army and for litigation in the courts. Contrary to its usual policy of indifferent toleration of all faiths that remained politically subservient, the Roman emperors declared Christianity to be an illicit religion. Imperial edicts outlawed Christian worship, charity, and education, as well as church government and law. Nevertheless, Christian leaders not only urged upon their Roman rulers law reform consonant with scriptural norms but also taught obedience to Roman law and loyalty to the emperor, within the limits set by the Christian faith. Beyond those limits, however, the church in those centuries generally taught civil disobedience and, if necessary, martyrdom.[9]

With the conversion of the Roman Emperor Constantine in 312, Christians came to enjoy an ample measure of religious toleration at Roman law. The famous imperial Edict of Milan (313), for the first time, guaranteed to Christians alongside all other faiths "freedom to follow whatever religion each one wished"; "a public and free liberty to practice their religion or cult"; and a "free permission to follow their own religion and worship as befits the peacefulness of our times." The Edict of Milan also recognized the rights of Christian groups to property and places of worship, "which belongs by right to their body—that is, to the churches not to individuals" and the right to sue for restitution of properties confiscated in earlier decades of persecution. Such guarantees of individual and group religious rights were granted, the edict provides, "so that the supreme Divinity, whose religion we obey with free minds, may be able to show in all matters His accustomed favour and benevolence towards us."[10]

Had this edict on the books remained the law in action, Rome would have instituted a regime of religious liberty that the West would not see again for more than a millennium. Even in Constantine's reign, however, and increasingly thereafter, the Roman emperors moved from a policy of open religious toleration of all to one of increasing preference for and control of Trinitarian Christianity. An imperial edict of 380 sealed this shift in policy, declaring as a matter of Roman law that:

> there is one Godhead, Father, Son, and Holy Spirit, in an equal Majesty and Holy Trinity. We order that those who follow this doctrine to receive the title of Catholic Christians, but others we judge to be mad and raving and worthy of incurring the disgrace of heretical teaching, nor are their assemblies to receive the name of churches. They are to be punished not only by Divine retribution but also by our own measures.[11]

This formal establishment of Trinitarian Christianity as the official religion of the Roman empire brought the church under the support and control of state authorities. On the one hand, orthodox clergy were given special military protection, legal privileges, and financial support to spread the faith, to educate the young, to care for the poor, and to build new churches and monasteries. Heretics, pagans, and Jews, in turn, were subject to many of the same policies of severe repression and legal disability that had earlier encumbered Christians.[12] On the other hand, the Roman emperor was made the supreme ruler of both civil and religious affairs. Constantine and his successors convoked and presided over church councils and synods, appointed and removed bishops and other higher clergy, and founded and administered churches and monasteries. Numerous imperial laws regulated the internal activities of the church, the lives of its clerics, and the acquisition and disposition of church property.[13]

Despite their claims to absolutism, the emperors did not rule the church without restriction. For all their authority, and even sanctity, the emperors were not ordained priests but laymen. During worship they sat in the congregation, and during the Eucharist they kneeled at the rail like all laity. They had no authority to administer the sacraments or to mete out ecclesiastical discipline. They were bound by the laws of the ecumenical councils, the teachings of the Bible, and the traditions of their predecessors. They also had to accept the church's instruction, judgment, and spiritual discipline. In 390, for example, Ambrose, Bishop of Milan, excommunicated the powerful Emperor Theodosius for massacring the people of Thessalonica and readmitted him to communion only after he had done public penance for his immoral act. In 494 Pope Gelasius I wrote to Emperor Anastasius:

> There are, indeed, most august Emperor, two powers by which the world is chiefly ruled: the sacred authority of the Popes and the royal power. Of these the priestly power is the more important, because it has to render account for kings of men themselves at [the Last Judgment]. For you know, our clement son, that although you have the chief place in dignity over the human race, yet you must submit yourself faithfully to those who have charge of Divine things, and look to them for the means of your salvation.[14]

This system of tempered imperial or royal rule within the church prevailed until the late eleventh century—more consistently and prominently in the Eastern (Byzantine) Empire, but increasingly as well in the Western Germanic kingdoms that prevailed after the collapse of the Western Roman Empire in the fifth century. Before their conversion, the pagan Germanic kings were considered to be divine and were the cult leaders, as well as the military leaders, of their people. Upon conversion to Christianity, they lost their divinity, yet continued as sacral rulers of the church within their respective territories. They found in Christianity an important source of authority in their efforts to extend their rule over the diverse peoples that made up their kingdoms and empires. The clergy not only supported the Germanic Christian kings in the suppression of tribal religions but also looked upon such leaders as the Frankish Emperor Charlemagne (r. 768–814) and the Anglo-Saxon King Alfred (r. 871–899) as their spiritual leaders. The kings, in turn, supported the clergy in the struggle against Christian heresies and gave them military protection.

The clergy of the first millennium did not generally constitute a political threat to the secular authority, for the dominant Christian outlook was essentially otherworldly. In St. Augustine's terms, the Christian believer was one who died to the earthly city and who lived in the eternal city of God. Germanic Christianity, like Eastern Orthodoxy, was not oriented toward a visible ecclesiastical unity or an independent ecclesiastical power. Its main message concerned the life of the world to come, heaven and hell. Its highest ideals were symbolized in monasticism, with its emphasis on spiritual withdrawal from the temporal world. Moreover, the clergy in the West were invested in their spiritual offices by kings and feudal lords. The church property that they administered was largely held "of" kings and feudal lords. Even the Bishop of Rome, who by tradition was the most prestigious and most independent of the higher clergy in the West, and whose consecration was eagerly sought by the Frankish-German kings and emperors of the eighth to early eleventh centuries, was at the same time almost wholly under their political domination.

The Papal Revolution

The relationship of church and state changed dramatically in the century between 1050 and 1150, when a large part of the clergy throughout Western Christendom united under the Bishop of Rome to form an independent polity, separate from the state authorities. This was what Harold J. Berman has called the Papal Revolution.[15] In his revolutionary manifesto called the Dictates of the Pope (1075), Pope Gregory VII proclaimed that emperors and kings had no authority over the church. Only the pope, Gregory VII declared, had authority to ordain, discipline, depose, and reinstate bishops, to convoke and control church councils, and to establish and administer abbeys and bishoprics. Only the pope had authority "to enact new laws according to the needs of the time." The papal court was "the court of the whole of Christendom" to which all Christians had a right to resort in matters within the ecclesiastical jurisdiction. The pope "may depose emperors," and "the pope is the only one whose feet are to be kissed by all princes."[16] Such a bold proclamation did not go unchallenged. For more than three generations thereafter, a good deal of Europe was locked in bitter religious and civil war, with the papacy and its supporters ultimately prevailing.

In the course of the twelfth century the Roman Catholic Church established itself as a unified, hierarchical, autonomous, political corporation. The "two powers" injunction of Pope Gelasius was transformed into a "two swords" doctrine. The pope and his clergy held the "spiritual" sword. Emperors, kings, feudal lords, urban rulers, and other political authorities held the "temporal" sword. By the Concordat of Worms (1122), which formally concluded the religious warfare, the secular authorities lost their right to invest priests and bishops with the symbols of their offices. The church also asserted its own independent property rights in the vast ecclesiastical holdings that eventually would constitute some one-third of the land of Western Europe. A dual system of government was introduced: Both political and ecclesiastical authorities ruled in the same territories and over the same people with overlapping jurisdictions.

By the end of the twelfth century, the Roman Catholic Church had emerged as the one universal sovereign of Western Christendom. The great nation-states of Western Europe were not yet born. The Holy Roman Empire was not yet real. In that interim, the Catholic Church came to hold preeminent legal and political authority throughout Western Christendom. The Church claimed a vast *jurisdiction*—a power to proclaim and enforce law, literally "to speak the law" *(jus dicere)*.[17] The Church claimed exclusive personal jurisdiction over clerics, pilgrims, students, heretics, Jews, and Muslims. It claimed subject matter jurisdiction over doctrine, liturgy, patronage, education, charity, inheritance, marriage, oaths, oral promises, and moral crimes. The Church predicated these jurisdictional claims in part on Christ's famous delegation of the keys to St. Peter (Matthew 16:18)—a key of knowledge to discern God's word and will and a key of power to implement and enforce that word and will by law. The Church also predicated these new claims on its traditional authority over the form and function of the Christian sacraments. By the fifteenth century, the Church had gathered whole systems of law around the seven sacraments of baptism, Eucharist, penance, orders, extreme unction, confirmation, and marriage. These church laws were enforced by a complex network of church courts that spread throughout the West.

The medieval Church's law, called *canon law*, was based, in part, on the concept of individual and corporate rights *(iura)*. The canon law defined the rights of the clergy to their liturgical offices and ecclesiastical benefices, their exemptions from civil taxes and duties, their immunities from civil prosecution and compulsory testimony. It defined the rights of ecclesiastical organizations like parishes, monasteries, charities, and guilds to form and dissolve, to accept and reject members, to establish order and discipline, to acquire, use, and alienate property. It defined the rights of church councils and synods to participate in the election and discipline of bishops, abbots, and other clergy. It defined the rights of the laity to worship, evangelize, maintain religious symbols, participate in the sacraments, travel on religious pilgrimages, and educate their children. It defined the rights of the poor, widows, and needy to seek solace, succor, and sanctuary within the church. A good deal of the rich latticework of medieval canon law was cast, substantively and procedurally, in the form and language of rights.[18]

To be sure, such rights were not unguided by duties. Nor were they available to all parties. Only the Catholic faithful—and, notoriously, not Jews, Muslims, or heretics—had full rights protection, and their rights were to be exercised with appropriate ecclesiastical and sacramental constraints.[19] But the basic medieval rights formulations of exemptions, immunities, privileges, and benefits, and the free exercise rights of religious worship, travel, speech, and education have persisted, with ever greater inclusivity, to this day.[20] Many of the common formulations of religious rights and liberties that came to prevail in the eighteenth-century American experiment were first forged not by a James Madison or a Thomas Jefferson but by obscure Catholic theologians and canon lawyers more than four centuries before them.

In the course of the fourteenth century and thereafter, this intricate system of religious rights, and of church-state relations, began to break down. Strong monarchs began to increase their control over the Church, and clerical authority began to wane—in part because of widespread corruption and compromise even at the highest levels of Church government. In 1309, the papal curia was moved from Rome to Avignon and there came under increasing constraint and control by the kings of France. In 1415, with rival popes in Avignon and Rome, and widespread confusion within the Church hierarchy, the German Emperor Sigismund convoked at Constance the first of a series of great Church councils that declared their authority over Church polity and canon law, despite papal disapproval. In England, the Statutes of Provisors (1351) and Praemunire (1353) truncated the original and appellate jurisdiction of the Church courts.[21] In the Pragmatic Sanction of Bourges (1438) and again in the Concordat of Bologna (1516), French kings banned various papal taxes, limited appeals to Rome, required French bishops to be elected by French Church councils called by the king, subjected the clergy in France to royal discipline, and increased royal control over Church property.[22] In Germany, strong princes and city councils began to pass "legal reformations" that placed limits on Church property and taxation, disciplined wayward clergy, and curtailed the jurisdiction of church courts over crime, family, inheritance, and contracts.[23] Fifteenth-century Spanish monarchs subordinated the ecclesiastical courts in Spain to the civil courts and assumed exclusive political and legal control, through the Spanish Inquisition, over the prosecution and execution of heretics, Jews, and Muslims.[24]

The Protestant Reformation

In retrospect, such developments could be seen as storm signals that announced the coming of the Protestant Reformation. The Reformation—inaugurated by Martin Luther's posting of the Ninety-Five Theses in 1517 and burning of the canon law books in 1520—began as a call for religious freedom. Luther, John Calvin, Thomas Cranmer, Menno Simons, and other sixteenth-century reformers all began their movements with a call for freedom from this ecclesiastical regime—freedom of the individual conscience from intrusive canon laws and clerical controls, freedom of political officials from ecclesiastical power and privileges, freedom of the local clergy from central papal rule and oppressive princely controls. "Freedom of the Christian" became the rallying cry of the early Reformation. It drove theologians and jurists, clergy and laity, princes and peasants alike to denounce canon laws and ecclesiastical authorities with unprecedented alacrity and to urge radical constitutional reforms. The reforms that they instituted, however, often simply reestablished new forms of Christian faith, now again under civil control.

The Protestant Reformation broke the unity of Western Christendom and eventually laid the foundations for the modern Western system of religious pluralism. The Lutheran Reformation *territorialized* the faith. Luther replaced the two swords theory of the Papal Revolution with a new two kingdoms theory. The "invisible" church of the heavenly kingdom, he argued, is a perfect community of saints, where all stand equal in dignity before God, all enjoy perfect Christian liberty, and all govern their affairs in accordance with the Gospel. The "visible" church of this earthly kingdom, however, embraces saints and sinners alike. Its members still stand directly before God and still enjoy liberty of conscience, including the liberty to leave the visible church itself. But, unlike the invisible church, the visible church needs both the Gospel and human laws to govern its members' relationships with God and with fellow believers. The clergy must administer the Gospel. But the magistrate must administer the law. For the magistrate is God's vice-regent, called to appropriate and apply God's law in all aspects of earthly life.[25]

This Lutheran understanding of the role of the magistrate in religious affairs, predicated in part on Roman law precedents, was cast into enduring constitutional form. The Peace of Augsburg (1555) established the principle of *cuius regio, eius religio* ("whose region, his religion") for much of Germany and surrounding polities. Under this principle, princes or city councils were authorized to establish by civil law the appropriate forms of religious doctrine, liturgy, charity, and education for their polities—with religious dissenters granted the right to worship privately in their homes or to emigrate peaceably from the polity. This new constitutional policy rendered Germany, with its approximately 350 distinct polities, a veritable honeycomb of religious pluralism.[26]

The Anglican Reformation *nationalized* the faith. Building in part on Lutheran precedents, King Henry VIII severed all ties between the Church in England and the pope. The Act of Succession (1534), which annulled Henry's marriage to Katherine of Aragon, denied papal authority over marriage and divorce. Succeeding acts effectively divested the Catholic Church of all its remaining jurisdiction and banned all tithes, annates, and appeals to Rome. The Supremacy Act (1534) declared the monarch to be "the only Supreme Head in Earth of the Church of England called *Anglicana Ecclesia*."[27] The Church in England had become the Church of England.

As spiritual and temporal heads of the Church of England, Henry VIII and his successors, through their parliaments, established a uniform liturgy, doctrine, and administration of the sacraments, issued *The Book of Common Prayer* (1559), and prepared the Authorized Version of the Bible (1611) in English translation, commonly called the King James Version. They also assumed legal responsibility for poor relief, education, and other activities that had previously been carried on under Catholic auspices. Communicant status in the Church of England was rendered a condition for citizenship status in the Commonwealth of England. Contraventions of royal religious policy were punishable both as heresy and as treason. Catholics and dissenting Protestants were subjected to severe repression, martyrdom in several instances.[28]

The Anabaptist Reformation *communalized* the faith by introducing what the Dutch Anabaptist leader Menno Simons once called the "*Scheidingsmaurer*"—literally, the "wall of separation" between the redeemed realm of religion and the fallen realm of the world. Anabaptist religious communities were ascetically withdrawn from the world into small, self-sufficient, intensely democratic communities. These ascetic religious communities were governed internally by biblical principles of discipleship, simplicity, charity, and Christian obedience. When such communities grew too large or too divided, they colonized themselves, eventually spreading the Anabaptist communities from Russia to Ireland to the furthest frontiers of North America—under such variant denominational labels as Amish, Hutterites, Mennonites, and Baptists.[29]

The Calvinist Reformation *congregationalized* the faith by introducing rule by a democratically elected consistory of pastors, elders, and deacons. During John Calvin's tenure from 1541 to 1564, the Geneva consistory was still an appointed body and held broad legal authority over all members of the city. By the later sixteenth century, however, Calvinist consistories in Geneva and other communities became elected, representative bodies within congregations. These consistories featured separation among the offices of preaching, discipline, and charity, and a fluid, dialogical form of religious polity and policing centered around collective worship, the congregational meeting, and the annual election of church officers.[30] This flexible form of ecclesiastical polity rendered the Calvinist churches and communities mobile and adaptable. They eventually spread throughout Europe under such labels as Scottish Presbyterians, English Puritans, Dutch Pietists, French Huguenots, and various Reformed groups.

The Protestant Reformation broke not only the unity of Western Christendom but also the primacy of corporate Christianity. Protestants gave new emphasis to the role of the individual believer in the economy of salvation and the individual rights that should attach thereto. The Protestant Reformation did not "invent" the individual or the concept of individual rights, as too many exuberant commentators still maintain.[31] But the sixteenth-century Protestant reformers, more than their Catholic contemporaries, gave new emphasis to the (religious) rights and liberties of the individual at both religious law and civil law.

This new emphasis upon individual religious piety was evident even in the more intensely communitarian Protestant traditions of Anglicanism and Anabaptism. The Anglican *Book of Common Prayer* (1559) was designed, in its principal author Thomas Cranmer's words, as a "textbook of liberty." The daily office of the lectionary, together with the vernacular Bible, encouraged the exercise of private devotion outside the church. The choices among liturgical rites and prayers within the *Book of Common Prayer* encouraged the exercise of at least some modest clerical innovation within the church, with such opportunities for variation and innovation increasing with the 1662 edition and 1789 (American) edition.[32]

The Anabaptist doctrine of adult baptism gave new emphasis to a voluntarist understanding of religion, as opposed to conventional notions of a birthright or predestined faith. The adult individual was now called to make a conscientious choice to accept the faith through adult baptism—metaphorically, to scale the wall of separation between the fallen world and the realm of religion to come within the perfection of Christ. Later Free Church followers converted this cardinal image into a powerful platform of liberty of conscience, free exercise of religion, and separation of church and state—not only for Christians but eventually for all peaceable believers. Such views would have a great influence on the formation of constitutional protections of religious liberty in North America.[33]

The Calvinist and Lutheran branches of the Reformation laid the basis for an even more expansive theory and law of rights and liberties. Classic Protestant theology teaches that a person is both saint and sinner. On the one hand, a person is created in the image of God and justified by faith in God. The person is called to a distinct vocation, which stands equal in dignity and sanctity to all others. The person is prophet, priest, and king and responsible to exhort, minister, and rule in the community. Every person, therefore, stands equal before God and before his or her neighbor. Every person is vested with a natural liberty to live, to believe, to serve God and neighbor. Every person is entitled to the vernacular Scripture, to education, to work in a vocation. On the other hand, the person is sinful and prone to evil and egoism. He needs the restraint of the law to deter him from evil and to drive him to repentance. She needs the association of others to exhort, minister, and rule her with law and with love. Every person, therefore, is inherently a communal creature, a member of a family, a church, a political community.[34]

Protestant groups in Europe and America cast these theological doctrines into democratic forms designed to protect rights. Protestant doctrines of the person and society were cast into democratic social forms. Since all persons stand equal before God, they must stand equal before God's political agents in the state. Since God has vested all persons with natural liberties of life and belief, the state must ensure them of similar civil liberties. Since God has called all persons to be prophets, priests, and kings, the state must protect their freedoms to speak, to preach, and to rule in the community. Since God has created persons as social creatures, the state must promote and protect a plurality of social institutions, particularly the church and the family. Protestant doctrines of sin were cast into democratic political forms. The political office must be protected against the sinfulness of the political official. Political power, like ecclesiastical power, must be distributed among self-checking executive, legislative, and judicial branches. Officials must be elected to limited terms of office. Laws must be clearly codified, and discretion closely guarded. If officials abuse their office, they must be disobeyed; if they persist in their abuse, they must be removed, even if by force. Such views would have a monumental influence on the theories of inalienable rights and political revolution in early modern Europe and eighteenth-century America.

Religious Establishment Versus Religious Freedom

The Reformation's splintering of Western Christendom into competing religious polities—each with its own preferred forms and norms of religious governance—was a recipe for religious warfare and persecution and for corresponding movements toward religious freedom.[35]

In the 1570s, for example, the Spanish monarch Philip II, who was also Lord of the Netherlands, ordered a bloody inquisition against the growing population of Dutch Protestants, ultimately killing some 10,000 to 20,000 of them and confiscating huge portions of their property. This sparked the revolt of the seven northern provinces, on the strength of Calvinist principles of revolution. Presaging American developments two centuries later, the Dutch revolutionaries established a confederate government by the Union of Utrecht of 1579, which included a provision that "each person must enjoy freedom of religion, and no one may be persecuted or questioned about his religion." The confederacy led the revolutionary war against the Spanish monarch. In 1581, the confederacy issued a Declaration of Independence, invoking "the law of nature" and the "ancient rights, privileges, and liberties" of the people in justification of its revolutionary actions. When the war was settled, each of the seven Dutch provinces instituted its own constitution. These provincial constitutions embraced the most benign forms of religious toleration of the day and helped to render the Netherlands a haven for religious dissenters from throughout Europe—and a common point of departure for American colonists, from the Mayflower Pilgrims of 1620 onward.[36] When comparing this sixteenth-century Dutch experience with the eighteenth-century American experience, John Adams wrote: "The originals of the two republics are so much alike, that the history of one seems but a transcript of that of the other."[37]

In the opening decades of the seventeenth century, much of northern Europe was locked in bitter religious warfare between and among Catholic and Protestant forces. This religious warfare finally ended with the Peace of Westphalia (1648). Confirming and extending the principles of the 1555 Peace of Augsburg, this new treaty authorized each ruler to establish by civil law either Catholicism, Lutheranism, or Calvinism in his territory. Dissenting religious groups, though denied the right to worship publicly, were granted special privileges to assemble and to worship privately and to educate their children in their own faith, eventually in their own private religious schools. The spiritual jurisdiction of the canon law and papal authority over clergy and church property were guaranteed for Catholic territories. But canon law was barred from use in the Protestant territories, and Catholic clerics and groups were divested of any remaining privileges of forum, tax exemptions, and other immunities in these Protestant territories.[38]

While this policy of balancing religious establishment with religious toleration proved effective to securing peace for a good deal of Europe for the remainder of the seventeenth century, it did not serve to constrain France and England, the two main national powers of the day.

In France, the monarchy gradually abandoned its earlier policies of religious toleration, particularly as they had been set out in the Edict of Nantes (1598), which had granted modest toleration to Calvinist and other Protestant nonconformists. Supported by the antipapalism of the revived Gallican party and by the new theories of absolute monarchy expounded by Jean Bodin and others on the strength of Roman law precedents, the French monarchs consolidated their control over a national Catholic church. The French monarchy sharply curtailed remaining papal power over church property, ecclesiastical courts, and clerical nomination. Louis XIV passed more than one hundred acts against Catholic and Protestant dissenters, confining their freedoms and imposing crushing taxes upon them. Finally, in the Edict of Fontainebleau (1685), Louis XIV ordered all Protestant churches and schools destroyed, proscribed all liturgies and theologies that deviated from officially sanctioned Gallicanism, and banished all dissenting clerics from France.[39] Protestants fled from France by the tens of thousands, many making their way to Belgium, the Netherlands, Switzerland, and Germany—and eventually to distant colonies in North America and South Africa.

Similarly, in early-seventeenth-century England, the Stuart monarchs, James I and Charles I, issued through their Parliaments a series of increasingly repressive laws against the few remaining Catholics and the growing numbers of Protestant dissenters in England. As official and unofficial persecution mounted in the 1620s and 1630s, tens of thousands of Puritans, Anabaptists, Lutherans, and other "sectaries" "flew out of England, as if out of Babylon" to make their way to the Continent, and often from there to North America.[40] When the English monarchy persisted in its abuse, the remaining Puritans, among others, led a revolutionary struggle against the English Crown. The revolutionaries ultimately deposed and executed King Charles I. In 1649, they passed a law "declaring and constituting the People of England to be a commonwealth and free state." They further outlawed the establishment of the Church of England and granted toleration to all Protestants—though not to Catholics or to Jews. This experiment was short-lived. In 1660 royal rule was restored, Anglicanism was reestablished, and dissenters were again repressed. But when the dissenters again rose up in revolt and threatened a new civil war, Parliament ultimately passed the Toleration Act of 1689 that guaranteed freedom of association and worship to all Protestants dissenting from the Church of England.[41] Many of the remaining legal restrictions on the civil and political liberties of Protestants fell into desuetude in the following decades. Catholicism and Judaism, however, continued to be formally proscribed by penal law until the Emancipation Acts of 1829 and 1833.

Colonization and Experimentation

This checkerboard of rival religious and political groups in early modern Europe was projected, in part, onto the New World. European powers, eager to extend their political and religious regimes, issued charters and privileges to colonial companies that would establish themselves in the New World, under the rule of the distant mother country and mother church. Thus Spanish and Portuguese Catholic rulers from the early sixteenth century onward extended their regimes through much of Latin America, the Caribbean, Mexico, and modern-day Florida. From the later sixteenth century onward, Jesuits and other missionaries made frequent forays into the American frontier, reaching north to the Carolinas and Virginia, and more successfully west to modern-day Alabama, Louisiana, New Mexico, and California. French Catholics sent colonists to Quebec and the Canadian Maritimes, and many of them migrated south into New England. By the eighteenth century, a number of Catholic families from Quebec had also settled in New York and Pennsylvania, and hundreds more had moved down the midwest corridor and the Mississippi River to Louisiana and westward. Dutch Protestant authorities chartered companies of Dutch Reformed to New York (called New Amsterdam) and parts of New Jersey and Pennsylvania. These companies, though only modestly successful, were amply bolstered in the eighteenth century by new waves of Reformed colonists from the German Palatinate. Swedish Lutheran monarchs sponsored scattered colonial companies to Delaware and eventually into Maryland, Pennsylvania, and New York as well.[42]

The most prominent colonizers of all, however, were the British, who established companies and colonies all along the Atlantic seaboard—from the north in Ontario and the Maritimes to the southern colonies of Virginia, the Carolinas, and Georgia. The British eventually assumed formal control of the Middle and New England colonies as well. The royal charters of all these colonies confirmed the rule of English laws and liberties, including its ecclesiastical laws. By the time of the American Revolution of 1776, there were Anglican churches in every American colony, and every American colony was formally under the jurisdiction of the Bishop of London and the Archbishop of Canterbury.[43]

Colonial America was not only a frontier for European establishments, however, but also a haven for European dissenters, many of whom introduced their own experiments in religious liberty. Both the Plymouth Colony of 1620 and the Massachusetts Bay Colony of 1629 were founded by Puritan dissenters from the Church of England and eventually became havens for Calvinist refugees from throughout Europe, though for few others until well into the eighteenth century.[44] Providence Plantation was established in 1636 as "a lively experiment [for] full liberty in religious concernments," in the words of its founder Roger Williams. The colony's policies of protecting "liberty of conscience" and "the free exercise and enjoyment of all their civil and religious rights" eventually attracted Anabaptists and other Christian dissenters from throughout Europe and other North American colonies.[45]

Maryland, too, was founded by the Catholic leader Lord Baltimore in 1633 as an experiment in Catholic and Protestant coexistence. Its famous Act of 1649 provided that "noe person . . . professing to believe in Jesus Christ, shall from henceforth bee any waies troubled . . . for his or her religion nor in the free exercise thereof . . . nor any way compelled to the beliefe or exercise of any other Religion against his or her consent."[46] Though ultimately frustrated by persistent Catholic-Protestant rivalries and slowly eclipsed by new Anglican establishment policies of the 1660s onward, the Maryland experiment provided ample inspiration during the constitutional debates of the next century.[47]

Equally inspirational was the Quaker leader William Penn's "holy experiment" in religious liberty instituted in Pennsylvania in 1681. The Great Law of 1682 captured Penn's cardinal convictions about Christian liberty:

> [N]o person now or at any time hereafter living in this province, who shall confess and acknowledge one almighty God to be the creator, upholder, and ruler of the world, and who profess himself or herself to be obliged in conscience to live peaceably and quietly under the civil government, shall in any case be molested or prejudiced for his or her conscientious persuasion or practice. Nor shall he or she at any time be compelled to frequent or maintain any religious worship, place, or ministry whatever contrary to his or her mind, but shall freely and fully enjoy his, or her, christian liberty in that respect, without any interruption or reflection.[48]

The eighteenth-century American experiment in religious freedom was thus, at once, very old and very new. For a nation to contemplate the disestablishment of religion altogether and to grant religious liberty to all without obstruction was, indeed, a novel exercise. But legal precedents for such an experiment lay closely at hand in the constitutional example of sixteenth-century Holland and more distantly in the imperial edicts of fourth-century Rome. And firm legal principles to implement this experiment—liberty of conscience, freedom of religious exercise, separation of religious and political authorities, guarantees of religious group rights, and the like—were readily at hand in Catholic canon law, Protestant civil law, and European peace treaties alike. But, as James Madison put it, "[i]t remained for North America to bring the great & interesting subject to a fair, & finally, to a decisive test."[49]

2

THE THEOLOGY AND POLITICS OF THE RELIGION CLAUSES

The religion clauses of the state constitutions and of the First Amendment, forged between 1776 and 1789, express both theological and political sentiments. They reflect both the convictions of the religious believers of the young American republic and the calculations of their political leaders. They manifest both the certitude of such eighteenth-century theologians as Isaac Backus and John Witherspoon and the skepticism of such contemporaneous philosophers as Thomas Jefferson and Thomas Paine. A plurality of theological and political views helped to inform the early American experiment.

The American experiment in religious liberty cannot be reduced to the First Amendment religion clauses alone, nor can the understanding of the framers be determined simply by studying the debates on these clauses in the First Session of Congress in 1789. Not only is the record of these debates very slender—a mere three pages in modern edition, as we shall see in Chapter 4—but the First Amendment religion clauses, by design, reflect only a part of the early constitutional experiment and experience. The religion clauses, on their face, define only the outer boundaries of appropriate governmental action respecting religion: Government may not prescribe ("establish") religion nor proscribe ("prohibit") its exercise. Precisely what governmental conduct short of outright prescription or proscription of religion is constitutionally permissible is left open for debate and development. Moreover, the religion clauses bind only the federal government ("Congress"), rendering prevailing state constitutional provisions and the sentiments of their drafters equally vital sources of the original understanding. Finally, the drafters of the religion clauses urged interpreters to look not to the drafters' intentions but, in James Madison's words, "to the text itself [and] the sense attached to it by the people in their respective State Conventions, where it received all the authority which it possesses."[1] The understanding of the state conventional delegates was derived from their own state constitutional experiments and experiences, which are reflected in contemporaneous pamphlets, sermons, letters, and speeches. A wide range of eighteenth-century textual and contextual materials must thus be consulted to come to terms with the prevailing sentiments on religious rights and liberties in the young American republic.[2]

Within the ample eighteenth-century sources at hand, two pairs of theological views on religious liberty were critical to constitutional formation: those of congregational *Puritans* and those of Free Church *Evangelicals*. Two pairs of contemporaneous political views were equally influential: those of *Enlightenment* thinkers and those of *Civic Republicans*. Exponents of these four views often found common cause and used common language, particularly during the constitutional convention and ratification debates. Yet each group offered its own distinct teachings on religious liberty and had its own preferences for their implementation at law. Together, these groups held up the four corners of a wide canopy of opinion about religious liberty in the eighteenth century.

The image of a "canopy" of opinions—which swayed and stretched even while covering the same basic ground—underscores the notion that the founders' views on religious liberty defy easy description and classification. Many other views on religious liberty besides these four circulated, and many other labels besides Puritan, Evangelical, Enlightenment, and Republican can be used to describe even these four views.[3] Moreover, the founders often moved freely between two or more perspectives, shifted their allegiances or alliances over time, or changed their tones and tunes as they moved from formal writing to the pulpit or to the political platform. John Adams, for example, expounded both Puritan and Republican views, depending on his audience. Massachusetts preacher Jonathan Edwards toed (and moved) the line between old light Puritan and new light Evangelical perspectives. John Witherspoon, signer of the Declaration of Independence and president of Princeton, moved freely between Evangelical and Republican camps. James Madison's early writings on religious liberty had the strong Evangelical flavor of Witherspoon, his teacher at Princeton; his political speeches often pulsed with Republican sentiments; his later writings, particularly after his presidency, were of increasingly firm Enlightenment stock.

Nonetheless, these four views were among the most distinct and distinguishable contributions to the eighteenth-century debates on religious liberty. The "original understanding" of the founders respecting government and religion cannot be reduced to any one of these views. It must be sought in the tensions among them and in the general principles that emerged from their interaction.

What follows in this chapter is a snapshot of these Puritan, Evangelical, Enlightenment, and Republican views on religious liberty. The next chapter provides a distillation of the first principles of religious liberty that they held in common.

Puritan Views

The Puritans of the New England states of Massachusetts, New Hampshire, Vermont, and Maine were the heirs of the theology of religious liberty taught by European Calvinists.[4] They had refined this European legacy through the efforts of John Winthrop, John Cotton, Cotton Mather, and others in the seventeenth century. They had liberalized some of this legacy through the writings of Jonathan Edwards, Charles Chauncy, Jonathan Mayhew, and others in the eighteenth century. They had propagated their views throughout colonial America through their relentless publications. But it was in New England, especially in the period from 1630 to 1730, that the Puritans had occasion to cast their Calvinist theological principles into constitutional practice.[5]

The Puritans who wrote on religious liberty were concerned especially with the nature of the church, of the state, and of the relationship between them. They conceived of the church and the state as two separate covenantal associations, two seats of Godly authority in the community. Each institution, they believed, was vested with a distinct polity and calling. The church was to be governed by pastoral, pedagogical, and diaconal authorities who were called to preach the word, administer the sacraments, teach the young, and care for the poor and the needy. The state was to be governed by executive, legislative, and judicial authorities who were called to enforce law, punish crime, cultivate virtue, and protect peace and order.

In the New England communities where their views prevailed, the Puritans adopted a variety of rules designed to foster this basic separation of the institutions of church and state. Church officials were prohibited from holding political office, serving on juries, interfering in governmental affairs, endorsing political candidates, or censuring the official conduct of a statesman. Political officials, in turn, were prohibited from holding ministerial office, interfering in internal ecclesiastical government, performing sacerdotal functions of clergy, or censuring the official conduct of a cleric. To permit any such officiousness on the part of church or state officials, Governor John Winthrop averred, "would confound those Jurisdictions, which Christ hath made distinct."[6]

Although church and state were not to be confounded, they were still to be "close and compact."[7] For, to the Puritans, these two institutions were inextricably linked in nature and in function. Each was an instrument of Godly authority. Each did its part to establish and maintain the community. As one mid-eighteenth-century writer put it, "I look upon this as a little model of the gloriou[s] kingdom of Christ on earth. Christ reigns among us in the commonwealth as well as in the church, and hath his glorious interest involved and wrapped up in the good of both societies respectively."[8] The Puritans, therefore, countenanced both the coordination and the cooperation of church and state.

State officials provided various forms of material and moral aid to churches and their officials. Public properties were donated to church groups for meetinghouses, parsonages, day schools, and orphanages. Tax collectors collected tithes and special assessments to support the ministers and ministry of the congregational church. Tax exemptions and immunities were accorded to some of the religious, educational, and charitable organizations that they operated. Special subsidies and military protections were provided for missionaries and religious outposts. Special criminal laws prohibited interference with religious properties and services. Sabbath day laws prohibited all forms of unnecessary labor and uncouth leisure on Sundays and holy days and required faithful attendance at worship services.

Church officials, in turn, provided various forms of material and moral aid to the state. Church meetinghouses and chapels were used not only to conduct religious services but also to host town assemblies, political rallies, and public auctions, to hold educational and vocational classes, to house the community library, to maintain census rolls and birth, marriage, and death certificates. Parsonages were used not only to house the minister and his family but also to harbor orphans, widows, the sick, the aged, and victims of abuse and disaster. Church officials preached obedience to the authorities and imposed spiritual discipline on parishioners found guilty of crime.[9] They encouraged their parishioners to be active in political affairs and each year offered "election day sermons" on Christian political principles. They offered learned expositions on the requirements of Godly law and occasionally offered advice to legislatures and courts, particularly on heated questions of public morality and law, such as the execution of criminals.[10]

Initially, the New England leadership left little room for individual religious experimentation. Despite their adherence to a basic separation of the offices of church and state, the New England authorities established a common Calvinist congregationalism for the community: Separatism for them did not connote disestablishment of one religion or the toleration of other religions. Already in the 1630s, dissidents from the established faith, such as Anne Hutchinson and Roger Williams, were summarily dismissed from the colony.[11] Immigration restrictions in Massachusetts Bay throughout the seventeenth century left little room to Catholics, Jews, "Familists, Antinomians, and other Enthusiasts"—especially Quakers.[12] Indeed, special laws in the late 1650s banned the Quakers and their teachings from the colony. Those Quakers who had newly arrived or newly converted were banished. Those who failed to leave were subject to flogging and the confiscation of their properties. The four Quakers who returned after banishment were hung in the Boston Common in 1659 and 1660.

Although Quakers remained unwelcome, Baptists, Episcopalians, and other Protestant groups came to be tolerated in the New England colonies—partly on account of the English Toleration Act (1689), which required all the colonies to be open to Protestant nonconformists. Though tolerated, these non-Puritan groups enjoyed limited political rights and social benefits and were subject to various tithe rates and restrictions on their properties and professions, which continued well into the nineteenth century.[13]

The growing presence of these religious nonconformists in New England, however, slowly shifted the Puritan understanding of liberty of conscience. Classic Calvinism taught that each person has the liberty to enter into a personal covenant relationship with God. Seventeenth-century Puritans had treated this covenant as something of a "divine adhesion contract."[14] God set the covenantal terms for salvation in the Bible; a person had the freedom only to accept or reject them. Such sentiments can be seen in a 1682 tract on "covenant liberty" by Samuel Willard, a leading Puritan systematizer of his day. Willard argued that every person has the "equal right," "title," "claim," "liberty," and "prerogative" "to enter and to enjoy every blessing of the covenant." But by the time Willard finished spelling out all the standard terms and conditions of the covenant, there seemed to be few at liberty to enter the covenant and little liberty left for those few who could.[15]

Confronted by the realities of religious pluralism, eighteenth-century Puritan writers began to view this covenantal relationship between God and persons in more open and voluntarist terms. The covenant was made more accessible to parties of various Christian faiths, and its terms were made more open to personal deliberation and innovation. Elisha Williams, a conservative Puritan theologian and jurist, put the matter thus in 1744:

> Every man has an equal right to follow the dictates of his own conscience in the affairs of religion. Every one is under an indispensable obligation to search the Scriptures for himself . . . and to make the best use of it he can for his own information in the will of God, the nature and duties of Christianity. And as every Christian is so bound; so he has the unalienable right to judge of the sense and meaning of it, and to follow his judgment wherever it leads him; even an equal right with any rulers be they civil or ecclesiastical.[16]

Such formulations became increasingly common among Puritan writers in the later eighteenth century.

It was only a short step from this formulation to the more generic and generous religious liberty guarantee of the 1780 Massachusetts Constitution:

> It is the right as well as the duty of all in society, publicly, and at stated seasons, to worship the Supreme Being, the great Creator and Preserver of the universe. And no subject shall be hurt, molested, or restrained, in his person, liberty, or estate, for worshipping God in the manner and season most agreeable to the dictates of his own conscience, or for his religious profession of sentiments; provided he doth not disturb the public peace or obstruct others in their religious worship.[17]

It was also a natural next step to find political, if not theological, virtue in the religious pluralism of the community. Zabdiel Adams put the prevailing opinion well in a sermon of 1782:

> Modes and forms of religion; sentiments concerning doctrines, etc., people should be indulged in, without molestation. If coer[c]ion would bring mankind to a uniformity of sentiment, no advantage would result therefrom. It is on the contrary best to have different facts and denominations live in the same societies. They are a mutual check and spy upon each other, and become more attentive to their principles and practice. . . . [W]here Papists and Protestants live intermingled together, it serves to meliorate them both. . . . With madmen and enthusiasts there can be no agreement, except among people as distracted as themselves. But even such, where they put on a religious guise, and do not interrupt the peace of society, are not to be disturbed by the civil arm. . . . [Only] that part of religion which has an immediate aspect on the good of the community falls under the cognizance of the ruler.[18]

Evangelical Views

Although the Evangelical tradition of religious liberty has its American roots in the seventeenth century—notably in Rhode Island founded by Roger Williams[19]—it did not emerge as a strong political force in America until after the Great Awakening of circa 1720–1780. Numerous spokesmen for the Evangelical cause rose up in the course of the later eighteenth century all along the Atlantic seaboard—Isaac Backus, John Leland, John Wesley, George Whitfield, and a host of other preachers and pamphleteers. Numerous denominational labels began to be attached to their followers—Baptists, Anabaptists, Moravians, Methodists, Enthusiasts, and German Protestants, among many others. Such labels sometimes signaled real differences in theological emphasis among these early groups, which later hardened into denominational divisions. Despite these theological differences, early Evangelicals were largely united in their insistence on liberty of conscience, disestablishment of religion, and separation of church and state. Although, outside of Rhode Island, the Evangelicals had fewer opportunities than the Puritans to institutionalize their views in the colonial era, their relentless preaching and pamphleteering had a formidable political influence on the early American experiment.[20]

Like the Puritans, the Evangelicals advanced a theological theory of religious liberty. They likewise advocated the institutional separation of church and state—the construction of "a wall of separation between the garden of the Church and the wilderness of the world," as Roger Williams put it famously in 1643.[21]

Most Evangelicals, however, went beyond the Puritans—and indeed battled with them in the New England states—both in their definition of the rights of religious individuals and groups and in their insistence on a fuller separation of the institutions of church and state. The Evangelicals sought to protect the liberty of conscience of every individual and the freedom of association of every religious group. Their preferred method for achieving these ends was to prohibit all legal establishments of religion and, indeed, all admixtures of religion and politics. John Leland, the fiery Baptist preacher, put it thus in a proposed amendment to the Massachusetts Constitution:

> To prevent the evils that have heretofore been occasioned in the world by religious establishments, and to keep up the proper distinction between religion and politics, no religious test shall ever be requested as a qualification of any officer, in any department of this government; neither shall the legislature, under this constitution, ever establish any religion by law, give any one sect a preference to another, or force any man in the commonwealth to part with his property for the support of religious worship, or the maintenance of ministers of the gospel.[22]

Later, Leland put the matter even more bluntly: "The notion of a Christian commonwealth should be exploded forever."[23]

Religious voluntarism lay at the heart of the Evangelical view. "[N]othing can be true religion but a voluntary obedience unto [God's] revealed will," declared Isaac Backus, the leading Baptist light of the eighteenth century.[24] God called the adult individual to make a conscientious choice to accept the faith. State coercion or control of this choice—either directly through persecution and repression or indirectly through withholding civil rights and benefits from those who made this choice—was an offense both to the individual and to God. A plurality of religions should coexist in the community. It was for God, not the state, to decide which of these religions should flourish and which should fade. "Religious liberty is a divine right," wrote the Evangelical preacher Israel Evans, "immediately derived from the Supreme Being, without the intervention of any created authority. . . . [T]he all-wise Creator invested [no] order of men with the right of judging for their fellow-creatures in the great concerns of religion."[25]

Autonomy of religious governance also lay at the heart of this Evangelical view. Every religious body, Evangelicals argued, should be free from state control of their assembly and worship, state regulations of their property and polity, state incorporation of their society and clergy, state interference in their discipline and government, state collection of religious tithes and taxes. "I am as sensible of the importance of religion and of the utility of it to human society as the Puritans are," Backus wrote. "And I concur with [them] that the fear and reverence of God and the terrors of eternity are the most powerful restraints upon the minds of men. But I am so far from thinking with [them] that these restraints would be broken down if equal religious liberty was established." Look at the long history of Christian establishment, where such forms of state intrusion on religious groups are countenanced, Backus wrote. It has led not to pure religion; instead "tyranny, simony, and robbery came to be introduced and to be practiced under the Christian name." Look at communities with no religious establishments; there religion, state, and society all flourish without fail. Look at the principles of the American revolution; "all America [was] up in arms" against taxation without representation. But just as certainly as we Americans were not represented in the British Parliament, so we religious dissenters are not represented among the established civil authorities. Yet we are still subject to their religious taxes and regulations. Look at the principles of the Bible:

> God has expressly armed the magistrate with the sword to punish such as work ill to their neighbors, and his faithfulness in that work and our obedience to such authority, is enforced [by the Bible]. But it is evident that the sword is excluded from the kingdom of the Redeemer. . . . [I]t is impossible to blend church and state without violating our Lord's commands to both together. His command to the church is, Put away from among yourselves that wicked person. His command to the state is, Let both grow together until the harvest. But it has appeared for these thousand years that pure Gospel discipline in the church is very little if at all known in state establishments of religion and that instead of letting conformists thereto, and dissenters therefrom, grow together or enjoy equal worldly privileges, the sword has been employed to root up, and to prepare war against all such as put not into the mouths of the established teachers who are the means of upholding such rulers as pervert all equity.[26]

Some Evangelicals extended the principle of church autonomy and disestablishment to argue against tax exemptions, civil immunities, property donations, and other forms of state support for all churches. Such Evangelicals feared state benevolence toward religion and religious bodies almost as much as they feared state repression. Those religious bodies that received state benefits would invariably become beholden to the state and distracted from their divine mandates. "[I]f civil Rulers go so far out of their Sphere as to take the

Care and Management of religious affairs upon them," reads a 1776 Baptist Declaration, "Yea . . . Farwel to 'the free exercise of Religion.'"[27]

The chief concern of the Evangelicals was theological, not political. Having suffered for more than a century as a religious minority in colonial America and more than two centuries in Europe, they sought a constitutional means to free all religion from the fetters of the law, to relieve the church from the restrictions of the state. In so doing, most Evangelicals of the founding era—save Isaac Backus, building on his seventeenth-century hero Roger Williams—developed only the rudiments of a political theory.[28] Most Evangelicals were content with a state that created a climate conducive to the cultivation of a plurality of religions and that accommodated all religious believers and religious bodies without conditions or controls.

Enlightenment Views

The Enlightenment movement in America provided a political theory that complemented the Evangelical theology of religious liberty. The Enlightenment was no single, unified movement, but a series of diverse ideological movements, in various academic disciplines and social circles throughout Europe and North America. Among its chief exponents were Montesquieu, Condorcet, and Voltaire in France, John Locke, Adam Smith, and David Hume in Britain, and a host of lesser-known writers. Among its leading lights in America were Thomas Jefferson and Thomas Paine, flanked on some causes by Benjamin Franklin and James Madison.[29] It was the American Revolution, especially, that catalyzed these American figures to convert Enlightenment ideals into constitutional imperatives.

The writings of English philosopher and theologian John Locke provided ample inspiration for this movement. In his famous *Letter Concerning Toleration* (1689) Locke had distilled the liberal English and Dutch learning of the seventeenth century into an elegant plea for church and state to end their corrosive alliances and to end their corrupt abridgments of the liberty of conscience.[30] The church, Locke wrote, is simply "a voluntary society of men, joining themselves together of their own accord in order to the public worshipping of God in such manner as they judge acceptable to Him, and effectual for the salvation of their souls." Church members are free to enter and free to exit this society. They are free to determine its order and organization and arrange its discipline and worship in a manner they consider most conducive to eternal life. "Nothing ought nor can be transacted in this society relating to the possession of civil and worldly power. No force is to be made use of upon any occasion whatsoever. For force belongs wholly to the civil magistrate."

State force, in turn, cannot touch religion, Locke argued. The state exists merely to protect persons in their outward lives, in their enjoyment of life, liberty, and property. "True and saving religion consists in the inward persuasion of the mind," which only God can touch and tend. A person cannot be compelled to true belief of anything by outward force—whether through "confiscation of estate, imprisonments, [or] torments" or through mandatory compliance with "articles of faith or forms of worship" established by law. "For laws are of no force without penalties, and penalties in this case are absolutely impertinent, because they are not proper to convince the mind." "It is only light and evidence that can work a change in men's [religious] opinions: which light can in no manner proceed from corporal sufferings, or any other outward penalties" inflicted by the state. Every person "has the supreme and absolute authority of judging for himself" in matters of faith.

Locke did not press this thesis to radical conclusions. His *Letter Concerning Toleration* presupposed a magistracy and community committed to a common Christianity. State laws directed to the common good, he believed, would only "seldom" "appear unlawful to the conscience of a private person" and would only seldom run afoul of conventional Christian beliefs and practices. Catholics, Muslims, and other believers "who deliver themselves up to the service and protection of another prince" have no place in this community. Moreover, "those are not at all tolerated who deny the being of a God"—for "promises, covenants, and oaths which are the bonds of human society, can have no hold upon an atheist." Locke strengthened these qualifications even more in his theological writings—arguing in *The Reasonableness of Christianity* for the cogency of a simple biblical natural law and endorsing in his several commentaries on St. Paul's epistles the utility of a moderate Christian republicanism.[31]

A century later and an ocean away, American Enlightenment writers pressed Locke's theses into more concrete legal and political forms.[32] The state, they taught, should not give special aid, support, privilege, or protection to religious doctrines or groups—through special tax appropriations or collections of tithes, special donations of goods and realty, special laws of religious incorporation, or special criminal laws against blasphemy, sacrilege, and Sabbath-breaking. The state should not predicate its laws on explicitly religious premises nor direct them to exclusively religious purposes. The state should not draw on the services of religious officials to discharge its political tasks nor interfere in the order, organization, or orthodoxy of religious bodies. As Madison put it in 1822: "[A] perfect separation between ecclesiastical and civil matters" is the best course, for "religion and Government will both exist in greater purity, the less they are mixed together."[33]

Like Locke, Madison did not press this logic to absolutist conclusions—particularly when it came to the "unessentials" of church-state relations. In an 1833 letter to Rev. Jaspar Adams, he wrote:

[I]t may not be easy, in every possible case, to trace the line of separation between the rights of Religion and the Civil authority, with such distinctness, as
to avoid collisions & doubts on unessential points. The tendency to a usurpation on one side, or the other, or to a corrupting coalition or alliance between
them, will be best guarded against by an entire abstinence of the Government
from interference in any way whatever, beyond the necessity of preserving
public order, & protecting each sect against trespasses on its legal rights by
others.[34]

Such views were based on both a skepticism about organized religion and
a fear of an autocratic state. To allow church and state to be unrestricted, it
was thought, would be to invite arbitrariness and abuse. To allow them to
combine would be to their mutual disadvantage—to produce, in Thomas
Paine's words, "a sort of mule-animal, capable only of destroying, and not
of breeding up."[35]

Such views were also based on the belief that a person is fundamentally
an individual being and that religion is primarily a matter of private reason
and conscience and only secondarily a matter of communal association and
corporate confession. Every person, Madison wrote, has the right to form
"a rational opinion" about the duty he owes the Creator and the manner in
which that duty is to be discharged.[36] Whether that religious duty is to be
discharged individually or corporately is of secondary importance.[37] Such
views were also based on a contractarian political philosophy that called
for the state to ensure the maximum liberty of citizens and their associations and to intervene only where one party's exercise of liberty intruded on
that of the other.

Postrevolutionary Virginia proved to be fertile ground for political exponents of the Enlightenment tradition to cultivate these views.[38] Article 16 of
the 1776 Virginia Bill of Rights, influenced in part by Madison, provided:

> That religion, or the duty which we owe to our Creator, and the manner of dis-
> charging it, can be directed only by reason and conviction, not by force or vio-
> lence; and therefore, all men are equally entitled to the free exercise of religion,
> according to the dictates of conscience; and that it is the mutual duty of all to
> practise Christian forbearance, love, and charity, towards each other.[39]

James Madison

The famous Virginia Statute for the Establishment of Religious Freedom,
drafted by Thomas Jefferson in 1779 and enacted in 1786, provided
stronger Enlightenment language. The statute begins by celebrating that
"Almighty God hath created the mind free; that all attempts to influence it
by temporal punishment, or burthens, or by civil incapacitations, tend only
to beget habits of hypocrisy and meanness, and are a departure from the
plan of the Holy Author of our religion." The statute recounts the ravages
of religious establishment and repression, and their resulting injuries to
God, religion, churches, states, and individuals. It then guarantees:

That no man shall be compelled to frequent or support any religious worship, place, or ministry whatsoever, nor shall be enforced, restrained, molested, or burthened, in his body or goods, nor shall otherwise suffer on account of his religious opinions or belief; but that all men shall be free to profess, and by argument to maintain, their opinions in matters of religion, and that the same shall in no wise diminish, enlarge or affect their civil capacities.[40]

These lofty protections of individual religious rights went hand in hand with the close restrictions on corporate religious rights that were also advocated by Enlightenment exponents. Before the turn of the nineteenth century, the Virginia legislature outlawed religious corporations, a prohibition still in place today in Virginia and West Virginia.[41]

The law of Virginia did not live entirely by the gospel of the Enlightenment, however. Even Jefferson supported the revision of Virginia's postrevolutionary laws, which included A Bill for Punishing Disturbers of Religious Worship and Sabbath Breakers; A Bill for Appointing Days of Public Fasting and Thanksgiving; and a Bill Annulling Marriages Prohibited by the Levitical Law, and Appointing the Mode of Solemnizing Lawful Marriage [in Church].[42]

Republican Views

The Civic Republicans, as they have come to be called in recent historical texts, were an eclectic group of politicians, preachers, and pamphleteers who strove to cultivate a set of common values and beliefs for the new nation.[43] Their principal spokesmen were George Washington, John Adams, Oliver Ellsworth, and other leaders—though the movement attracted considerable support among the spiritual and intellectual laity of the young republic as well. Many of the core ideas of this movement were grounded in earlier Anglican ideals of a Christian commonwealth. By the later eighteenth century, Republican leaders found their most natural theological allies among the Puritans, just as most Enlightenment leaders found their most natural allies among the Evangelicals.

To be sure, Civic Republicans shared much common ground with Evangelical and Enlightenment exponents. They, too, advocated liberty of conscience for all and state support for a plurality of religions in the community. They, too, opposed religious intrusions on politics that rose to the level of political theocracy and political intrusions on religion that rose to the level of religious establishment. But, contrary to Evangelical and Enlightenment writers and consistent with the Puritans, Republican writers sought to imbue the public square with a common religious ethic and ethos—albeit one less denominationally specific and rigorous than that countenanced by the Puritans.

"Religion and Morality are the essential pillars of Civil society," George Washington declared. "Of all the dispositions and habits which lead to political prosperity, religion and morality are indispensable supports."[44] "[W]e have no government," John Adams echoed, "armed with power capable of contending with human passions unbridled by morality and religion."[45] "Religion and liberty are the meat and the drink of the body politic," wrote Yale President Timothy Dwight.[46] According to Republican lore, society needs a fund of religious values and beliefs, a body of civic ideas and ideals, that are enforceable both through the common law and through communal suasion. This was what Benjamin Franklin in 1749 had called the "Publick Religion" (and what is now called the "civil religion") of America, which undergirded the plurality of sectarian religions.[47] This "Publick Religion" taught a creed of honesty, diligence, devotion, public spiritedness, patriotism, obedience, love of God, neighbor, and self, and other ethical commonplaces taught by various religious traditions at the time of the founding. Its icons were the Bible, the Declaration of Independence, the bells of liberty, and the Constitution. Its clergy were public-spirited ministers and religiously devout politicians. Its liturgy was the proclamations of prayers, songs, sermons, and Thanksgiving Day offerings by statesmen and churchmen. Its policy was government appointment of legislative and military chaplains, government sponsorship of general religious education and organization, and government enforcement of a religiously based morality through positive law.

These Republican views found favor in the Continental Congress, which authorized the appointment of tax-supported chaplains to the military, tax appropriations for religious schools and missionaries, diplomatic ties to the Vatican, and recitations of prayer at its opening sessions and during the day of Thanksgiving.[48] The Continental Congress also passed the Northwest Ordinance in 1787, which provided, in part: "Religion, morality and knowledge, being necessary to good government and the happiness of mankind, schools and the means of education shall forever be encouraged."[49]

These Republican views also found strong support among the states. Republicans countenanced state support and accommodation for religious institutions, for they were regarded as allies and agents of good government. "[R]eligion and its institutions are the best aid of government," declared Nathan Strong, "by strengthening the ruler's hand, and making the subject faithful in his place, and obedient to the general laws."[50] Similarly, Connecticut Senator Oliver Ellsworth declared: "Institutions for the promotion of good morals, are objects of legislative provision and support: and among these . . . religious institutions are eminently useful and important."[51] Republicans, therefore, endorsed tax exemptions for church properties and tax support for religious schools, charities, and missionaries; donations of public lands to religious organizations; and criminal protections against blasphemy, sacrilege, and interruption of religious services.[52]

The 1780 Constitution of Massachusetts, which John Adams drafted, was an influential example of the Republican effort to balance the freedom of all private religions with the "mild and equitable establishment" of one public religion. We must certainly begin "by setting the conscience free," Adams wrote. For "[w]hen all men of all religions consistent with morals and property, shall enjoy equal liberty, . . . [and] security of property, and an equal chance for honors and power . . . we may expect that improvements will be made in the human character and the state of society." But we must just as certainly begin by "setting religion at the fore and floor of society and government," Adams wrote. "Statesmen may plan and speculate for liberty, but it is religion and morality alone which can establish the principles upon which freedom can securely stand." A common "religion and virtue are the only foundations, not only of republicanism and of all free government, but of social felicity under all governments and in all the combinations of human society."[53]

The Massachusetts Constitution reflected this attempted balance.[54] Article II provided: "It is the right as well as the duty of all men in society, publickly, and at stated seasons to worship the SUPREME BEING, the great Creator and preserver of the Universe." Article III stated the reason: "[T]he public worship of GOD and instructions in piety, religion, and morality . . . promote their happiness, and secure . . . the good order and preservation of their government."[55] The same constitution also insisted that all persons, particularly political leaders, maintain rigorous moral and religious standards, which they confirmed in their oaths of office. It also rendered these same moral qualities essential ingredients of education within the state, since "the encouragement of arts and sciences, and all good literature, tends to the honor of GOD, the advantage of the Christian religion, and the great benefit of this and the other United States of America."[56]

These four views—Puritan, Evangelical, Enlightenment, and Republican—helped to inform the early American experiment in religious rights and liberties. Each view was liberally espoused by federal and state leaders in the early American republic, informally in their letters and pamphlets, and formally in the constitutional convention and ratification debates. Each left indelible marks on the documents and developments of early American constitutionalism.

3

THE ESSENTIAL RIGHTS
AND LIBERTIES OF
RELIGION

Puritans, Evangelicals, Republicans, and Enlightenment exponents—these four groups of founders held up the four corners of the wide and swaying canopy of opinion on religious liberty in eighteenth-century America. Beneath this canopy were gathered what they called the "essential rights and liberties" of religion: (1) liberty of conscience; (2) free exercise of religion; (3) religious pluralism; (4) religious equality; (5) separation of church and state; and (6) disestablishment of religion.[1]

These six principles appear regularly in the debates over religious liberty in the eighteenth century, though with varying definitions and priorities. They were also commonly incorporated into the original state and federal constitutions, though with different emphases and applications. They remain at the heart of the American experiment today—as central commandments of the American constitutional order and as cardinal axioms of a new American logic of religious liberty.

The common goal of these six principles was to replace the inherited tradition of religious establishments with a new experiment in religious liberty. To be sure, a number of founders were reluctant to extend the pale of religious liberty to Catholics and Jews—let alone to believers in African or Native American religions. These restrictive views are sometimes betrayed in the draft religion clauses of the state and federal constitutions. A number of founders understood "religion" to mean Christianity (or even Protestantism). Accordingly, their discussion of "religious liberty" was cast in terms of the "liberties" or "rights" of (Protestant) Christians.[2] And, to be sure, some states continued to support what John Adams called a "mild and equitable" establishment of religion—consisting principally in the collection of tithes for favored churches and clerics and the administration of religious oaths for high political offices. Before 1789, eleven of the original thirteen states extracted such oaths from high officials, and four collected religious tithes.[3]

Such seeming compromises of religious liberty, however, must be judged on their own terms, not on ours. It is easy enough to weigh eighteenth-century practices against twentieth-century norms and to find many of them wanting—just as twenty-second-century historians will doubtless weigh our practices against their norms and find many of them wanting. But such chronological snobbery is ultimately fruitless.

Judged by eighteenth-century Western standards, the American experiment in religious liberty was remarkably advanced. First, its efforts to extend the pale of religious liberty to the vast majority of the population were almost unprecedented. Many of the new constitutional provisions on religious rights and liberties were cast in broad terms—and applied on their face to "all persons" rather than simply to the narrow band of "citizens." Those constitutional provisions that were more denominationally specific could easily be extended to other religious groups, as later state courts and constitutional conventions repeatedly demonstrated. Second, the "mild and equitable" establishments of religions that remained were not the repressive regimes of earlier eras, featuring pogroms, inquisitions, persecutions, and religious wars. They were instead the constitutional expression of the Republican argument that each community must establish by law some form of public religion, some image and ideal of itself, some common values and beliefs to undergird and support the plurality of private religions. The notion that a state and society could remain neutral and purged of any religion was, for many founders, a philosophical fiction. Absent of a commonly adopted set of values and beliefs, politicians would invariably hold out their private convictions as public ones. It was thus essential for each community to define the basics of its public religion, even while guaranteeing essential religious rights and liberties for all it subjects.[4]

Virtually all the founders embraced religious liberty as the "first liberty" and the "first freedom" of the new constitutional order.[5] Religious liberty is "the most inalienable and sacred of all human rights," wrote Thomas Jefferson.[6] "Religious liberty, both civil and ecclesiastical, is the greatest blessing of the kind, that we can enjoy," wrote the Puritan preacher Jonathan Parsons, "and therefore to be deprived of either, is the greatest injury that we can suffer."[7]

At the same time, virtually all writers denounced the bloody persecution and repression of previous eras of religious establishment. James Iredell, a leading lawyer from North Carolina, reflected commonplaces of the day when he wrote:

Our guarantee of religious liberty for all . . . is calculated to prevent evils of the most pernicious consequences to society. Every person in the least conversant in the history of mankind, knows what dreadful mischiefs have been committed by religious persecutions. Under the color of religious tests the utmost cruelties have been exercised. Those in power have generally considered all wisdom centered in themselves, that they alone had a right to dictate to the rest of mankind, and that all opposition to their tenets was profane and impious. The consequence of this intolerant spirit had been, that each church has in turn set itself up against every other, and persecutions and wars of the most implacable and bloody nature have taken place in every part of the world. America has [now] set an example to mankind to think more modestly and reasonably; that a man may be of different religious sentiments from our own, without being a bad member of society.[8]

Liberty of Conscience

Liberty of conscience was the general solvent used in the early American experiment in religious liberty. It was almost universally embraced in the young republic—even by the most rigid of establishmentarians.[9] The phrase "liberty of conscience" is of ancient vintage, rooted in early Roman and Christian sources, and laden with multiple meanings in canon law, common law, and civil law alike.[10] The plasticity of the phrase was not lost on the American founders. Like their predecessors, they often conflated or equated the phrase with other favorites, such as "free exercise of religion," "religious freedom," "religious liberty," "religious privileges," and "religious rights." James Madison, for example, simply rolled into one linguistic heap "religious freedom" or "the free exercise of religion according to the dictates of conscience."[11] In another passage, he spoke of "liberty of conscience" as the "religious rights and privileges . . . of a multiplicity of sects."[12] Such patterns of interwoven language appear regularly in writings of the day. One term often implicated and connoted several others.[13] To read the original guarantee of liberty of conscience too dogmatically is to ignore its inherent plasticity.

That said, the founders did ascribe distinct content to the phrase "liberty of conscience," which won wide assent in the early republic.

First, for most founders, liberty of conscience protected *voluntarism*— "the unalienable right of private judgment in matters of religion," the unencumbered ability to choose and to change one's religious beliefs and adherences.[14] The Puritan theologian and jurist Elisha Williams put the matter strongly already in 1744:

Every man has an equal right to follow the dictates of his own conscience in the affairs of religion. Every one is under an indispensable obligation to search the Scripture for himself . . . and to make the best use of it he can for his own information in the will of God, the nature and duties of Christianity. And as every Christian is so bound; so he has the inalienable right to judge of the sense and meaning of it, and to follow his judgment wherever it leads him; even an equal right with any rulers be they civil or ecclesiastical.[15]

Every person must be "left alone" to worship God "in the manner and season most agreeable to the Dictates of his own conscience," John Adams echoed. For the rights of conscience are "indisputable, unalienable, indefeasible, [and] divine."[16] James Madison wrote more generically in 1785: "The Religion then of every man must be left to the conviction and conscience of every man; and it is the right of every man to exercise it as these may dictate."[17] The Evangelical leader John Leland echoed these sentiments in 1791:

> Every man must give an account of himself to God, and therefore every man ought to be at liberty to serve God in that way that he can reconcile it to his conscience. . . . It would be sinful for a man to surrender to man [that] which is to be kept sacred for God. A man's mind should be always open to conviction, and an honest man will receive that doctrine which appears the best demonstrated; and what is more common for the best of men to change their minds?[18]

Puritan, Republican, *Philosophe,* and Evangelical alike could agree on this core meaning of liberty of conscience.[19]

Second, and closely related, liberty of conscience *prohibited* religiously based *discrimination* against individuals. Persons could not be penalized for the religious choices they made nor swayed to make certain choices because of the civil advantages attached to them. Liberty of conscience, Ezra Stiles opined, permits "no bloody tribunals, no cardinal inquisitors-general, to bend the human mind, forcibly to control the understanding, and put out the light of reason, the candle of the Lord in man."[20] Liberty of conscience also prohibits more subtle forms of discrimination, prejudice, and cajolery by state, church, or even other citizens. "[N]o part of the community shall be permitted to perplex or harass the other for any supposed heresy," wrote a Massachusetts pamphleteer. "[E]ach individual shall be allowed to have and enjoy, profess and maintain his own system of religion."[21]

Third, in the view of some founders, liberty of conscience guaranteed "a freedom and *exemption* from human impositions, and legal restraints, in matters of religion and conscience."[22] Persons of faith were to be "exempt from all those penal, sanguinary laws, that generate vice instead of virtue."[23] Such laws not only included the onerous criminal rules that traditionally encumbered and discriminated against religious nonconformists, and led to fines, whippings, banishments, and occasional executions of dissenting colonists. They also included more facially benign laws that worked injustice to certain religious believers—conscription laws that required religious pacifists to participate in the military, oath-swearing laws that ran afoul of the religious scruples of certain believers, tithing and taxing laws that forced believers to support churches, religious schools, and other causes that they found religiously odious.[24] Liberty of conscience required that persons be exempt or immune from civil duties and restrictions that they could not, in good conscience, accept or obey.[25] As Henry Cumings put it: "Liberty of conscience requires not [only] that persons are . . . exempt from hierarchical tyranny and domination, from the usurped authority of pope and prelates, and from every species of persecution on account of religion." It also requires that they "stand on equal ground, and behaving as good members of society, may equally enjoy their religious opinions, and without molestation, or being exposed to fines or forfeitures, or any other temporal disadvantages."[26]

It was commonly assumed in the eighteenth century that the laws of conscientious magistrates would not often tread on the religious scruples of their subjects.[27] As George Washington put it in a letter to a group of Quakers: "In my opinion the conscientious scruples of all men should be treated with great delicacy and tenderness: and it is my wish and desire, that the laws may always be as extensively accommodated to them, as a due regard for the protection and essential interests of the nation may justify and permit."[28] It was also commonly understood that the growing pluralization of American religious life might make such inherent accommodation of all religions increasingly difficult. Where general laws and policies did intrude on the religious scruples of an individual or group, liberty of conscience demanded protection of religious minorities through exemptions from such laws and policies.[29] Whether such exemptions should be accorded by the legislature or by the judiciary and whether they were per se a constitutional right or simply a rule of equity—the principal bones of contention among a raft of recent commentators[30]—the eighteenth-century sources at my disposal do not dispositively say.

All the early state constitutions included a guarantee of liberty of conscience for all.[31] The Delaware Constitution had typical language:

> That all men have a natural and inalienable right to worship Almighty God according to the dictates of their own consciences and understandings; and that no man ought or of right can be compelled to attend any religious worship or maintain any religious ministry contrary to or against his own free will and consent, and that no authority can or ought to be vested in, or assumed by any power whatever that shall in any case interfere with, or in any manner controul the right of conscience and free exercise of religious worship.[32]

The Pennsylvania Constitution added a protection against religious discrimination: "Nor can any man, who acknowledges the being of a God, be justly deprived or abridged of any civil right as a citizen, on account of his religious sentiments or peculiar mode of religious worship." It also provided an exemption for conscientious objectors: "Nor can any man who is conscientiously scrupulous of bearing arms, be justly compelled thereto, if he will pay such equivalent."[33] The Constitution of New York addressed both state and church intrusions on conscience, endeavoring "not only to expel civil tyranny, but also to guard against that spiritual oppression and intolerance . . . wherewith the bigotry and ambition of weak and wicked priests have scourged mankind." It thus declared, "that the free exercise and enjoyment of religious profession and worship, without discrimination or preference, shall forever hereafter be allowed, within this State, to all mankind."[34] The Constitution of New Jersey provided exemptions from religious taxes, using typical language: "nor shall any person . . . ever be obliged to pay tithes, taxes, or any other rates, for the purpose of building or repairing any other church, . . . or ministry, contrary to what he believes to be right."[35]

The principle of liberty of conscience also informed some of the federal constitutional debates on religion. Article VI of the Constitution explicitly provides: "[N]o religious Test [oath] shall ever be required as a qualification" for public office, thereby protecting the religiously scrupulous against oath-swearing.[36] Early versions of the First Amendment religion clauses included such phrases as the following: "That any person religiously scrupulous of bearing arms ought to be exempted, upon payment of an equivalent to employ another to bear arms in his stead";[37] "[t]he civil rights of none shall be abridged on account of religious belief or worship . . . nor shall the full and equal rights of conscience be in any manner, or on any pretext, infringed";[38] "no State shall violate the equal rights of conscience"[39]; and "Congress shall make no law . . . to infringe the rights of conscience."[40] Such phrases were ultimately abandoned (though not argued against in the extant records) for the more pregnant language: "Congress shall make no law . . . prohibiting the free exercise [of religion]." This language does not leave conscience unprotected, but more protected. Since Congress cannot "prohibit" the free exercise, the public manifestation, of religion, it follows that Congress cannot "prohibit" a person's private liberty of conscience and the precepts embraced therein.

Liberty of conscience was the cardinal principle for the new experiment in religious liberty. Several other "essential rights and liberties of religion" built directly on this core principle.

Free Exercise of Religion

Liberty of conscience was inextricably linked to free exercise of religion and was a guarantee to be left alone to choose, to entertain, and to change one's religious beliefs. Free exercise of religion was the right to act publicly on the choices of conscience once made, without intruding on or obstructing the rights of others or the general peace of the community. This organic tie between religious conscience and religious exercise was well known in the Western tradition and was not lost on English and American writers.[41] Already in 1670, the Quaker leader William Penn had linked these two guarantees, insisting that religious liberty entails "not only a mere Liberty of the Mind, in believing or disbelieving . . . but [also] the Exercise of ourselves in a visible Way of Worship."[42] In the next century, this organic linkage was commonplace. Religion, Madison wrote, "must be left to the convictions and conscience of every man; and it is the right of man to exercise it as these may dictate."[43] For most eighteenth-century writers, religious belief and religious action went hand in hand, and each deserved legal protection.

Although eighteenth-century writers, or dictionaries, offered no universal definition of "free exercise," the phrase generally connoted various forms of free public religious action—religious worship, religious speech, religious assembly, religious publication, and religious education, among others. Free exercise of religion also embraced the right of the individual to join with like-minded believers in religious societies, which were free to devise their own modes of worship, articles of faith, standards of discipline, and patterns of ritual.[44] The founders did not use the phrases "religious group rights" or "corporate free exercise rights," which are commonplace today. But they did regularly call for "ecclesiastical liberty," "the equal liberty of one sect . . . with another," and the right "to have the full enjoyment and free exercise of those purely spiritual powers . . . which, being derived only from CHRIST and His Apostles, are to be maintained, independent of every foreign, or other, jurisdiction, so far as may be consistent with the civil rights of society."[45]

Virtually all the early state constitutions guaranteed "free exercise" rights—adding the familiar caveat that such exercise not violate the public peace or the private rights of others.[46] Most states limited their guarantee to "the free exercise of religious worship" or the "free exercise of religious profession"—thereby leaving the protection of other noncultic forms of religious expression and action to other constitutional protections, if any. A few states provided more generic free exercise guarantees. The Constitution of Virginia, for example, guaranteed "the free exercise of religion, according to the dictates of conscience"[47]—thereby expanding free exercise protection to cultic and noncultic religious expression and action, provided these were mandated by conscience. The Constitution of Georgia provided even more flatly: "All persons whatever shall have the free exercise of their religion; provided it be not repugnant to the peace and safety of the State."[48] The First Amendment drafters chose the expansive language of "free exercise [of religion]"—without defining or delimiting the kinds of religious exercises that might be protected, as some of the states had done.

Religious Pluralism

The founders regarded "multiplicity," "diversity," or "plurality" as an equally essential dimension of religious rights and liberties. Two kinds of pluralism were distinguished.

Evangelical and Enlightenment writers stressed the protection of *confessional pluralism*—the maintenance and accommodation of a plurality of forms of religious expression and organization in the community. Evangelical writers advanced a theological argument for this principle, emphasizing that it was for God, not the state, to decide which forms of religion should flourish and which should fade. "God always claimed it as his sole prerogative to determine by his own laws what his worship shall be, who shall minister in it, and how they shall be supported," Isaac Backus wrote.[49] "God's truth is great, and in the end He will allow it to prevail."[50] Confessional pluralism served to respect and reflect this divine prerogative.

Enlightenment writers advanced a rational argument for this principle. "Difference of opinion is advantageous in religion," Thomas Jefferson wrote. "The several sects perform the office of a *Censor morum* over each other. Is uniformity attainable? Millions of innocent men, women, and children, since the introduction of Christianity, have been burnt, tortured, fined, imprisoned; yet we have not advanced one inch towards uniformity. . . . Reason and persuasion are the only practicable instruments."[51] When Jefferson seemed to be wandering from these early sentiments, John Adams wrote to his Monticello friend: "Checks and balances, Jefferson"—in the political as well as the religious sphere—"are our only Security, for the progress of Mind, as well as the Security of Body. Every Species of these Christians would persecute Deists, as [much] as either Sect would persecute another, if it had unchecked and unbalanced Power. Nay, the Deists would persecute Christians, and Atheists would persecute Deists, with as unrelenting Cruelty, as any Christians would persecute them or one another. Know thyself, human Nature!"[52] Madison wrote similarly that "freedom arises from the multiplicity of sects, which pervades America, and which is the best and only security for religious liberty in any society. For where there is such a variety of sects, there cannot be a majority of any one sect to oppress and persecute the rest."[53] Other writers added that the maintenance of multiple faiths is the best protection of the core guarantee of liberty of conscience.[54]

Puritan and Republican writers, while endorsing confessional pluralism, also urged the protection of *social pluralism*—the maintenance and accommodation of a plurality of associations to foster religion. Churches and synagogues were not the only "religious societies" that deserved constitutional protection. Families, schools, charities, and other learned and civic societies were equally vital bastions of religion and equally deserving of the special protections of religious liberty. These diverse social institutions had several redeeming qualities. They provided multiple forums for religious expressions and actions, important bulwarks against state encroachment on natural liberties, particularly religious liberties, and vital sources of theology, morality, charity, and discipline in the state and broader community.[55] John Adams put it thus:

> My opinion of the duties of religion and morality comprehends a very extensive connection with society at large. . . . The benevolence, charity, capacity and industry which exerted in private life, would make a family, a parish or a town happy, employed upon a larger scale, in support of the great principles of virtue and freedom of political regulations might secure whole nations and generations from misery, want and contempt.[56]

Benjamin Rush concurred:

> Religion is best supported under the patronage of particular societies. . . . Religion could not long be maintained in the world without [these] forms and the distinctions of sects. The weaknesses of human nature require them. The distinction of sects is as necessary to the perfection and government of the whole as regiments and brigades are in an army.[57]

Pluralism was thus not just a sociological fact for the founders. It was also a constitutional condition for the guarantee of religious liberty. This was a species and application of Madison's famous argument about the virtues of republican pluralism in *Federalist Papers No. 10* and *No. 51*. In a federalist republic, Madison had argued in *Federalist Paper No. 10:*

> The influence of factious leaders may kindle a flame within their particular States but will be unable to spread a general conflagration through the other States. A religious sect may degenerate into a political faction in a part of the Confederacy; but the variety of sects dispersed over the entire face of it must secure the national councils against any danger from that source.[58]

He summarized this general point crisply in Paper No. 51: "In a free government, the security for civil rights must be the same as that for religious rights; it consists in the one case in the multiplicity of interests, and in the other in the multiplicity of sects."[59]

Religious Equality

The efficacy of liberty of conscience, free exercise of religion, and religious pluralism depended on a guarantee of equality of all peaceable religions before the law. For the state to single out one pious person or one form of faith for either preferential benefits or discriminatory burdens would skew the choice of conscience, encumber the exercise of religion, and upset the natural plurality of faiths. Many of the founders therefore called for equality of all religions before the law. James Madison captured well the prevailing sentiment: "A just Government . . . will be best supported by protecting every Citizen in the enjoyment of his religion, with the same equal hand which protects his person and property; by neither invading the equal rights of any sect, nor suffering any sect to invade those of another."[60] John Adams concurred: "[A]ll men of all religions consistent with morals and property [must] enjoy equal liberty, . . . security of property . . . and an equal chance for honors and power."[61] Isaac Backus wrote similarly that religious liberty requires that "each person and each [religious] society are equally protected from being injured from others, all enjoying equal liberty to attend the worship which they believe is right."[62]

The founders's argument for religious equality became particularly pointed in their debates over religious test oaths as a condition for holding federal political office and positions of public trust. Oaths were commonly accepted in the early republic as "one of the principal instruments of government." They induce "the fear and reverence of God, and the terrors of eternity," one Puritan preacher put it, and thus impose "the most powerful restraints upon the minds of men."[63] Following colonial custom, eleven of the original thirteen states prescribed such oaths. These ranged in specificity from a general affirmation of belief in God or in (Protestant) Christianity to the Trinitarian confession required by Delaware: "I, A. B., do profess faith in God the Father, and in Jesus Christ His only Son, and in the Holy Ghost, one God, blessed for evermore; and I do acknowledge the holy scriptures of the Old and New Testament to be given by divine inspiration."[64] A number of Quakers, Moravians, Baptists, and other groups, before and after the Revolution, had condemned such oaths as a violation of the liberty of conscience and as an "invading of the essential prerogatives of our Lord Jesus Christ."[65] The few Jewish voices of the day protested oaths as a violation of their liberty of conscience and civil rights.[66] In response, most colonies and states exempted Quakers (and sometimes others with conscientious objections) from the oaths in deference to the principle of liberty of conscience.

The addition of an argument from religious equality proved particularly persuasive in outlawing religious test oaths. The argument first came to prominence in the federal constitutional convention and in the ratification debates that followed. Article VI of the Constitution provided that "no religious Test shall ever be required as a Qualification to any office or public Trust under the United States." James Iredell of North Carolina offered a quite typical defense of this provision: "This article is calculated to secure universal religious liberty, by putting all sects on a level."[67] Fellow Carolinian Richard Spaight elaborated the argument: "No sect is preferred to another. Every man has the right to worship the Supreme Being in the manner that he thinks proper. No test is required. All men of equal capacity and integrity are equally eligible to offices."[68] Such an argument for equality proved persuasive enough to garner state ratification of Article VI of the Constitution in 1789. It also helped to outlaw some of the state religious test oaths: Georgia (1789), Delaware (1792), and Vermont (1793) dropped their test oaths. Pennsylvania (1790) extended theirs to include Jews. The new state constitutions of Kentucky (1792) and Tennessee (1796) included no religious test oaths, although they still required that political officials be theists, if not Christians.[69]

Most founders extended the principle of equality before the law to all peaceable religions—though sometimes only grudgingly conceding its application to Jews and Muslims. A few founders pressed the principle further, arguing for the equality of religions and nonreligions—particularly on issues of test oaths and religious taxes. Luther Martin of Maryland grumbled about this solicitude for the nonreligious shown during the debates over religious test oaths:

> The part of the system which provides, that no religious test shall ever be required as a qualification to any office or public trust under the United States, was adopted by a great majority of the convention, and without much debate; however, there were some members so unfashionable as to think, that a belief of the existence of a Deity, and of a state of future rewards and punishments would be some security for the good conduct of our rulers, and that, in a Christian country, it would be *at least decent to hold out some distinction between the professors of Christianity and downright infidelity or paganism.*[70]

Similarly, James Madison, in protesting the proposed tax scheme for religious teachers in Virginia, wrote:

> Above all are they to be considered as retaining an "equal title to the free exercise of religion according to the dictates of conscience." While we assert for ourselves a freedom to embrace, to profess and to observe the religion which we believe to be of divine origin, *we cannot deny an equal freedom to those whose minds have not yet yielded to the evidence which has convinced us.* If this freedom be abused, it is an offence against God, not against man.[71]

The founders's principal concern, however, was directed to equality among religions, not equality between religion and nonreligion.[72] Benjamin Huntington indicated during the House debate over the disestablishment and free exercise clauses of the First Amendment that "he hoped the amendment would be made in such a way to secure the rights of conscience, and a free exercise of the rights of religion but *not to patronize those who professed no religion at all.*"[73] Likewise, in the House debates about including conscientious objection among the rights of conscience, Representative Scott stated firmly, without rejoinder: "There are many sects I know, who are religiously scrupulous in this respect; I do not mean to deprive them of any indulgence. . . . [M]y design is to guard against those who are of no religion."[74]

This principle of equality of all peaceable religious persons and bodies before the law found its way into a number of early state constitutions. New Jersey insisted that "there shall be no establishment of any one religious sect in . . . preference to another."[75] Delaware guaranteed Christians "equal rights and privileges"—a guarantee soon extended to all religions.[76] Maryland insisted that Christians "are equally entitled to protection in their religious liberty."[77] Virginia guaranteed that "all men are equally entitled to the free exercise of religion."[78] New York guaranteed all persons "free exercise and enjoyment of religious profession and worship, without discrimination or preference."[79] Even Massachusetts, which maintained a "slender" establishment, nonetheless guaranteed that "all religious sects and denominations, demeaning themselves peaceably, and as good citizens of the commonwealth, shall be equally under the protection of the law; and no subordination of one sect or denomination to another shall ever be established by law."[80]

The principle of equality also found its place in early drafts of the First Amendment religion clauses, yielding such phrases as: "nor shall the full and equal rights of conscience be in any manner, or on any pretext, infringed";[81] "Congress shall make no law establishing One Religious Sect or Society in preference to others";[82] and "Congress shall make no law establishing any particular denomination of religion in preference to another."[83] Madison, in fact, regarded protection of the "equal rights of conscience" as the "most valuable" guarantee for religious liberty, and he argued that it should be guaranteed specifically against the states.[84] These provisions and arguments were abandoned for the more generic guarantees of disestablishment and free exercise at the federal level—guarantees that presumably are to apply equally to all religions.

Separation of Church and State

"Separation of church and state" was a familiar Western principle, especially among Protestant writers. Martin Luther, for example, had spoken of "a paper wall . . . between the spiritual estate [and] the temporal estate."[85] John Calvin had argued that the "political kingdom" and "spiritual kingdom" must always be "considered separately." For there is "a great difference between the ecclesiastical and civil power" and it would be "unwise to mingle these two which have a completely different nature."[86] Such early Protestant views were repeated in New England Puritan writings and laws.[87] European Anabaptist writers had also spoken of the necessary separation between the fallen world and the redeemed church. Such views recurred in Roger Williams's image of "a wall of separation between the garden of the Church and the wilderness of the world" and were repeated by later Evangelical writers in the eighteenth century, notably Isaac Backus.[88]

The principle of separation of church and state also had solid grounding in political sources that appealed to American Enlightenment and Republican writers. James Burgh, for example, a Scottish Whig who was popular among several American founders, pressed for the principle in his influential writings of the 1760s and 1770s.[89] Burgh lamented the "ill consequences" of the traditional "mixed-mungrel-spiritual-secular-eccesiastical establishment." Such conflations of church and state, said Burgh, lead to "follies and knaveries," and make "the dispensers of religion despicable and odious to all men of sense, and will destroy the spirituality, in which consists the whole value, of religion." "Build an impenetrable wall of separation between sacred and civil," Burgh enjoined. "Do not send the graceless officer, reeking from the arms of his trull [i.e., prostitute], to the performance of a holy rite of religion, as a test for his holding the command of a regiment. To profane, in such a manner, a religion, which you pretend to reverence, is an impiety sufficient to bring down upon your heads, the roof of the sacred building you thus defile."[90]

Tunis Wortman, a Jeffersonian, also wrote boldly:

> It is your duty, as Christians, to maintain the purity and independence of the church, to keep religion separate from politics, to prevent an union between the church and the state, and to preserve the clergy from temptation, corruption and reproach. . . . Unless you maintain the pure and primitive spirit of Christianity, and prevent the cunning and intrigue of statesmen from mingling with its institutions, you will become exposed to a renewal of the same dreadful and enormous scenes which have not only disgraced the annals of the church, but destroyed the peace, and sacrificed the lives of millions. . . . Religion and government are equally necessary, but their interests should be kept separate and distinct.[91]

Such quotes, from both theological and political sources, reflect the central understanding of the principle of separation in the founding era: The offices and officers of the churches and states must break their traditional alliances. "Upon no plan, no system," wrote Wortman, "can they become united, without endangering the purity and usefulness of both—the church will corrupt the state, and the state pollute the church."[92]

On the one hand, separation of church and state guarantees "ecclesiastical purity and liberty"—the independence and integrity of the internal processes of religious bodies. Elisha Williams spoke for many churchmen when he wrote: "[E]very church has [the] right to judge in what manner God is to be worshipped by them, and what form of discipline ought to be observed by them, and the right also of electing their own officers" without interference from political officials.[93]

On the other hand, separation guarantees "political and social stability"—the protection of individual rights and social cohesion. James Madison put this well in discussing church and state:

> Their jurisdiction is both derivative and limited. It is limited with regard to the co-ordinate departments; more necessarily is it limited with regard to the constituents. The preservation of a free government requires not merely, that the metes and bounds which separate each department of power be invariably maintained; but more especially that neither of them be suffered to overleap the great barrier which defends the rights of the people.[94]

The principle of separation of church and state was also readily understood by the founders as a means to protect the liberty of conscience of the religious believer. Thomas Jefferson, for example, in his famous 1802 letter to the Danbury Baptist Association, tied the principle of separationism directly to the principle of liberty of conscience:

> Believing with you that *religion is a matter which lies solely between a man and his God,* that he owes account to none other for his faith or his worship, that the [legitimate] powers of government reach actions only, and not opinions, I contemplate with sovereign reverence that the act of the whole American people which declared that their legislature should "make no law respecting an establishment of religion, or prohibiting the free exercise thereof," *thus building a wall of separation between church and State.* Adhering to this expression of the supreme will of the nation *in behalf of the rights of conscience,* I shall see with sincere satisfaction the progress of those sentiments which tend to *restore to man all his natural rights,* convinced he has no natural right in opposition to his social duties.[95]

Separatism thus assured individuals of their natural, inalienable right of conscience, which could be exercised freely and fully to the point of breaching the peace or shirking social duties. Jefferson is not talking here of separating politics and religion altogether. Indeed, in the very next paragraph of his letter, President Jefferson performed an avowedly religious act of offering prayers on behalf of his Baptist correspondents: "I reciprocate your kind prayers for the protection and blessing of the common Father and Creator of man."[96] This was consistent with a number of his other political acts in support of religion, both as governor of Virginia and as president of the United States.[97]

Disestablishment of Religion

For some founders, particularly the New England Puritans who defended their "mild and equitable establishments," the roll of "essential rights and liberties" ended here. Many other founders, however, combined several of these principles into a call for the disestablishment of religion.

The term "establishment of religion" was an ambiguous phrase—in the eighteenth century, as much as today. In the dictionaries and common parlance of the founders' day, to "establish" meant "to settle firmly," "to fix unalterably," "to settle in any privilege or possession," "to make firm," "to ratify," "to ordain," "to enact," "to set up," to "build firmly."[98] Such was the basic meaning of the term, for example, when used in the 1787 Constitution—"We the people of the United States, in order to form a perfect union, to *establish* justice . . . do ordain and *establish* this Constitution" (preamble); Congress shall have power "[t]o *establish* an uniform rule of naturalization" and "[t]o *establish* post offices" (Art. I.8); Governmental offices "shall be *established* by law" (Art. II.2); Congress may "ordain and *establish* . . . inferior courts" (Art. III.1); the ratification of nine states "shall be sufficient for the *establishment* of this Constitution" (Art. VI).[99]

Following this basic sense of the term, the founders understood the establishment of religion to mean the actions of government to "settle," "fix," "define," "ordain," "enact," or "set up" the religion of the community—its religious doctrines and liturgies, its religious texts and traditions, its clergy and property. The most notorious example of this, to their minds was the establishment by law of Anglicanism. English ecclesiastical law formally required use of the Authorized (King James) Version of the Bible and of the liturgies, rites, prayers, and lectionaries of the *Book of Common Prayer*. It demanded subscription to the Thirty-Nine Articles of Faith and the swearing of loyalty oaths to the Church, Crown, and Commonwealth of England. When such ecclesiastical laws were rigorously applied—as they were in England in the early Stuart period of the 1610s–1630s, and again in the Restoration of the 1660s–1670s, and intermittently in the American colonies—they led to all manner of state controls of the internal affairs of the established church, and all manner of state repression and coercion of religious dissenters.

Many of the founders who called for the disestablishment of religion sought to outlaw this traditional form of religious establishment. To them, such an establishment of religion violated a number of first principles of religious liberty—notably liberty of conscience, equality and plurality of religion, and the separation of church and state.

Disestablishment of religion, under this understanding, served to protect the principle of liberty of conscience by foreclosing government from coercively prescribing mandatory forms of religious belief, doctrine, and practice. As both the Delaware and Pennsylvania constitutions put it: "[N]o authority can or ought to be vested in, or assumed by any power whatever, that shall in any case interfere with, or in any manner controul, the right of conscience in the free exercise of religious worship."[100]

Disestablishment of religion further protected the principles of equality and pluralism by preventing government from singling out certain religious beliefs and bodies for preferential treatment. This concept of disestablishment came through repeatedly in both state and federal debates. In the Virginia Ratification Convention, for example, both Madison and Edmund Randolph stressed that religious pluralism would "prevent the establishment of any one sect in prejudice, to the rest, and will forever oppose all attempts to infringe religious liberty."[101] South Carolina conventioneer Francis Cummins likewise stated that it was "his duty and honor to oppose the ideas of religious establishments; or of states giving preference to any religious denomination."[102] The New Jersey Constitution provided "there shall be no establishment of any one religious sect ... in preference to another."[103] Both the New York and the Rhode Island Ratifying Conventions suggested amendments to the Constitution that "no religious sect or society ought to be favored or established by law in preference to others."[104] Two drafts of the religion clauses debated in the First Congress included a similar guarantee: "Congress shall make no law establishing one religious sect or society in preference to others"[105] and "Congress shall make no law establishing any particular denomination of religion in preference to another."[106]

Disestablishment of religion also served to protect the basic principle of separation of church and state. Disestablishment, in Jefferson's words, prohibited government "from intermeddling with religious institutions, their doctrines, discipline, or exercises" and from "the power of effecting any uniformity of time or matter among them. Fasting & prayer are religious exercises. The enjoining them is an act of discipline. Every religious society has a right to determine for itself the times for these exercises, & the objects proper for them, according to their own peculiar tenets."[107] To allow such governmental intermeddling in the affairs of religious bodies would inflate the competence of government. As Madison wrote, it "implies either that the Civil Magistrate is a competent judge of religious truth; or that he may employ religion as an engine of civil policy. The first is an arrogant pretension falsified by the contradictory opinions of rulers in all ages, and throughout the world, the second an unhallowed perversion of the means of salvation."[108] Governmental interference in religious affairs also compromises the pacific ideals of most religions. Thomas Paine, who is usually branded as a religious skeptic, put this well:

All religions are in their nature mild and benign, and united with principles of morality. They could not have made proselytes at first, by professing anything that was vicious, cruel, persecuting or immoral. . . . Persecution is not an original feature in any religion; but it is always the strongly marked feature of all law-religions, or religions established by law. Take away the law-establishment, and every religion reassumes its original benignity.[109]

The question that remained controversial—in the eighteenth century as much as in our own—was whether more gentle and generic forms of state support for religion could be countenanced. Did disestablishment of religion prohibit governmental support for religion altogether, or did it simply require that such governmental support be distributed nonpreferentially among religions?

It takes a bit of historical imagination to appreciate this question in eighteenth-century terms. In eighteenth-century America, government patronized religion in a variety of ways. Officials donated land and personalty for the building of churches, religious schools, and charities. They collected taxes and tithes to support ministers and missionaries. They exempted church property from taxation. They incorporated religious bodies. They outlawed blasphemy and sacrilege, unnecessary labor on the Sabbath and on religious holidays. They administered religious test oaths.[110]

Historically, such forms of state patronage of religion were reserved to the established church alone. All other faiths, if tolerated at all, were left to depend on their own resources. In the course of the eighteenth century, the growth of religious freedom often entailed the gradual extension of these forms of state privilege and patronage to other faiths—often in a piecemeal fashion: benefit by benefit, congregation by congregation. By the later eighteenth century, the hard constitutional questions became this: Should state patronage for religion end altogether? Or should state patronage be extended to all religions indiscriminately, rather than granted only in this piecemeal fashion? Given the overwhelmingly Christian, indeed Protestant, character of the new nation, a policy of nonpreferential governmental support for virtually all religions could be quite realistically envisioned—particularly if some accommodation were made for Jewish sabbatarian beliefs and Quaker aversions to religious oaths. (No founder seriously thought of having to accommodate the African religions of the slaves or the traditional religions of the Native Americans.)

The question of whether disestablishment of religion outlaws all governmental support for religion or only preferential governmental support for some religions was not resolved in the eighteenth century. The founders were divided on the question. A number of Evangelical and Enlightenment writers viewed the principle of disestablishment as a firm bar on state support, particularly financial support, of religious beliefs, believers, and bodies.[111] James Madison, for example, wrote late in his life: "Every new & successful example ... of a perfect separation between ecclesiastical and civil matters, is of importance. And I have no doubt that every new example, will succeed, as every past one has done, in shewing that religion & Govt. will both exist in greater purity, the less they are mixed together."[112] Similar sentiments can be found in contemporaneous Baptist tracts, particularly those of Isaac Backus and John Leland.[113] Puritan and Republican writers often viewed such principles only as a prohibition against direct financial support for the religious worship or exercise of one particular religious group. General governmental support for religion—in the form of tax exemptions to religious properties, land grants and tax subsidies to religious schools and charities, tax appropriations for missionaries and military chaplains, and similar general causes—were considered not only licit but necessary for good governance.

The state constitutions were likewise divided on the question. A number of states explicitly authorized such support in their original constitutions. The constitution of Maryland (1776) was typical. It included strong guarantees of religious liberty that touched each of the principles of religious liberty we have rehearsed. "[A]ll persons, professing the Christian religion, are equally entitled to protection in their religious liberty." This includes freedom from "molestation" "on account of his religious persuasion or profession, or for his religious practice"; "nor ought any person to be compelled to frequent or maintain, or contribute, unless on contract [i.e., by agreement] to maintain any particular place of worship, or any particular ministry." But, the constitution continues, without pause, to provide that "the Legislature may, in their discretion, lay a general and equal tax, for the support of the Christian religion; leaving to each individual the power of appointing the payment over of the money, collected from him, to the support of any particular place of worship or minister, or for the benefit of the poor of his own denomination, or the poor in general of any particular county."[114] Similar provisions were included in the original constitutions of Massachusetts, New Hampshire, and Connecticut.[115] The other original state constitutions simply repeated the general principles of religious liberty, without touching the issue of whether government could support religion(s). Similarly, none of the drafts nor the final version of the First Amendment addresses the question directly, beyond simply prohibiting "the" or "an" "establishment of religion."

Interdependence of Principles

For all the diversity of opinion one finds in the constitutional convention debates, pamphlets, sermons, editorials, and broadsides of the eighteenth century, most influential writers embraced this roll of "essential rights and liberties of religion"—liberty of conscience, free exercise of religion, religious pluralism, religious equality, separation of church and state, and disestablishment of religion. To be sure, many of these terms carried multiple meanings in the later eighteenth century. And to be sure, numerous other terms and norms were under discussion, often with widely discordant and confusing implications. But in the range of eighteenth-century sources at my disposal, these principles were the most commonly discussed and embraced.

On the one hand, eighteenth-century writers designed these principles to provide an interwoven shield against repressive religious establishments. Liberty of conscience protected the individual from coercion and discriminatory treatment by church or state officials and guaranteed unencumbered, voluntary choices of faith. Free exercise of religion protected the individual's ability to discharge the duties of conscience through religious worship, speech, publication, assembly, and other actions without necessary reference to a prescribed creed, cult, or code of conduct. Pluralism protected multiple forms and forums of religious belief and action, in place of a uniformly mandated religious doctrine, liturgy, and polity. Equality protected religious individuals and bodies from special benefits and from special burdens administered by the state or by other religious bodies. Separationism protected individual believers, as well as religious and political officials, from undue interference or intrusion on each other's processes and practices. Disestablishment precluded governmental prescriptions of the doctrine, liturgy, or morality of one faith and compromises of the principles of liberty of conscience, free exercise, equality, pluralism, or separationism.

On the other hand, eighteenth-century writers designed these principles to be mutually supportive and mutually subservient to the highest goal of guaranteeing "the essential rights and liberties of religion" for all. No single principle could by itself guarantee such religious liberty. Simple protection of liberty of conscience provided no protection of religious actions or organizations. Pure pluralism could decay into religious relativism and render the government blind to the special place of religion in the community and in the Constitution. Simple guarantees of the equality of religion could render governments indifferent to the widely divergent needs of different forms of religion. Pure separationism could deprive the church of all meaningful forms and functions and deprive states of an essential ally in government and social service. Pure nonestablishment could readily rob society of all common values and beliefs and the state of any effective religious role. Eighteenth-century writers, therefore, arranged these multiple principles into an interlocking and interdependent shield of religious liberties and rights for all. Religion was simply too vital and too valuable a source of individual flourishing and social cohesion to be left unguarded on any side.

4

FORGING THE FIRST AMENDMENT RELIGION CLAUSES

Four views drove much of the early American experiment in religious liberty—Puritan, Evangelical, Enlightenment, and Republican. Six principles of religious liberty were held in common among them—liberty of conscience, free exercise of religion, religious pluralism, religious equality, separation of church and state, and disestablishment of religion. It is in the context of this plurality of opinions and panoply of principles that the First Amendment religion clauses should, in my view, be understood.

In an effort to come to terms with the range of original views on religious liberty, the two previous chapters have touched intermittently on speeches and acts made in the Continental Congress of 1774–1789, the Constitutional Convention of 1787, and the First Session of Congress of 1789. This chapter will digest more carefully the work of these federal bodies up to the final formulation of the First Amendment religion clauses on September 26, 1789. The federal record, in this early period, is rather spare. I shall quote extensively from what is said therein about religion and religious liberty, and then sketch the range of plausible meanings that can be assigned to the final text of the First Amendment: "Congress shall make no law respecting an establishment of religion, or prohibiting the free exercise thereof."

Religion and the Continental Congress

The Continental Congress, comprised of delegates from the colonies, met for the first time on September 5, 1774, to respond to the increasingly harsh economic measures imposed by the British mother country.[1] Its second session, commencing on May 10, 1775, was devoted to coordinating the Revolutionary War against Great Britain. During this session, the Congress also began to emerge as the provisional federal government of the budding new nation, a status confirmed by the Articles of Confederation of 1781. The Congress's principal mandate was to deal with pressing issues of the military, interstate relationships, national commerce, foreign diplomacy, and the like. But in the course of its work from 1774 to 1788, the Continental Congress did issue a few acts touching religion.

Early in the first session, the Continental Congress resolved to open its daily sessions with prayer. During the second session, the Congress appointed and funded legislative chaplains to offer these prayers, as well as chaplains to serve in the military forces. On June 12, 1775, the Congress issued the first of its four fast-day proclamations, urging a "day of publick humiliation, fasting, and prayer; that we may, with united hearts and voices, unfeignedly confess and deplore our many sins"; that we may "be ever under the care and protection of a kind Providence, and be prospered"; and "that virtue and true religion may revive and flourish throughout our land."[2] On November 1, 1777, the Congress issued its first of what would become annual Thanksgiving Day proclamations. This first proclamation was an overtly Trinitarian Christian statement, providing that "it is the indispensable Duty of all men to adore the superintending Providence of Almighty God; to acknowledge with Gratitude their Obligation to him for Benefits received, and to implore such farther Blessings as they stand in need of." The proclamation set aside a day each year of "solemn thanksgiving and praise":

> That at one Time and with one Voice, the good People may express the grateful Feelings of their Hearts, and consecrate themselves to the Service of their Divine Benefactor; and that, together with their sincere Acknowledgements and Offerings, they may join the penitent Confession of their manifold Sins, whereby they had forfeited every Favour; and their humble and earnest Supplication that it may please God through the Merits of Jesus Christ, mercifully to forgive and blot them out of Remembrance: That it may please him graciously to afford his Blessing on the Governments of these States respectively, and prosper the public Council of the whole: To inspire our Commanders, both by Land and Sea, and all under them, with that Wisdom and Fortitude which may render them fit instruments, under the Providence of Almighty God, to secure for these United States, the greatest of all human Blessings, Independence and Peace: That it may please him, to prosper the Trade and Manufactures of the People, and the Labour of the Husbandman, that our Land may yield its Increase: To take Schools and Seminaries of Education, so necessary for cultivating the Principles of true Liberty, Virtue and Piety, under his nurturing Hand; and to prosper the Means of Religion, for the promotion and enlargement of that Kingdom, which consisteth *"in Righteousness, Peace, and Joy, in the Holy Ghost."*[3]

The Continental Congress expressed ample concern about their Catholic neighbors to the north in Quebec. Initially, their views were hostile. In 1763, Quebec had come to be a British colony. In the Quebec Act of 1774, the British Parliament had guaranteed to these new subjects "free exercise of the religion of the Church of Rome, subject to the king's Supremacy."[4] The Congress denounced this act "for establishing the Roman Catholick religion." It expressed "astonishment that a British Parliament should ever consent to *establish* in that country a religion that has deluged your island in blood, and dispersed impiety, bigotry, persecution, murder and rebellion through every part of the world."[5] During the Revolutionary War with Britain, however, the Congress reversed its sentiments abruptly. Congress sent two letters to their Catholic neighbors in Quebec, urging them to cede from the British and to join the budding American union. In their overtures, they guaranteed them, inter alia, religious freedom. To press their case, Congress also sent a distinguished delegation to the north, with this instruction:

> You are further to declare that we hold sacred the rights of conscience and may promise to the whole people, solemnly in our name, the free and undisturbed exercise of their religion; and, to the clergy, the full, perfect, and peaceable possession and enjoyment of all their estates. That the government of everything relating to their religion and clergy, shall be left entirely in the hands of the good people of that province and such legislature as they shall constitute: provided, however, that all other denominations of Christians be equally entitled to hold offices and enjoy civil privileges and the free exercise of their religion and be totally exempt from the payment of any tythes or taxes for the support of any religion.[6]

Also during the Revolutionary War, the Congress sought to encourage defection of German mercenaries who were fighting for Great Britain. It offered would-be defectors guarantees of liberty, security, and property. It also ordered all states to receive these soldiers, and ensure that they "be protected in the free exercise of their respective religions."[7]

On September 11, 1777, a narrow majority of the Congress voted to import 20,000 Bibles for distribution in the new states. Absent sufficient funds and strong political support, no federal action to procure the Bibles was ever taken. Instead, the Congress resolved tepidly in 1780: "That it be recommended to such of the States who may think it convenient for them that they take proper measures to procure one or more new and correct editions of the Old and New Testament to be printed."[8] Thereafter, the Congress also endorsed a privately funded translation of the Bible, directed the legislative and military chaplains to make use of it, and recommended "this edition of the Bible to the inhabitants of the United States."[9]

On November 15, 1778, the Congress approved the Articles of Confederation, which came to govern the body in 1781. Article III bound the states to "assist each other, against all force offered to, or attacks made upon them, or any of them, on account of religion."[10]

Three treaties adopted by the Congress included religious liberty clauses. The Treaty with the Netherlands (1782) provided that "there shall be an entire and perfect liberty of conscience allowed to the subjects and inhabitants of each party, and their families; and no one shall be molested in regard to his worship, provided he submits, as to the public demonstration of it, to the laws of the country."[11] The language recurs almost verbatim in a treaty with Sweden (1783). A 1785 treaty with Prussia provided: "the most perfect freedom of conscience and of worship is granted to the citizens or subjects of either party within the jurisdiction of the other, without being liable to molestation in that respect for any cause other than an insult on the religion of others."[12] The final peace treaty with England (1783) was also made "[i]n the name of the Most Holy and Undivided Trinity."[13]

The 1787 Northwest Ordinance, establishing a new territorial government for the midwestern frontier, set forth various "fundamental principles of civil and religious liberty," including: "No person, demeaning himself in a peaceable and orderly manner, shall ever be molested on account of his mode of worship, or religious sentiments"; and "Religion, morality and knowledge, being necessary to good government and the happiness of mankind, schools and the means of education shall forever be encouraged."[14]

The record of the Continental Congress also includes other scattered acknowledgments and endorsements of public worship, Christian thanksgiving, Sunday observance, and confession of sin. The record is also amply peppered with genial references to and invocations of God and Christianity. The most famous of these divine invocations was the Declaration of Independence of 1776, with its references to "the Laws of Nature and Nature's God," "the Creator," "the Supreme Judge of the world," and "a firm reliance on the protection of Divine Providence."

The 1787 Constitutional Convention

The United States Constitution—debated and drafted by the Constitutional Convention from May 25 to September 17, 1787—was largely silent on questions of religion and religious freedom. The preamble to the Constitution speaks generically of the "Blessings of Liberty." Article I, section 7 recognizes the Christian Sabbath: "If any Bill should not be returned by the President within ten days (Sundays excepted) after it shall have been presented to him, the Same shall be a Law." Article VI provides "no religious Test shall ever be required as a Qualification to any Office or public Trust under the United States." A reference to "the Year of our Lord" sneaks into the dating of the instrument. But nothing more. The "Godless Constitution" has been both celebrated and lamented ever since.[15]

The seeming impiety of the work of the 1787 Constitutional Convention must be understood in political context. It was commonly assumed at the convention that questions of religion and of religious liberty were for the states and the people to resolve, not the budding federal government. By 1784, eleven of the thirteen states had already crafted detailed constitutional provisions on religious liberty. The two remaining states, Rhode Island and Connecticut, retained their colonial charters, which also had religious liberty clauses. The mandate of the 1787 convention was to create a new national sovereign with enumerated powers and delineated procedures. What was not specifically given to this new federal sovereign was to be retained by the sovereign states and the sovereign people.

Federal power over religion was not considered part of this new constitutional calculus. As James Madison put it to the Virginia Ratification Convention: "There is not a shadow of right in the general government to intermeddle with religion. Its least interference with it, would be a most flagrant usurpation."[16] James Iredell concurred in the North Carolina Ratification Convention, arguing that the federal branches of government "certainly have no authority to interfere in the establishment of any religion whatsoever, and I am astonished that any gentleman should conceive they have."[17]

Federal protection of religion was also considered beyond the mandate of the 1787 convention. Both the natural checks and balances inherent in the nation's religious pluralism and the new religious liberty provisions of the state constitutions were considered to be ample protection.[18] For the emerging federal constitution to guarantee religious and civil rights was viewed to be otiose, if not odious. James Wilson put the case famously in the Pennsylvania Ratification Convention:

> [A] bill of rights is neither an essential nor a necessary instrument in framing a system of government, since liberty may exist and be as well secured without it. But it was not only unnecessary, but on this occasion it was found impracticable—for who will be bold enough to undertake to enumerate all the rights of the people?—and when the attempt to enumerate them is made, it must be remembered that if the enumeration is not complete, everything not expressly mentioned will be presumed to be purposely omitted.[19]

Alexander Hamilton warned further in *Federalist Paper No. 84* that to specify federal rights was "not only unnecessary in the proposed Constitution, but would even be dangerous. They would contain various exceptions to powers not granted; and, on this very account, would afford a colorable pretext to claim more than was granted. For why declare that things shall not be done which there is no power to do?"[20]

Accordingly, the three weak attempts to introduce federal protections of religion and religious liberty into the new constitution were quickly quashed. Early in the convention debates, on May 29, 1787, Charles Pinckney of South Carolina submitted to the convention a draft constitution, which included a religion clause: "The Legislature of the United States shall pass no Law on the subject of Religion."[21] Although many of Pinckney's proposed provisions helped to shape the debates and the final form of the Constitution, his religious liberty clause was passed over without comment and died silently in committee. On September 12, five days before the conclusion of the convention, George Mason and Eldridge Gerry moved to designate a committee to attach a bill of rights to the largely completed Constitution. The motion failed 10–0.[22] On September 14, James Madison and Charles Pinckney sought to ascribe to Congress a power "to establish an University, in which no preferences or distinctions should be allowed on account of religion."[23] The motion failed 6–4.

Even Benjamin Franklin's motion to have the convention sessions open with prayer garnered virtually no support. On June 28, the elderly Franklin, exasperated by the casuistic debates in the convention to date, had issued a short sermon to his fellow delegates on the importance of prayer:

> [W]e have not hitherto once thought of humbly applying to the Father of lights to illuminate our understandings. In the beginning of the Contest with G. Britain, when we were sensible of danger we had daily prayer in this room for the divine protection. . . . And have we now forgotten that powerful friend? or do we imagine that we no longer need his assistance? I have lived, Sir, a long time, and the longer I live, the more convincing proofs I see of this truth—*that God governs in the affairs of men*. And if a sparrow cannot fall to the ground without his notice, is it probable that an empire can rise without his aid? We have been assured, Sir, in the sacred writings, that "except the Lord build the House they labour in vain that build it." I firmly believe this; and I also believe that without his concurring aid we shall succeed in this political building no better than the Builders of Babel: We shall be divided by our little partial local interests; our projects will be confounded, and we ourselves shall become a reproach and bye word down to future ages. And what is worse, mankind may hereafter from this unfortunate instance, despair of establishing Governments by Human Wisdom and leave it to chance, war and conquest.
>
> I therefore beg leave to move—that henceforth prayers imploring the assistance of Heaven, and its blessings on our deliberations, be held in this Assembly every morning before we proceed to business, and that one or more of the Clergy of this City be requested to officiate in that service.

Franklin's motion failed, the record reads, for fear it might "1. bring on it some disagreeable animadversions. & 2. lead the public to believe that the embarrassments and dissentions within the convention, had suggested this measure." Moreover, another delegate pointed out, there were no funds to pay for a chaplain to pray.[24]

The only proposal about religion to receive support was Charles Pinckney's proposal that religion not be considered a condition for federal office. On August 20, Pinckney had proposed a freestanding provision in the Constitution prohibiting religious tests or qualifications for federal office.[25] On August 30, he moved to amend a clause specifying the oath of office with the words that would eventually find their way into Article VI of the Constitution: "but no religious test shall ever be required as a qualification to any office or public trust under the authority of the U. States." Only one delegate objected to the motion—not because he favored religious test oaths but because he thought "it unnecessary, the prevailing liberality being a sufficient security against such tests." Pinckney's motion, however, was seconded and passed, with one dissent.[26]

During the ratification debates and thereafter, the no religious test provision of Article VI was sometimes denounced as an invitation to "Papists" and "Mahometans," and even "infidels" and "pagans," to hold federal office. It was defended, as we saw (pages 46–47), on principles both of liberty of conscience and equality of faiths before the federal law.[27] But in the 1787 convention itself, the almost casual passage of the prohibition against religious tests for federal office was testimony to the commonality of the assumption that religion and religious liberty were beyond the pale of federal authority.

Ratification and Proposed Amendments

The Constitutional Convention completed its draft Constitution on September 17, 1787. The Continental Congress approved it by unanimous vote on September 28 and sent it on to the states for ratification. Article VII of the proposed Constitution required ratification by the "Conventions of nine States." The Constitution was ratified on July 2, 1788, when the ninth vote, from the New Hampshire ratification convention, was recorded.[28]

The absence of a bill of a rights to the Constitution, however, was a point of considerable controversy in the state ratification debates. Despite the repeated assurances of the federalists that Congress could not exercise power over subjects like religion that were not specifically enumerated in the Constitution, only four states would ratify the instrument without a federal bill of rights. The remaining states ratified the Constitution only on the promise that the First Session of Congress would prepare a bill of rights to amend the Constitution. Seven states ultimately proposed provisions to be included in a federal bill of rights. Of these, six proposed religious liberty clauses, with some overlap in content. Four of these proposed amendments on religious liberty, tendered in the summer of 1788, were critical.[29]

On June 21, 1788, New Hampshire proposed the following religious liberty amendment:

[1] Congress shall make no laws touching religion, or to infringe the rights of conscience.[30]

On June 26, 1788, Virginia—stating its concern "that no right of any denomination" may be violated and "among other essential rights, the liberty of conscience, and of the press, cannot be cancelled, abridged, restrained, or modified, by any authority of the United States"—proposed the following amendment:

[2] That religion, or the duty which we owe to our creator, and the manner of discharging it, can be directed only by reason and conviction, not by force or violence, and therefore all men have an equal, natural and unalienable right to the free exercise of religion according to the dictates of conscience, and that no particular religious sect or society ought to be favored or established by law in preference to others.[31]

On July 26, 1788, New York proposed:

[3] That the people have an equal, natural, and unalienable right freely and peaceably to exercise their religion, according to the dictates of conscience; and that no religious sect or society ought to be favored or established by law in preference to others.[32]

On August 1, 1788, North Carolina—resolving to protect the "great principles of civil and religious liberty"—repeated the Virginia provision (with only cosmetic changes in punctuation), prefaced by a conscientious objection clause:

[4] That any person religiously scrupulous of bearing arms ought to be exempted, upon payment of an equivalent to employ another to bear arms in his stead.[33]

Rhode Island repeated North Carolina's language in its proposed amendment, belatedly tendered on June 16, 1790.[34]

Drafting the First Amendment Religious Clauses

It was up to the First Session of Congress to cull from these proposals, and the broader traditions that they represented, a suitable amendment on religious rights and liberties. The record of the Congress's effort is considerably slimmer than is apt for such a momentous act. Neither the House nor the

Senate kept an official record of its proceedings in this first year. The Senate met in closed session and merely kept a journal of brief minutes of its resolutions. The House debates were sometimes open to visitors; much of what appears in the *Annals of Congress* for the First Session of 1789 is drawn from the inexactly taken and transcribed notes of newspaper reporter Thomas Lloyd.[35] These minutes and notes do include several drafts of the religion clauses that were considered intermittently between June 8 and September 26, 1789. They also include summaries and paraphrases of a few of the House debates on August 15, 17, and 20. But for the critical stages of deliberation in late August and September 1789 when these various drafts and speeches were pressed into the final text of the First Amendment, the record is exceedingly cryptic and conclusory—leaving courts and commentators ever since with ample room for speculation and interpolation.[36]

On June 8, 1789, James Madison, a newly elected representative from Virginia, proposed to the House of Representatives that they take up the task of preparing a bill of rights to the United States Constitution. He had reduced the multiple state proposals for rights provisions into a draft, which included two religion clauses. These he put to the House for consideration:

[5] The civil rights of none shall be abridged on account of religious belief or worship, nor shall any national religion be established, nor shall the full and equal rights of conscience be in any manner, or any pretext infringed.

[6] No state shall violate the equal rights of conscience, or the freedom of the press, or the trial by jury in criminal cases.[37]

The House agreed to give formal consideration to Madison's proposals in due course. But debate was postponed for several weeks, as Congress devoted itself to the immediate task of organizing the new government.[38]

On July 21, again prompted by Madison, the House finally turned to Madison's proposals and appointed a committee comprised of one representative of each of the eleven states represented in the First Congress.[39] Madison, representing Virginia, was included. This committee of eleven put forward its proposed rights provisions on July 28, including three separate provisions on religion:

[7] no religion shall be established by law, nor shall the equal rights of conscience be infringed.

[8] no person religiously scrupulous shall be compelled to bear arms.

[9] no State shall infringe the equal rights of conscience, nor the freedom of speech or of the press, nor of the right of trial by jury in criminal cases.

The committee's report was tabled without any recorded discussion. On August 13, the House, sitting as a committee of the whole, took up the report, one provision at a time.

On August 15, the House reached the first of the three committee provisions on religion: "no religion shall be established by law, nor shall the equal rights of conscience be infringed." The House ultimately approved an amended version of the same. The full record of their debate, highlighting the amended provision, reads thus:

Mr. SYLVESTER had some doubts of the propriety of the mode of expression used in this paragraph. He apprehended that it was liable to a construction different from what had been made by the committee. He feared it might be thought to have a tendency to abolish religion altogether.

Mr. VINING suggested the propriety of transposing the two members of the sentence.

Mr. GERRY said it would read better if it was, that no religious doctrine shall be established by law.

Mr. SHERMAN thought the amendment altogether unnecessary, inasmuch as Congress had no authority whatever delegated to them by the constitution to make religious establishments; he would, therefore, move to have it struck out.

Mr. [Daniel] CARROLL. As the rights of conscience are, in their nature, of peculiar delicacy, and will little bear the gentlest touch of governmental hand; and as many sects have concurred in opinion that they are not well secured under the present constitution, he said he was much in favor of adopting the words. He thought it would tend more towards conciliating the minds of the people to the Government than almost any other amendment he had heard proposed. He would not contend with gentlemen about the phraseology, his object was to secure the substance in such a manner as to satisfy the wishes of the honest part of the community.

Mr. MADISON said, he apprehended the meaning of the words to be, that Congress should not establish a religion, and enforce the legal observation of it by law, nor compel men to worship God in any manner contrary to their conscience. Whether the words are necessary or not, he did not mean to say, but they had been required by some of the State Conventions, who seemed to entertain an opinion that under the clause of the constitution, which gave power to Congress to make all laws necessary and proper to carry into execution the constitution, and the laws made under it, enabled them to make laws of such a nature as might infringe the rights of conscience, and establish a national religion; to prevent these effects he presumed the amendment was intended, and he thought it as well expressed as the nature of the language would admit.

Mr. HUNTINGTON said that he feared, with the gentleman first up on this subject, that the words might be taken in such latitude as to be extremely hurtful to the cause of religion. He understood the amendment to mean what had been expressed by the gentleman from Virginia; but others might find it convenient to put another construction upon it. The ministers of their congregations to the Eastward were maintained by the contributions of those who belonged to their society; the expense of building meetinghouses was contributed in the same manner. These things were regulated by by-laws. If an action was brought before a Federal Court on any of these cases, the person who had neglected to perform his engagements could not be compelled to do it; for a support of ministers, or building of places of worship might be construed into a religious establishment.

By the charter of Rhode Island, no religion could be established by law; he could give a history of the effects of such a regulation; indeed the people were now enjoying the blessed fruits of it. He hoped, therefore, the amendment would be made in such a way as to secure the rights of conscience, and a free exercise of the rights of religion, but not to patronize those who professed no religion at all.

Mr. MADISON thought, if the word national was inserted before religion, it would satisfy the minds of honorable gentlemen. He believed that the people feared one sect might obtain a pre-eminence, or two combine together, and establish a religion to which they would compel others to conform. He thought if the word national was introduced, it would point the amendment directly to the object it was intended to prevent.

Mr. LIVERMORE was not satisfied with that amendment; but he did not wish them to dwell long on the subject. He thought it would be better if it was altered, and made to read in this manner, that [10] **Congress shall make no laws touching religion, or infringing the rights of conscience.**

Mr. GERRY did not like the term national, proposed by the gentleman from Virginia, and he hoped it would not be adopted by the House. It brought to his mind some observations that had taken place in the conventions at the time they were considering the present constitution. It had been insisted upon by those who were called antifederalists, that this form of Government consolidated the Union; the honorable gentleman's motion shows that he considers it in the same light. Those who were called antifederalists at that time complained that they had injustice done them by the title, because they were in favor of a Federal Government, and the others were in favor of a national one; the federalists were for ratifying the constitution as it stood, and the others not until amendments were made. Their names then ought not to have been distinguished by federalists and antifederalists, but rats and antirats.

Mr. MADISON withdrew his motion, but observed that the words "no national religion shall be established by law," did not imply that the Government was a national one; **the question was then taken on Livermore's motion, and passed in the affirmative,** thirty-one for, and twenty against it.[40]

On August 17, the House came to the second provision on religion in the committee report: "no person religiously scrupulous shall be compelled to bear arms." The record of their debate, which ended inconclusively, reads thus:

Mr. GERRY—This declaration of rights, I take it, is intended to secure the people against the mal-administration of the Government; if we could suppose that, in all cases, the rights of the people would be attended to, the occasion for guards of this kind would be removed. Now, I am apprehensive, sir, that this clause would give an opportunity to the people in power to destroy the constitution itself. They can declare who are those religiously scrupulous, and prevent them from bearing arms. . . . Now, if we give a discretionary power to exclude those from militia duty who have religious scruples, we may as well make no provision on this head. For this reason, he wished the words to be altered so as to be confined to persons belonging to a religious sect scrupulous of bearing arms.

Mr. JACKSON did not expect that all the people of the United States would turn Quakers or Moravians; consequently, one part would have to defend the other in case of invasion. Now this, in his opinion, was unjust, unless the constitution secured an equivalent: for this reason he moved to amend the clause, by inserting at the end of it, "upon paying an equivalent, to be established by law."

Mr. SMITH, of South Carolina, inquired what were the words used by the conventions respecting this amendment. If the gentleman would conform to what was proposed by Virginia and Carolina, he would second him. He thought they were to be excused provided they found a substitute.

Mr. JACKSON was willing to accommodate. He thought the expression was, "No one, religiously scrupulous of bearing arms, shall be compelled to render military service, in person, upon paying an equivalent."

Mr. SHERMAN conceived it difficult to modify the clause and make it better. It is well known that those who are religiously scrupulous of bearing arms are equally scrupulous of getting substitutes or paying an equivalent. Many of them would rather die than do either one or the other; but he did not see an absolute necessity for a clause of this kind. We do not live under an arbitrary Government, said he, and the States, respectively, will have the government of the militia, unless when called into actual service; besides, it would not do to alter it so as to exclude the whole of any sect, because there are men amongst the Quakers who will turn out, notwithstanding the religious principles of the society, and defend the cause of their country. Certainly it will be improper to prevent the exercise of such favorable dispositions, at least whilst it is the practice of nations to determine their contests by the slaughter of their citizens and subjects.

Mr. VINING hoped the clause would be suffered to remain as it stood, because he saw no use in it if it was amended so as to compel a man to find a substitute, which, with respect to the Government, was the same as if the person himself turned out to fight.

Mr. STONE inquired what the words "religiously scrupulous" had reference to: was it of bearing arms? If it was, it ought so to be expressed.

Mr. BENSON moved to have the words "but no person religiously scrupulous shall be compelled to bear arms," struck out. He would always leave it to the benevolence of the Legislature, for, modify it as you please, it will be impossible to express it in such a manner as to clear it from ambiguity. No man can claim this indulgence of right. It may be a religious persuasion, but it is no natural right, and therefore ought to be left to the discretion of the Government. If this stands part of the constitution, it will be a question before the Judiciary on every regulation you make with respect to the organization of the militia, whether it comports with this declaration or not. It is extremely injudicious to intermix matters of doubt with fundamentals.

I have no reason to believe but that the Legislature will always possess humanity enough to indulge this class of citizens in a matter they are so desirous of; but they ought to be left for their discretion.

The motion for striking out the whole clause being seconded, was put, and decided in the negative—22 members voting for it, and 24 against it.[41]

Later that same day of August 17, the House debated the third of the provisions recommended by the committee: "no State shall infringe the equal rights of conscience, nor the freedom of speech or of the press, nor of the right of trial by jury in criminal cases." It approved a slightly amended version:

Mr. TUCKER.—This is offered, I presume, as an amendment to the constitution of the United States, but it goes only to the alteration of the constitutions of particular States. It will be much better, I apprehend, to leave the State Governments to themselves, and not to interfere with them more than we already do; and that is thought by many to be rather too much. I therefore move, sir, to strike out these words.

Mr. MADISON conceived this to be the most valuable amendment in the whole list. If there was any reason to restrain the Government of the United States from infringing upon these essential rights, it was equally necessary that they should be secured against the State Governments. He thought that if they provided against the one, it was as necessary to provide against the other, and was satisfied that it would be equally grateful to the people.

Mr. LIVERMORE had no great objection to the sentiment, but he thought it not well expressed. He wished to make it an affirmative proposition; [11] **"the equal rights of conscience, the freedom of speech or of the press, and the right of trial by jury in criminal cases, shall not be infringed by any State."**

This transposition being agreed to, and Mr. TUCKER's motion being rejected, **the clause was adopted.**[42]

Up to this point, the House had considered its rights amendments as individual provisions to be inserted at appropriate places in the body of the Constitution. On August 20, the House agreed to consolidate these multiple rights provisions, including those on religion, into a more systematic and uniform "supplement" to the Constitution—a separate bill of rights.[43] The three provisions on religion discussed to date were distilled into two provisions. The brief record of the debate on these two provisions on August 20, follows:

On motion of Mr. AMES, the fourth amendment was altered so as to read: [12] **"Congress shall make no law establishing religion, or to prevent the free exercise thereof, or to infringe the rights of conscience."** This being adopted, the first proposition was agreed to.

Mr. SCOTT objected to the clause in the sixth amendment, "No person religiously scrupulous shall be compelled to bear arms." He observed that if this becomes part of the constitution, such persons can neither be called upon for their services, nor can an equivalent be demanded; it is also attended with still further difficulties, for a militia can never be depended upon. This would lead to the violation of another article in the constitution, which secures to the people the right of keeping arms, and in this case recourse must be had to a standing army. I conceive it, said he, to be a legislative right altogether. There are many sects I know, who are religiously scrupulous in this respect; I do not mean to deprive them of any indulgence the law affords; my design is to guard against those who are of no religion. It has been urged that religion is on the decline; if so, the argument is more strong in my favor, for when the time comes that religion shall be discarded, the generality of persons will have recourse to these pretexts to get excused from bearing arms.

Mr. BOUDINOT thought the provision in the clause, or something similar to it, was necessary. Can any dependence, said he, be placed in men who are conscientious in this respect: or what justice can there be in compelling them to bear arms, when, according to their religious principles, they would rather die than use them? He adverted to several instances of oppression on this point, that occurred during the war. In forming a militia, an effectual defence ought to be calculated, and no characters of this religious description ought to be compelled to take up arms. I hope that in establishing this Government, we may show the world that proper care is taken that the Government may not interfere with the religious sentiments of any person. Now, by striking out the clause, people may be led to believe that there is an intention in the General Government to compel all its citizens to bear arms.

Some further desultory conversation arose, and it was agreed to insert the words "in person" to the end of the clause; after which it was adopted. (This yielded [13] "No person religiously scrupulous shall be compelled to bear arms in person.")[44]

On August 22, these two provisions on religion, along with other amendments, were referred to a House style committee.[45] Two days later, the committee issued its final report. The report included the first religion provision, introduced by Fisher Ames on August 20, but slightly revised. It omitted the second provision, without explanation. This final House version, sent to the Senate on August 25, reads thus:

[14] Congress shall make no law establishing religion, or prohibiting the free exercise thereof, nor shall the rights of conscience be infringed.[46]

On September 3, the Senate took up debate of this religion clause proposed by the House. No record of their debate survives. The *Journal of the Senate* reports that separate motions first to adopt and later to strike the House provision on religion were defeated.[47] The journal then reports that three alternative drafts of the religion clauses were proposed and defeated. These read seriatim:

[15] Congress shall make no law establishing One Religious Sect or Society in preference to others, nor shall the rights of conscience be infringed.[48]

[16] Congress shall not make any law, infringing the rights of conscience, or establishing any Religious Sect or Society.[49]

[17] Congress shall make no law establishing any particular denomination of religion in preference to another, or prohibiting the free exercise thereof, nor shall the rights of conscience be infringed.[50]

Although none of these version passed, the Senate did agree to a fourth proposal on September 3:

[18] Congress shall make no law establishing religion, or prohibiting the free exercise thereof.[51]

Agreement on this clause, however, was short-lived. On September 9, the Senate passed a rather different version of the religion clause, now combined with clauses on free speech, press, and assembly.

> [19] **Congress shall make no law establishing articles of faith or a mode of worship, or prohibiting the free exercise of religion,** or abridging the freedom of speech, or the press, or the right of the people peaceably to assemble, and petition to the Government for the redress of grievances.[52]

That same day, September 9, the Senate sent this final version to the House for approval.

The House rejected this version. A joint committee, composed of three representatives and three senators was appointed to forge a consensus draft. Representing the House were three members of the original committee of eleven that had prepared the draft religion clauses of July 28—Madison; Roger Sherman, a Puritan from Connecticut; and John Vining, a Republican from Delaware. Representing the Senate were Oliver Ellsworth, a Connecticut Republican; William Patterson, an Evangelical from New Jersey; and Charles Carroll, a Catholic from Maryland.[53] No record of their debate survives. On September 24, 1789, they reported the final text that came to be the First Amendment:

> [20] **Congress shall make no Law respecting an establishment of Religion, or prohibiting the free exercise thereof.**[54]

On September 25, the Senate concurred in the House resolution to send the draft bill of rights, including this religion clause, to President Washington. It was sent the following day, and the president sent it to the states for ratification. The final vote needed for ratification, from Virginia, was recorded on December 15, 1791, rendering the amendments effective from that day forward.

The Final Text

Determining the original understanding of the First Amendment has been the perennial challenge of the American experiment ever since. The final text has no plain meaning. The congressional record holds no Rosetta Stone for easy interpretation. Twenty separate drafts of the religion clauses (highlighted and numbered above) came under Congress's consideration— four tendered by the states, ten debated in the House, five more debated in the Senate, and the final draft forged by the joint committee. The congressional record holds no dispositive argument against any one of the nineteen interim drafts and few clear clues on why the sixteen words that comprise the final text were chosen.

A Thinner Reading

One plausible reading is that the final text is a compromise agreement only on the outer boundaries of appropriate congressional action on religion. *Congress* may not *prescribe* religion. *Congress* may not *proscribe* religion. Nothing more—and to try to impute more to the text is to over-read the unreliable record of debates in the First Congress.

On this reading, the First Amendment leaves open to later discussion and development what governmental bodies, besides Congress, might be bound. Earlier drafts of the religion clauses had bound the states by name—"no state may infringe [or "violate"] the equal rights of conscience" (Draft Nos. 6, 9, 11). Other drafts had been written in the passive voice and were thus potentially applicable to all government officials—"no religion shall be established by law, nor shall the equal rights of conscience be infringed"; "the people have an equal, natural, and unalienable right freely and peaceably to exercise their religion according to the dictates of conscience" (Nos. 2–5, 7, 8, 13). But in the final text, Congress alone is singled out for special limitation, in a way that no other Amendment in the Bill of Rights seeks to do.

On this reading, the First Amendment also leaves open to later discussion and development what conduct short of prescribing or proscribing religion is outlawed. Earlier drafts of the disestablishment clause had included much more sweeping language: Congress was not to "touch" or "favor" religion; not to give "preference" to any religious sect society, or denomination; not to "establish" any articles of faith or mode of worship (Nos. 1–3, 10, 15–17, 19). Such provisions were left aside for the more blunt provision that Congress should simply not do anything that would point to ("respect") an establishment of religion. It is an open question whether congressional conduct favorable toward religion, but not of a sort traditionally associated with an established religion, is outlawed by the instrument.

Likewise, the first seventeen drafts of the free exercise clause had included much more sweeping guarantees: Congress was not to "touch," "infringe," "abridge," "violate," "compel" or "prevent" the exercise of religion or the rights and freedom of conscience. Again, such provisions were left aside for a more blunt provision: Congress should simply not "prohibit" the free exercise of religion. It is an open question whether conduct short of outright prohibition of religious exercise is outlawed.

Such a thin reading of the religion clauses comports with the eighteenth-century ideal that the new Constitution is a blueprint of government, not a code of governmental conduct. The First Amendment simply sets the outer boundaries to appropriate congressional action—no prescription and no proscription of religion. But it leaves the middle way between these outer boundaries open to constitutional discussion and development. The founders knew that this middle way was not uncharted and that the discussion was not unprincipled. After all, the nineteen earlier drafts of the religion clauses included five of the six main principles of religious liberty regularly discussed in the founding era. Concern for the liberty (or rights or scruples) of conscience appear in fifteen drafts. Free exercise appears in nine drafts, religious equality in nine, religious pluralism in six, disestablishment in twelve. (Conspicuously absent from all the drafts is the principle of separation of church and state.)

It is instructive, on this thinner reading, that Congress chose the terms "free exercise" and "establishment" to define the outer boundaries of proper congressional conduct. As we saw (pages 42–44, 51–55), these were the broadest terms at hand to describe the principles and province of religious liberty. "Free exercise" was at once a source, summary, and synonym for "liberty of conscience," "religious equality," "religious pluralism," and "separation of church and state." "Non-" or "disestablishment" was broadly defined as a general guarantee of religious equality, liberty of conscience, and separation of church and state. The religion clauses, therefore, set only outside limits to Congress's action respecting religion. But the guarantees of disestablishment and free exercise together had embodied—incorporated—within them the full range of first principles of religious liberty prized by the founders. And these first principles would help set the metes and bounds of the proper constitutional way between these two outer boundaries.

Thicker Readings

The record of the debates over the religion clauses can also support somewhat more nuanced interpretations. The temptation to self-serving present-mindedness, of course, increases as one thickens the interpretation. But even a cautious reading of the spare record suggests a bit more about the original understanding of some of the words and phrases.

"Congress." The specification of *"Congress"* underscored the founders' general agreement that the religion clauses were binding not on the states but on the most dangerous branch of the new federal government. This was the strong sentiment of the 1787 Constitutional Convention and the state ratification debates. It was repeated in the surviving speeches of Sherman, Livermore, Gerry, and Tucker in the House.

The first draft of the religion clauses, submitted by New Hampshire, had specified "Congress" (No. 1). The three other state drafts submitted in the summer of 1788 included general guarantees of religious liberty that could be read to bind both federal and state governments. In his June 8, 1789, consolidated draft, Madison had sought to accommodate both readings—

by outlawing a "national" establishment and by prohibiting states from infringing on conscience (Nos. 5, 6). This construction failed, despite Madison's two arguments for it in the August 15 debate. The original New Hampshire focus on "Congress" became the norm.

In his same June 8 draft, Madison had also included generic guarantees of religious liberty without specifying the government entity bound thereby—"the full and equal rights of conscience shall not be infringed" and "the civil rights of none shall be abridged on account of religion" (No. 5). Such provisions, too, died without explanation. By August 20, Fisher Ames's draft (No. 12) specified Congress alone, and the Senate held to this.

"Shall Make." The phrase "shall make no law" is rather distinctive—written in a future active imperative voice, as our grammar teachers would say. In eighteenth-century parlance, "shall," as opposed to "will," is an imperative; it is an order, rather than a prediction, about what Congress does in the future. "Shall" is so used fifteen times in the Bill of Rights alone. But why the construction "shall make no law," which is a phrasing unique to the First Amendment? Could it be that Congress could make no new laws on religion but could confirm laws that had already been made—before the First Amendment was passed, or by the Continental Congress before it?

Such a reading seems fanciful until one notes the exchange in the House, on September 25, 1787, the very day the House approved the final text of the religion clauses. Elias Boudinot of New Jersey, who chaired the recorded House debates on the religion clauses, announced that "he could not think of letting the session pass over without offering an opportunity to all the citizens of the United States of joining, with one voice, in returning to Almighty God their sincere thanks for the many blessings he had poured down upon them." He then moved that both houses of Congress request the president to set aside a day of "public thanksgiving and prayer, to be observed by acknowledging . . . the many signal favors of Almighty God." Aedanus Burke of South Carolina thought this too redolent of a military European custom, which made "a mere mockery of thanksgiving." Thomas Tucker, also of South Carolina, objected that "it is a business with which Congress ha[s] nothing to do; it is a religious matter, and, as such, is proscribed to us. If a day of thanksgiving must take place, let it be done by the authority of the several States; they know best what reason their constituents have to be pleased with the establishment of the Constitution." Roger Sherman countered that the tradition of offering such public prayers was "laudable," and after citing a few biblical precedents for it, declared the practice "worthy of Christian imitation on the present occasion." Boudinot defended his motion on grounds that it was "a measure both prudent and just" and quoted "further precedents from the practice of the late

Congress" to drive home his point. The motion passed in the House, and later also in the Senate.[55] President Washington set aside a Thanksgiving Day and gave a robust proclamation on October 3, 1789. This Thanksgiving tradition has continued virtually uninterrupted ever since.

This was not the only such inherited tradition touching religion that the First Congress confirmed and continued. On April 15, 1789, before deliberating the religion clauses, the Congress voted to appoint "two Chaplains of different denominations" to serve Congress, one in each house.[56] On April 27, the Congress ordered, relevant to the pending inauguration of President Washington: "That after the oath shall have been administered to the President, he, attended by the Vice President, and members of the Senate, and House of Representatives, proceed to St. Paul's Chapel, to hear divine service, to be performed by the Chaplain of Congress already appointed."[57] These chaplains served the Congress throughout the period of the debates on the religion clauses. On September 22, 1789, just as the joint committee was polishing the final draft of the religion clauses, Congress passed an act confirming their appointment and stipulating that the chaplains were to be paid a salary of $500 per annum.[58] Similarly, on August 7, 1789, after the committee of eleven had put to the House its three proposed religion clauses, the Congress reenacted without issue the Northwest Ordinance, with its two religion clauses: "No person, demeaning himself in a peaceable and orderly manner, shall ever be molested on account of his mode of worship, or religious sentiments"; and "Religion, morality and knowledge, being necessary to good government and happiness of mankind, schools and other means of education shall forever be encouraged."[59]

One cannot lean too heavily on this construction of the phrase "shall make no law." First, the congressional record is too blunt and cryptic to decide whether such a subtle play on words was deliberate. Second, it must be remembered that the First Congress served as both a legislature and a constitutional drafter in 1789. Its legislative acts were driven by the fleeting necessities of the time, its constitutional amendments by the enduring needs of the nation. And the two kinds of acts should not be conflated.

Nonetheless, it is rather clear that the First Session of Congress had little compunction about confirming and continuing the Continental Congress's tradition of supporting chaplains, prayers, Thanksgiving Day proclamations, and religious education. And, in later sessions in the 1790s and 1800s, the Congress also continued the Continental Congress's practice of including religion clauses in its treaties, condoning the American edition of the Bible, funding chaplains in the military, and celebrating religious services officiated by congressional chaplains—all with very little dissent or debate.[60] The ease with which Congress passed such laws does give some guidance on what forms of religious support the First Congress might have condoned.

"Respecting an Establishment." The phrase *"respecting an establish-ment of religion"* has long been the most hotly contested phrase of the First Amendment. We certainly cannot resolve all the modern contests on a read-ing of the congressional record alone. But at least three plausible lines of in-terpretation that speak to perennial questions of the relationship of religion and government can be made out.

Thirteen of the nineteen drafts of the religion clauses included disestab-lishment clauses. The only recorded debate is that of August 15 on the for-mulation: "no religion shall be established by law" (No. 7). Although all the words of the final text of the disestablishment clause appear and recur in earlier drafts, the word "respecting" is new. It is a studiously ambiguous term, variously defined in the day as: "to look at, regard, or consider"; to "heed or pay attention to"; "to regard with deference, esteem, or honor"; to "expect, anticipate, look toward."[61]

One plausible reading of the final text is that Congress shall make no laws "respecting" a *state establishment* of religion. In 1789, six states still had some form of religious establishment, which both their state legisla-tures and constitutional conventions defined and defended, often against strong opposition from religious dissenters. Moreover, Virginia had just passed Jefferson's bill "for the *establishment* of religious freedom," also against firm opposition by defenders of the traditional establishment of Anglicanism. Having just defended their state establishments at home, the new members of Congress were not about to relinquish control of them to the new federal government. There was special concern to prevent Congress, the lawmaking body, from passing laws that might interfere in such religious matters—particularly through the "necessary and proper clause" of Article I, which Madison in the August 15 debate signaled as the danger point. There was also some concern—reflected both in Hunt-ington's second intervention on August 15 and in Benson's intervention on August 17—about state actions on religion being adjudicated in "fed-eral courts."

To be sure, the First Congress had already quite explicitly rejected those drafts of the religion clauses that bound the states directly and those that were cast in general terms and thus potentially binding on the states. And to be sure, the Tenth Amendment (which was under discussion in the Con-gress at the same time) guaranteed generally: "The powers not delegated to the United States by the Constitution . . . are reserved to the States respec-tively, or to the people." But perhaps on so sensitive an issue as religion, it was best to be triply sure—and explicitly outlaw any congressional interfer-ence in the states' establishments of religion or of religious freedom. Per-haps, in the final House-Senate committee of six, it was the hard political issue of federal versus state power that was resolved by adding the curious phrase "respecting an establishment." Congress could simply make no law that "looked at," "regarded," or "paid attention to" a state establishment of religion—whether benignly or unfavorably.

This reading of the disestablishment clause would be considerably easier to press if the final draft said "a *state* establishment," rather than "*an establishment.*" But since reference to "state establishments" had not appeared before in the drafts, perhaps the final committee thought it prudent to avoid introducing a new contested term so late in the debate—particularly given the squabbling over the term "*national* establishment" in the August 15 House debate.

A second plausible reading is that Congress could neither establish religion outright nor make laws that would "point toward," "anticipate," or "reflect" such an establishment. On this reading, Congress could not pass a comprehensive new religion law defining the texts, doctrines, and liturgies of the nation's faith and/or governing religious polity, clergy, and property. Such a law, reflective of prevailing English ecclesiastical laws, would clearly be unconstitutional. But that was not the founders' only fear, according to this reading. Congress could also not make more discrete laws that might "respect"—that is, point toward, anticipate, or reflect—such an establishment. The First Congress's concern was to prevent not only a single comprehensive law that established a national religion but also piecemeal laws that would move incrementally toward the same.

The disestablishment clause, on this reading, was not necessarily a prohibition against all laws "touching" religion, as some earlier drafts had indicated. After all, Congress had already passed several such laws (supporting chaplains, prayers, religious education, and the like). Such laws presumably did not point toward or reflect an established religion but simply reflected commonplaces of the day about what was proper for the young nation. But the disestablishment clause was a rather firm barrier against a large number of laws touching religion that might move toward an establishment.

This reading turns on a crucial judgment about why the First Congress had rejected earlier drafts that were more specific about defining a religious establishment. On August 15, the House debated whether to outlaw "religious establishment" per se (No. 7). There seemed to be consensus on this, as Roger Sherman said early in the debate. The moment that the representatives began to specify what they meant by religious establishment, however, the conversation broke down: Gerry was concerned about establishing religious doctrines, Huntington about forced payments of religious tithes, Madison about compulsory worship of God and giving preeminence to one sect—all of which were features of a traditional establishment of religion. The initial compromise was Livermore's clause that sought "no law touching religion" at all (No. 10). By August 20, the House had returned to the language that opened the August 15 debate: "no law establishing religion" (No. 12). That was the language sent to the Senate. The Senate also could not nuance this "no establishment" formulation—failing to reach agreement on clauses that would outlaw the establishment of "one Religious Sect or Society" or "articles of faith or a mode of worship" or that would outlaw the preference of one religious sect, society, or denomination (Nos. 15–17, 19). On this second reading of the disestablishment clause, the word "respecting," therefore, becomes something of an umbrella term for these and other features of a religious establishment. Congress could not agree on what specifics of religious establishment to outlaw—and so they simply outlawed the establishment of religion altogether and anything that "pointed to" or "moved toward" the same.

On the first reading, the disestablishment clause is a limited prohibition against congressional interference with state controls of religion. This leaves little guidance for what Congress might do at the federal level respecting (an establishment of) religion. On the second reading, the disestablishment clause is a comprehensive prohibition against any congressional inclination toward establishing religion. This leaves a little room for Congress to pass laws "touching religion," but not much. Between these two readings of "respecting an establishment" of religion, one can find in the literature a whole host of alternatives.

Among the more popular of such intermediate readings is that of "non-preferentialism." The disestablishment clause, on this reading, simply outlaws preferential support for a "national religion" but allows for "nonpreferential" support for multiple religions. On this reading, the feature of "establishment" that concerned Congress most was not a grand scheme of ecclesiastical law as prevailed in England; that was clearly beyond the pale, and no one was seriously advocating this for America in the 1780s. Congress's real concern was to avoid official "preferences" for certain religious sects, denominations, doctrines, or modes of worship. Six drafts of the religion clauses, including the penultimate one, sought to formulate this directly by outlawing various types of "preferential" establishments by name (Nos. 2, 3, 15–17, 19). None of these drafts passed muster. But Congress accomplished its goal of outlawing preferential support more efficiently by simply prohibiting laws against "an" establishment of this sort—rather than prohibiting laws against "the" establishment of religion altogether.[62] On this formulation, Congress could certainly "touch religion"—rather generously in fact—so long as it did so in a way that would not prefer one religious sect or society above another. And Congress demonstrated what such nonpreferential support meant by appointing and funding chaplains from different denominations, supporting general "religious education," and condoning pious but nondenominational prayers and Thanksgiving Day proclamations.

This "nonpreferential" reading of the disestablishment clause, while certainly plausible, relies heavily on Madison's rejected concern about "national establishment." It does rather little to explain the insertion of the curious word "respecting." It also relies heavily on a clever distinction between "an" and "the" establishment of religion—words on which the sloppy congressional record slipped more than once.[63]

"Prohibiting Free Exercise."   Although the origins of the disestablishment clause have long occupied commentators, the origins of the free exercise clause have only recently come into prominent discussion. A modern controversy has driven much of the new interest—the weakening of the free exercise clause, culminating in the Supreme Court case of *Employment Division v. Smith* (1990) and Congress's attempt in the Religious Freedom Restoration Act (1993) to restore a more rigorous free exercise test. Here, too, as in the case of the disestablishment clause, the record does not resolve all modern questions. Indeed, in the case of the free exercise clause, the congressional record raises as many questions as it answers.

First, as we noted in the "thinner" reading above, the free exercise clause merely outlaws congressional acts that "prohibit" the free exercise of religion. Earlier drafts had included much more embracive protections, outlawing laws that would "touch," "infringe," "abridge," "violate," "compel" or "prevent" the same. All this is replaced by the seemingly minimalist guarantee that Congress not "prohibit" the free exercise of religion.

Second, the free exercise clause is not matched by a liberty of conscience clause. The first seventeen drafts of the religion clauses had included a provision protecting the liberty or rights of conscience, sometimes generally, sometimes specifically with respect to religious scruples against bearing arms. The final recorded House debates on August 20 show agreement on both such protections: "Congress shall make no law establishing religion, or to prevent the free exercise thereof, or to *infringe the rights of conscience*" (No. 12). And again, "no person *religiously scrupulous* shall be compelled to bear arms in person" (No. 13). The Senate included such a guarantee in its first three drafts but then abruptly dropped it for good at the end of September 3 (No. 18). We are left with the final spare free exercise clause.

Third, it must be remembered that while formulating the free exercise clause, Congress was also formulating the free speech, free press, and free assembly clauses. The House had combined the speech, press, and religion clauses already on July 28 (Nos. 9, 11). The Senate combined these and the assembly clause on September 9 (No. 19), and thereafter, they were considered together. The House debates on these other First Amendment provisions make rather clear that religious speech, religious press, and religious assembly were covered by these three clauses.[64] The free exercise clause could not be merely redundant of these attendant clauses. So what is protected by the free exercise clause beyond free religious speech, free religious press, and free religious assembly?

To read the free exercise clause too minimally is hard to square with the widespread solicitude for rights of conscience and free exercise reflected in the First Congress's debates. All four state drafts of the religion clauses included such protections. The Virginia and North Carolina drafts, as we saw, went on at length: "That religion, or the duty which we owe to our creator, and the manner of discharging it, can be directed only by reason and conviction, not by force or violence, and therefore all men have an equal, natural and unalienable right to the free exercise of religion according to the dictates of conscience" (No. 2). New York's draft was also effusive: "That the people have an equal, natural, and unalienable right freely and peaceably to exercise their religion, according to the dictates of conscience" (No. 3).

These favorable sentiments are reflected in the August House debates that have survived. Daniel Carroll spoke eloquently that "the rights of conscience are, in their nature of such peculiar delicacy, and will little bear the gentlest touch of government." Benjamin Huntington warned against anything "hurtful to religion" and hoped the "amendment would be made in such a way as "to secure the rights of conscience and a free exercise of the right of religion." Elias Boudinot gave the final resounding word of the House on August 20: "I hope that in establishing this Government, we may show the world that proper care is taken that the Government may not interfere with the religious sentiments of any person."

How does all this enthusiasm in the First Congress for the rights of conscience and freedom of exercise square with the seemingly crabbed guarantee that "Congress shall make no law . . . prohibiting the free exercise" of religion?

The free exercise clause is somewhat less crabbed when read in eighteenth-century terms, rather than ours. The word "prohibiting," in eighteenth-century parlance, was as much a synonym as a substitute for the terms "infringing," "restraining," or "abridging." As Michael McConnell has ably shown, both dictionaries and political tracts of the day conflated these terms. To flip from one to the other, particularly in the charged political rhetoric of the First Congress, might well have been driven more by aesthetics and taste than by substantive calculation.[65]

One can see this conflation of terms in the original draft submitted by the Virginia Ratification Convention in the summer of 1788. In the preface to its proffered amendments, the convention cites its main concern—"that essential rights, the liberty of conscience, and of the press, cannot be cancelled, abridged, restrained, *or* modified, by any authority." Commenting on this passage in 1800, Madison argued that the point of listing all these verbs was simply to underscore "that the liberty of conscience and the freedom of press were equally and completely exempted from all authority whatever of the United States." And such rights, in Madison's view, were equally and completely protected by the First Amendment, despite its use of the alternative terms, "prohibiting" and "abridging." To read the First Amendment otherwise would lead to silly results:

> [I]f Congress may regulate the freedom of the press, provided they do not abridge it, because it is said only "they shall not abridge it," and is not said, "they shall make no law respecting it," the analogy of reasoning is conclusive that Congress may regulate and even abridge the free exercise of religion, provided they do not prohibit it; because it is said only "they shall not prohibit it," and is not said "they shall make no law respecting, or no law abridging it."[66]

One cannot lean too heavily on this construction, since the primary meaning of "prohibit" in the eighteenth century was still to "forbid," "prevent," or "preclude." But awareness both of the elasticity of the term in the day and of the inexactitude of the congressional record helps to explain what the First Congress may have been about.

Moreover, the word "free exercise," in eighteenth-century parlance, was both a source and a summary of a whole range of principles of religious rights and liberties. "Free exercise" did have a distinct meaning in the eighteenth century, as we saw (pages 42–44). It was conventionally understood to protect the religious speech, press, assembly, and other activities of individuals, and the actions respecting the religious property, polity, discipline, and clergy of religious groups.[67] But, as we also saw, "free exercise" was just as much an umbrella term that connoted protections of liberty of conscience, religious equality and pluralism, and (in some formulations) separation of church and state. In earlier drafts of the religion clauses, Congress sought to spell out these various principles separately—listing liberty of conscience fifteen times, free exercise and religious equality nine times each, and religious pluralism six times. Perhaps in an attempt to avoid giving priority to any particular construction, Congress thought it best to use the generic term "free exercise" and leave its specific province open to ongoing constitutional development and application. This is a speculative reading, but plausible even on the thin congressional record.

The record of the First Congress does give a better indication of why the clause on conscientious objection to bearing arms might have been excluded. The North Carolina ratification convention had introduced this provision in 1788 (No. 4). The House committee of eleven had repeated it on July 28 (No. 8). The House debated the clause on August 17 and 20. It was clearly controversial—passing only 24–22 in the full House on August 20, before being silently dropped by the House style committee four days later. Both Gerry and Scott objected because such an open-ended clause might well be abused, with the military and the nation thereby imperiled. Both Scott and Jackson thought it unfair that "one part" of the nation "would have to defend the other in case of invasion." Chairman Boudinot ultimately carried the slender majority with an impassioned speech: "what justice can there be in compelling them to bear arms, when, according to their religious principles, they would rather die than use them?"

But three of the representatives had suggested a legislative alternative that may have ultimately led to the quiet disappearance of this clause after August 20. Sherman hinted at this by saying the clause was not "absolutely necessary." Scott said more explicitly that conscientious objection status was not a constitutional but a "legislative right." Benson elaborated this view, advising that such questions be left "to the benevolence of the Legislature," to the "discretion of the Government." "If this stands part of the constitution," Benson reasoned, "it will be before the Judiciary on every regulation you make with respect to the organization of the militia." Such a reading has proved prophetic. The contentious issue of conscientious objection status in the military has remained almost consistently subconstitutional ever since—handled by statute and regulation, rather than by direct free exercise inquiry.[68]

"Religion." "What is religion?" is today a recurrent refrain that echoes through much First Amendment law. The issue is as intractable at modern law as it is in modern theology, philosophy, sociology, and anthropology. At law, a claim or claimant must be deemed religious to seek the protection of the free exercise clause. A government action must be deemed religious to trigger the remedies of the disestablishment clause. With the remarkable pluralism of modern America, featuring more than 1,000 denominations, charting the course between religion and nonreligion can be a hazardous exercise, as we shall see (pages 186–187, 203–208, 229–230).

The issue was a good bit simpler in the eighteenth century. As we saw (pages 37–39), the founders recognized and celebrated a plurality of Protestant Christian faiths. The issue was how much further to extend the pale of recognized religion and thus of constitutional protection. Some set the legal line at Protestantism. Others set the legal line at Christianity, thereby including Catholics and Eastern Orthodox. Others set the legal line at theism, thereby including Jews, Muslims, and Deists. No founders writing on religious rights and liberties argued seriously about setting the line any further—to include African or Native American religions, let alone nontheistic faiths from the East, such as Buddhism.[69]

The First Congress did little more than repeat this conventional lore. The House debates repeated the general endorsement of a plurality of sects, societies, and denominations but touched by name only Quakers and Moravians. They also alluded to a distinction between religion and nonreligion, seeking to reserve the protections of constitutional religious rights to the former. In the House debates, Sylvester expressed concern about "abolishing religion altogether" by crafting too broad a disestablishment clause. Huntington wished "to secure the rights of conscience, and a free exercise of the rights of religion, but not to patronize those who professed no religion at all." Scott wanted to prevent misuse of the conscientious objection clause by "those who are of no religion." But precisely what constituted religion and nonreligion and where the line was to be drawn between them, the congressional record simply does not say.

Summary and Conclusions

In the foregoing four chapters, we have taken our stand with the founders in 1789 and looked backward to appreciate both the genesis and the genius of the American experiment in religious liberty. James Madison tells us what the founders saw and what they initially had in mind:

> In most of the governments of the old world, the legal establishment of a particular religion and without any, or with very little toleration of others, makes a pa[c]t of the political & civil organization; & there are few of the most enlightened judges who will maintain that the system has been favourable either to Religion or to government. Until Holland ventured on the experiment of combining a liberal toleration, with the establishment of a particular creed, it was taken for granted that an exclusive & intolerant establishment was essential, and notwithstanding the light thrown on the subject by the experiment, the prevailing opinion in Europe, England not excepted, has been that Religion could not be preserved without the support of Government, nor Government be supported witht. an established Religion, that there must be at least an alliance of some sort between them. It remained for North America to bring the great & interesting subject to a fair, & finally, to a decisive test.[70]

The "decisive test" of the American founders was to press the earlier European and colonial experiments with religious toleration and disestablishment to their theological and political conclusions. Theologians and jurists, believers and skeptics, churchmen and statesman all participated in this exercise—Puritans, Evangelicals, Republicans, and Enlightenment exponents most prominently and consistently. Their efforts, while often independent and wide-ranging, collectively yielded several "first principles" to guide the new American experiment—liberty of conscience, free exercise of religion, religious equality, religious pluralism, separation of church and state, and disestablishment of religion. These first principles, some of ancient Western vintage, were collectively called "the essential rights and liberties of religion."

These essential rights and liberties of religion came to fullest expression and experimentation in the eleven new state constitutions forged between 1776 and 1784. No state constitution embraced all six of these principles equally, nor did they institute them without the kind of qualifications we would regard as improper, if not unconstitutional, today. Most states still retained some semblance of a traditional religious establishment—usually by favoring certain religious ceremonies and moral codes; sometimes by instituting religious tithes, taxes, and test oaths; occasionally by condoning only certain modes and manners of religious worship and organization. Most of the states still retained ample constraints on the free exercise of religion—usually by prohibiting breaches of the peace and public morality; sometimes by curbing religious speech that was deemed blasphemous, religious assemblies that were considered dangerous, or religious allegiances that were judged unpatriotic, if not treasonous.

These essential rights and liberties of religion were also incorporated into the First Amendment to the United States Constitution. The founders regarded religion as special and assigned it a distinct place in the Bill of Rights, with its own unique protections.[71] Today, this First Amendment is taken as the source and summary of much of the nation's law on religious liberty. We have thus taken the time to watch its birth carefully and to parse its words closely, for they will be our principal occupation for much of the remainder of the volume.

It must be stressed, however, that in the founding era, the First Amendment religion clauses were only a small part of the American experiment. The religion clauses bound only the national government ("Congress"). They set only hazy outer boundaries to constitutional congressional conduct respecting religion. These religion clauses were designed in part to legitimate, and to live off, the state constitutional guarantees of religious rights and liberties. The twin guarantees of disestablishment and free exercise depended for their efficacy both on each other and on other religious rights and liberties that the founders regarded as "essential." The guarantees of disestablishment and free exercise standing alone—as they came to be during the 1940s when the Supreme Court "incorporated" these two guarantees into the due process clause of the Fourteenth Amendment—could legitimately be read to have multiple principles incorporated within them.

Indeed, it might not be too strong to say that the "first incorporation" of religious rights and liberties was engineered not by the Supreme Court in the 1940s but by the First Congress in 1789 when it drafted the First Amendment religion clauses. This "first incorporation"—if it can be so called—had two dimensions. First, the pregnant language that "Congress shall make no law *respecting an establishment* of religion" can be read as a confirmation and incorporation of prevailing state constitutional precepts and practices. Such state practices included "the slender establishments" of religion in New England and the Carolinas, which nonetheless included ample guarantees of liberty of conscience, free exercise, religious equality, religious pluralism, and separation of church and state. Such practices also included the "establishment of religious freedom" that had prevailed in Virginia since 1786. The First Amendment drafters seem to have contemplated and confirmed a plurality of constitutional constructions "respecting" religion and its establishment.

Second, the embracive terms "free exercise" and "establishment" can be read to incorporate the full range of "essential rights and liberties" discussed in the eighteenth century. The founders often used the term "free exercise" synonymously with liberty of conscience, religious equality, religious pluralism, and separation of church and state. They similarly regarded "nonestablishment" or "disestablishment" as a generic guarantee of liberty of conscience, religious equality, and separation of church and state. Read in historical context, therefore, the cryptic religion clauses of the First Amendment can be seen to "embody"—to "incorporate"—multiple expressions of the essential rights and liberties of religion.

5

RELIGION AND
THE STATES BEFORE 1947

For the first 150 years of the republic, principal responsibility for the American experiment in religious rights and liberties lay with the states. The First Amendment religion clauses applied only to Congress, and Congress made rather little law respecting an establishment of religion or prohibiting the free exercise thereof. Various attempts to develop a national law on religious liberty applicable to the states and enforceable in the federal courts—most notably the agitation in 1875–1876 for Congress to pass the Blaine Amendment to the United States Constitution—were defeated.[1] Most questions of religious liberty were left to the states to resolve, each in accordance with its own state constitution. This remained the norm until the landmark cases of *Cantwell v. Connecticut* (1940) and *Everson v. Board of Education* (1947) applied the First Amendment religion clauses to state and local governments—thereby catalyzing the development of a national law on religious liberty, enforceable in the federal courts.

The making of state constitutions was a brisk business in the period from 1787 to 1947—with 135 different state constitutions featured. Each of the thirteen original states, save Massachusetts and New Hampshire, adopted at least one new constitution in this period—Georgia leading the way with eight new constitutions, the last in 1945. Thirty-five new states joined the union in this period, each adding its own new constitution. Seventeen of these thirty-five new states retained their original constitutions; eighteen adopted at least one replacement constitution before 1947—Louisiana leading the way with ten, the last in 1921.[2] Every such constitution empowered the state courts to hear constitutional cases from its own citizens or subjects. Literally thousands of state cases came before these courts raising questions of state power over religious matters or of religious liberties from this exercise of state power.

A comprehensive analysis of this state constitutional law on religious liberty—both on the books and in action—could easily fill several dozen thick volumes. For our purposes, we shall focus primarily on the patterns of religious rights and liberties protected formally in the state constitutions until 1947.[3] Our particular concern will be to watch the treatment of the six main principles of religious liberty forged in the founding period. A table in Appendix 2 summarizes each state's treatment of these and related principles.

Liberty of Conscience and Free Exercise

Forty-two of the forty-eight state constitutions in effect before 1947 had a general clause explicitly protecting the liberty and/or right of conscience. Sometimes the language was direct and efficient, as in the 1851 Constitution of Indiana:

> All men shall be secured in the natural right to worship Almighty God according to the dictates of their own consciences. No law shall, in any case whatever, control the free exercise and enjoyment of religious opinions, or interfere with the rights of conscience. No preference shall be given, by law, to any creed, religious society or mode of worship; and no man shall be compelled to attend, erect or support any place of worship, or to maintain any ministry, against his consent. No religious test shall be required as a qualification for any office of trust or profit. . . . No person shall be rendered incompetent as a witness, in consequence of his opinion on matters of religion.[4]

Sometimes the language was more florid, as was the 1843 Rhode Island Constitution's paraphrase of Jefferson's Bill for the Establishment of Religious Freedom:

> Whereas Almighty God hath created the mind free; and all attempts to influence it by temporal punishments or burdens, or by civil incapacitations, tend to beget habits of hypocrisy and meanness; and whereas a principal object of our venerable ancestors, in their migration to this country and their settlement of this state, was, as they expressed it, to hold forth a lively experiment, that a flourishing civil state may stand and be best maintained with full liberty in religious concernments: We, therefore, declare that no man shall be compelled to frequent or to support any religious worship, place, or ministry whatever, except in fulfillment of his own voluntary contract; nor enforced, restrained, molested, or burdened in his body or goods; nor disqualified from holding any office; nor otherwise suffer on account of his religious belief; and that every man shall be free to worship God according to the dictates of his own conscience, and to profess and by argument to maintain his opinion in matters of religion; and that the same shall in no wise diminish, enlarge or affect his civil capacity.[5]

Six constitutions lacked an express liberty or rights of conscience clause—those of Alabama, Iowa, Maryland, Oklahoma, South Carolina, and West Virginia. Of these six constitutions, however, four expressly outlawed compulsory participation in, or support for, religion. Three expressly added a clause protecting those with religious scruples against bearing arms—this being a day where state involvement in the military was still commonly assumed. The Constitution of Oklahoma (1907), though lacking both a conscientious objection and a compulsory support clause, nonetheless provided: "Perfect toleration of religious sentiment shall be secured, and no inhabitant of the State shall ever be molested in person or property on account of his or her mode of religious worship; and no religious test shall be required for the exercise of civil or political rights."[6]

Only twenty-five state constitutions included an explicit free exercise clause. Of these, nine couched this as "the free exercise" or the "(free) enjoyment" of "religious profession," "religious sentiment," or "religious worship." Delaware and Vermont spoke of "the free exercise of religious worship" alone. Oregon and Indiana spoke of "the free exercise of religious opinion." Idaho spoke of "the free exercise of religious faith and worship." The remaining state constitutions had more open-ended free exercise clauses.

The relative rarity and restrictiveness of these free exercise clauses is explained in part by the detail of most state constitutional provisions on religion. Rather than using the umbrella term "free exercise," as did the First Amendment, most state constitutions spelled out the meaning of religious freedom in some detail. Twenty-nine state constitutions outlawed state coercion or compulsion in matters of religion, particularly compulsory attendance at religious worship or in religious exercises. Twenty-two state constitutions had explicit provisions exempting those with religious scruples from bearing arms.[7] Nineteen state constitutions explicitly outlawed mandatory payments of religious tithes, taxes, or other forms of compulsory support for religion; none, after 1833, required such support. Fifteen state constitutions provided in more general terms that a person's civil and political rights could not be affected or comprised by his or her religious beliefs or affiliations. Three states, Colorado, New Jersey, and Kentucky, specifically outlawed religious discrimination within public schools.

Religious test oaths for holding political office remained a highly contested issue among the states—and, indeed, would remain so until outlawed by the United States Supreme Court in *Torcaso v. Watkins* (1961).[8] Twenty-four states explicitly banned religious test oaths for political or public office altogether; but of these states, six required that political officers must believe in God. Seven state constitutions provided explicitly that the guarantees of religious freedom did not foreclose the state from administering religious test oaths. In practice, these latter six states plus the remaining states that lacked constitutional provisions on political test oaths generally continued to administer religious test oaths, of varying rigor, at least for the governor.[9]

Controversies over the application of religious tests and oaths spilled over into other areas of public involvement as well. Twenty-four state constitutions banned such oaths and tests as a condition for sitting on juries and/or testifying in criminal and civil cases; two states insisted that such tests could continue. Eight states also banned religious tests as a condition for voting in political elections.

A number of state constitutions, following eighteenth-century precedents, set firm limits to the rights of conscience and free exercise of religion. Seventeen constitutions indicated that these guarantees would not excuse "licentious" actions or conduct that violated the peace, safety, order and/or security of the state. Two other states added "morals" to this list. Four states added that one person's exercise of religious rights could not violate "the natural, civil, or religious rights" of others.[10] The Connecticut Constitution (1818) spelled out in some detail the relative rights of religious groups and religious individuals in an instance of dispute.

The constitutions of five Western states, Arizona, Montana, New Mexico, Idaho, and Utah, following congressional mandates, explicitly foreclosed religious liberty protection to bigamy or polygamy—Idaho aggressively so. Every other state had criminal laws against polygamy, but their constitutions did not touch on the religious liberty implications of these laws.

Religious Pluralism and Equality

In the eighteenth century, explicit guarantees of religious pluralism were considered critical to ensuring religious liberty. Religious pluralism, in the founders's view, served as a natural check both on the monopolistic inclination of any church and on the establishment tendencies of any state. In the state constitutions of the nineteenth and early twentieth centuries, religious pluralism was more a sociological fact than a constitutional condition of religious liberty. Most state constitutions included clauses that simply acknowledged the existence of confessional pluralism—the multiplicity of religious sects, societies, and/or denominations within the community. Most also included clauses that acknowledged the existence of social pluralism—the multiple "institutions," "societies," "associations," and/or "corporations" that religious groups operated besides places of worship: lower schools, colleges, seminaries, charities, cemeteries, hospitals, asylums, poor houses, mission societies, religious clubs, and other such voluntary religious associations.

Thirty-six state constitutions included affirmative guarantees of equality for these multiple religious institutions. Of these, thirty-two constitutions formulated this as a general "no preference" clause. The Constitution of Arkansas (1874) had typical language: "Religion, morality and knowledge being essential to good government, the General Assembly shall enact suitable laws to protect every religious denomination in the peaceable enjoyment of its own mode of public worship . . . and no preference shall be given, by law, to any religious establishment, denomination or mode of worship above any other."[11] Seven state constitutions couched this as a guarantee of "equality of faiths" before the law or "equal protection under the law" for all faiths. Eight state constitutions included compacts with the United States that guaranteed "a perfect toleration" of all religious sects and sentiments. The constitutions of New Hampshire (1784) and Connecticut (1818) were alone in restricting their equality guarantee to "every denomination of Christians"—though in practice these provisions were extended to all theistic religious groups.[12]

Few state constitutions went much beyond these general guarantees of equality to specify the affirmative constitutional rights of religious groups. The Delaware Constitution guaranteed the "rights, privileges, immunities, and estates of religious societies."[13] Kansas included a right of religious groups to incorporate and to hold corporate property. Louisiana and Maryland protected the rights of religious trusts and charities to receive donations. Maine and Massachusetts provided that religious societies had freedom to enter contracts with their ministers. New Mexico explicitly protected the church authority's right to acquire and use sacramental wines. But most states left the issue of particular religious group rights to statutory, rather than constitutional, formulation.[14]

Two pairs of state constitutions imposed explicit disabilities on religious bodies. Virginia and West Virginia banned the right of religious groups to organize themselves as corporations, thereby foreclosing to them the property, liability, inheritance, and tax advantages that attached to corporate status. This disability, though challenged both in state and federal courts, remains the law in these states today.[15] Maryland and Tennessee both expressly prohibited clergy from holding political office—prohibitions that remained on the book in Tennessee until outlawed by the United States Supreme Court in *McDaniel v. Paty* (1978).[16]

Separation of Church and State

Whereas today the principle of separation of church and state is regarded as indispensable to the American experiment in religious liberty, historically the principle was considered more dispensable. None of the twenty drafts of the First Amendment religion clauses in 1788 and 1789 had included the principle, as we saw in Chapter 4. This trend continued among the state constitutional drafters. Only the Constitution of Utah (1896) included a general guarantee: "There shall be no union of Church and State, nor shall any church dominate the State or interfere with its functions."[17]

Although they did not use the language of separation of church and state, a number of state constitutions effectively adopted this principle in part in the context of education and state funding. Thirty-five state constitutions insisted that state and local governments grant no funds to religious schools—provisions often motivated by a strong bias against emerging Catholic primary and secondary schools.[18] Fifteen state constitutions insisted that state schools remain free from "sectarian influence" or from the control of religious officials and institutions. Few constitutions included affirmative guarantees for religious education. The Constitution of Missouri (1945) required that the Bible be taught in public schools. The constitutions of New York (1895) and New Jersey (1947) provided that "the legislature may provide for the transportation of children to or from any school or institution of learning."[19] Six other states repeated the platitudes of the Northwest Ordinance without comment—"Religion, morality, and knowledge being necessary for good government and the happiness of mankind, schools and the means of education shall for ever be encouraged."

Twenty-nine state constitutions broadened this no-state-funding rule to apply not only to religious schools but to all religious causes and institutions. The Nevada Constitution (1864), for example, provided briefly: "No public funds of any kind or character whatever, State, county, or municipal, shall be used for sectarian purpose."[20] Several states echoed the strong language of the 1870 Illinois Constitution:

> Neither the General Assembly nor any county, city, town, township, school district or other public corporation shall ever make any appropriation or pay from any public fund whatever, anything in aid of any church or sectarian purpose, or to help support or sustain any school, academy, seminary, college, university or other literary or scientific institution, controlled by any church or sectarian denomination whatever; nor shall any grant or donation of land, money or other personal property ever be made by the State or any such public corporation to any church or for any sectarian or religious purpose.[21]

In most states, however, this constitutional prohibition against state funding of religion was matched by a new constitutional right to tax exemptions for religious properties and/or associations. Thirty-three state constitutions exempted from general taxation all properties devoted to religious worship, charity, education, and other public uses.[22] As we shall see in Chapter 9, such tax exemptions of religious properties and bodies were justified in part on grounds of the separation of church and state.

Disestablishment of Religion

In the eighteenth century, as we saw (pages 51–54, 77–80), disestablishment of religion was a broad, multilayered guarantee. At its core, this principle prohibited government from defining by law the religious doctrines, liturgies, texts, and traditions of a community. But as an umbrella term, disestablishment outlawed governmental violations of a number of other principles of religious liberty—particularly liberty of conscience, religious equality, and separation of church and state.

Only seven of the state constitutions before 1947 included an explicit disestablishment clause. The constitutions of New Jersey and Maine cast the clause thus: "[N]o subordination nor preference of any one sect or denomination shall ever be established by law." The constitutions of Iowa, Louisiana, South Carolina, and Utah simply emulated the First Amendment: "The General Assembly shall make no law respecting an establishment of religion." Only the Alabama Constitution of 1901 had a direct and general guarantee: "[N]o religion shall be established by law."

This relative rarity of state disestablishment clauses is explained in part by the pervasive religious pluralism among most of the states. Pluralism made the establishment of one state religion too remote a prospect to outlaw. In the new, thinly populated western states, however, the threat of such a religious establishment was quite real. These states sought to avert this threat not by adopting a disestablishment clause but by entering a compact with the United States that guaranteed a "perfect toleration" among all religious sects and sentiments.[23]

This relative rarity of state disestablishment clauses is also explained in part by the detail of state religious freedom guarantees. Most state constitutions, as we have seen, had lengthy provisions on liberty of conscience, free exercise of religion, and religious pluralism and equality. Most also respected the separation of church and state at least to the point of granting religious institutions their autonomy and equality, and in a number of states, also barring them from interfering in state education and from receiving state funds. With the express outlawing of these features of a traditional established religion, a general disestablishment clause was often considered unnecessary, if not dangerous.

The danger was that a general prohibition against establishment might conflict with a number of other provisions in the state constitutions favorably touching religion. A good illustration of this comes from Massachusetts.[24] Massachusetts is usually described as the last state to disestablish religion—by passage of its famous Amendment XI of 1833.[25] But this 1833 amendment said nothing about disestablishment. It simply replaced Article III of the original 1780 Constitution, which had mandated the payment of tithes and supports for religion. The 1833 amendment, in fact, commended theistic religion, even while confirming the principles of religious equality and freedom of exercise. The full text of Amendment XI reads thus:

> As the public worship of GOD and instructions in piety, religion, and morality, promote the happiness and prosperity of a people, and the security of a republican government; therefore, the several religious societies of this commonwealth, whether corporate or incorporate, at any meeting legally warned and holden for that purpose, shall ever have the right to elect their pastors or religious teachers, to contract with them for their support, to raise money for erecting and repairing houses for public worship, for the maintenance of religious instruction, and for the payment of necessary expenses; And all persons belonging to any religious society shall be taken and held to be members, until they shall file with the clerk of such society, a written notice declaring the dissolution of their membership, and thenceforth shall not be liable for any grant or contract which may be thereafter made, and denominations, demeaning themselves peaceably, and as good citizens of the Commonwealth, shall be equally under the protection of the law; and no subordination of one sect or denomination to another shall ever be established by law.

The 1833 amendment left untouched many provisions in the Massachusetts Constitution, still in place today, that commend religious ceremony and morality. The preamble, for example, refers to the constitution as "a covenant" or "compact" between the people and God:

> [T]he people of Massachusetts, acknowledging, with grateful hearts, the goodness of the great Legislator of the universe, in affording us, in the course of His providence, an opportunity, deliberately and peaceably, without fraud, violence, or surprise, of entering into an original, explicit, and solemn compact with each other; and of forming a new constitution of civil government for ourselves and Posterity; and devoutly imploring His direction in so interesting a design, do agree upon, ordain and establish the following *Declaration of Rights and Frame of Government*.

This is a classic covenant ceremony, rooted in the Hebrew Bible and in a New England tradition going back to the Mayflower Compact of 1620.[26]

The moral implications of this covenant are set out elsewhere in the Massachusetts Constitution. Article II of the Declaration of Rights states: "It is the right as well as the duty of all men in society, publicly, and at stated seasons to worship the SUPREME BEING, the great Creator and Preserver of the Universe." Article XVIII rendered adherence to moral duties integral to the character of public offices and public officials:

> A frequent recurrence to the fundamental principles of the constitution, and a constant adherence to those of piety, justice, moderation, temperance, industry, and frugality, are absolutely necessary to preserve the advantages of lib-

erty, and to maintain a free government. The people ought, consequently, to have a particular attention to all those principles, in the choice of their officers and representatives: and they have a right to require of their lawgivers and magistrates an exact and constant observance of them, in the formation and execution of the laws necessary for the good administration of the commonwealth.

For, as Article VII put it: "Government is instituted for the common good; for the protection, safety, prosperity, and happiness of the people."

Such moral qualities were also regarded as essential ingredients of state-funded public education. Chapter V of the Frame of Government provides:

> Wisdom, and knowledge, as well as virtue, diffused generally among the body of the people, [are] necessary for the preservation of their rights and liberties. . . . [It is thus] the duty of Legislatures and magistrates in all future periods of this commonwealth to cherish the interests of literature and sciences, and all seminaries of them; . . . to encourage private societies and public institutions, rewards and immunities, for the promotion of [education]; . . . to countenance and inculcate the principles of humanity and general benevolence, public and private charity, industry and frugality, honesty and punctuality in their dealings; sincerity, good humor, and all social affections, and generous sentiments among the people.

The same Chapter V confirmed and commended the incorporation of Harvard College, since "the encouragement of arts and sciences, and all good literature, tends to the honor of GOD, the advantage of the Christian religion, and the great benefit of this and the other United States of America." All these constitutional provisions remain in place in the Massachusetts Constitution still today.[27]

To be sure, the 1780 Massachusetts Constitution was unusual in the rigor and detail of its continued endorsement of religion. And the thick religious language, crafted in the days of Puritan hegemony, might well have been more tempered had the Massachusetts Constitution been reissued by a more heterogeneous nineteenth-century state convention. Nonetheless, this language attests to a pervasive understanding among the states about the salutary, even necessary, role of religion in public life.

Like Massachusetts, forty-three of the forty-eight state constitutions in place before 1947 included in their preamble some ceremonial expression of gratitude to "Almighty God" (or the "Supreme Legislator" or "Supreme Being" or "Supreme Ruler of the Universe" or "Sovereign Ruler of Nations"). Most of these preambles were a brief line or two, but several went on for a paragraph. The New Jersey Constitution of 1947, for example, which was the last constitution ratified in this period, provided: "We, the people of New Jersey, grateful to Almighty God for the civil and religious liberty which He hath so long permitted us to enjoy, and looking to Him for a blessing upon our endeavors to secure and transmit the same unimpaired to succeeding generations, do ordain and establish this Constitution."

Endorsements of religious morality also appear in some of the state constitutions. Connecticut, Delaware, and Maryland followed Massachusetts in providing that it was the right as well as the duty of the person to worship Almighty God. The 1902 Constitution of Virginia retained its original 1776 religious liberty clause with its concluding admonition that "it is the mutual duty of all to practice Christian forbearance, love, and charity towards each other."[28] Six state constitutions repeated the language that "religion, morality, and knowledge" are necessary for good government and the happiness of mankind. Three state constitutions made provisions for chaplains in prisons and the legislatures, two others for observance of the Christian Sabbath and of religious holidays.

Faith, Freedom, and the Frontier

The constitutional law on the books, of course, does not describe the law in action. But the foregoing provisions of the state constitutions of 1787–1947 do give some indication of the prevailing pattern of religious rights and liberties among the states in the nineteenth century. The dominant pattern was that states sought to balance the general freedom of all private religions with the general patronage of one common public religion—increasingly relying on the frontier as a release valve for the tensions between this private religious freedom and public religious patronage.

On the one hand, state and local governments granted basic freedoms of conscience, exercise, and equality to most religious groups and religious practices, at least those that conformed with common culture and average temperament. Most religious individuals were granted rights to assemble, speak, publish, parent, educate, travel, and the like on the basis of their religious beliefs. Most religious groups were generally afforded the rights to incorporate, to hold property, to receive private donations, to enforce religious laws, and to maintain buildings, schools, and charities for their voluntary members.

Many states, however, still dealt discriminately with religious minorities, particularly those of high religious temperature or low cultural conformity. The New England states, for example, continued to resist the missionizing efforts of Quakers, Baptists, and Methodists, routinely delaying delivery of their corporate charters, tax exemptions, and educational licenses. New York, New Jersey, and Pennsylvania were similarly churlish with Unitarians, Adventists, and Christian Scientists, often turning a blind eye to private abuses against them. Virginia and the Carolinas tended to be hard on conservative Episcopalians and upstart Evangelicals alike. Many of the southern states were notorious in their resistance to Catholic churches, schools, missions, and literature. Few legislatures and courts, outside of the main cities on the eastern seaboard, showed much respect for the religious rights of the few Jews or Muslims about, let alone the religious rights of Native Americans or enslaved African Americans.[29]

On the other hand, state and local governments patronized a "public" religion that was generally Christian, if not Protestant, in character. A "mass of organic utterances," as the Supreme Court later put it, attest to the typical features of this system.[30]

State and local governments endorsed religious symbols and ceremonies. "In God We Trust" and similar confessions appeared on governmental seals and stationery. The Ten Commandments and favorite Bible verses were inscribed on the walls of court houses, public schools, and other public buildings. Crucifixes were erected in state parks and on statehouse grounds. Flags flew at half mast on Good Friday. Christmas, Easter, and other holy days were official holidays. Sundays remained official days of rest. Government-sponsored chaplains were appointed to the state legislatures, military groups, and state prisons, asylums, and hospitals. Prayers were offered at the commencement of each session of many state legislatures and at city council meetings. Thanksgiving Day prayers were offered by governors, mayors, and local officials. Election day sermons were offered, especially in rural and town churches, throughout the nineteenth century.

State and local governments also afforded various forms of aid to religious groups. Subsidies were given to Christian missionaries on the frontier. States and municipalities occasionally underwrote the costs of Bibles and liturgical books for poorer churches and donated land and services to them. Property grants and tax subsidies were furnished to Christian schools and charities. Special criminal laws protected the property, clergy, and worship services of the churches. Tax exemptions were accorded to the real and personal properties of many churches, clerics, and charities. Tax revenues supported the acquisition of religious art and statuary for state museums and other public buildings.

State and local governments predicated some of their laws and policies on biblical teachings. Many of the first public schools and state universities had mandatory courses in the Bible and religion and compulsory attendance in daily chapel and Sunday worship services. Employees in state prisons, reformatories, orphanages, and asylums were required to know and to teach basic Christian beliefs and values. Polygamy, prostitution, pornography, and other sexual offenses against Christian morals and mores were prohibited. Blasphemy and sacrilege were still prosecuted. Gambling, lotteries, fortune-telling, and other activities that depended on fate or magic were forbidden. In many jurisdictions, these and other laws were predicated on explicitly religious grounds. It was a commonplace of nineteenth-century American legal thought that "Christianity is a part of the common law."[31]

This prevalent pattern of balancing the freedom of all private religions with the patronage of one public religion worked rather well for the more religiously homogeneous times and towns of the early republic. The established public religion confirmed and celebrated each community's civic unity and confessional identity. It also set natural limits to both political action and individual freedom—limits that were enforced more by communal reprobation than by constitutional litigation.

One of the saving assumptions of this system was the presence of the frontier, and the right to emigrate thereto.[32] Religious minorities who could not abide a community's religious restrictions or accept its religious patronage were not expected to stay long to fight the local establishment as their European counterparts had done. They moved—sometimes at gunpoint—to establish their own communities on the frontier, often on the heels of missionaries and schoolmasters who had preceded them. Mormons moved from New York to Ohio, to Missouri, to Illinois, before finally settling in Utah and thereafter colonizing Nevada, California, Idaho, and Wyoming. Catholics moved to California, the Dakotas, Illinois, Louisiana, Montana, Nevada, and New Mexico. Baptists and Methodists poured into the southern states from Georgia and Tennessee to Mississippi and Missouri. Free spirits escaped to the mountainous frontiers of Wyoming, Montana, Washington, and Oregon.[33]

The right—sometimes the duty—to emigrate was a basic assumption of the American experiment in religious liberty. Many first-generation Americans had left their Europeans faiths and territories to gain their freedom. Accordingly, they embraced the right to leave—to exit their faith, to abandon their blood and soil, to reestablish their lives, beliefs, and identities afresh—as a cardinal axiom of religious freedom. Escape to the frontier provided the release valve for the common state system of balancing freedom for all private religions with patronage of one public religion.

As the American populace became more pluralized and the American frontier more populated, however, this system became harder to maintain. The Second Great Awakening of c.1800–1860 introduced to the American scene a host of newly minted faiths—Adventists, Christian Scientists, Disciples, Holiness Churches, Jehovah's Witnesses, Mormons, Pentecostals, Unitarians, and Universalists.[34] The Second Great Awakening also fueled what Edwin S. Gaustad has aptly called "the reconquest" of the original eastern seaboard states by evangelical Baptists and Methodists as well as by Roman Catholics.[35] The American Civil War (1861–1865) permanently divided Lutherans, Presbyterians, and other denominations into northern and southern branches. The 13th, 14th, and 15th Amendments (1865–1870)

TABLE 5.1   Proportional Numbers of Mainline Churches 1780–1900

	Percent Anglican	Percent Calvinist	Percent Evangelical	Percent Lutheran	Percent Catholic
1780	14.8	50.2	16.7	8.7	2.1
1820	5.5	30.1	49.4	7.3	1.1
1860	4.1	18.6	61.2	4.1	4.9
1900	3.8	14.3	63.7	6.6	6.3

not only outlawed slavery but also liberated a host of long-cloaked African beliefs and rituals, some in pure African forms, many inculturated with various Christian traditions. After the 1840s, the great waves of European emigration brought new concentrations and forms of Catholicism and Protestantism from Ireland, Germany, and Great Britain, joined by a number of Catholic emigrants from Mexico. After the 1880s, fresh waves of emigrants from Eastern Europe and Russia brought new forms and concentrations of Catholicism, Judaism, and Orthodox Christianity. At the same time, a growing number of emigrants from across the Pacific introduced Buddhism, Confucianism, Hinduism, and other Eastern religions to the western states.

These movements of new inspiration, immigration, and invention radically recast the American religious map in the course of the nineteenth century—with the traditional Calvinist and Anglican strongholds of the early republic giving way, especially to precocious new forms of Evangelical Baptists and Methodists. Table 5.1 shows the change over time in the relative numbers of the main founding churches: (1) Anglican (later called Episcopalian); (2) Calvinist (Congregationalist, Presbyterian, and Reformed); (3) Evangelical (mostly Methodist and Baptist); (4) Lutheran (Swedish, German, and Swiss); and (5) Roman Catholic.[36] Note the huge percentage increase in Evangelical churches and the corresponding drop in Calvinist and Anglican churches between 1780 and 1860.

Throughout this period, Quakers remained a consistent minority, attracting one to two percent of the population. By 1850, and increasingly thereafter, new religious groups became prominent—notably, Adventists, Christian Scientists, Holiness Churches, Mormons, Pentecostals, Unitarians, and Universalists.

This radical reconfiguration of the American religious map in the nineteenth century eventually challenged state constitutional patterns of religious liberty. In particular, state policies of patronizing a public religion became increasingly difficult to maintain with the growing plurality of the populace and the growing political strength of groups who opposed such policies. Many Evangelical churches, both Baptist and Methodist, insisted that states adhere more firmly to principles of disestablishment and separatism; in a number of states, they gained the political power to revise the constitutions accordingly. Religious minorities in many communities—whether Protestant, Catholic, Orthodox, Jewish, Adventist, or Mormon—also began to ally themselves in opposition to this system, particularly the patronage of a common Protestantism within the public schools. Some of these minority religious communities refused to conform or to assimilate. Others refused to live or leave quietly. Still others began to crusade actively against the system.

When neither assimilation nor accommodation policies proved effective, state and local legislatures began to clamp down on these dissenters. At the turn of the twentieth century and increasingly thereafter, local officials began routinely denying Roman Catholics their school charters, Jehovah's Witnesses their preaching permits, Eastern Orthodox their canonical freedoms, Jews and Adventists their Sabbath-day accommodations, non-Christian pacifists their conscientious objection status. As state courts and legislatures turned an increasingly blind eye to their plight, religious dissenters began to turn to the federal courts for relief.

6

RELIGION AND THE
SUPREME COURT,
1815–1947

The United States Supreme Court has long held the power to review federal and state laws. Article III of the United States Constitution provides: "The judicial power shall extend to all Cases, in Law and Equity, arising under this Constitution." In the landmark case of *Marbury v. Madison* (1803), the Court ruled that this provision empowered it to review and invalidate *federal* laws that violated any provision of the Constitution.[1] In a trio of cases from 1810 to 1821, the Court ruled further that it had similar power to review and overturn state laws.[2]

Before 1940, however, the Supreme Court made only modest use of this power to review laws touching religion. The first application of the free exercise clause to federal law came in *Reynolds v. United States* (1879), the first application of the disestablishment clause in *Bradfield v. Roberts* (1899). In both these cases, and in the dozen federal cases to follow before 1940, the Court found no First Amendment violation. It held for Congress in each instance, often employing rudimentary analysis of the religion clauses in so holding.

Before 1940, the Supreme Court did review a number of state and local laws touching religion—but not under the First Amendment religion clauses. The First Amendment, by its terms, governed "Congress," and in its earliest cases on point, the Court insisted that this language be read literally: "The Constitution makes no provision for protecting the citizens of the respective states in their religious liberties; this is left to the state constitutions and laws."[3] The Court did have power to review state laws touching religion under other provisions of the Constitution or under general principles of law and fairness. Particularly determined parties, therefore, who exhausted their remedies at state law, could appeal to the Supreme Court for final relief. The Court heard seventeen such cases from the states from 1815 to 1939.[4]

Ironically, it was these early cases arising from the states, not the early First Amendment cases reviewing congressional laws, that provided the more sophisticated analysis of religious rights and liberties. The cases from 1815 to 1914 developed the principles of free exercise of religion, religious pluralism and equality, and separation of church and state in a manner that would be critical to later First Amendment law. The cases from 1923 to 1939 also cast the concept of religious liberty as a fundamental liberty to be protected against both federal and state action. These latter cases laid the foundation for *Cantwell v. Connecticut* (1940) and *Everson v. Board of Education* (1947) that incorporated the First Amendment religion clauses into the due process clause of the Fourteenth Amendment, and thereby applied them to the states.

Review of Federal Laws Touching Religion

Polygamy

The Court's first application of the free exercise clause came in *Reynolds v. United States* (1879).[5] In that case, and in a pair of cases in 1890, the Court offered an extremely narrow reading of the free exercise clause to uphold congressional restrictions on the preaching and practice of polygamy.

Each of the cases involved the Church of Jesus Christ of Latter-Day Saints. This was one of numerous new churches to emerge during the Second Great Awakening of c. 1800–1860. Its founder, Joseph Smith, had developed, under divine inspiration, a new Scripture to supplement the Bible—the *Book of Mormon*, which he published in 1830. He had further developed a separate *Book of Commandments* in 1833, which described followers of the *Book of Mormon* as a new chosen people. The Mormon faith prescribed the formation of new communities centered on a temple, devoted to a common "Law of Consecration and Stewardship," and committed especially to mission. This faith also featured a number of novel teachings, such as the efficacy of proxy baptism for the dead, the pre-existence of man, and a metaphysical materialism that stood in tension with the traditional biblical story of the creation *ex nihilo*. Such novel teachings and practices, and the ardent advocacy of them by missionaries, soon led to severe repression of the LDS Church. The church was driven first from New York to Ohio, then to Missouri and Illinois. After severe rioting and the murder of Joseph Smith and his brother in 1844, the LDS members escaped to the frontier under the new leadership of Brigham Young, establishing themselves in what became in 1850 the Territory of Utah.

Far on the frontier, the LDS Church may well have been left to itself, like many other new religious communities born of the Second Great Awakening. But in 1852, the church leadership issued a manifesto commending polygamy. For one man to have several wives, the church taught, was an appropriate and biblical form of communal living. It also increased the opportunities for women to enjoy the spiritually salutary steps of marriage and motherhood. To set an example for the reticent, the church's leaders took several wives. They further reported that Joseph Smith and other church leaders had done the same in the 1830s and 1840s.[6]

When word of this policy of polygamy reached Washington, D.C., it prompted instant denunciation and a mounting political crusade against the LDS Church. Since Utah and some of the other western areas where the Mormons settled were still United States territories, Congress had general authority to pass laws that touched on issues of marriage, family, and sexuality, and Congress exercised this authority with increasing sternness. An 1862 law made polygamy a federal crime in United States territories.[7] An 1882 law disqualified polygamists, as well as men cohabiting with more than one woman, from holding political office, voting in elections, and sitting on juries, among other rights.[8] Related statutes required parties to swear oaths denying any practice or advocacy of polygamy and subjected them to close scrutiny for suspected participation or even belief in the same.[9] An 1887 law called for the forfeiture of the LDS Church's property altogether if it persisted in its preaching and practice of polygamy.[10]

Three main cases challenged these congressional laws as violations of the free exercise clause. In *Reynolds v. United States* (1879), a Mormon appealed a conviction under the criminal law against bigamy. In *Davis v. Beason* (1890), a Mormon appealed a conviction for false swearing of a mandatory oath renouncing polygamy.[11] In *Church of Jesus Christ of Latter Day Saints v. United States* (1890), the LDS Church challenged the government's dissolution of its corporate charter and confiscation of its property.[12]

The Supreme Court upheld congressional law in each instance and would hear nothing of the Mormons' free exercise arguments. In *Reynolds*, Chief Justice Waite took Jefferson's adage of "building a wall of separation between church and State . . . almost as an authoritative declaration of the scope and effect of the [first] amendment thus secured." The free exercise clause protects religious beliefs, not religious actions, he argued. "Congress was deprived of all legislative power over mere opinion, but was left free to reach [religious] actions which were in violation of social duties and subversive of good order."[13] This congressional "freedom," the Court continued in *Davis* (1890), could not be compromised by judicial creations of a free exercise exemption from general antipolygamy legislation. To exempt Mormons, particularly from criminal prohibitions against polygamy, Justice Field thundered for the Court, would be "to shock the moral judgment of the community . . . [and] offend the common sense of mankind."[14]

Justice Bradley drove home these sentiments in the Court's opinion in *Latter Day Corporation:* "The organization of a community for the spread and practice of polygamy is, in a measure, a return to barbarism. It is contrary to the spirit of Christianity and of the civilization which Christianity has produced in the Western world." It is a "sophistical plea" to claim free exercise protection for this "nefarious doctrine." For the Court to grant free exercise protection in this case would invite all manner of specious evasions of the criminal law—even religious excuses for human sacrifice and suicide. "The state has a perfect right to prohibit polygamy, and all other open offenses against the enlightened sentiment of mankind, notwithstanding the pretense of religious conviction by which they may be advocated and practiced."[15]

Confronted by these realities in 1890, Wilford Woodruff, the presiding officer of the LDS Church, issued a manifesto disavowing any further participation in polygamy and urging church members to follow. On October 6, 1890, an LDS Church conference accepted the manifesto, although a group that insisted on traditional doctrine split off from the main church and relocated, quietly maintaining their polygamous practices to this day.[16] Congress returned the church's property in 1894. Utah became a state in 1896, its new constitution prohibiting polygamy and featuring the only clause on separation of church and state to appear among the state constitutions before 1947.[17] In time, the church began to develop its distinctive ethical code, featuring abstinence from tobacco, alcohol, and caffeine and strict codes for dress, diet, hygiene, and sexual practice. It also routinized its theology and practice of mission, becoming one of the fastest growing faiths in twentieth-century America.[18]

These early cases did little to embellish the meaning of the free exercise clause. The Court had effectively reduced the free exercise clause to a minimalist guarantee of liberty of conscience alone—and even that was now cast as a mere freedom to have one's opinion, not as a protection against being forced on demand to swear oaths, to give testimony about one's religious opinion, or to have one's right to vote denied if associated with Mormonism. The Court gave short shrift to free exercise arguments that individuals are entitled to preach or practice polygamy peaceably and privately, or even to associate with those who were suspected of the same. The free exercise clause protected religious opinions about polygamy; it gave no protection to actions taken upon such beliefs by individuals or groups. Congress had power to regulate all such religious actions, and it had declared all such actions related to polygamy to be dangerous and criminal. Congress had power to incorporate the Mormon church; it also had power to dissolve this corporation if it persisted in its crime. For the Court, this was the end of the matter. Very little in the text or the history of the free exercise clause supported such a narrow reading.[19]

Pacifism

In a series of cases from 1918 to 1945, the Court used similar logic to address the free exercise claims of pacifists to conscientious objection to war. Belief in pacifism was constitutionally protected; actions or omissions taken upon those beliefs were not. Congress had full power to decide whether and which pacifists might be excused from military preparation or participation, or oaths attesting to the same. And it was simply not "within the province of the courts to make bargains" with individuals whose religious scruples were not sufficiently respected by Congress.[20]

In *Arver v. United States* (1918), a pacifist challenged the 1917 Selective Draft Act in which Congress had granted conscientious objector status only to ordained ministers and theology students and to members of "any well recognized religious sect or organization whose existing creed or principles forbids its members to participate in war."[21] The petitioner contended that the Selective Draft Act violated both the free exercise and the disestablishment clauses by privileging religious pacifists over nonreligious and by preferring some religious pacifists over others. The Court dismissed this argument out of hand: "We pass without anything but statement the proposition that an establishment of a religion or an interference with the free exercise thereof repugnant to the First Amendment resulted from the exemption clauses . . . because we think its unsoundness is too apparent to require us to do more."[22]

In *United States v. Schwimmer* (1929) and *United States v. Macintosh* (1931), the Court denied relief to parties who were denied naturalized citizenship status solely because of their failure to swear an oath that they would take up arms in defense of the country. Schwimmer was a 49-year-old, well-educated Hungarian woman who wrote and lectured on pacifism. Macintosh was a Baptist divinity professor at Yale and former military chaplain in the Canadian armed forces. Both were ineligible for the military under then current draft laws. Both were otherwise eligible for citizenship. Both were willing to swear full allegiance to the nation but could not swear they could bear arms in defense of the same because of their religious pacifism. Both were denied citizenship and appealed to the Supreme Court. Both lost.

In *Schwimmer,* Justice Butler defended the military power of Congress as "a fundamental principle of the Constitution" and described pacifism as a danger to the same. "The common defense was one of the purposes for which the people ordained and established the Constitution," he wrote for the Court. "It empowers the Congress to provide for such defense, to declare war, to raise and support armies, to maintain a navy, to make rules for the government and regulation of the land and naval forces, to provide for organizing, arming and disciplining the militia." Pacifists can be dangerous, for they are "apt to be more detrimental than their mere refusal to bear arms. The fact that, by reason of sex, age, or other cause, they may be unfit to serve does not lessen their purpose or power to influence others."[23]

In *Macintosh*, Justice Sutherland, speaking for the Court, added that conscientious objection status was a legislative privilege, not a natural right. The status "comes not from the Constitution, but from the acts of Congress. That body may grant or withhold the exemption as in its wisdom it sees fit." Moreover, it was for Congress, not for the individual subject, to judge the religious and moral propriety of the nation's military policy and the role of its citizens therein:

> We are a Christian people according to one another the equal right of religious freedom, and acknowledging with reverence the duty of obedience to the will of God. But, also, we are a nation with the duty to survive; a nation whose Constitution contemplates war as well as peace; whose government must go forward upon the assumption, and safely can proceed upon no other, that unqualified allegiance to the nation and submission and obedience to the laws of the land, as well those made for war as those made for peace, are not inconsistent with the will of God.[24]

Chief Justice Hughes wrote a strong dissent in *Macintosh*, arguing that the Court had trespassed even the narrow view of liberty of conscience set out in the Mormon polygamy cases as well as the policy reflected in the "no religious test oath" in Article VI. This argument failed to convince the *Macintosh* Court. It also failed to convince three subsequent Courts that heard comparable cases on the rights of pacifism.[25] Fifteen years later, however, in *Girouard v. United States* (1946), Chief Justice Hughes's argument, particularly his rendering of the no religious test oath clause, convinced a slender majority of the Court to outlaw such military test oaths as part of the application for naturalized citizenship status.[26]

Though perhaps harsh, the Court's reading of the free exercise clause in these pacifism cases stood on somewhat firmer historical ground. As we saw (pages 64, 65, 68–69, 70–71, 82–83), three drafts of the First Amendment religion clauses had included an explicit conscientious objection clause. But the clause was perennially controversial and eventually dropped from the First Amendment. The most persuasive argument against it came from Representative Benson in the House debate of August 17, 1789: Questions of conscientious objection to military service must be left "to the benevolence of the Legislature" and to the "discretion of the Government," he declared. "If this stands part of the constitution, it will be before the Judiciary on every regulation you make with respect to the organization of the militia." Although the Court made no reference to this history, its dismissive treatment of the claim of a constitutional right to pacifism seemed to be driven in part by this concern. It was for the legislature, not the Court, to decide the rights and limits of the pacifist.

In these early cases, the Court was firm in maintaining Congress's strict limits on pacifism. In a series of cases in the 1960s and 1970s, arising from the Vietnam War, the Court was equally firm in enforcing to the fullest extent possible Congress's generous extension of conscientious objector status to anyone who was a pacifist "by reason of religion and belief."[27]

Funding

Bradfield v. Roberts (1899) was the Court's first disestablishment clause case. In *Bradfield,* Congress had made available some $30,000 to build two new hospital buildings in the District of Columbia. The funding was given to a nonprofit hospital, properly incorporated in 1864. The hospital, though open to the public, was operated by an order of nuns under the auspices of the Roman Catholic Church. A taxpayer and citizen of the District challenged the funding as a violation of the disestablishment clause. The Court rejected the challenge out of hand. On the one hand, the Court stated, "a law respecting a religious establishment" is not necessarily "a law respecting an establishment of religion." Moreover, in this instance, the recipient hospital was not a religious establishment but simply a hospital devoted to medical services that happened to be run by religious folks.

> [T]he fact that its members . . . are members of a monastic order or sisterhood of the Roman Catholic [Church], and the further fact that the hospital is conducted under the auspices of the said church, are wholly immaterial. . . . Whether the individuals who compose the corporation under its charter happen to be all Roman Catholics, or all Methodists, or Presbyterians, or Unitarians, or members of any other religious organization, or of no organization at all, is not of the slightest consequence with reference to the law of its incorporation, nor can the religious beliefs upon religious matters of the various incorporators of the religious body be inquired into.[28]

The Court used similar reasoning in *Quick Bear v. Leupp* (1908). In treaties with the Sioux Indians, Congress had agreed to hold money in trust to be used later for the Indians' education—as partial consideration for the tribal lands that the federal government had confiscated. The treaties entitled the Sioux to designate the schools for which the money should be spent. When the Sioux requested that the funds be spent on Catholic schools that would serve their communities, however, taxpayers objected. Such payments were alleged to violate both a governing statute and the "spirit of the Constitution" that required that government must "always be undenominational [and] never act in a sectarian capacity." Citing *Bradfield,* the Court dismissed this argument, saying that Congress was not establishing religion or prohibiting its free exercise but discharging its treaty obligations to pay for the Sioux's education—a patently secular governmental function.[29]

Review of State Laws Touching Religion

Before 1940, the United States Supreme Court did not apply the First Amendment religion clauses to the states. But the Court did review (or at least issue federal common law respecting) state and local laws touching religion under other provisions of the Constitution as well as under general principles of law and equity. Seventeen such cases reached the Court.

Church Property and Polity

Nine of these seventeen cases involved disputes over church property. In *Terrett v. Taylor* (1815), its first case touching religion, the Supreme Court declared null and void an 1801 Virginia act that rescinded the corporate charter of the Episcopal Church issued in 1776 and required the church to sell its vacant glebe lands and turn over the proceeds to the poor. The act, even if consistent with the Constitution of Virginia, Justice Story wrote for the Court, violated "fundamental principles of natural justice." Religious groups, like all other legal associations, must be allowed to retain a corporate charter once lawfully given and must be allowed to use their properties in any lawful manner they deem apt, without undue interference by the state.[30]

In a trio of cases in 1852, 1856, and 1887, the Court upheld the corporate property rights of a communitarian Christian group against the claims of defecting members. The Harmony Society, an intensely communitarian sect of German Anabaptist origin and orientation, professed and practiced a policy of holding all property in common. Members were expected to give up their private properties and to accept a new ethic and practice of communal sharing and caring. Most parties signed a document to this effect upon joining the group. In each of the three cases that reached the Court, members who defected from the Harmony Society sought to recover the private property that they had contributed—in two cases alleging fraud on the part of the religious leadership in acquiring and retaining the once-private property. The Court held for the Harmony Society in each instance, resolving each case using basic laws of contract and association.[31]

The Court distilled the rationale of these cases in *Order of St. Benedict v. Steinhauser* (1914).[32] There, a monastic order that practiced community property claimed title to the estate of a deceased life-long member. The

Court upheld the order's right to the property on the strength of these earlier Harmony Society cases and set out its basic method of adjudication:

> We are not concerned in the present case with any question of ecclesiastical requirement or monastic discipline. The question is solely one of civil rights. The claim in suit rests upon the constitution of the complainant corporation, and the obligations inherent in membership. . . . [T]he question here is not one of canon law or ecclesiastical polity. The requirement of complainant's constitution [respecting community property] must be read according to its terms, and its validity must thus be determined.[33]

The Court extended this logic in another trio of cases in 1853, 1871, and 1872, each involving disputes over property between two factions within a church. "Religious organizations come before us in the same attitude as other voluntary associations for benevolent or charitable purposes," Justice Miller wrote for the Court in *Watson v. Jones* (1871), "and their rights of property, or contract, are equally under the protection of the law, and the actions of their members subject to its restraints."[34] State courts could thus hear such intrachurch dispute cases and grant equitable or legal relief as was apt.[35] But in determining which of the two factions is entitled to the property, a civil court should defer to the judgment of the highest religious authority:

> [W]e think the rule of action which should govern the civil courts, founded in a broad and sound view of the relations of church and state . . . is, that, whenever the questions of discipline, or of faith or ecclesiastical rule, custom, or law have been decided by the highest of these church judicatories to which the matter has been carried, the legal tribunals must accept such decisions as final and binding on them, in their application of the case before them.[36]

In *Watson v. Jones*, Justice Miller offered a crisp rendition of the basics of individual and corporate religious rights and liberties that supported these holdings:

> In this country the full and free right to entertain any religious belief, to practice any religious principle, and teach any religious doctrine which does not violate the laws of morality and property, and which does not infringe personal rights, is conceded to all. The law knows no heresy, and is committed to the support of no dogma, the establishment of no sect. The right to organize voluntary religious associations to assist in the expression and dissemination of any religious doctrine, and to create tribunals for the decision of controverted questions of faith within the association . . . is unquestioned.[37]

Justice Strong amplified the principles of liberty of conscience and separation of church and state in *Bouldin v. Alexander* (1872), stating for the Court: "[W]e have no power to revise or question ordinary acts of church discipline, or of excision of church membership. . . . [W]e cannot decide who ought to be members of the church, nor whether the excommunicated have been regularly or irregularly cut off."[38]

Although they did not involve application of the First Amendment, these early Supreme Court cases reviewing state laws on religion underscored the principles of religious equality and pluralism and separation of church and state: First, religion is both individual and corporate in character, and both these forms of religious identity and expression are deserving of legal protection. Second, religious groups are entitled to acquire, use, maintain, and alienate their properties in accordance with their own internal religious strictures, so long as these abide by general laws of property that prevail within the state. Third, religious groups are entitled to govern their own internal affairs, at least with respect to property, without interference or review by secular courts. These holdings helped to lay an important foundation for later developments of religious group rights in matters of property, education, employment, and discipline.[39]

Cummings v. Missouri (1866) was the only nonproperty case touching religion to come to the Court from the states in the nineteenth century. A state statute, adopted in the aftermath of the American Civil War, required various licensed professionals, including clergy, to swear an oath disavowing support or sympathy for the cause of the Confederate states against the United States. A Roman Catholic priest was fined $500 for preaching without having sworn the oath. On appeal, a sharply divided Court held that the law violated Article I, section 10 of the United States Constitution that no state shall "pass any Bill of Attainder, ex post facto Law, or Law impairing the Obligation of Contracts." The majority said nothing of the oath violating the priest's religious liberty, save one line: "It would be strange, indeed, if a minister of the Gospel, whose sympathies are with all the children of men—the good, the sinful, the happy, and the sorrowing—might not manifest such sympathy by an act of charity or a word of consolation."[40] The dissenting justices saw the case as a specious attempt to impose First Amendment values onto the states, even though nothing in the Constitution "interposes any such protection between the State governments and their own citizens."[41]

Fundamental Religious Liberty and Incorporation

In several cases in the 1920s and 1930s, the Supreme Court began to review state and local laws touching religion under an emerging standard of "fundamental religious liberty."[42] These cases first stated the concept of fundamental religious liberty in the abstract, then tied it to the Fourteenth Amendment guarantee that no state shall "deprive any person of life, liberty, or property, without due process of law." The Supreme Court began to outlaw state laws touching religion because they violated the liberty guarantee of the Fourteenth Amendment.

The first reference to this standard of religion as a "fundamental liberty" came in *Meyer v. Nebraska* (1923). The state of Nebraska, like several other states in the aftermath of World War I, began to clamp down on German Protestants, exposing them to a number of increasingly onerous registration and taxation policies and often turning a blind eye to private violence against them. At issue in *Meyer* was a new state law that mandated English instruction in all grade schools. Teachers in private Protestant grade schools were convicted under this statute for allowing the reading of Bible stories in German. The Supreme Court reversed the conviction, mostly on grounds of the rights of the parents to direct the education of their children. But the Court noted in a passing dictum that such an action also violated the Fourteenth Amendment due process clause that protected, among others, the defendant's right "to worship God according to the dictates of his own conscience."[43]

The Court touched on this standard again in *Pierce v. Society of Sisters* (1925). Oregon had passed a law mandating that all eligible students must attend public schools. The Oregon law, like that of many states at the time, was enacted, in part, to drive out of existence emerging Catholic and other private religious schools and to give new impetus to the development of public schools. The Society of Sisters, which owned and operated several private Catholic schools that were jeopardized by the new Oregon law, challenged this law as a violation of the right of the parents, children, schools, and school teachers alike. The Court struck down the Oregon law and upheld the rights of the parents and of the religious schools. Again, the Court offered a suggestive dictum about protecting the fundamental liberty interests at stake: "rights guaranteed by the Constitution may not be abridged by legislation which has no reasonable relation to some purpose within the competency of the state. The fundamental theory of liberty upon which all governments in this Union repose excludes any general power of the state to standardize its children by forcing them to accept instruction from public teachers only." It also forecloses "unwarranted compulsion . . . over present and future patrons" of the religious schools.[44] These principles were echoed in two subsequent cases.[45]

In *Hamilton v. Board of Regents* (1934), the Court stated this principle of fundamental liberty more explicitly. State university students objected to mandatory R.O.T.C. training in violation of their conscientious scruples to participation in war, or preparation for the same. One basis of their challenge was the explicit guarantee of liberty in the Fourteenth Amendment due process clause. Although the Court rejected the students's appeal, they did accept this constitutional basis for review. As Justice Butler put it for the Court: "There need be no attempt to enumerate or comprehensively to define what is included in the 'liberty' protected by the due process clause [of the Fourteenth Amendment]. Undoubtedly it does include the right to entertain the beliefs, to adhere to the principles, and to teach the doctrines" of a faith.[46] Justice Cardozo concurred in the result but added even more directly: "I assume for present purposes that the religious liberty protected by the First Amendment against invasion by the nation is protected by the Fourteenth Amendment against invasion by the states."[47]

Three years later, in *Palko v. Connecticut* (1937), Justice Cardozo sharpened this view of fundamental liberty. The due process clause of the Fourteenth Amendment, he argued, requires that all state and local governments must adhere to the "fundamental principles of liberty and justice which lie at the base of all our civil and political institutions." An authoritative definition of these principles of liberty and justice is set forth in the Bill of Rights attached to the United States Constitution. The first eight amendments of the Bill of Rights, by their terms, bind the federal government. But, as authoritative statements of fundamental principles of liberty, they might also be understood to bind the states. The Court, in interpreting and applying the "liberty" provision of the Fourteenth Amendment due process clause may thus selectively apply various provisions of the federal Bill of Rights to test state and local ordinances.[48]

In *Lovell v. City of Griffin* (1938) and *Schneider v. Town of Irvington* (1939), the Court selectively applied the free speech and free press clauses of the First Amendment to invalidate a series of municipal ordinances that prohibited the distribution of religious literature. Freedoms of speech and press, Chief Justice Hughes declared for the *Lovell* Court, are "among the fundamental personal rights" that neither federal nor state officials have power to abridge.[49]

In *Cantwell v. Connecticut* (1940), the Court for the first time applied the free exercise clause to a local ordinance. In *Cantwell*, Jehovah's Witnesses appealed their conviction under a city licensing law, among others. The law required all parties who wished to solicit for "any alleged religious, charitable or philanthropic cause" to procure a license in advance. Local administrators could deny a license to those whose cause did not seem to be in good faith. The Witnesses were convicted for preaching and soliciting without having procured such a license. They appealed, arguing, in the Court's words, that the statute "was offensive to the due process clause of the Fourteenth Amendment because, on its face and as construed and applied, it denied them freedom of speech and prohibited their free exercise of religion."[50]

With matter-of-fact simplicity, the Court applied the free exercise clause to the local ordinance and held for the Witnesses. Justice Roberts wrote for the Court:

We hold that the statute, as construed and applied to the appellants, deprives them of their liberty without due process of law in contravention of the Fourteenth Amendment. The fundamental concept of liberty embodied in that Amendment embraces the liberties guaranteed by the First Amendment. The First Amendment declares that Congress shall make no law respecting an establishment of religion or prohibiting the free exercise thereof. The Fourteenth Amendment has rendered the legislatures of the states as incompetent as Congress to enact such laws.[51]

The Court went on to soften the wooden belief-action distinction of its earlier free exercise cases and to restate a number of basic principles of religious liberty that were at work in its earlier cases reviewing state laws touching religion:

The constitutional inhibition of legislation on the subject of religion has a double aspect. On the one hand, it forestalls compulsion by law of the acceptance of any creed or the practice of any form of worship. Freedom of conscience and freedom to adhere to such religious organization or form of worship as the individual may choose cannot be restricted by law. On the other hand, it safeguards the free exercise of the chosen form of religion. Thus the Amendment embraces two concepts,—freedom to believe and freedom to act. The first is absolute but, in the nature of things, the second cannot be. Conduct remains subject to regulation for the protection of society. The freedom to act must have appropriate definition to preserve the enforcement of that protection. In every case the power to regulate must be so exercised as not, in attaining a permissible end, unduly to infringe the protected freedom.[52]

Seventeen cases over the next six years drove home the lessons of *Cantwell*—that the free exercise clause applied as readily to the states as to the federal government and that the clause required states to respect the principles of liberty of conscience and the equality of a plurality of faiths before the law.[53] Most of these early free exercise cases, as we shall see in the next chapter, simply adjusted the American experiment by protecting the rights of newly emergent religious groups against recalcitrant local officials. Jehovah's Witnesses, the Court held repeatedly, could not be denied licenses to preach, parade, or pamphleteer just because they were unpopular. Public school students could not be compelled to salute the flag or recite the pledge if they were conscientiously opposed. Other parties, with scruples of conscience, could not be forced to swear oaths before receiving citizenship status, property tax exemptions, state bureaucratic positions, social welfare benefits, or standing in courts. Such free exercise remedies are often condemned as a corruption of the federalism inherent in the religion clauses. But read more charitably, they can be seen as an effort to make the traditional state systems of religious governance more "mild and equitable" for the many new private religions on the American scene.

In *Everson v. Board of Education* (1947), the Court signaled a more radical change to the American experiment. *Everson* formally incorporated the First Amendment disestablishment clause into the Fourteenth Amendment due process clause and applied it to the states. After a long recitation of the history and purpose of the religion clauses, Justice Black declared for the Court:

> The meaning and scope of the First Amendment, preventing [an] establishment of religion or prohibiting the free exercise thereof, in light of its history and the evils it was designed forever to suppress, have been several times elaborated by the decisions of this Court prior to the application of the First Amendment to the states by the Fourteenth. The broad meaning given the Amendment by these earlier cases has been accepted by this Court in its decisions concerning an individual's religious freedom [of exercise]. . . . There is every reason to give the same application and broad interpretation to the "establishment of religion" clause.[54]

Like the *Cantwell* Court, the *Everson* Court went on to state a preliminary standard of review for future disestablishment cases. But the *Everson* Court, unlike the *Cantwell* Court, did not have a brace of earlier Supreme Court cases on which to call—only *Bradfield* and *Quick Bear,* neither of which offered much guidance. The disestablishment standard that the Court chose in this opening case was the strong separationist standard already in place in some of the state constitutions and initially proposed in the defeated Blaine Amendment of 1875–1876. In Justice Black's famous words:

> The "establishment of religion" clause of the First Amendment means at least this: Neither a state nor the Federal Government can set up a church. Neither can pass laws which aid one religion, aid all religions, or prefer one religion over another. Neither can force nor influence a person to go or to remain away from church against his will or force him to profess a belief or disbelief in any religion. No person can be punished for entertaining or professing religious beliefs or disbeliefs, for church attendance or non-attendance. No tax in any amount, large or small, can be levied to support any religious activities or institutions, whatever they may be called, or whatever form they may adopt to teach or practice religion. Neither a state nor the Federal Government can, openly or secretly, participate in the affairs of any religious organizations or groups, or vice versa. In the words of Jefferson, the clause against establishment of religion by law was intended to erect "a wall of separation between church and state." . . . That wall must be kept high and impregnable. We could not approve the slightest breach.[55]

Justice Black, and Justice Rutledge in dissent in *Everson*, described these sentiments as the "original intent of the eighteenth century framers."[56] But in determining the intent of the framers, they turned only to Enlightenment writers—principally Jefferson and Madison—and read primarily the constitutional history of Virginia, where these writers had their greatest influence.[57] The justices did not consider the multiple opinions of Puritans, Evangelicals, or Republicans nor the constitutional experiments or experiences of other early states besides Virginia. The justices also did not consider the nuances of even the sternest Enlightenment writers on religion, who were concerned with other "essential rights and liberties" besides separation of church and state. The disestablishment clause, the Court declared, demanded a strict separationism. Henceforth, all federal and state laws would be held to this strong principle or struck down as unconstitutional.

Everson was an open invitation to litigation. Numerous state and local policies on religion that were promulgated under a regime dominated by eighteenth-century Puritan and Civic Republican sentiments were now open to challenge. Scores of establishment cases poured into the lower federal courts after the 1940s. More than fifty cases ultimately have reached the Supreme Court on appeal. The subject matter of these cases in the early years was predictable enough: challenges to traditional laws and policies involving state endorsements of religious symbols and services; challenges to traditional laws and policies that afforded state aid to religious missions, schools, charities, and others; challenges to traditional laws explicitly predicated on (Protestant) Christian morals and mores. The new application of the First Amendment religion clauses to the states, through incorporation doctrine, encouraged such extensive litigation. The *Everson* Court's separationist interpretation of the disestablishment clause demanded it.

By so incorporating the First Amendment religion clauses into the Fourteenth Amendment due process clause, the Court set in motion the creation of a new national law on religious liberty, governed by the federal courts and enforceable against federal, state, and local governments alike.[58] Viewed in isolation, this development might seem to be a rather remarkable attack on the basic principle of federalism built in the text of the First Amendment ("*Congress* shall make no law . . . "). But this development was of a piece with other movements of the day—the growing federalization of the society and the economy through the New Deal legislation and case law, the pressing need for national solidarity in the face of World War II and in the Cold War to follow, the grim lessons about religious and cultural bigotry learned through the Holocaust and the gulag.

Incorporation doctrine was a small part of an emerging constitutional nationalism that insisted on the guarantees of fundamental liberty and rule of law for all and that would brook neither local bigotry nor local favoritism even in the name of federalism. Before 1940, a number of other provisions of the Bill of Rights had already been selectively incorporated into the Fourteenth Amendment due process clause and applied to the states.[59] Given the grim lessons about unchecked religious bigotry taught by the death camps of World War II, it was almost culturally inevitable, even if not constitutionally ineluctable, that the religion clauses be incorporated as well.

7

MODERN FREE
EXERCISE LAW

The incorporation of the First Amendment religion clauses into the Four-teenth Amendment due process clause shifted final authority over the American experiment from the states to the United States Supreme Court. In the first 150 years of the republic, the Court issued 32 cases on religious liberty—none of them applying the First Amendment religion clauses to state and local governments. In the past 60 years, the Court has issued more than 150 decisions on religious liberty—more than 100 of them ap-plying the First Amendment to state and local governments.

The incorporation doctrine has not foreclosed the states from participa-tion in the American experiment. State and local legislatures have contin-ued to issue numerous laws touching religion—from prison regulations governing the religious exercises of state inmates, to regulations of religious expression in public schools and the public square, to criminal laws pro-hibiting violations of life, limb, and property in the name of religion, among many other laws. State courts have kept an ample docket of religion cases, adjudicating them under their own state constitutional provisions on religious liberty.[1]

Since the 1940s, however, most laws in America that touch religion have become subject to First Amendment influence, if not scrutiny. And most ju-dicial interpretations of religious liberty—both by lower federal courts and by state courts—have sought to follow the precedents laid down by the United States Supreme Court. Every major Supreme Court case on religious liberty produces numerous lower court progeny. And every major shift in prevailing Supreme Court law on religious liberty can take years to trickle down into the constitutional calculus of the lower courts.

It is no small challenge to master the Supreme Court's modern First Amendment cases. Not only are some of the Court's opinions rife with casuistry and contradiction. But particularly in the cases of the past decade, a bitterly divided Court has issued a barrage of lengthy concurring and dissenting opinions—often bristling with long historical and jurisprudential debates and disquisitions that go far beyond the constitutional issues at hand. No amount of summarizing can ultimately substitute for sitting down and reading the cases for oneself. A table of Supreme Court cases is provided in Appendix 3 herein.[2] Several good collections of cases are at hand.[3]

Two tasks are before us in this chapter on modern free exercise law and in the following chapter on modern disestablishment law. First, I shall map the main shifts in doctrine in the Supreme Court cases since the 1940s. Under both clauses, the Court has developed various doctrinal approaches or tests that are driven, in part, by broader constitutional concerns over federalism, judicial review, and separation of powers. To provide some guidance to these broader constitutional dimensions of First Amendment law, this chapter, and the next, will open by mapping the main doctrinal issues and tests at work before analyzing various groups of cases touching religion. Second, in analyzing these cases, I shall review especially the Supreme Court's treatment of the first principles of the American experiment—not only the principles of free exercise and disestablishment per se but also the allied principles of liberty of conscience, religious equality, religious pluralism, and separation of church and state.

Mapping Modern Free Exercise Doctrine

Government Power Versus Free Exercise Rights

At the heart of a modern free exercise case is a basic conflict between the exercise of governmental power and the exercise of a private party's religion. The private party challenges the exercise of governmental power as a violation of its rights protected by the free exercise clause.

The challenged governmental entity can be at any level—federal, state, county, or municipal. The governmental action that is challenged can be executive, legislative, or regulatory in nature. But it must be governmental, not private, conduct that is at issue. When private entities or individuals violate another private party's religious rights, such conduct is addressed by civil suits and/or criminal prosecution, not by free exercise litigation.

The claimant in a free exercise case can be a religious individual or a religious group. Their claim is that the law at issue somehow "prohibits" the freedom of their religious exercise. The law infringes upon their beliefs of conscience. It inhibits their acts of worship or of religious speech, press, or association. It commands them to do something, or to forgo something, that conflicts with the demands of their individual consciences or collective faiths. It discriminatorily singles out their activities or properties for duties or exclusions that are not imposed on other individuals or groups similarly situated. In brief, government unduly "burdens" their religion.[4]

Free exercise claimants must meet the usual requirements for pressing any constitutional case against the government. The claimants must state an actual "case or controversy"—not an issue that has become moot or requests only an advisory opinion from the Court. They must have standing to bring the suit—showing an actual injury to themselves. They must raise a constitutional issue on which a court may sit—not a "political question" that is better addressed by other branches of government.[5]

In addition, free exercise claimants must demonstrate that it is their *religious* exercise that has been improperly burdened. In many instances, the religious qualities of the claim are easy enough to make out. A Jehovah's Witness is discriminately denied a license to preach.[6] An atheist is indiscriminately required to swear an oath reciting his belief in God.[7] A Jewish officer is forbidden from wearing his yarmulke on an Air Force base.[8] A Muslim prisoner is kept from prayer at the appointed hour of the day or from collective Friday worship.[9] These are core free exercise cases involving religious individuals. A religious school is required to hire a teacher who does not share its faith.[10] A religious crusader is fined for selling religious articles without collecting sales and use taxes.[11] A bishop is denied his *cathedra* and cathedral because a state religious incorporation law does not recognize the foreign religious authority that appoints him and governs his church.[12] These are core free exercise cases involving religious groups.

In a number of cases, however, the free exercise interest can appear more attenuated. An applicant for a temporary agency refuses a job because it might require him to work on Sunday, his day for "rest," though not for worship. He claims unemployment compensation, is denied, and appeals.[13] A furniture store owner, who is a strict Saturday sabbatarian, opens his store on Sunday in violation of Sunday blue laws that prohibit all but "necessary labor." He is fined, and appeals, claiming that the law burdens his free exercise rights to observe his Saturday sabbath.[14] A religious university discriminates against African American employees and students on the understanding that the Bible requires that races be kept separate. The school is stripped of its federal tax exempt status, and appeals, claiming that its free exercise rights have been violated just because its beliefs are not popular.[15] A manufacturing company, owned and operated by devout religious believers, requires all its employees to participate in regular devotional activities on company time. The federal Equal Employment Opportunity Commission forbids them from imposing this requirement on a recalcitrant employee. The company owners appeal, alleging violations of their free exercise rights to practice a holistic faith.[16] In each of these cases, from the internal claimant's perspective, the religious interests may be no less central and sincere. But from the external legal perspective, the religious interests at stake are viewed as more penumbral and attenuated. Sometimes they will not prove sufficient to meet threshold requirements to press a free exercise claim.

The Supreme Court has generally allowed individuals to press free exercise claims that are "sincere"—even if they are inconsistent, incoherent, idiosyncratic, or newly acquired.[17] In some cases, this sincerity test "cannot completely escape the distinctly bad aroma of an inquisition," in Ira Lupu's apt phrase.[18] It can lead judges or juries to inquire intrusively into the faith of a person or a group or to play to their prejudices against unpopular or exotic religions.[19] But, if the Court is to be protected from fraudulent or sham claims under the free exercise clause, some measured inquiry into the claims of faith is unavoidable.

The Court has provided less guidance to decide the free exercise standing of religious groups. It is easy enough when a church, synagogue, mosque, or temple alleges free exercise violations. But what if the group deliberately mixes religious and secular functions and forms?[20] What if the group's religiosity seems thin, transient, or contrived? What if the claimant is a large family that describes itself as a naturalist faith and wishes to have tax exemptions for farmland, which it calls a religious shrine?[21] Absent Supreme Court direction, lower courts have developed a range of tests to decide the free exercise standing of such religious groups.[22]

Resolving the Conflict

Assuming that the claimant can meet the threshold requirements to press a free exercise claim, how does the Court resolve this basic conflict between government power and religious rights, both anchored in the constitution? Two principal methods seem to be at work in the Court's free exercise cases of the past sixty years: (1) "case-by-case balancing," which has led to clusters of free exercise cases; and (2) "definitional balancing," which has led to shifting standards of judicial review under the free exercise clause.

One way to read the Court's free exercise cases is that they reflect a tradition of case-by-case balancing of these conflicting constitutional interests.[23] Thin lines and then clusters of cases have slowly emerged as the Court has adjudicated cases with comparable fact patterns and built on its immediate precedents. Accordingly, today there are clusters of cases upholding free exercise rights to engage in proselytism, worship, and other forms of religious expression; to receive unemployment compensation when discharged from work for religious reasons; to gain equal access to public schools, public forums, and public benefits. There are also clusters of cases dealing with failed free exercise claims to exemptions from military, prison, and taxation laws. A relatively consistent internal logic governs each cluster of cases, and the Court will sometimes reach back several decades to retrieve or distinguish a precedent in that cluster.[24] But it is harder to make out a common free exercise logic that applies across these clusters of cases. Under this reading, proper categorization of the dispute in advance is critical to locking one's position into the cluster of cases most advantageous to one's cause.[25]

A second, more complicated, way to read these cases is that they represent a series of shifting definitions of how the free exercise clause is to be applied across the board. In a few cases, the Court has said explicitly, as it did in *Prince v. Massachusetts* (1944): "Our ruling does not extend beyond the facts the case presents."[26] But in other cases, the Court has defined a standard of review to be used to adjudicate future free exercise cases, even with decidedly different facts. Subsequent cases have applied this same standard of review until the Court determines that the experiment requires a new standard. What sometimes seems to trigger a change in the standard of review is an extreme application of the prior standard by an overreaching litigant or by an overindulgent Court.[27]

Defining general standards of review to resolve constitutional conflicts between powers and rights is not unique to the free exercise clause. The Supreme Court has engaged in this exercise in many cases arising under the Bill of Rights and the Fourteenth Amendment. Particularly in the past half century, the Court has developed a whole spectrum of standards of review, from low-level to high-level scrutiny of the law that is challenged.[28]

1. Under low-level scrutiny, the Court will uphold the challenged law so long as:

   A. it is in pursuit of a *legitimate* governmental interest; and
   B. it is *reasonably related* to that interest.

This test, often called the *rational basis test*, involves high judicial deference to the legislature. It provides a loose safety net to protect parties against governmental caprice and abuse by allowing a Court to strike down patently discriminatory and arbitrary laws.

2. Under high-level scrutiny, a Court will uphold the challenged law only if:

   A. it is in pursuit of a *compelling* or overriding *governmental interest*; and
   B. it is *narrowly tailored* to achieve that interest, not intruding on the claimant's rights any more than is absolutely necessary.

This test, often called the *compelling state interest test*, involves close judicial inquiry into the purposes and provisions of the law. It empowers a Court to strike down the law altogether or to tailor it in a manner that will cause less harm to the claimant.

3. Between these forms of review, the Court has developed a category of "heightened" scrutiny. Under this standard, the Court will uphold the challenged law if:

A. it is in pursuit of an *important* or significant *governmental interest*; and
B. it is *substantially related* to that interest.

This test, often called the *intermediate scrutiny test*, is neither as deferential to the legislature as the rational basis test nor as penetrating in its scrutiny as the compelling state interest test.[29]

These standards of review can be easily contracted or conflated. A strong rational basis test can slide into a intermediate scrutiny test.[30] A strong intermediate scrutiny test can fold into a compelling state interest test. The three "tests" are not so much insular modes of analysis as general stopping points on a continuum. Viewed as such, they guide the Court in resolving the constitutional conflict before it, and they help predict the outcome of a case. The lower the level of scrutiny, the more likely it is that government will win. The higher the scrutiny, the more likely it is that the rights claimant will win.[31]

This spectrum of standards of review helps us to gain another picture of the Supreme Court's free exercise doctrine. Since its first free exercise case in 1879, the United States Supreme Court has ranged across this entire spectrum of review. Although not all free exercise cases fit on this spectrum, a number of the main cases do. By plotting them (see Figure 7.1), we can at

Rational Basis Test	*Intermediate Scrutiny Test*	*Compelling State Interest Test*
legitimate interest	significant interest	compelling interest
rational link	substantial link	narrowly tailored
Reynolds (1879)		
	Cantwell (1940)	
		Sherbert (1963)
Smith (1990)		
		RFRA (1993)
Boerne (1997)		*Boerne?* (1997)

FIGURE 7.1   Trends in Modern Free Exercise Law

least get a rough picture of the main shifts in the Court's application of the free exercise clause.

In *Reynolds v. United States* (1879), the Court applied a very low level of scrutiny. The Court's only stated concern was whether the laws outlawing polygamy were "authorized," "reasonable," and "general" and whether they properly reached the actions of the parties.[32] This standard of review recurred in the pacifism cases from *Arver v. United States* (1918) onward, where the Court several times upheld military oaths and training as "legitimate," "authorized," and "necessary and proper" exercises of congressional power over national security and the military. Every case that applied this standard of review found for the government.

In *Cantwell v. Connecticut* (1940), the Court for the first time applied a heightened level of scrutiny in its application of the free exercise clause. The Court cordoned off areas of religion that government could not regulate unless they were clearly criminal: religious beliefs, worship, and assembly. Regulation of other religious conduct was "permissible" so long as it was by "general and non-discriminatory legislation" and did not "unduly infringe" upon this exercise.[33] Later *Cantwell* progeny stated that government could not infringe on religious conduct on "such slender grounds" as "rational basis" or other "modest estimates of governmental competence." The law at issue, as the Court later put it, must "serve a significant governmental interest" to withstand free exercise scrutiny.[34] More than two dozen cases in the next two decades—often combining free exercise and free speech analysis—generally applied this intermediate standard of review. The cases were roughly evenly divided in holding for government and for the free exercise claimant.

In *Sherbert v. Verner* (1963), the Court for the first time applied a strict scrutiny standard of review in applying the free exercise clause. Not only was the law at issue to be general, as the rational basis test required. Not only was the law to be nondiscriminatory on religious grounds and not touch religious beliefs, as the intermediate scrutiny test required. The law was now also (1) to serve a compelling state interest; and (2) to be narrowly tailored to achieve that interest with the least possible intrusion on free exercise rights.[35] Under this standard, the *Sherbert* Court reviewed both the general law and its particular application to this free exercise claimant. Finding no compelling reason to apply the general law to this claimant, the Court ordered her exempt from the general law and entitled to receive the state unemployment compensation benefits that had been withheld from her. The Supreme Court used this strict scrutiny test of free exercise in ten cases after 1963, six times finding for the religious claimant, four times for the government.[36]

In *Employment Division v. Smith* (1990), the Court formally rejected the strict scrutiny test of free exercise and adopted a lower-level scrutiny test. Building on a trio of cases in the later 1980s that had avoided application of the *Sherbert* strict scrutiny test, the *Smith* Court held that "the right of free exercise does not relieve an individual of the obligation to comply with a 'valid and neutral law of general applicability on the ground that the law proscribes (or prescribes) conduct that his religion prescribes (or proscribes).'"[37] If a law is neutral and generally applicable, it is constitutional, even if it burdens a central aspect of the claimant's religion.[38] But if a law is not neutral or not generally applicable, it must be justified by a compelling governmental interest and narrowly tailored to achieve that interest. This latter caveat rendered the *Smith* test somewhat more protective of religious interests than the original *Reynolds* test. The Court in *Reynolds* and its progeny readily upheld patently discriminatory laws that targeted the Mormons. In 1993, the Supreme Court used the *Smith* test to strike down discriminatory laws that transparently targeted the slaughtering practices of Santerians.[39]

The weakening of free exercise scrutiny introduced by *Smith* was widely denounced as a travesty to religious liberty.[40] In reaction, a virtually unanimous Congress passed the Religious Freedom Restoration Act (1993) (RFRA). The stated purpose of the act was to "restore the compelling state interest test" of *Sherbert* and progeny—which the act called "a workable test for striking sensible balances between religious liberty and competing prior governmental interests." The act provided: "(a) In General [—] Government shall not substantially burden a person's exercise of religion even if the burden results from a rule of general applicability, except as provided in subsection (b). (b) Exception [—] Government may substantially burden a person's exercise of religion only if it demonstrates that application of the burden to the person (1) is in furtherance of a compelling governmental interest; and (2) is the least restrictive means of furthering that compelling governmental interest."[41] RFRA has been applied in more than 150 free exercise cases since 1993, the majority of them filed by state and federal prisoners. It has not brought ready victory to religious rights claimants; only about 15 percent of RFRA claims have succeeded.[42]

The Religious Freedom Restoration Act was a bold attempt to restore a stricter standard of review for free exercise cases. Its formulation was supported by a remarkably broad spectrum of religious and political groups. But the act soon drew sharp opposition, even from critics who were alarmed by *Smith*. Critics began to charge that Congress had overstepped its authority in violation of both federalism and separation of powers principles, that it had created something of an individual religious veto of general laws in violation of the disestablishment clause, that it had inflicted on the courts endless and expensive litigation, among many other charges.[43]

In *City of Boerne v. Flores* (1997), the Supreme Court declared the Religious Freedom Restoration Act unconstitutional, at least as applied to the states. Congress had passed RFRA on the strength of section 5 of the Fourteenth Amendment, which empowered Congress to "enforce" the liberty provisions of the Amendment, using "appropriate legislation." In the

Court's judgment: "Legislation which alters the meaning of the Free Exercise Clause cannot be said to be enforcing the Clause."[44] The act, in the Court's judgment, fundamentally changed the free exercise law and was thus unconstitutional. With respect to free exercise claims against state and local laws, the *Smith* lower-level scrutiny test is again the law.[45]

The *Boerne* case, however, left the Religious Freedom Restoration Act standing as applied to review of federal laws. Lower federal courts have continued to apply the strict scrutiny test of RFRA, particularly in free exercise cases challenging the new application of federal laws of bankruptcy to religious parties.[46] It is an open question whether the Court will allow this two-tracked approach to free exercise litigation to continue for long. The sharpness of the *Boerne* Court's rebuke of Congress seems to go beyond the majority opinion's stated concerns for federalism and congressional overreaching under section 5 of the Fourteenth Amendment.[47]

For now, *Boerne* might be viewed as a step along the way to a more traditional understanding of free exercise jurisprudence, where federal and state laws are subject to separate forms of religious liberty review. The federal government will be held to the stricter free exercise standard of RFRA. State and local governments will be held to the looser free exercise standard of *Smith*. In its current form, this two-tracked approach to religious rights and liberties is not a reversal of *Cantwell*'s incorporation doctrine. But it is something of a revival of the federalism values built into the text of the First Amendment. As such, it is of a piece with the Court's new concern for federalism in several other areas of constitutional law, most notably in its interpretation of the commerce clause of Article I of the Constitution.[48]

The two foregoing readings give us two pictures of the Court's modern free exercise doctrine—one as a collection of case clusters, a second as a series of shifting standards of review. Both readings account for most of the free exercise cases of the modern era, but not all. Occasionally, the Court has defied the common logic of a factual cluster—as it did in the *Smith* case, which was after all another unemployment compensation case in the *Sherbert* cluster. Occasionally, the Court has wandered from a general standard of review—as it did in several cases holding against protections of Jewish Sabbath Day observance, Muslim Friday worship, and Native American religious rites and sites. Occasionally, the Court has simply decided a case categorically—as it did in holding that pacifism is a statutory privilege and not a free exercise right or that religious oaths impugn religious beliefs and are thus categorically prohibited.

The Multiple Principles of Modern Free Exercise Law

The Supreme Court's modern free exercise cases are, in part, small skirmishes in great constitutional battles over principles of federalism, judicial review, and separation of powers. The Court's free exercise opinions thus sometimes reflect and project grand constitutional causes and conundrums that seem far removed from a litigant's simple petition for protection of the sources, sanctions, or sanctuaries of faith.

The Supreme Court's modern free exercise cases are also, however, small laboratories for carrying on the great American experiment in religious liberty. It is thus apt to read the Court's main free exercise cases not only in light of broader constitutional movements but also in terms of the founding principles of the American tradition of religious liberty. Such a reading produces a rather different picture of modern free exercise law. The main cases fall into clusters around the four main founding principles that are incorporated into the free exercise clause—principles that have, since 1980, been slowly reduced to a single concern for neutrality.

The eighteenth-century founders, as we saw (pages 42–44, 80–83), regarded the principle of free exercise as a basic protection for religious speech, press, and assembly—what is today called freedom of religious expression. They also regarded "free exercise" as an umbrella term that incorporated the principles of liberty of conscience, separation of church and state, and equality of a plurality of faiths.

In its first modern case on point, *Cantwell v. Connecticut* (1940), the Court effectively read each of these principles into the free exercise clause, as well as the free speech clause as applied to religion. This First Amendment guarantee, the *Cantwell* Court declared, protects "[f]reedom of conscience and freedom to adhere to such religious organization or form of worship as the individual may choose." It "safeguards the free exercise of the chosen form of religion," the "freedom to act" on one's beliefs. It protects a "plurality of forms and expressions" of faith, each of which deserves equal protection under the law. "In the realm of religious faith, and in that of political belief," the Court wrote, "sharp differences arise."

> But the people of this nation have ordained in light of history, that, in spite of the probability of the excesses and abuses, these liberties are, in the long view, essential to enlightened opinion and right conduct on the part of the citizens of the democracy. The essential characteristic of these liberties is, that under their shield many types of life, character, opinion and belief can develop unmolested and unobstructed. Nowhere is this shield more necessary than in our own country for a people composed of many races and of many creeds.[49]

In a number of free exercise cases from the early 1940s onward, the Supreme Court elaborated each of these founding principles of religious liberty.

Freedom and Equality of Religious Expression

The *Cantwell* Court gave clear guidance as to the meaning and measure of the freedom of religious expression. All religious expression, Justice

Roberts wrote for Court, "remains subject to regulation for the protection of society."

> In every case the power to regulate must be so exercised as not, in attaining a permissible end, unduly to infringe the protected freedom. No one would contest the proposition that a State may not, by statute, wholly deny the right to preach or to disseminate religious views. Plainly such a previous and absolute restraint would violate the terms of the guarantee. It is equally clear that a State may by general and non-discriminatory legislation regulate the times, the places, and the manner of [religious expression] . . . without unconstitutionally invading the liberties protected by the Fourteenth Amendment. . . . No one would have the hardihood to suggest . . . that religious liberty connotes the privilege to exhort others to physical attack upon those belonging to another sect. When clear and present danger of riot, disorder, interference with traffic upon the public streets, or other immediate threat to public safety, peace, or order appears, the power of the State to prevent or punish is obvious. Equally obvious is it that a State may not unduly suppress free communication of views, religious or other, under the guise of conserving desirable conditions.[50]

These were the keys to adjudicating free exercise claims: (1) outright prohibitions and prior restraints on religious expression that effectively foreclosed it were forbidden; (2) discriminatory regulations of religious expression were also forbidden; but (3) general regulations that properly protected public safety and security were permissible. The Court elaborated on these sentiments in a long series of cases following *Cantwell*. Most of these cases were raised by the indefatigable Jehovah's Witness—a newly prominent Christian missionary group, for whom strong religious preaching, proselytism, pamphleteering, and public demonstrations of biblical beliefs were vital exercises of faith.[51]

The Court readily struck down outright prohibitions on religious proselytism and other forms of religious expression. In *Cantwell* itself, the Court held that merely unpopular preaching on the public streets of a religious neighborhood could not be prohibited or punished as a breach of the peace. In *Jamison v. Texas* (1943) and *Martin v. Struthers* (1943), the Court struck down ordinances that prohibited distribution of religious pamphlets in the public square and door to door. "The state may prohibit the use of the streets for the distribution of purely commercial leaflets," Justice Black declared for the *Jamison* Court. But "they may not prohibit the distribution of handbills in pursuit of a clearly religious activity merely because the handbills invite the purchase of books for the improved understanding of the religion or because the handbills seek in a lawful fashion to promote the raising of funds for religious purposes."[52] Three years later, the Court extended this ruling to company- and government-owned towns: per se prohibitions and criminal penalties levied on such religious expression violate the free exercise and free speech clauses.[53]

The Court also struck down taxing schemes on religious preaching as "prior restraints" on the freedom of religious expression. In the leading case, *Murdock v. Pennsylvania* (1943), a Jehovah's Witness challenged the constitutionality of a city ordinance that required all persons soliciting or selling goods to procure a license for a day or for a one, two, or three week period. Each license required payment of a fee: from $1.50 for a day to $20 for three weeks—more than nominal fees by 1943 standards. Jehovah's Witnesses were convicted and fined for soliciting, distributing religious literature, and collecting donations in the town without a license. They appealed, arguing that this was a tax laid specifically on the exercise of their religion.

The *Murdock* Court agreed. "The hand distribution of religious tracts is an age-old form of missionary evangelism," Justice Douglas wrote for the Court. It "occupies the same high estate under the First Amendment as do worship in the churches or preaching from the pulpits. It has the same claim to protection as the more orthodox and conventional exercises of religion." The freedom to engage in such religious activity is "available to all, not merely to those who can pay their own way." The tax imposed by the city, "is a flat license tax, the payment of which is a condition for the exercise of these constitutional privileges. The power to tax the exercise of a privilege is the power to control or suppress its enjoyment. Those who can tax the exercise of this religious practice can make its exercise so costly as to deprive it of the resources necessary for its maintenance."[54] The *Murdock* Court thus struck down this licensing scheme. Three other early cases struck down comparable schemes, even with more nominal fees, that taxed the solicitation, distribution, and sale of religious literature and articles by Jehovah's Witnesses.[55]

Consistent with the dicta of *Cantwell*, the Court did allow general "time, place, and manner" regulations of religious expression—so long as they did not target religious expression per se, and so long as local officials implementing the statute had clear standards for implementation and no discretion to discriminate on religious grounds. In *Cantwell* itself, the city licensing regulation failed because it targeted religion and gave officials discretion to deny licenses to unpopular religious applicants. In *Kunz v. New York* (1951), the denial of a license to a Baptist minister to preach in a public park was struck down because local officials had open discretion to deny the licenses.[56] In *Niemotko v. State of Maryland* (1951), the denial of a permit to use a public park for "Bible talks" was struck down because the statute lacked clear criteria for such denials.[57] In *Fowler v. Rhode Island* (1953), an ordinance that prohibited religious speech but allowed for religious services in a public park was struck down because it was religiously discriminatory.[58]

In *Poulos v. New Hampshire* (1953), the Court upheld a municipal regulation of religious expression, and it used the case to underscore the kinds of regulation of religious expression that were permissible under the free exercise and free speech clauses. In this case, a New Hampshire town provided what the Court considered a properly "uniform, non-discriminatory, and consistent administration of . . . licenses for public meetings." Any parties intending to use public streets or parks for "theatrical or dramatic representation," "parades or processions," or "open air public meetings" were required to procure a license by written application in advance. A sliding fee of up to $300 would be charged for the license to pay for police protection, crowd control, and cleanup. Officials had no discretion to deny an application based on the nature of the applicant's activities. Parties would be charged with a set fine of $20 if they failed to procure a license for such an occasion.

A group of Jehovah's Witnesses seeking to use the public park for a religious meeting challenged the statute. The Court upheld it as a valid regulation of religious expression. What impressed the Court was that "the state left to the licensing officials no discretion as to granting permits, no power to discriminate, no control over speech. . . . The ordinance merely calls for the adjustment of unrestrained exercise of religions with the reasonable convenience and comfort of the whole city." This was licit even in the face of strong claims to religious expression. Justice Reed wrote for the Court:

> The principles of the First Amendment are not to be treated as a promise that everyone with opinions or beliefs to express may gather around him at any public place and any time a group for discussion or instruction. It is a non sequitur to say that First Amendment rights may not be regulated because they hold a preferred position in the hierarchy of the constitutional guarantees of the incidents of freedom. This Court has never so held and indeed has definitely indicated the contrary. It has indicated approval of reasonable nondiscriminatory regulation by government authority that preserves peace, order and tranquillity without deprivation of the First Amendment guarantees of free speech, press and the exercise of religion. . . . There is no basis for saying that freedom and order are not compatible. That would be a decision of desperation. Regulation and suppression are not the same, either in purpose or result, and courts of justice can tell the difference.[59]

Several subsequent cases have upheld this standard, on both free exercise and free speech grounds.[60]

The Court upheld regulations of religious expression even more readily when such expression threatened the life and limb of others or violated criminal law. In the leading case, *Prince v. Massachusetts* (1944), the Court upheld a state criminal law against a Jehovah's Witness, who with her nine-year-old ward distributed religious literature on the public streets in the evening. This was in technical violation of a state criminal law against the use of child labor after certain set hours. The woman was arrested and fined for violation of the statute. She appealed, claiming violation of both her and her ward's free exercise rights, as well as her parental rights to raise her ward in her own faith. She claimed further that the distribution of religious literature was not "labor" under the applicable statute but a form of religious exercise under the First Amendment. Given the gravity of the state interest in protecting children, who had historically been abused in the workplace, the Court applied the child labor statute literally and held for the state. Justice Rutledge stated the "delicate balance" struck by the Court:

> On one side is the obviously earnest claim for freedom of conscience and religious practice. With it is allied the parent's claim to authority in her own household and in the rearing of her children. The parent's conflict with the state ... is serious enough when only secular matters are concerned. It becomes the more so when an element of religious conviction enters. Against these sacred private interests, basic in a democracy, stand the interests of society to protect the welfare of children. ... [N]either rights of religion nor rights of parenthood are beyond limitation. Acting to guard the general interest in youth's well being, the state as *parens patriae* may restrict the parent's control by requiring school attendance, regulating or prohibiting the child's labor, and in many other ways. Its authority is not nullified merely because the parent grounds his claims to control the child's course of conduct on religion or conscience. ... The right to practice religion freely does not include liberty to expose the community or the child to communicable disease or the latter to ill health or death.[61]

The Court thus held for the state. With this precedent, it was very easy for the Court, a few years later, to affirm a lower court decision that a child of Jehovah's Witness parents could receive a blood transfusion, despite the religious objection of conscientiously opposed parents.[62]

Liberty of Conscience

This brings us to the second main principle protected by the free exercise clause—the individual's liberty of conscience. At the heart of this principle is what the founders had called "the unalienable right of private judgment in matters of religion."[63] Liberty of conscience, as understood at American law today, embraces the freedom of the person to choose or to change religious beliefs or practices without coercion or control by government and without facing discrimination or penalties for the religious choices once made.

The Supreme Court came only gradually to this understanding of liberty of conscience in its interpretation of the free exercise clause. The Court's early dicta, well before *Cantwell*, were promising enough. In *Watson v. Jones* (1871), Justice Miller had declared for a unanimous Court: "In this country the full and free right to entertain any religious belief, to practice any religious principle, and to teach any religious doctrine which does not violate the laws of morality and property, and which does not infringe personal rights, is conceded to all. The law knows no heresy, and is committed to the support of no dogma, the establishment of no sect."[64] Eight years later, in *Reynolds v. United States* (1879), the Court had underscored this principle by declaring that "Congress was deprived of all legislative power over mere [religious] opinion."[65]

Although it endorsed the liberty of conscience, the Court did little to protect it in these early free exercise cases. The polygamy cases from 1879 to 1890 upheld congressional laws that penalized Mormons for their practices, as well as their beliefs in polygamy, and demanded from them all manner of confessions and exculpatory oaths (see pages 102–105). The early pacifism cases from 1918 to 1934 would hear nothing of a party's constitutional right to be protected from swearing oaths to, or training for service in, the military—no matter how devout and developed a party's conscientious scruples (see pages 105–107).

This discordance of principle and practice continued in the early years after *Cantwell*. In *Cantwell* itself, Justice Roberts had declared confidently for the Court that the free exercise clause was "absolute" in forestalling "compulsion by law of the acceptance of any creed or the practice of any form of worship."[66]

But in its next case, *Minersville School Board v. Gobitis* (1940), decided two weeks later, the Court betrayed this very principle. The children of a Jehovah's Witness were expelled from a public school because they refused to salute the American flag or pledge their allegiance. The Bible, in their understanding and that of their coreligionists, prohibited such acts as forms of false worship. To compel them to such acts, their parents argued, was a violation of the liberty of conscience. The Supreme Court disagreed. The purpose of the school policy was to promote national unity and loyalty, said the Court, not to institute a false form of worship. "To stigmatize legislative judgment in providing for this universal gesture of respect for the symbol of our national life in the setting of the common school as a lawless inroad on that freedom of conscience which the Constitution protects," Justice Frankfurter wrote for a divided Court, "would amount to no less than the pronouncement of pedagogical and psychological dogma in a field where courts possess no marked and certainly no controlling competence."[67]

Three years later, in *West Virginia State Board of Education v. Barnette* (1943), the Court overruled *Gobitis* and read the First Amendment to exempt parties from mandatory participation in rituals to which they were conscientiously opposed. *Barnette* raised similar facts to those of *Gobitis*: Jehovah's Witness children were again expelled from public school for their failure to salute the flag and recite the pledge of allegiance, and now faced fines if they persisted in their recalcitrance. While acknowledging the importance of teaching national loyalty and unity in public schools, the Court held that the compulsory participation in such civic ceremonies violated the liberty of conscience. As Justice Jackson wrote for the Court:

> If there is any fixed star in our constitutional constellation, it is that no official, high or petty, can prescribe what shall be orthodox in politics, nationalism, religion, or other matters of opinion or force citizens to confess by word or act their faith therein. If there are any circumstances which permit an exception, they do not now occur to us.[68]

Although in a pair of cases immediately thereafter the Court again stumbled on this principle of liberty of conscience, *Barnette* soon became the rule.[69] The Court has since held that government officials cannot require a party who is conscientiously opposed to swear an oath before receiving citizenship status[70] or a property tax exemption.[71] In *Torcaso v. Watkins* (1961), the Court extended this principle to say that a professed atheist could not be required to swear an oath attesting to his belief in God as part of his initiation into a state bureaucratic position.[72] "The Free Exercise Clause categorically forbids government from regulating, prohibiting, or rewarding religious beliefs as such," the Court later put it in summary of the case.[73]

In *Sherbert v. Verner* (1963), the Court widened this liberty of conscience reading of the free exercise clause. Not only could the free exercise clause exempt conscientious parties from participation in oathswearing and other ceremonies that ran afoul of their conscientious beliefs, but the free exercise clause could also exempt them from adherence to other general laws and regulations that unduly burdened their consciences.

Sherbert posed a conflict between the right of religious conscience and the right to a state benefit. A Seventh Day Adventist was discharged from employment, and foreclosed from reemployment, because of her conscientious refusal to work on Saturday, her Sabbath Day. She was denied unemployment compensation from the state, for she had been, according to the applicable statute, discharged "for cause" and was thus disqualified from the benefit. She appealed, arguing that the disqualifying provisions of the statute "abridged her right to the free exercise of her religion." If she exercised her religious right to Saturday sabbatarianism, she would lose her civil right to a state benefit. If she was to receive her civil right to a state benefit, she would have to forgo her religious right to Saturday sabbatarianism. Such a conflict, she argued, violated her free exercise rights.

The Supreme Court agreed. As Justice Brennan put it for the Court: "To condition the availability of [state] benefits upon this appellant's willingness to violate a cardinal principle of her religious faith effectively penalizes the free exercise of her constitutional liberties."[74] The Court ordered Ms. Sherbert exempt from the general strictures on payment and entitled to unemployment compensation benefits.

In a trio of cases, the Court extended the technical *Sherbert* holding. One case involved a Jehovah's Witness who had individual scruples, not shared by fellow Witnesses, against production of hardware that would be used for military tanks.[75] Another case involved a new convert to Seventh-Day Adventism who began to insist on the right to observe her Saturday Sabbath.[76] A third case involved a Christian party who refused a temporary position because it might require him to work on his Sabbath.[77] Each of these parties lost their employment. Each was denied unemployment compensation benefits on the general rule that they had been discharged for cause. Each successfully appealed to the Court for a free exercise exemption from this general rule and was found entitled to unemployment compensation. Neither the novelty nor the idiosyncrasy of a religious belief changed the core violation of the liberty of conscience. As Chief Justice Burger put it for the Court in *Thomas v. Review Board* (1981): "Where the state conditions receipt of an important benefit upon conduct proscribed by a religious faith, or where it denies such a benefit because of conduct mandated by religious belief, thereby putting substantial pressure on an adherent to modify his behavior and to violate his beliefs, a burden upon religion exists." This violates the liberty of conscience values of the free exercise clause and entitles the claimant to an exemption.[78]

In *McDaniel v. Paty* (1978), the Court extended this analysis to the political sphere. The original Constitution of Tennessee (1796) prohibited clergy from holding political office in the state. The purpose of this prohibition was "to assure the success of a new political experiment, the separation of church and state." With the growing religious pluralism of their societies, other states had eventually struck such clauses from their constitutions. Tennessee alone retained it. An otherwise qualified Baptist minister was enjoined from running for a political position. He appealed, arguing that this prohibition violated his free exercise rights. It posed a direct conflict between his religious rights to ministry and his civil rights to run for political office. The Court agreed. Quoting both *Sherbert* and James Madison, the Court held that "the State is 'punishing a religious profession with the privation of a civil right.'"[79] The state constitutional prohibition was struck down as a violation of the free exercise clause.

Separation of Church and State

The heart of the principle of liberty of conscience is the individual's "right of private judgment" in matters of faith. The heart of the principle of separation of church and state is a religious group's right to define for itself what *Cantwell* had called its "religious organization and form of worship." Separation of church and state, as we shall see in the next chapter, has been a critical principle for interpretation of the disestablishment clause. But it has also been a valuable principle for interpretation of the free exercise clause: It protects a religious group's rights to organize its worship, property, and polity without interference from the state.

Before *Cantwell,* the Court had issued more than a dozen cases that protected the general common law rights of religious groups to acquire, use, and alienate property without confiscation or undue interference by the state. It had also upheld the common law rights of religious groups to organize their own internal polities, to regulate the internal activities of their religious officials, and to set standards for the entrance and exit of their voluntary members.[80]

After *Cantwell,* the Court converted some of these early common law rules into constitutional principles protected by the free exercise clause.[81] A trio of cases held that religious groups must have autonomy to decide their own internal disputes, and courts must defer to the judgment of the highest religious authorities among such disputants.

In *Kedroff v. Saint Nicholas Cathedral* (1952), the Court struck down a New York religious corporation law, passed in the Cold War era, that rejected the authority of the Moscow Patriarch to appoint a bishop in a local Russian Orthodox Church. Justice Reed declared for the Court:

> Here there is a transfer by statute of control over churches. This violates our rule of separation between church and state. . . . [It also violates] a spirit of freedom for religious organizations, an independence from secular control or manipulation, in short, power to decide for themselves, free from state interference, matters of church government as well as those of faith and doctrine. Freedom to select the clergy, where no improper methods of choice are proven, we think, must now be said to have federal constitutional protection as a part of the free exercise of religion against state interference.[82]

In *Presbyterian Church of the United States v. Hull Presbyterian Church* (1969), the Court reversed the Georgia Supreme Court, which had resolved an internal church dispute over property by inquiring whether either party had departed from orthodox doctrine. In outlawing such a "departure-from-doctrine" test, Justice Brennan put the matter firmly for a unanimous Court:

> First Amendment values are plainly jeopardized when church property litigation is made to turn on the resolution by civil courts of controversies over religious doctrine and practice. If civil courts undertake to resolve such controversies in order to adjudicate the property dispute, the hazards are ever present of inhibiting the free development of religious doctrine and of implicating secular interests in matters of purely ecclesiastical concern.[83]

In *Orthodox Diocese v. Milivojevich* (1976), the Court outlawed even "marginal review" by a civil court of an ecclesiastical decision that might appear "arbitrary, collusive, or fraudulent." Justice Brennan again spoke for the Court: "Indeed, it is the essence of religious faith that ecclesiastical decisions are reached and are to be accepted as matters of faith whether or not rational or acceptable by objective criteria." The Constitution allows "religious organizations to establish their own rules and regulations for internal discipline and government, and to create tribunals for adjudicating disputes over these matters. When this choice is exercised and ecclesiastical tribunals are created to decide disputes . . . the Constitution requires that civil courts accept their decisions as binding."[84]

The Court also extended this concern for religious group rights in other contexts. Already in *Pierce v. Society of Sisters* (1925), the Court had upheld the "fundamental right" of religious schools to exist and to educate children in the faith without undue interference by the state.[85] In *National Labor Relations Board v. Catholic Bishop* (1979), the Court used this same principle to deny the NLRB jurisdiction over a Catholic school's teachers.[86] In the same vein, *Corporation of the Presiding Bishop v. Amos* (1987) upheld the exemption provision of the Civil Rights Act, which allowed a religious employer to discriminate on religious grounds in the selection or retention of its employees.[87]

In *Wisconsin v. Yoder* (1972), the Court extended this concern for religious group identity and autonomy even further. The Court required that Old Order Amish parents and communities be exempted from full compliance with compulsory school attendance laws for their children, in order to preserve their ascetic, agrarian religious communitarianism. What seemed to impress the Court was that the Amish "lifestyle" was "not merely a matter of personal preference, but one of deep religious conviction, shared by an organized group, and intimately related to daily living" and that these "religious beliefs and attitudes towards life, family and home . . . have not altered in fundamentals for centuries." In the Court's view, compliance with the compulsory school attendance law "carries with it a very real threat of undermining the Amish community and religious practice as they exist today; they must either abandon belief and be assimilated into society at large, or be forced to migrate to some other and more tolerant region."[88]

Religious Pluralism

The point of all these protections of individual and corporate free exercise was to encourage and protect a plurality of religions before the law. "The essential characteristic of these liberties" of the free exercise clause, Justice Roberts wrote in *Cantwell*, "is, that under their shield many types of life, character, opinion and belief can develop unmolested and unobstructed.

Nowhere is this shield more necessary than in our own country for a people composed of many races and of many creeds."[89]

Even Justice Frankfurter and Justice Black, whose interpretations of the First Amendment religion clauses have often been criticized, earnestly defended the principle of religious pluralism. "Propagation of belief—or even disbelief in the supernatural—is protected, whether in church or chapel, mosque or synagogue, tabernacle or meetinghouse," wrote Justice Frankfurter wisely in his otherwise unwise *Gobitis* opinion. "Likewise the Constitution assures generous immunity to the individual from imposition of penalties for offending, in the course of his own religious activities, the religious views of others, be they a minority or those dominant in government."[90] The free exercise clause, Justice Black echoed, mandates that government "cannot exclude individual Catholics, Lutherans, Mohammedans, Baptists, Jews, Methodists, Non-believers, Presbyterians, or the members of any faith, *because of their faith, or lack of it*, from receiving the benefits of public welfare legislation."[91]

Justice Douglas underscored the difficulty of living up to these constitutional mandates as the nation's religions had pluralized and its welfare laws had proliferated. He wrote in concurrence in *Sherbert v. Verner:*

> Religious scruples of Moslems require them to attend a mosque on Friday and to pray five times daily. Religious scruples of a Sikh require him to carry a regular or a symbolic sword. Religious scruples of a Jehovah's Witness teach him to be a colporteur, going from door to door, from town to town, distributing his religious pamphlets. Religious scruples of a Quaker compel him to refrain from swearing [an oath] and to affirm instead. Religious scruples of a Buddhist may require him to refrain from partaking of any flesh. The examples could be multiplied . . . to show that many people hold beliefs alien to the majority of our society—beliefs that are protected by the First Amendment but which could easily be trod upon under the guise of "police" or "health" regulations reflecting the majority's views.[92]

Neutralizing the Free Exercise Clause

From 1940 to the early 1980s, the Supreme Court read the free exercise clause in expansive terms. The clause not only protected the freedom of religious exercise or expression. It also protected the attendant principles of liberty of conscience, separation of church and state, and equality of plural faiths before the law. The rigor and range of the Court's free exercise inquiry did not always bring victory to religious claimants. They lost as many cases as they won, particularly when their religious exercise touched on fundamental issues of public policy or criminal law. But the free exercise clause provided what *Cantwell* had called for: "a multi-layered shield" to protect many forms and forums of individual and corporate religious life.

In the course of the 1980s, the Supreme Court slowly reduced the free exercise clause to a single and simple principle of neutrality. The Court's earlier concerns to protect the conscience of the religious individual and the autonomy of the religious group from state intrusions slowly fell aside. The Court's earlier decisions to strike down laws that imposed taxes or discriminatory restrictions on religious expression also fell aside. In a series of cases culminating in *Employment Division v. Smith* (1990), the Court systematically read each of these constitutive principles out of the free exercise clause, reducing it to a single and simple principle of neutrality.

The Court's first step on the path to neutrality came in *Jones v. Wolf* (1979). This was another intrachurch dispute case. Three years before, in *Milivojevich*, the Court had confirmed, in strong terms, its century-long sentiment that religious groups must be left to resolve their own internal disputes over polity and property without state interference. The Court had ordered lower courts to defer to the resolution offered by the highest religious authority and to forgo even "marginal review" of that religious authority's decision. Since the *Kedroff* case of 1952, the Court had said that this deferential approach to religious groups was mandated by the First Amendment.

In *Jones v. Wolf*, however, the Court held that intrachurch disputes could be resolved on the basis of "neutral principles of law." With little attempt to distinguish these earlier cases, Justice Blackmun declared for the Court: Nothing in "the First Amendment requires States to adopt a rule of compulsory deference to religious authority in resolving church property disputes." In most instances, courts can resolve these cases without reference to the religious sources or dimensions of the dispute.

> The primary advantages of the neutral principles approach are that it is completely secular in operation, and yet flexible enough to accommodate all forms of religious organization and polity. The method relies exclusively on objective, well-established concepts of trust and property law familiar to lawyers and judges.[93]

Since *Jones v. Wolf* was issued, intrachurch disputes over everything from consecrated sanctuaries and cemeteries to church storage sheds and campgrounds have been resolved under the simple "neutral principles" approach.[94]

In *Goldman v. Weinberger* (1986), the Court took a further step down this neutrality path. The Court held that the free exercise clause permitted the Air Force to prohibit a rabbi from wearing his yarmulke as part of his military uniform. The Court so held even though the petitioner served as a psychologist in the mental health clinic of a military base (not on the front lines), even though for three years earlier he was accorded this "privilege," and even though numerous other exemptions for religious garb, including crucifixes, were accorded by the 190-page military dress code. The requirements for military discipline and uniformity, in the Court's view, outweighed the countervailing religious interests—however deep-seated and essential they were to the petitioner.[95]

In *Bowen v. Roy* (1986), the Court pressed this concern for uniformity and neutrality from the military context to the regulatory context. A Native American objected to having a Social Security number assigned to his daughter, arguing, in the Court's words, that "he must keep her person and spirit unique and that the uniqueness of the Social Security number as an identifier, coupled with the other uses of the number over which she has no control, will 'rob the spirit' of his daughter and prevent her from attaining greater spiritual power." He requested an exemption for his daughter, until she reached sufficient spiritual maturity at the age of sixteen. Although it acknowledged the sincerity and substance of the parent's claim, the Court found for the government. Chief Justice Burger's opinion for the Court was in striking contrast to his highly solicitous tone in *Wisconsin v. Yoder* (1972):

> Never to our knowledge has the Court interpreted the First Amendment to re-quire the Government *itself* to behave in ways that the individual believes will further his or her spiritual development or that of his or her own family. The Free Exercise Clause simply cannot be understood to require the Government to conduct its own internal affairs in ways that comport with the religious beliefs of particular citizens. . . . Government meets its burden when it demonstrates that a challenged requirement for governmental benefits, neutral and uniform in its application, is a reasonable means of promoting a legitimate public interest.[96]

In *O'Lone v. Estate of Shabazz* (1987), the Court extended this logic to prison officials, holding that a change in prison policy that deprived Muslim inmates from attending Jumu'ah, their Friday collective worship service, did not violate their free exercise rights. Here the requirements for security, protection of other prisoners, and other "reasonable penological objectives," in the Court's view, outweighed the free exercise rights of the Muslim prisoners. Moreover, said the Court quoting *Bowen v. Roy* and other precedents, it is wrong to impose a "special burden on prison officials to prove 'that no reasonable method exists by which [prisoners'] religious rights can be accommodated.'" So long as the prison's regulations are "neutral and reasonable," they pass constitutional muster.[97]

In *Lyng v. Northwest Indian Cemetery Protective Association* (1988),[98] the Court extended this neutrality logic to the actions of the United States Forest Service. The Court held that the free exercise clause does not prohibit the Forest Service's construction of a road through a sacred site used for centuries by Indians—notwithstanding the protective policy of the American Indian Religious Freedom Act,[99] and the Court's recognition that this construction "will have severe adverse effects of the practice of their religion."[100] Citing *Roy* and *O'Lone*, Justice O'Connor defended this holding with blunt literalism:

> The crucial word in the constitutional text is "prohibit": "For the Free Exercise Clause is written in terms of what the government cannot do to the individual". . . . However much we might wish that it were otherwise, government simply could not operate if it were required to satisfy every citizen's religious needs and desires. A broad range of government activities—from social welfare programs to foreign aid to conservation policies—will always be considered essential to the spiritual well-being of some citizens, often on the basis of sincerely-held religious beliefs. Others will find the very same activities deeply offensive, and perhaps incompatible with their own search for spiritual fulfillment and with the tenets of their religion. The First Amendment must apply to all citizens alike, and it can give to none of them a veto over public programs that do not prohibit the free exercise of religion. The Constitution does not, and courts cannot, offer to reconcile the various competing demands on government, many of them rooted in sincere religious belief, that inevitably arise in so diverse a society as ours.[101]

The following term, in *Jimmy Swaggart Ministries v. Board of Equalization of California* (1990), the Court pressed this logic further and upheld the retroactive imposition of sales and uses taxes on the sales of religious articles by a religious ministry. Swaggart Ministries argued that the imposition of such taxes was a prior restraint on the exercise of its religion—which the Court had explicitly outlawed in *Murdock v. Pennsylvania* (1943) and its progeny. The Court rather speciously distinguished these earlier cases: These earlier cases, Justice O'Connor wrote for the Court, dealt with "prior" restraints on free exercise, not post hoc collections of taxes. (The Court said nothing about the future collection of such taxes on Swaggart Ministries.) They addressed specific flat taxes on religious solicitation, not general state taxes imposed on all sales of goods. (The Court ignored that the earlier tax schemes were imposed on all solicitors, not just religious ministers, and in some schemes had sliding fee scales depending on the number of days the license was to be used.) By contrast, the state's tax challenged in this case is not "a flat tax, represents only a small fraction of any retail sale, and applies neutrally to all retail sales of tangible personal property." To drive home her point, Justice O'Connor also questioned whether there was a real free exercise burden here: "There is no evidence in this case that collection and payment of the tax violates appellant's sincere religious beliefs. . . . The only burden on appellant is the claimed reduction in income."[102]

The foregoing cases had, in effect, written out of the free exercise clause the multiple principles that had earlier informed the Court's free exercise opinions. *Bowen v. Roy* and *O'Lone v. Estate of Shabazz* undercut the Court's earlier solicitude for liberty of conscience. *Jones v. Wolf* and *Lyng* undercut the Court's concerns for the rights of religious groups captured in the principle of separation of church and state. *Lyng, O'Lone,* and *Goldman v. Weinberger* undercut the Court's earlier solicitude for the equality of plural religious faiths, particularly the needs of religious minorities to be protected against general legislation. All these cases, most notably *Lyng* and *Swaggart Ministries,* reduced the Court's nuanced interpretations of the freedom of religious expression to a blunt inquiry into simple neutrality.

While these cases may have been isolated to their facts, *Employment Division v. Smith* (1990) wove their holdings into a new and narrow understanding of the free exercise clause.[103] Smith, a Native American, ingested peyote as part of the sacramental rite of the Native American church of which he was a member. Discharged from employment at a drug rehabilitation center because of this practice, he applied for unemployment compensation from the State of Oregon. Such compensation was denied on grounds that peyote ingestion was disqualifying criminal misconduct. Smith appealed, ultimately to the Supreme Court, claiming a violation of his free exercise rights.

The *Smith* Court rejected his argument, even though the case fell within the holdings of unemployment compensation cases from *Sherbert* to *Frazee.* More importantly, the Court denied the validity of the *Sherbert* "compelling state interest" test altogether and explained away its application in subsequent cases. Henceforth, Justice Scalia wrote for the majority, "the right of free exercise does not relieve an individual of the obligation to comply with a 'valid and neutral law of general applicability.'"[104] Such laws, when promulgated under proper procedures, must prevail—regardless of the nature of the state's interest and regardless of any intrusion on the interest of a religious believer or body. Religious petitioners whose beliefs or practices are burdened by such neutral, generally applicable laws must seek redress in the legislatures, not the courts.

Smith effectively reduced the free exercise guarantee to the single principle of neutrality. This is not an entirely toothless provision, as the Court showed in its next free exercise case, *Church of Lukumi Babalu Aye, Inc. v. City of Hialeah* (1993).[105] The *Hialeah* case posed a free exercise challenge to a city ordinance that singled out local followers of the Santerian faith for special restrictions and penalties for engaging in the ritual slaughter of animals—a central practice of their faith. Even using the *Smith* test, the Court struck down the statute in question, for it was neither a general law nor neutrally applied. It transparently targeted Santerian believers and practices for special prohibitions, in pursuit of no compelling state interest.

As we saw in our mapping of free exercise doctrine (pages 123–125), *Smith* remains the law—at least for all free exercise challenges to state and local laws. But virtually all the earlier free exercise cases that had offered a more multiprincipled reading of the free exercise clause also remain good law. A few of these cases were distinguished by *Smith* and its predecessors, but none were overturned. This collection of cases will provide a formidable arsenal of free exercise protections if and when redeployed. But, for now, these earlier free exercise cases have been effectively set aside in favor of the prevailing neutrality test.

Free Speech and Statutory Protections of Religion

With the neutralization of the free exercise clause, religious claimants have sought other forms and forums of protection. Two forums have been particularly important—the First Amendment free speech clause and new federal and state statutes.

Free Speech and Religion

It is no small irony that today the free speech clause affords considerably more protection to religious liberty than the free exercise clause. But it must be noted that the free speech clause has long been invoked for the protection of religious liberty.[106] The free speech clause has been used to review state and local laws since 1925.[107] Before *Cantwell v. Connecticut* (1940), both the Supreme Court and lower federal courts used the free speech clause to outlaw patently discriminatory laws that closed local public squares to religious preaching and pamphleteering.[108] In *Cantwell* and in several cases thereafter, religious claimants seeking protection of their religious expression used both the free exercise and free speech clauses to assert their rights. The two clauses afforded comparably rigorous standards of review, and it often proved safer, even if sometimes redundant, to predicate one's claim on both clauses. To be sure, there were dimensions of free exercise protection—notably claims of conscience and of church autonomy—that the free speech clause did not and could not reach. But at least on questions of freedom of religious expression, claimants often sought free speech and free exercise protection simultaneously.

With the gradual weakening of the free exercise clause in the course of the 1980s and 1990s, religious claimants have turned increasingly to the free speech clause alone for protection. Three main cases have introduced a new doctrine of religious equality—that religious individuals and groups must be given "equal access" to facilities and benefits generally afforded to nonreligious groups.[109]

The opening case in this sequence was *Widmar v. Vincent* (1981). The state university in Missouri at Kansas City had a policy of opening its facilities to voluntary student groups. More than 100 student groups organized themselves in the year at issue. A voluntary student group, organized for private religious devotion and charity, sought access to the university facilities that year. The group was denied access, in application of the university's written policy that its buildings and grounds were not to be used "for purposes of religious worship or religious teaching." The student group appealed, arguing that this policy of exclusion violated their free exercise, free speech, and equal protection rights. The university countered that it had a compelling state interest in maintaining the "strict separation of church and state" as both the First Amendment and the state constitution required.

The *Widmar* Court found for the religious student group. Drawing on free speech precedents, the Court held that where a state university creates a limited public forum open to voluntary student groups, religious groups must be given "equal access" to that forum. Justice Powell wrote for the Court that the university "has discriminated against student groups and speakers based on their desire to use a generally open forum to engage in religious worship and discussion. These are forms of speech and association protected by the First Amendment. In order to justify discriminatory exclusions from a public forum based on the religious content of the group's intended speech" the university must show that "its regulation is necessary to serve a compelling state interest and that it is narrowly drawn to achieve that end." In the Court's view, a general desire to keep a strict separation of church and state was not a sufficiently compelling state interest. The religious groups would enjoy only "incidental benefits" from this ruling. The values of "equal treatment and access" for religious groups outweighed the hypothetical dangers of a religious establishment.[110]

In *Lamb's Chapel v. Center Moriches Union Free School District* (1993), the Court extended the "equal access" principle of the free speech clause to other religious groups besides students. A local school board, pursuant to state policy, opened its school facilities, during nonschool time, for various "social, civic, recreational, and political uses" by voluntary groups in the community. The school board policy stated explicitly, however, that the "school premises shall not be used by any group for religious purposes." An evangelical church twice applied for use of the facilities to show a film series that discussed traditional family values from a Christian perspective. Their application was denied. Lamb's Chapel appealed, arguing that such exclusion violated their free speech rights.

The *Lamb's Chapel* Court agreed. Relying on *Widmar* and other free speech cases, the Court found that Lamb's Chapel had been discriminatorily denied access to this limited public forum. As Justice White put it for the Court:

The film series involved here no doubt dealt with a subject otherwise permissible, . . . and its exhibition was denied solely because the film series dealt with the subject from a religious standpoint. The principle that has emerged from our cases "is that the First Amendment forbids the government to regulate speech in ways that favor some viewpoints or ideas at the expense of others."[111]

Again, the school district's concern for protecting against the establishment of religion was not considered a sufficient reason for denying equal access to this religious group.

In *Rosenberger v. Rector and Visitors of the University of Virginia* (1995), a sharply divided Court extended this equal access principle to hold that a voluntary group of religious students in a state university was entitled to the same funding made available to nonreligious student groups. The University of Virginia encouraged student groups to organize themselves for extracurricular activities. Each student group was required to petition for the right to be recognized as such a group, to pledge that it would not discriminate in its membership, and to include in all communications a disclaimer that the group and its activities were independent of the university. In the year in question, 343 such voluntary student groups were organized.

Properly registered student groups were permitted to apply for funding from a general student activity fund to facilitate their activities. The funds could be used for a variety of purposes, including the costs of printing and distributing the group's literature. All such funds were to be paid to outside contractors. Of the 343 properly registered student groups, 118 received funds, and 15 were denied funds.

One of the groups denied funds was a religious student group that was properly registered at the university. The group printed an overtly religious newspaper, called "Wide Awake: A Christian Perspective at the University of Virginia." The group's request for funds to defray printing costs was denied, on grounds that the student activity fund could not be used for "religious activities." Such activities were defined in the school's regulations as "any activity 'that primarily promotes or manifests a particular belief in or about a deity or an ultimate reality.'" The group appealed, arguing that such discriminatory treatment violated, among other things, their free speech rights.

The *Rosenberger* Court agreed and held that the University of Virginia had violated these students' free speech rights. The state university policy, Justice Kennedy wrote for the Court, improperly "selects for disfavored treatment those student journalistic efforts with religious editorial viewpoints." The denial of funding to this otherwise qualified student group "is based upon viewpoint discrimination not unlike the discrimination the

school district relied upon in *Lamb's Chapel* and that we found invalid."
The principle of equal access applied as much to state university funding as
to state university facilities.

Justice Kennedy elaborated:

> Vital First Amendment speech principles are at stake here. The first danger to
> liberty lies in granting the State the power to examine publications to deter-
> mine whether or not they are based on some ultimate idea and if so for the
> State to classify them [as religious]. The second, and corollary, danger is to
> speech from the chilling of individual thought and expression. That danger is
> especially real in the University setting, where the State acts against a back-
> ground and tradition of thought and experiment that is at the center of our in-
> tellectual and philosophic tradition. . . . For the University, by regulation, to
> cast disapproval on particular viewpoints of its students risks the suppression
> of free speech and creative inquiry in one of the vital centers for the nation's
> intellectual life, its college and university campuses.[112]

In a sharply worded dissent, Justice Souter, joined by three others, argued
that the Court had used the equal access principle of the free speech clause
to undermine a cardinal principle of the disestablishment clause. "Using
public funds for the direct subsidization of preaching the word is categorically forbidden under the Establishment Clause, and if the Clause was
meant to accomplish nothing else, it was meant to bar this use of public
money."[113]

Statutes and Religion

These three "equal access" cases point to a second way in which religious
liberty has come to be protected—through federal and state statutes. The
Court has repeatedly upheld statutes that protect vital religious interests,
terming these a proper governmental accommodation, rather than an improper governmental establishment, of religion.[114]

Some legislative accommodations of vital religious interests have long enjoyed constitutional protection. Already in *Arver v. United States* (1918),
the Court rejected a disestablishment clause challenge to the Selective
Service Act that exempted clergy, seminary students, and members of certain faiths from military service. This legislative accommodation of pacifism has continued to this day, and the Court has rebuffed disestablishment
clause challenges to the same.[115] In *Zorach v. Clauson* (1952), the Court
upheld a public school program allowing religious students release time to
attend religious classes off the school's premises—calling this a "suitable
accommodation . . . to spiritual needs."[116] In *Walz v. Tax Commission*
(1970), the Court sustained a state tax exemption of church property
against a taxpayer challenge that this was an establishment of religion.[117]

In *Transworld Airlines v. Hardison* (1977), the Court upheld Title VII provisions that required employers to make "reasonable accommodations" to their employees' religious needs.[118] In *Presiding Bishop v. Amos* (1987), the Court sustained a 1972 amendment to the Civil Rights Act that exempted religious organizations from the general prohibition against religious discrimination.[119] Several lower federal courts have sustained, against disestablishment clause challenges, provisions in the federal Fair Housing Act that allow religious organizations to favor their own coreligionists and state laws that allow religious schools and charities to favor their own coreligionist pupils and patrons.

Furthermore, the Court has repeatedly said in cases from *Sherbert* to *Rosenberger*—where it used the free exercise and free speech clauses to create exemptions for religious interests—that a statute could have included such an accommodation of religion without running afoul of the disestablishment clause.

Since the early 1980s, Congress and state legislatures have seized upon these precedents with new vigor in an effort to offset the narrowing of free exercise protections. The most dramatic example of this trend is provided by the "equal access" principle itself. A week after the 1981 *Widmar v. Vincent* case, the Court declined to review a case in which a lower court denied that a voluntary group of public high school students organized for religious devotions must have equal access to school facilities.[120] Congress responded in 1984 with the Equal Access Act that effectively imposed the *Widmar* principle on public high schools:

> It shall be unlawful for any public secondary school which receives Federal financial assistance and which has a limited open forum to deny equal access or a fair opportunity to, or discriminate against, any students who wish to conduct a meeting within that limited open forum on the basis of the religious, political, or other content of the speech at such meetings.[121]

In *Westside Community Schools v. Mergens* (1990), the Court upheld the Equal Access Act against charges that it was an establishment of religion.[122]

Other statutes have undone the results of some of the Court's more controversial free exercise cases. Following *Goldman v. Weinberger* (1986), for example, Congress in 1988 amended the military dress code such that it would allow the wearing of a yarmulke: "a member of the armed forces may wear an item of religious apparel while wearing the uniform of the member's armed force."[123] Similarly, following *Employment Division v. Smith* (1990), the State of Oregon amended its criminal code to allow for the ingestion of peyote as part of a Native American religious ceremony.

Not all such legislative accommodations of religion have been sustained or have proven equally effective.[124] For example, in an attempt to grant further protections to the religious interests of Native Americans, Congress in 1978 passed the American Indian Religious Freedom Act (AIRFA). The act was only a resolution—not a statute with specific rights and duties set forth. Nonetheless, AIRFA provided, in pertinent part: "It shall be the policy of the United States to protect and preserve for American Indians their inherent right of freedom to believe, express, and exercise the traditional religions of the American Indians . . . including but not limited to access to sites, use and possession of sacred objects, and the freedom to worship through ceremonials and traditional rites."[125] The Native American claims at issue in *Bowen v. Roy*, *Lyng v. Protective Association*, and *Employment Division v. Smith* all fell easily within the preferred policy of AIRFA. The Court could have used the language of the act as a basis for extending free exercise protections to these claims, without undue worry of creating precedents for numerous new non-Native American claims. The Court chose instead to dismiss the act with wooden language, declaring in *Lyng*: "Nowhere in the law is there so much as a hint of any intent to create a cause of action or any judicially enforceable individual rights."[126]

In 1993, Congress passed a statute that did "create a cause of action and judicially enforceable individual rights"—the Religious Freedom Restoration Act (1993) designed to offset the *Smith* Court's narrow neutrality reading of the free exercise clause. But in the *City of Boerne v. Flores* (1997), as we saw (pages 124–125), the Court struck down RFRA as a violation of section 5 of the Fourteenth Amendment.

The majority of the *Boerne* Court did not address whether the Religious Freedom Restoration Act constituted an establishment of religion.[127] It is now an open—and hotly contested—question whether Congress should pass a comprehensive new statute on religious freedom using alternative constitutional bases (such as the commerce, treaty, or taxing and spending clauses) or pass a series of more narrowly gauged acts protecting religious freedom, using section 5 of the Fourteenth Amendment.[128] Whatever the basis and scope of the new statute(s), the precedents of the past two decades suggest that the disestablishment clause leaves ample room for such forms of legislative accommodation of religion.

Conclusions

It must be said in conclusion that neither free speech nor statutory protections of religious liberty can ultimately substitute for a more rigorous free exercise clause. To be sure, the development of these doctrines testifies both to the ingenuity of litigants and legislators and to the flexibility of the constitutional process to accommodate the pressing spiritual needs of citizens. And to be sure, the development of these doctrines has provided some religious minorities with forms and forums of relief hitherto foreclosed to them.

These can only be temporary refuges for religious liberty, however. Speech is only one form of religious exercise; equality is only one principle that the free exercise clause protects. Even generously defined, "speech" cannot embrace many forms of individual and corporate religious exercise—from the silent meditations of the sages to the noisy pilgrimages of the saints, from the corporate consecration of the sanctuary to the ecclesiastical discipline of the clergy. Even expansively interpreted, "equality" cannot protect the special needs of religious individuals and religious groups. These needs were traditionally protected by the principles of liberty of conscience and separation of church and state and traditionally reflected in the exemptions and exclusions countenanced and created by the free exercise clause.[129]

Likewise, statutory provisions cannot substitute for constitutional principles of free exercise. It is an elementary, but essential, political reality that statutes generally privilege the views of the majority, not the minority. They are passed by elected officials who must be as vigilant in reflecting popular opinion as protecting constitutional imperatives. The free exercise clause, by contrast, is designed to protect the needs of the minority as much as the majority. Its provisions are enforced by appointed officials who must be more vigilant about protecting constitutional imperatives than reflecting popular opinion. The free exercise clause is designed to provide remedies for individuals and groups with insufficient political strength to have their religious views or practices reflected in or protected by statutes.

The original vision of the founders was that religion was special and that it was deserving of special protection.[130] The founders thus placed the free exercise clause alongside the free speech, press, and assembly clauses to provide religious claimants with a special pathway to relief. They incorporated within this free exercise clause the principles of liberty of conscience, freedom of religious expression, religious equality and pluralism, and separation of church from the state. Both individuals and groups were thus protected in their most fundamental religious rights.

One need not necessarily endorse a jurisprudence of originalism to embrace this multiprincipled reading of the free exercise clause. This was, after all, the vision articulated by the Supreme Court in *Cantwell v. Connecticut* (1940), the case that opened the modern era of free exercise jurisprudence. And this was the Court's vision of the free exercise clause for more than forty years thereafter.

The majority of the Supreme Court has to date shown little willingness to overturn the 1990 *Smith* case that sealed the Court's rejection of this multiprincipled reading of the free exercise clause. In *Church of Lukumi Babalu Aye v. Hialeah* (1993), which applied the free exercise clause, a six-member majority applied the *Smith* test, with only Justices Souter, O'Connor, and Blackmun objecting thereto.[131] In *City of Boerne v. Flores* (1997), which outlawed the Religious Freedom Restoration Act, again only three justices argued that the *Smith* test should be reconsidered.[132] A solid majority of the Court has shown little indication that it will change its position any time soon.

Therefore, further free speech and statutory protections of religious liberty must be vigilantly pursued in the short term, along with more rigorous state constitutional laws. But, at the same time, religious claimants must continue to press their free exercise cases in federal courts, inviting the Supreme Court slowly to draw the sting from *Smith* and to isolate it, if not overturn it.

8

MODERN
DISESTABLISHMENT LAW

Modern free exercise law has moved from a multiprincipled to a single-principled reading of the "essential rights and liberties of religion" incorporated into the First Amendment. In its early free exercise cases, the Court applied the principles of liberty of conscience, freedom of religious expression, religious pluralism and equality, and separation of church from state. Since the mid-1980s, the Court has reduced the free exercise clause to the single principle of neutrality, which Congress is now struggling mightily to unmake.

Modern disestablishment law has moved in the opposite direction. In its early disestablishment cases, the single principle of separation of church and state dominated the Court's reasoning, occasionally rebuffed by historical arguments for accommodation of religion. Since the mid-1980s, however, individual justices have slowly imported into their analysis new principles of religious equality and liberty of conscience, which the Court is now struggling mightily to integrate.

Following the style of Chapter 7, this chapter first maps the Court's rather convoluted disestablishment cases from 1947 onward. It then reviews the Court's treatment of the first principles of the American experiment in the more than fifty cases that have addressed the meaning of the phrase: "Congress shall make no law respecting an establishment of religion."

Mapping Modern Disestablishment Doctrine

The Challenge

At the heart of a modern disestablishment case is a claimant's challenge that the government has made a law establishing religion or "respecting" the same. The challenged government entity or official can be at the federal, state, or local level. The law at issue can involve the exercise of executive, legislative, or regulatory power.

The claimant's challenge is that the government has improperly funded, supported, or endorsed religion. It has coerced parties to participate in religious worship, indoctrination, or education. It has made improper use of religious sanctuaries, symbols, or services. It has improperly allied itself with religious causes, clerics, or corporations. It has discriminately favored or preferred some religious interests, individuals, or institutions over others. In brief, government has taken one or more steps down the road toward the establishment of religion.

As in free exercise so in disestablishment cases, claimants must meet the usual requirements for pressing any constitutional case. In particular, claimants must state an actual "case or controversy" justiciable by a court, and they must have "standing" to bring the suit. But the Supreme Court has softened these threshold requirements considerably for disestablishment cases.

In free exercise and other cases, the Court has read the "case and controversy" rules strictly: "It is a fundamental rule of judicial restraint, that this Court will not reach constitutional questions in advance of the necessity of deciding them."[1] But in modern disestablishment cases, the Court has not always shown such restraint. In *Epperson v. Arkansas* (1968), for example, a school teacher challenged a state criminal law that prohibited the teaching of evolution in a public school or state university. The law had not been enforced against the teacher. Stating that the teacher "faced at least a literal dilemma" of whether the state law established the teaching of creationism, the *Epperson* Court addressed the constitutional issue and found that the state law violated the disestablishment clause.[2]

In *Zobrest v. Catalina Foothills School District* (1993), the Court also relaxed the case and controversy rule, this time to find no constitutional violation. A student attending a religious high school challenged a state decision not to afford him disability services. The case below turned largely on interpretation of applicable state and federal disability statutes. On appeal, the student raised the question whether a state's furnishing him with disability services in a religious high school would constitute an establishment of religion. Four dissenters argued that the Court "should vacate and remand this case for consideration of various threshold questions, statutory and regulatory, that may moot the constitutional question."[3] The majority judged otherwise: "The fact that there may be buried in the record a nonconstitutional ground for decision is not by itself enough to invoke this rule."[4] The Court addressed the constitutional question and found no establishment of religion.[5]

Not only "case and controversy" rules but also "standing" rules have been relaxed in modern disestablishment cases. The Court's traditional standing rules, formulated in 1923, required that a party pressing a constitutional case "must be able to show that he has sustained or is in immediate danger of sustaining some direct injury as a result of the statute's enforcement and not merely that he suffers in some indefinite way in common with people generally."[6] In its early disestablishment cases, the Court applied this traditional rule.[7] In 1963, however, the Court declared that "the requirements for standing to challenge state action under the Establishment Clause, unlike those relating to the Free Exercise Clause, do not include proofs that particular *religious freedoms* are infringed."[8] In 1968, the Court held further that federal taxpayers could challenge any government programs that involved taxing and spending in aid of religion—opening federal courts to an ample tide of disestablishment cases.[9] In 1982, the Court stemmed this tide somewhat by holding that a religious liberty organization by itself lacked standing to challenge a federal agency's action that caused it no direct and obvious injury.[10] But it remains relatively easy for tax-paying citizens to challenge government actions under the disestablishment clause.

Some critics charge that these unique standing rules effectively empower a single secular party to "veto" popular laws touching religion that cause him or her only the most tangential injury. Such criticisms have become more pointed now that the Court no longer reads the free exercise clause to grant individual exemptions from neutral and generally applicable laws. Today, a secular claimant can use the disestablishment clause to overturn a carefully calibrated local law that happens to touch religion too favorably.[11] But a religious claimant cannot use the free exercise clause to claim an individual exemption from a discretionary regulatory decision that happens to "virtually destroy" its religion.[12]

Defenders of these unique rules counter that such open standing is precisely what the disestablishment clause requires. "History makes it clear," Justice Brennan argues, "that the federal taxpayer is a singularly 'proper and appropriate party to invoke a federal court's jurisdiction' to challenge a federal bestowal of largesse as a violation of the Establishment Clause. Each, and indeed every, federal tax payer suffers precisely the same injury: . . . a continuing and intolerable burden on his pocketbook, his conscience, and his constitutional rights."[13] All such parties, whether religious or secular, must be given their day in court. To grant them standing is not necessarily to find an establishment of religion. But to deny them standing is to defy a cardinal purpose of the First Amendment: to enable citizens of any religion or of no religion to keep legislative majorities from taking a single step toward the establishment of religion.

Resolving the Conflict

The government claims the constitutional power to make or enforce a law. A citizen challenges the law as a form of religious establishment. How does the Court resolve this basic constitutional conflict?

We saw in Chapter 7 that in its modern free exercise cases, the Court used three interrelated methods: (1) "case-by-case balancing," which led to factually and logically related clusters of free exercise cases; (2) "definitional balancing," which led to shifting standards of judicial review under the free exercise clause and groups of cases under each of them; and (3) "principled balancing," which led to varying treatment of the first principles of liberty of conscience, freedom of religious expression, religious equality and plurality, and separation of church from state.

These three methods avail us rather little in mapping modern disestablishment law. The only factual cluster in which the Court has kept a rather steady line of logic concerns the role of religion in public education; even in this cluster, the Court's rationale of late has begun to shift. The only formal "standard of review" the Court has developed is the so-called *Lemon* test of 1971, which has been severely twisted in recent cases and simply disregarded in others. The only "first principle" that the Court has consistently invoked is that of "separation of church and state," a phrase that has become stretched to the point of cliché. Indeed, in the minds of many today, "separation of church and state" is a synonym for "disestablishment of religion."

To address disestablishment challenges, the Court has developed a number of unique, and often sharply juxtaposed, approaches. From 1947 to the mid-1980s, these approaches were respectively labeled: (1) "separationism," (2) "accommodationism," and (3) "neutrality." Since the mid–1980s, the Court has added several new formulas to test for establishment, respectively labeled: (4) "endorsement," (5) "coercion," and (6) "equal treatment." For each of these formulas, one or more justices has offered lengthy historical and jurisprudential apologiae. But history has also become something of a "wild card" in modern disestablishment contests. In one recent case, the Court upheld on purely historical grounds a state legislature's hiring of a Presbyterian chaplain to offer prayers at the General Assembly; the Court's precedents would have easily outlawed this as an establishment of religion.[14] Figure 8.1 roughly illustrates the main shifts and juxtapositions of these approaches and a few of the main cases upholding them.

Separationism

One of the main formulas at work in modern disestablishment law is that of strict separation of church and state. This formula has firm historical roots, especially in the writings of eighteenth-century Enlightenment and Evangelical groups. Both these groups of founders had called for religious and political authorities to end their alliances and rivalries, to distinguish their forms and functions. The state, they argued, should not give special

Establishment		No Establishment
Separationism		Accommodationism
McCollum (1948)		*Zorach* (1952)

Wholesome Neutrality
Schempp (1963)

Strict Neutrality		Benevolent Neutrality
Lemon (1971)		*Walz* (1970)

Aguilar (1985)		
Texas Monthly (1989)		*Mueller* (1983)
		Kendrick (1988)

Endorsement
Mergens (1990)

Neutrality		Coercion
Kiryas Joel (1994)		*Weisman* (1992)

Equal Treatment
Pinette (1995)
Rosenberger (1995)

FIGURE 8.1   Trends in Modern Disestablishment Law

aid, support, privilege, or protection to religious doctrines or groups—through special tax appropriations or government donations of lands and goods. The state should not predicate its laws on religious premises nor direct them to religious purposes. The state should not draw on the services of religious groups nor seek to interfere in their order, organization, or orthodoxy. Religion should be left alone to flourish in the conscience of each individual and in the voluntary assemblies that individuals convene.

Enlightenment formulations of this separationist doctrine emphasized the need to protect politics and the state from the intrusions of religion and the church. Evangelical formulations emphasized the need to protect religion and the church from the intrusions of politics and the state. Both views were united, however, in their opposition to the traditional interlacings of religion and politics and the traditional alliances of church and state. Both had a formidable influence on the development of eighteenth-century state and federal laws on religious liberty. Both came to special prominence in some states during the later nineteenth and early twentieth centuries—particularly in state constitutional provisions prohibiting governmental aid to religious causes and religious aid to public schools.[15]

The Court's first modern formulation of this separationist doctrine was offered by Justice Black in *Everson v. Board of Education* (1947):

The "establishment of religion" clause of the First Amendment means at least this: Neither a state nor the Federal Government can set up a church. Neither can pass laws which aid one religion, aid all religions, or prefer one religion over another. Neither can force nor influence a person to go or to remain away from church against his will or force him to profess a belief or disbelief in any religion. No person can be punished for entertaining or professing religious beliefs or disbeliefs, for church attendance or non-attendance. No tax in any amount, large or small, can be levied to support any religious activities or institutions, whatever they may be called, or whatever form they may adopt to teach or practice religion. Neither a state nor the Federal Government can, openly or secretly, participate in the affairs of any religious organizations or groups, or vice versa. In the words of Jefferson, the clause against establishment of religion by law was intended to erect "a wall of separation between church and state."[16]

In later cases, Justice Black stressed that "a union of government and religion tends to destroy government and to degrade religion." "Religion is too personal, too sacred, [and] too holy, to permit its 'unhallowed perversion' by a civil magistrate."[17] Religion is also too powerful, too sinister, and too greedy to permit its unhindered pervasion of a civil magistracy. "[T]he same powerful religious propagandists," who are allowed to succeed in making one inroad on the state and its laws, Justice Black wrote, "doubtless will continue their propaganda, looking toward complete domination and supremacy of their particular brand of religion. And it is nearly always by insidious approaches that the citadels of [religious] liberty are more successfully attacked."[18] "The First Amendment has erected a wall of separation between church and state. That wall must be kept high and impregnable. We could not approve the slightest breach."[19]

Separationist logic found its strongest and most consistent application in a long series of cases outlawing religious officials, texts, ceremonies, and symbols from public schools. Separationism has also had an influence on other areas of government and religion, notably in cases dealing with tax support and tax exemption for religious organizations and religious causes.[20] Until 1971, separationist logic was applied directly. Since then, it has often expressed itself in a "separationist reading" of the *Lemon* test (discussed below).[21]

Accommodationism

Accommodationists are the modern heirs of eighteenth-century Puritan and Civic Republican groups. Both these groups of founders had argued that every polity must support some form of public religion, some common morals and mores to undergird and support the plurality of protected private religions. Both groups supported state appointment of chaplains for the legislature, military, and prison, state sanctions against blasphemy, sacrilege, and iconoclasm, state administration of tithe collections, test oaths, and clerical appointments, state sponsorship of religious schools, charities, and other societies.

Puritan exponents of this accommodationist doctrine were inclined to a more specifically Christian public religion, Civic Republicans to a less denominationally rigorous theism. Puritan exponents tended to be more churlish in their toleration of private religions that strayed far from the mainstream; Civic Republicans were generally more charitable. Both formulations had a formidable influence on state and federal constitution-making in the eighteenth century and on both state and federal constitutional decisions in the nineteenth and early twentieth centuries.

The Court's first modern formulation of this accommodationist doctrine came in *Zorach v. Clauson* (1952), which upheld the constitutionality of granting students release time from public schools to attend religious education or services. Justice Douglas wrote for the Court:

> We are a religious people whose institutions presuppose a Supreme Being. We guarantee the freedom to worship as one chooses. We make room for as wide a variety of beliefs and creeds as the spiritual needs of man deem necessary. We sponsor an attitude on the part of government that shows no partiality to one group and that lets each group flourish according to the zeal of its adherents and the appeal of its dogma. When the state encourages religious instruction or cooperates with religious authorities by adjusting the schedule of public events to sectarian needs, it follows the best of our traditions. For it then respects the religious nature of our people and accommodates the public service to their spiritual needs. To hold that it may not would be to find in the Constitution a requirement that government show a callous indifference to religious groups. That would be preferring those who believe in no religion over those who do believe. Government may not finance religious groups nor undertake religious instruction nor blend secular and sectarian education nor use secular institutions to force one or some religion on any person. But we find no constitutional requirement which makes it necessary for government to be hostile to religion and to throw its weight against efforts to widen the effective scope of religious influence. The government must be neutral when it comes to competition between sects. It may not thrust any sect on any person. It may not make a religious observance compulsory. It may not coerce anyone to attend church, to observe a religious holiday, or to take religious instruction.[22]

Later formulations of this accommodationist doctrine counseled against too zealous an application of separationist logic.[23] To restrict all religious exercises in the public school and public square, Justice Stewart wrote, "is seen, not as the realization of state neutrality, but rather as the establishment of a religion of secularism, or at the least, as government support of beliefs of those who think that religious exercises should be conducted only in private."[24] Justice Rehnquist added: "The 'wall of separation between church and state' is a metaphor based on bad history, a metaphor that has proved useless as a guide to judging." The disestablishment clause was designed only to prohibit government "from asserting a preference for one religious denomination or sect over others." It does not mandate "government to be strictly neutral between religion and irreligion, nor does the Clause prohibit Congress or the States from pursuing legitimate secular ends through non-discriminatory sectarian means."[25]

Accommodationists share ample common ground with separationists. Both forbid formal government alliances with religious groups. Both forbid government coercion of religious teaching or observance. Both agree that a plurality of religions must stand equal before the law. Both agree that government must not discriminate on religious grounds.

But separationists and accommodationists differ at crucial points. Separationists forbid any government aid to religion; accommodationists allow aid that is equally or nonpreferentially distributed among religions. Separationists forbid any government participation in religious worship, education, or charity. Accommodationists allow such participation so long as citizens are not coerced into participation. Separationists forbid religious and political institutions from cooperating; accommodationists allow for such cooperation in the delivery of charity, education, and other social services.

Accommodationist logic found its strongest hold in some of the Court's pre-*Everson* cases on the place and role of government in religious schools. The Court repeated the logic and holdings of these cases a few times after *Everson*, although these early cases stood in rather awkward juxtaposition to the Court's more dominant separationist tendencies. Since the mid–1980s, this accommodationist logic has returned in the form of a "benevolent neutrality" reading of the *Lemon* test and in cases upholding various legislative accommodations and uses of religious services and symbols.[26]

Neutrality

After a generation of vacillation between these juxtaposed separationist and accommodationist formulas, the Supreme Court in the early 1960s sought a middle way between them. In both its separationist and accommodationist opinions in these early years, the Court spoke intermittently about the need for government to adhere to a policy of religious neutrality. Separationists tended to formulate this as government neutrality between religion and nonreligion, accommodationists as governmental neutrality among religions. But they held this concern for neutrality in common.[27]

Beginning in the early 1960s, the Court made neutrality the new operative principle of disestablishment. Strict separation between church and state, the Court argued, is impossible in today's society, even if it could have been possible in the eighteenth century. But even-handed accommodation and acknowledgment of religion is impossible in today's religiously heterogeneous society, even if it could have been permitted in the more religiously homogeneous eighteenth century.

"Wholesome 'neutrality,'" Justice Clark announced for the Court in *Abington School District v. Schempp* (1963), is now the watchword. The disestablishment clause forbids the exercise of "all legislative power respecting religious belief or the expression thereof." Hereafter, if the stated purpose or primary effect of a law "either is the advancement or the inhibition of religion then the enactment exceeds the scope of legislative power as circumscribed by the Constitution."[28]

In *Walz v. Tax Commission* (1970) and *Lemon v. Kurtzman* (1971), the Court sharpened this "neutrality" approach into a formal test. In order to pass constitutional muster, Chief Justice Burger wrote in both cases, a challenged law (1) must have a secular purpose, (2) must have a primary effect that neither advances nor inhibits religion, and (3) must foster no excessive entanglement between church and state. Incidental religious "effects" or modest "entanglements" of church and state are tolerable. But defiance of any of these three criteria is constitutionally fatal.

The "three main evils," Chief Justice Burger declared, are "sponsorship, financial support, and active involvement of the sovereign in religious activity." These are categorically forbidden. But beyond that, the "line of separation, far from being a 'wall', is a blurred, indistinct and variable barrier depending on all the circumstances of a particular relationship."[29]

From the start, the *Lemon* test proved itself amenable to both accommodationist and separationist readings. For all of its seeming formalism, the test left ample room for interpretation. The "secular purpose" of a statute could be determined by its words alone or by a full review of its legislative history.[30] The *"primary* effect" of the statute could be determined from the perspective of the plaintiff alone or by a full inquiry into the law in action. Whether an "entanglement" between church and state proved *excessive* depended very much upon what Chief Justice Burger called "all the circumstances of a particular relationship." In the hands of skillful counsel, the *Lemon* test was subject to a variety of readings and applications.[31]

In *Walz v. Tax Commissioner* (1970), the Court gave this test an accommodationist reading and upheld a state law granting tax exemption to church property. "The course of constitutional neutrality in this area cannot be an absolutely straight line," Chief Justice Burger wrote for the *Walz* Court. "The general principle" is that "we will not tolerate either governmentally established religion or government interference with religion.

Short of those expressly proscribed government acts, there is ample room for play in the joints productive of a *benevolent neutrality* which will permit religious exercise to exist without sponsorship and without interference." Neutrality demands that we outlaw "the kind of involvement that would tip the balance toward government control of churches or government restraint on religious practice."[32] A general state policy of granting tax exemptions for the properties of churches, alongside charities, schools, and other public institutions, involves no such government control or restraint of the religious bodies that are exempt. To the contrary, it reflects a spirit of benevolent neutrality toward religion, which also ensures the separation of church and state. It is not a religious establishment.

This "accommodationist reading" of the *Lemon* test fell into desuetude for much of the 1970s and early 1980s. But it began to reappear in the Court's cases on government and religious education, beginning with *Mueller v. Allen* (1983).[33] Its most forceful exposition came in *Bowen v. Kendrick* (1988), which upheld federal funding of Catholic counseling centers for pregnant teenagers, in implementation of the Adolescent Family Life Act.[34]

In *Lemon v. Kurtzman* (1971) itself, the Court gave the *Lemon* test a separationist reading, and struck down a state policy that reimbursed religious schools for some of the costs of teaching secular subjects that the state prescribed. The challenged state policy was restricted to religious schools that served students from lower-income families. Reimbursements were allowed only for clearly specified secular subjects and were limited to 15 percent of the costs. The Court declared that this policy fostered an "excessive entanglement between church and state." The Catholic schools, in question, were notably religious—closely allied with nearby parish churches, filled with religious symbols, and staffed primarily by nuns who were under "religious control and discipline." "[A] dedicated religious person, teaching at a school affiliated with his or her faith and operated to inculcate its tenets, will inevitably experience great difficulty in remaining religiously neutral." She will be tempted to teach secular subjects with a religious orientation in violation of state policy. "A comprehensive, discriminating, and continuing state surveillance will inevitably be required to ensure that these restrictions are obeyed and the First Amendment otherwise obeyed." This is precisely the kind of excessive entanglement between church and state that the disestablishment clause outlaws.[35]

This "separationist reading" of the *Lemon* test guided most of the Court's disestablishment cases for the next fifteen years—not only for religion and education cases but also for cases raising other issues. The Court's most forceful expositions came in *Wallace v. Jaffree* (1985), which outlawed moments of silence in public schools, and in *Texas Monthly v. Bullock* (1989), which outlawed state tax exemptions for the sale of religious periodicals.[36]

The increasingly wide disparities of logic and results in the Court's cases in the later 1970s and 1980s undercut the rationale for devising the *Lemon* test in the first place—to strike more of a predictable middle way between separationism and accommodationism. Since the mid–1980s, individual justices have begun to experiment with alternative approaches to disestablishment. Three such approaches—"endorsement," "coercion," and "equal treatment"—have emerged as well as a reformulation of the neutrality approach. None of these approaches has consistently captured a majority of the Court. But each has attracted considerable support among the justices, and each has led the Court in at least one recent case.

Endorsement

The endorsement approach is largely the creation of Justice O'Connor. The disestablishment clause, she argues, forbids governmental endorsement or disapproval of religion. "We live in a pluralistic society. Our citizens come from diverse religious traditions or adhere to no particular religious beliefs at all."[37] "[G]overnment may generally not treat people differently based on the God or gods they worship, or don't worship."[38] It may not "make adherence to religion relevant to a person's standing in the political community. Direct government action endorsing religion or a particular religious practice is invalid under this approach because it 'sends a message to nonadherents that they are outsiders, not full members of the political community, and an accompanying message to adherents that they are insiders, favored members of the community.'"[39]

Government accommodations of religion, if indiscriminately applied, are acceptable, Justice O'Connor writes. "What makes accommodation permissible, even praiseworthy, is not that the government is making life easier for some particular religious group as such. Rather, it is that the government is accommodating a deeply held belief."[40] This fosters equal protection for all, religious and nonreligious alike.[41]

Justice O'Connor has applied this endorsement reasoning in a dozen opinions since 1984. This approach came to strongest expression in the plurality opinion of *Board of Education v. Mergens* (1990), where the Court upheld the constitutionality of the Equal Access Act, which we discussed in the last chapter (page 145). Usually, Justice O'Connor has expressed her endorsement views in concurring opinions, joined by one or two other justices. Governmental support of religious symbols prominently displayed on its own buildings signals endorsement, she has argued.[42] But governmental accommodation of private religious displays in public parks and squares does not.[43] Governmental programs that give religious students equal access to state funding or facilities, or that support the secular functions of religious organizations, or that accommodate the special core needs of religious individuals or groups are necessary protections against outright hostility to religion.[44] But equality and accommodation give way to endorsement when the boundary of a public school district follows exactly the boundary of an exclusively religious community. In such an instance, religion does affect a person's standing in the political community.[45]

Justice O'Connor's endorsement approach is the most original of the Court's latest disestablishment offerings. But it has not captured the imagination of a majority of the Court. Justice O'Connor's early formulations of this approach were criticized for inviting judicial inquiry into an elusive "legislative intent respecting religion" and for substituting rigorous judicial analysis of the constitutionality of governmental action with the "perceptions" of a "reasonable outsider" or "objective observer."[46] Her later formulations quietly dropped inquiries into "legislative intent" and the "objective observer."[47] But by removing these inquiries, fellow justices now charge, her approach invites judges to make an abstract, subjective inquiry whether a government policy happens to favor religion. Such an approach is, at minimum, unpredictable. But, without requiring close inquiry into the context in which a law was made, the endorsement approach might now well require judges to outlaw the very legislative accommodations for religion that Justice O'Connor has so strongly favored.[48]

Coercion

Justice Kennedy regards "coercion" as the central concern of the disestablishment clause. In his view, "government may not coerce anyone to support or participate in any religion or its exercise; and it may not, in the guise of avoiding hostility or callous indifference, give direct benefits to religion in such a degree that it in fact 'establishes a religion or religious faith, or tends to do so.'"[49]

The disestablishment clause is designed to protect liberty of conscience and the autonomy of religious groups, Justice Kennedy argues, not to purge the public square or public policy of all religion. "[P]reservation and transmission of religious beliefs and worship is the responsibility and a choice committed to the private sphere, which itself is promised freedom to pursue its mission."[50] "Government policies of accommodation, acknowledgement or support for religion are an accepted part of our political and cultural heritage" and should be maintained in a pluralistic manner.[51] Only where such accommodations of religion effectively coerce public participation in religious exercises such as prayer or merge "political and religious lines" and institutions should they be struck down.[52] These latter policies invariably invite the kind of religious stigmatizing that impairs true liberty of conscience and autonomy of religious governance. Parties will choose to participate in the prayer or to abide by the religious line-drawing not out of voluntary conviction but because of the civil and social advantages attached to them.[53]

A majority of the Court used this coercion test in *Lee v. Weisman* (1992) to outlaw prayers at a public middle school graduation ceremony. In this case, the school principal engaged a local rabbi to offer the prayers—instructing him to be "nonsectarian" and furnishing him with published guidelines to illustrate an appropriate prayer. The graduation ceremony took place on public school grounds. The prayer followed the public recitation of the pledge of allegiance, with participants standing. Although students were not required to participate in the graduation ceremony, or in the prayer, most did.

Speaking for the Court, Justice Kennedy found the state's action doubly coercive. The state was dictating to the rabbi the content of his prayer. It was also effectively coercing all students to participate in its recitation. Although he adduced earlier cases that outlawed prayer in schools, Justice Kennedy did not dwell on their separationist reasoning. Although he did not apply the *Lemon* test, he explicitly rejected the recommendation of the parties and the dissent to bury it.[54]

Neutrality

According to Justice Souter, the endorsement approach is not predictable enough, and the coercion approach is not embracive enough to outlaw more subtle forms of religious discrimination or favoritism. In Justice Souter's view, the disestablishment clause mandates "governmental neutrality" among religions and between religion and nonreligion. The *Lemon* test can be a helpful guide, but it is no dispositive method for judging whether government has acted neutrally.

Justice Souter's neutrality approach would outlaw a variety of forms of governmental accommodation of religion or cooperation with religious officials in the public school or the public square, for such actions favor religion over nonreligion.[55] Religiously neutral policies that afford an incidental benefit to the religious beliefs or bodies are acceptable.[56] Governmental programs that support secular institutions along with religious institutions delivering secular services are also acceptable—so long as there is "a searching enquiry to ensure that the institution kept the secular activities separate from its sectarian ones, with any direct aid flowing only to the former and never the latter."[57] But direct government funding of any religious activities is "categorically prohibited," for taxpayers either of different or of nonreligious persuasion are being forced to pay for the religious activities of another.[58]

Justice Souter's neutrality approach carried a plurality of the Court in *Kiryas Joel Village School District v. Grumet* (1994). That case outlawed

New York's creation of a new public school district that followed exactly the boundaries of an Hasidic Jewish community. The state had created this special school district in order to offer handicapped students in the Hasidic community the remedial services mandated by federal and state law, without forcing these students into the gentile world. All students in these remedial programs were Hasidic, and the school officials could respect the community's religious laws, particularly those mandating separate sex education. Writing for the Court, Justice Souter found this policy in violation of the disestablishment clause. It favors religious over nonreligious students. It subordinates and delegates the state's educational responsibility to the religious leadership and preferences of the community. Both features of the program fail to meet the neutrality required by the disestablishment clause.[59]

Equal Treatment

An emerging fourth approach to disestablishment has been called "equal treatment."[60] This approach overlaps heavily in terminology and interpretation with the neutrality approach and is also consistent somewhat with the endorsement approach.[61] But whereas Justice Souter's formulation of neutrality forbids government funding or alliances with religion, equal treatment exponents allow such funding and alliances so long as nonreligious parties similarly situated receive comparable treatment.[62]

Equal treatment of religion, of course, is no recent invention and no monopoly of the disestablishment clause. Already in 1899, the Court upheld a federal grant to a religious hospital alongside others.[63] More recently, the Court has upheld construction grants to religious schools and religious charities as part of broader programs that fund nonreligious institutions as well.[64] The Court has upheld school bus transportation and textbook loans for religious students alongside nonreligious students.[65] It has upheld tax exemptions to church properties alongside those of schools, charities, and other associations.[66] And it has said that it is no establishment of religion for religious workers to receive the same access to unemployment compensation benefits afforded other workers.[67] The Court's rationale for these earlier holdings, however, was not stated in terms of "equality." These were forms of religious accommodation, protections of free exercise, expressions of benevolent neutrality, or suitable means of implementing secular policy.

In recent cases, however, the Court has said more explicitly that religious institutions and individuals are not "disabled by the First Amendment" from equal access to forums open to others, or from equal participation in government programs in which nonreligious parties participate.[68] Thus in *Capitol Square v. Pinette* (1995) the Court upheld the private display of a cross in a public square that was "open to all on *equal terms*."[69] And in

Rosenberger v. University of Virginia (1995), the Court upheld the equal access of a voluntary religious secular student groups to state university funding for its publications, which was available to more than 100 nonreligious student groups similarly situated.

Endorsement, coercion, neutrality, and equal treatment—these are the four main alternative approaches that the Court has recently imported into its disestablishment clause calculus. All of these approaches have aimed to replace the *Lemon* neutrality test and to nuance the underlying separationist and accommodationist approaches that antedate and inform the *Lemon* test. None of these approaches has, as yet, commanded a consistent majority of the Court, and none has interred the *Lemon* test entirely.

The juxtaposition of these approaches has led the Court of late to issue a number of sharply divided and discordant decisions. Each of the Court's disestablishment cases in the 1990s has produced at least four separate judicial opinions, many bristling with all manner of polemic against the approaches of fellow justices. The Court has been struggling mightily for more than a decade to bring this unwieldy mass of precedents to some semblance of order and predictability. But for the moment, an integrated law of disestablishment remains only a distant ideal. In this chaotic context, litigants and judges in disestablishment cases—let alone law professors teaching the same—are rarely left without an argument for any number of positions.

The Dominant Principle of Separation of Church and State

The Supreme Court's modern disestablishment cases are not only forums for the contestation of rival judicial approaches. They are also laboratories for the application of the first principles of the American experiment in religious rights and liberties. In the foregoing section, I have used the Court's terms of art and forms of analysis to map modern disestablishment doctrine. In this section, I trace the Court's interpretation and application of the first principles of the American experiment in its more than fifty disestablishment cases issued since 1947.

The founders viewed the disestablishment clause as both a source and a summary of religious freedom. At minimum, disestablishment of religion meant foreclosing government from defining and enforcing by law the religion of the community—its religious texts and traditions, its doctrines and liturgies, its lectionaries and prayers—as European ecclesiastical laws had done for centuries before. More fully conceived, disestablishment of religion meant foreclosing government from coercing citizens to participate in religious exercises and affiliations in violation of the principle of liberty of conscience. It foreclosed government from discriminating among its citizens on religious grounds in violation of the principle of equality of plural religions before the law. It foreclosed government from allying or involving itself in the offices and activities of religious bodies, in violation of the principle of separation of church and state. The guarantee of disestablishment of religion, like the guarantee of free exercise of religion, was an umbrella term. It protected at once the principles of liberty of conscience, equality of a plurality of religions, and separation of church and state.

There was ample debate, both in the founding era and in the generations to follow, about the relative rigor and priority of each of these constitutive principles of disestablishment. One issue that was particularly divisive was whether all government aid to religion was categorically forbidden or whether governmental aid could be given nonpreferentially among religions. Both interpretations could be plausibly drawn from the debates surrounding the formation of the religion clauses.[70] Both interpretations came to vigorous expression in nineteenth- and early twentieth-century state constitutions.[71]

The Emergence of Separationism

In *Everson v. Board of Education* (1947), the case that opened the modern era of disestablishment, the Supreme Court reiterated each of the first principles that the founders had incorporated into the disestablishment clause. This can be seen if one parses phrase by phrase Justice Black's famous summary in *Everson:* "The 'establishment of religion' clause of the First Amendment means at least this," Justice Black wrote. No federal or state government (1) "can set up a church"—a violation of the core disestablishment principle; (2) "can force or influence a person to go or to remain away from church against his will or force him to profess a belief or disbelief in any religion"—a violation of liberty of conscience; (3) can "punish [a person] for entertaining or professing religious beliefs or disbeliefs, for church attendance or non-attendance"—a violation of both liberty of conscience and religious equality; (4) "can, openly or secretly, participate in the affairs of any religious organizations or groups, or *vice versa*"—a violation of the principle of separation of church and state.[72] Justice Black also underscored the founders' principle of religious pluralism, declaring that government may not exclude "individual Catholics, Lutherans, Mohammedans, Baptists, Jews, Methodists, Nonbelievers, Presbyterians, or the members of any faith, *because of their faith, or lack of it,* from receiving the benefits of public welfare legislation."[73] Liberty of conscience, religious equality, religious pluralism, and separation of church and state were all considered part of the disestablishment clause in the Court's initial formulation.

On the perennially contested issue of government aid to religion, however, the *Everson* court came down four-square against it and linked its "no-aid" formulation to the principle of separation of church and state.

Government, Justice Black wrote, may pass no laws "which aid one religion, aid all religions, or prefer one religion over another. No tax in any amount, large or small, can be levied to support any religious activities or institutions, whatever they may be called, or whatever form they may adopt to teach or practice religion." "[T]he clause against establishment of religion by law was intended to erect a wall of separation between church and state."[74]

It was this latter move by the *Everson* Court that set the tone for much of the Court's early interpretation and application of the disestablishment clause. Disestablishment of religion meant no government aid to religion. No government aid to religion was best accomplished by separating government from religion altogether. Disestablishment, separation, and no aid were increasingly linked in the Court's opinions under the general rubric of "separationism." The other founding principles of disestablishment were increasingly lost in the Court's opinions for the next forty years.

Religion and Public Education

In its first generation of cases in the modern era, the Court enforced this separationist reading of the disestablishment clause repeatedly in the context of education. This was not so unusual a first forum for separationist logic. By 1947, thirty-three state constitutions prohibited state and local governments from granting funds and other aid to religious schools. Fifteen state constitutions insisted further that state schools remain free from "sectarian influence" or from the control of religious officials and institutions.[75] At the turn of the century, and thereafter, various Protestant, Catholic, and other religious constituencies had led campaigns to reinvigorate the religion of the public schools—calling for the enhancement of biblical teaching, the appointment of Christian teachers, the reinvigoration of religious ceremonies and symbols, and much else. By 1947, these issues had occupied state courts and constitutional conventions for more than a half century—with widely varying results.[76]

After 1947, the Supreme Court took firm control of these controversies and systematically outlawed the use of religious teachers, texts, ceremonies, and symbols in the public schools. In its early cases, the Court developed a general logic that was specific to the issue of government support of religion in public education. The public school is one of the most visible and well-known arms of the state in any community, the cases repeatedly argued. One primary purpose of the public school is to stand as a model of constitutional democracy and to provide a vehicle for the communication of democratic values and abilities to its students. The state compels its students to be at schools. These students are perforce young and impressionable. As a consequence, the public schools must cling closely to core constitutional and democratic values. One such core value is the separation of church and state taught by the disestablishment clause. Some relaxation of constitutional values, even disestablishment values, might be possible in other public contexts—where mature adults can make informed assessments of the values being transmitted. But no such relaxation can occur in public schools with their impressionable youths who are compelled to be there. In public schools, the constitutional values of the disestablishment clause must be vigorously protected.

The case that opened this series was *McCollum v. Board of Education* (1948). The state action at issue was a "release time" program, adopted by a local public school board for fourth through ninth grade students. For 30 to 45 minutes once a week, students were released from their regular classes to be able to participate in religious classes, if their parents consented to their participation. Students could choose among three such religious classes, taught respectively by qualified Protestant, Catholic, or Jewish teachers. These religious teachers were not employed by the school but were approved by its superintendent. Students whose parents did not consent to their participation continued their "secular studies" during this release time period.

A parent of one student challenged the release time program as a violation of the disestablishment clause. The *McCollum* Court agreed. Writing for the majority, Justice Black declared that this was precisely the kind of conflation of church and state that *Everson* sought to allow—using "tax-supported property for religious instruction and the close cooperation between school authorities and the religious council in promoting religious education."

> The operation of the State's compulsory education system thus assists and is integrated with the program of religious instruction carried on by separate religious sects. Pupils compelled by law to go to school for secular education are released in part from their legal duty upon the condition that they attend the religious classes. This is beyond all question a utilization of the tax-established and tax-supported public school to aid religious groups to spread their faith. And it falls squarely under the ban of the First Amendment [that] . . . had erected a wall of separation between Church and State.[77]

In a strongly worded concurrence, Justice Frankfurter underscored the importance of rigorous application of the principle of separationism in the realm of public education. After lamenting that public schools of late had become "hostage" to "sectarian control," Justice Frankfurter wrote:

> Separation means separation, not something less. Jefferson's metaphor in describing the relation between Church and State speaks of a "wall of separation," not of a fine line easily overstepped. The public school is at once the

symbol of our democracy and the most pervasive means for promoting our common destiny. In no activity of the State is it more vital to keep out divisive influences than in its schools, to avoid confusing, not to say fusing, what the Constitution sought to keep strictly apart. "The great American principle of eternal separation"—Elihu Root's phrase bears repetition—is one of the vital reliances of our Constitutional system for assuring unities among our people stronger than our diversities. It is the Court's duty to enforce this principle in its full integrity.[78]

In *Engel v. Vitale* (1962), the Court extended this separationist reasoning to outlaw prayer in schools. The State Board of Regents of New York had adopted a nondenominational prayer to be recited by public school teachers and their students at the commencement of each day: "Almighty God, we acknowledge our dependence upon Thee, and we beg Thy blessings upon us, our parents, our teachers, and our Country." Students who did not wish to participate in the prayer could remain silent or be excused from the room during its recitation. The parents of ten students challenged both the state's creation of the prayer and its use in the public school classroom, as violations of the disestablishment clause.

The *Engel* Court agreed. Again Justice Black wrote for the majority:

It is no part of the business of government to compose official prayers for any group of the American people to recite as part of a religious program carried on by government. . . . There can be no doubt that New York's state prayer program officially establishes the religious beliefs embodied in the Regents prayer. . . . Neither the fact that the prayer may be denominationally neutral nor the fact that its observance on the part of the students is voluntary can serve to free it from the Establishment Clause. . . . When the power, prestige, and financial support of government is placed behind a particular religious belief, the indirect coercive pressure upon religious minorities to conform to the prevailing officially approved religion is plain.

This is plainly unconstitutional, Justice Black concluded. It violates the "first and most immediate" principle of the disestablishment clause: "a union of government and religion tends to destroy government and to degrade religion."[79] This prohibition on prayer in public schools remains the law, as the Court underscored most recently in *Lee v. Weisman* (1992).[80]

In *Abington Township School District v. Schempp* (1963), the Court extended this reasoning to outlaw Bible reading in the public schools.[81] Following general state law, a public school district mandated that each school open its day with the reading of ten Bible verses. Either a teacher or a student who volunteered would read the text. Each reader was permitted to choose the text of the day. No commentary or discussion of the Bible reading were allowed. In some schools, a common reading was broadcast throughout the school; in other schools, the reading was done in individual classrooms. In some schools, this reading was followed by public recitation of the Lord's Prayer and of the pledge of allegiance. Students whose parents did not consent could again refuse to participate or leave the room during these religious exercises.

Against the backdrop of *Engel v. Vitale*, the *Schempp* Court found this case an easy violation of the disestablishment clause. The policy in question was an overtly religious exercise, mandated by the State, for impressionable youths required to be in school, with no realistic opportunity for the average student to forgo participation. "[I]t is no defense that the religious practices here may be relatively minor encroachments on the First Amendment," Justice Clark wrote for the Court. "The breach of neutrality that is today a trickling stream may all too soon become a raging torrent."

Justice Clark emphasized that to ban religion from the public school was not to ban it from society altogether:

> The place of religion in our society is an exalted one, achieved through a long tradition of reliance on the home, the church, and the inviolable citadel of the individual heart and mind. We have come to recognize through bitter experience that it is not within the power of government to invade that citadel, whether its purpose or effect be to aid or oppose, to advance or retard. In the relationship between man and religion, the state is firmly committed to a position of neutrality.[82]

Responding to Justice Stewart's sharply worded dissent that the Court's neutrality stance effectively established "secularism" as the religion of the public school, Justice Clark offered a conciliatory word about the objective value of religion in public education:

> We agree of course that the State may not establish a "religion of secularism" in the sense of affirmatively opposing or showing hostility to religion. . . . We do not agree, however, that this decision in any sense has that effect. In addition, it might well be said that one's education is not complete without a study of comparative religion or the history of religion and its relationship to the advancement of civilization. It certainly may be said that the Bible is worthy of study for its literary and historic qualities. Nothing we have said here indicates that such study of the Bible or of religion, when presented objectively as part of a secular program of education, may not be effected consistently with the First Amendment.[83]

In two subsequent cases, however, the Court closed the door firmly against symbolic and objective forms of religion in the public school. In *Stone v. Graham* (1980), the Court struck down a state statute that required the posting of a plaque bearing the Ten Commandments on the wall of each public school classroom. The plaques were donated and hung by private groups in the community. There was no public reading of the commandments nor any evident mention or endorsement of them by teachers or school officials. Each plaque bore a small inscription that sought to immunize it from charges of religious establishment: "The secular application of the Ten Commandments is clearly seen in its adoption as the fundamental legal code of Western Civilization and the Common Law of the United States."

The Court struck down the displays as a form of religious establishment. It found the statute mandating the Decalogue display had no "secular legislative purpose" but was "clearly religious." The Ten Commandments are sacred in Jewish and Christian circles, and they command "the religious duties of believers." It made no constitutional difference, said the Court, that the Ten Commandments were passively displayed rather than formally read or that they were privately donated rather than purchased with state money. The very display of the Decalogue served only a religious purpose and was thus per se unconstitutional.[84]

In *Edwards v. Aguillard* (1987), the Court pressed this logic further to strike down a Louisiana act requiring a "Balanced Treatment for Creation-Science and Evolution-Science in Public School Instruction." The statute mandated that a public school teacher could not teach "evolution-science" without teaching "creation-science" and vice-versa. Teachers were not required to teach a theory of origins, but if they did, they had to give equal time to "the scientific evidences" for both evolutionary and creationist accounts of origins. The stated legislative purpose of the act was "to promote academic freedom" in allowing teachers to explore various theories of origins, including religious theories.

The *Edwards* Court declared the act unconstitutional. After rehearsing the legislative history at length, the Court concluded that the act had no real secular purpose but was a thinly veiled attempt to import religious teachings into the curriculum. The act evinced a "discriminatory preference for the teaching of creation and against the teaching of evolution," Justice Brennan wrote for the Court. Its "preeminent purpose" was "clearly to advance the religious viewpoint that a supernatural being created humankind. The term 'creation science' was defined as embracing this particular religious doctrine. ... In this case, the purpose of the Creationism Act was to restructure the science curriculum to conform with a particular religious viewpoint." This was not a proper objective teaching of religion but an unconstitutional establishment of religion.[85]

In *Wallace v. Jaffree* (1985), the Court stretched its separationist logic to its furthest point. At issue in the case was a state statute that authorized a moment of silence at the beginning of each school day for "meditation or voluntary prayer." On rehearsing the legislative history, the Court found that the statute revealed no secular purpose but a "legislative intent to return prayer to the public schools." "The addition of 'or voluntary prayer'" to the statute, Justice Stevens wrote for the Court, "indicates that the State intended to characterize prayer as a favored practice. Such an endorsement is not consistent with the established principle that Government must pursue a course of complete neutrality toward religion."[86]

Government and Religious Education

From the start, the principle of separation of church and state dominated the Court's opinions on the role of religion in public education. This principle came only to more gradual application in the Court's opinions on the role of government in religious education.

In the decades before *Everson*, the Court had already several times countenanced general protection and support for religious schools.[87] In *Quick Bear v. Leupp* (1908), the Court upheld the allocation of federal funds to Catholic schools that offered education to Native Americans. In *Meyer v. Nebraska* (1923), the Court held that states could not forbid religious schools from teaching or reading the Bible in a foreign language. In *Pierce v. Society of Sisters* (1925), the Court held that a state government could not mandate that all students attend public schools; religious schools were a vital and viable alternative form of education that was constitutionally protected. In *Farrington v. Tokushige* (1927), the Court held that states could not impose unduly intrusive and stringent accreditation and regulatory requirements on religious and other private schools. In *Cochran v. Board of Education* (1930), the Court held that a state policy of supplying textbooks to all students could also supply them to religious school students.[88]

This accommodation of religious schools and students initially continued in the modern disestablishment cases. *Everson* itself, for all its sweeping separationist dicta, nonetheless held that it was no establishment of religion for states to provide school bus transportation to religious and public school children alike. Moreover, it was no establishment of religion for the state to reimburse the parents of religious and public school children alike for the costs of using school bus transportation. "[C]utting off church schools [and their students] from these services, so separate and indisputably marked off from the religious function, would make it far more difficult for the schools to operate," Justice Black wrote. "But such obviously is not the purpose of the First Amendment. The Amendment requires the State to be neutral in its relations with groups of religious believers and non-believers; it does not require the state to be their adversary."[89]

The Court struck a similar tone in *Board of Education v. Allen* (1968). The State of New York had a policy of lending prescribed textbooks in science, mathematics, and other "secular subjects" to all students in the state, whether attending public or private schools. Many of the private school recipients of the textbooks were religious schools. A taxpayer thus challenged the policy as a violation of the disestablishment clause. Citing the 1930 *Cochran* case, the Court upheld this policy, emphasizing that it was the students and parents, not the religious schools, that directly benefited. "Perhaps free books make it more likely that some children choose to attend a sectarian school," Justice White wrote for the Court, "but that was true of the state-paid bus fares in *Everson*, and does not alone demonstrate an unconstitutional degree of support for a religious institution."[90]

The Court continued this accommodationist tone in a trio of cases upholding the payment of government construction grants and revenue bonds to religious colleges and universities.[91] In *Tilton v. Richardson* (1971), the Court rebuffed a challenge to federal grants that supported construction of library, science, and arts buildings at four church-related colleges. The grants were made as part of the federal Higher Education Facilities Act (1963), which sponsored new college and university buildings throughout the nation. Chief Justice Burger wrote for the Court: "The Act itself was carefully drafted to ensure that the federally-subsidized facilities would be devoted to the secular and not the religious functions of the recipient institution."[92] This feature, together with the reality that most funding was directed to state, not religious, universities and colleges was sufficient to save them from charges of religious establishment.

In *Roemer v. Board of Public Works* (1977), the Court upheld a state construction grant program that aided five church-related schools among its seventeen grant recipients. The Court counseled against too zealous an application of separationist principles. In Justice Blackmun's words:

> A system of government that makes itself felt as pervasively as ours could hardly be expected never to cross paths with the church. In fact, our State and Federal Governments impose certain burdens upon, and impart certain benefits to, virtually all our activities, and religious activity is no exception. The Court has enforced a scrupulous neutrality by the State, as among religions, and also as between religious and other activities, but a hermetic separation of the two is an impossibility [and] it has never been required. . . . [R]eligious institutions need not be quarantined from public benefits that are neutrally available to all. . . . Just as *Bradfield [v. Roberts* (1899)] dispels any notion that a religious person can never be in the State's pay for a secular purpose, so *Everson* and *Allen* put to rest any argument that the State may never act in such a way that has the incidental effect of facilitating religious activity.[93]

Outside of these cases, however, the Court's accommodationist tones ended abruptly in 1971. With its adoption of the *Lemon* test that year, the Court began to apply the separationist logic of its public education cases to the religious education cases as well. *Lemon v. Kurtzman* (1971) itself, as we saw, used the separationist policy of the "no excessive entanglement between church and state" prong to strike down a state policy that reimbursed religious schools for up to 15 percent of the costs of teachers's salaries, plus the costs of textbooks and other instructional materials for prescribed secular subjects.

Lemon left open the question whether the state could give aid directly to religious students or to their parents—as the Court had allowed in earlier cases. Two years later, the Court closed this door tightly. In *Committee for Public Education v. Nyquist* (1973) and *Sloan v. Lemon* (1973), the Court struck down state policies that allowed low-income parents to seek reimbursements from the state for some of the costs of religious school tuition. *Nyquist* further struck down a state policy that allowed low-income parents to take tax deductions for the costs of sending their children to non-public schools. In *Nyquist*, Justice Powell characterized such policies as just another "of the ingenious plans of channelling state aid to sectarian schools." Responding to the State argument that "grants to parents, unlike grants to [religious] institutions, respect the 'wall of separation' required by the Constitution," the Court declared that "the effect of the aid is unmistakeably to provide desired financial support for non-public, sectarian institutions."[94] This violates the second prong of the *Lemon* test that outlaws any policy whose primary effect is to advance religion.

Lemon also left open the question of whether the state could give textbooks, educational materials, or other aid to religious schools for the teaching of mandatory secular subjects, or the administration of state-mandated tests and other programs. The Court struck down most such policies, save the lending of textbooks, which had been upheld since the 1930 *Cochran* case. In a long series of increasingly tedious cases, from 1973 to 1985, the Court held that states could not reimburse religious schools for most costs incurred to administer standardized tests or to prepare mandated state records[95]—although the "actual costs" for certain tests could be recouped.[96] States could loan textbooks on secular subjects to religious schools, but not if those schools discriminated on racial grounds.[97] States could not loan or furnish religious schools with various supplies and films, and various counseling and other personnel, even if those were mandated by state policy.[98] States could not use public school teachers to hold remedial educational programs to indigent children in classrooms leased from religious schools.[99] States could not lend public school personnel to teach remedial and enrichment courses in religious schools.[100]

By 1985, these cases on the relationship between government and religious schools began increasingly to "partake of the prolixity" of a bizarre byzantine code. Justice Rehnquist summarized the law:

> [A] State may lend to parochial school children geography textbooks that contain maps of the United States, but the State may not lend maps of the United

States for use in geography class. A State may lend textbooks on American colonial history, but it may not lend a film of George Washington, or a film projector to show it in history class. A State may lend classroom workbooks, but may not lend workbooks in which the parochial school children write, thus rendering them nonreusable. A State may pay for bus transportation to religious schools, but may not pay for bus transportation from the parochial school to the public zoo or natural history museum for a field trip. A State may pay for diagnostic services conducted in the parochial school but therapeutic services must be given in a different building; speech and hearing "services" conducted by the State inside the sectarian school are forbidden, but the State may conduct speech and hearing testing inside the sectarian school. Exceptional parochial school students may receive counseling, but it must take place outside of the parochial school, such as in a trailer parked down the street. A State may give cash to a parochial school to pay for administration of State-written tests and State-ordered reporting services, but it may not provide funds for teacher-prepared tests on secular subjects. Religious instruction may not be given in public school, but the public school may release students during the day for religion classes [in the sectarian school], and may enforce attendance of those classes with its truancy laws.[101]

Already in a 1948 education case, Justice Jackson had warned his brethren that if the Court did not set strict limits to federal jurisdiction over these education cases, it would soon have "to accept the role of a super board of education for every school district in the nation." "And more importantly," he warned, "we are likely to make the legal 'wall of separation between church and state' as winding as the famous serpentine wall designed by Mr. Jefferson for the University he founded."[102] Within four decades, such warnings had proved painfully prescient.

Religion and the Public Square

The Court's separationist logic in its education cases set the tone for adjudicating other disestablishment cases as well. The Supreme Court itself heard very few disestablishment cases that did not involve questions of religion and education. But many lower federal and state courts did. These courts used the Supreme Court's separationist logic to outlaw all manner of traditional government subsidies for religious charities, social services, and mission works; government use of religious services, facilities, and publications; government protections of Sundays and Holy Days; government enforcement of blasphemy and sacrilege laws; government participation in religious rituals and religious displays.[103]

It often did not take law suits to implement this separationist logic. Particularly local governments, sensitive to the costs of constitutional litigation, often voluntarily ended their prayers, removed their decalogues, and closed their coffers to religion long before any case was filed against them.

This voluntary "First Amendmentization" of religion and politics seemed to be what the Court's separationist reading of the disestablishment clause required.

The few Supreme Court disestablishment cases outside the realm of education underscored this popular impression. *Larkin v. Grendel's Den* (1982) was a good case in point. A Massachusetts law required that no facility within 500 feet of a school or church could receive a liquor license if "the governing body of such school or church files written objection thereto." Grendel's Den was denied a liquor license because a neighboring church had objected. Grendel's Den appealed, claiming that the licensing law was an establishment of religion. The Court agreed. "Jefferson's idea of a 'wall,'" Chief Justice wrote for the Court, "was a useful figurative illustration to emphasize the concept of separateness. Some limited and incidental entanglement between church and state authority is inevitable in a complex modern society, but the concept of a 'wall' of separation is a useful signpost. Here that 'wall' is substantially breached by vesting discretionary governmental power in religious bodies."[104]

Writing in lonely dissent, Justice Rehnquist termed this "a silly case." This is a sound and sensible zoning law, he argued, not an establishment of religion. Massachusetts could have, like many states, simply banned altogether the serving of liquor within stated distances of schools and religious institutions—and this ban would easily pass constitutional muster. Instead of imposing this flat ban, the state here chose to leave it to schools or churches to decide whether they wanted to have this common protection from the sale of liquor in their immediate surroundings. Here, one church simply said that it wanted such protection, and the state gave it to them. This is hardly a "fusion of governmental and religious functions" or a "delegation of essential governmental powers" to religious bodies, Justice Rehnquist wrote, but an equitable application of a valid rule of law. The Massachusetts law in question "does not encourage, much less compel anyone to participate in religious activities or to support religious organizations." "The heavy First Amendment artillery that the Court fires at this sensible and unobjectionable Massachusetts statute is both unnecessary and unavailing."[105]

Toward Multiple Principles of Disestablishment

Justice Rehnquist's lonely 1982 dissent against too strict a separationist reading of the disestablishment clause increasingly became the norm for the Court in the later 1980s and thereafter. While holding fast to separationism in most of its public education cases, the Court has been slowly retreating from this principle in other cases.

The Court's retreats have often been rather clumsy exercises—featuring inventive twists of the *Lemon* test in some cases, tendentious distinctions of precedent in others, and the rather haphazard introduction of new approaches and terms, such as endorsement, coercion, neutrality, and equal treatment. Moreover, in this process of retreat, the Court has issued a number of blatantly contradictory decisions. In successive years, the Court upheld the constitutionality of federal funding of Catholic teenage pregnancy counseling centers but struck down a state tax exemption for sales of religious periodicals.[106] The Court upheld the constitutionality of a federal law exempting religious employers from Title VII prohibitions on religious discrimination but struck down the constitutionality of a state law allowing religious employees to claim exemptions from working on their sabbath.[107] The Court upheld the constitutionality of state funding of a legislative chaplain who opened each General Assembly session with prayer but struck down a county's policy of allowing a privately funded Christmas display in the foyer of its courthouse.[108] While some of these decisions can be partially explained by close attention to their facts, they collectively betray ample evidence of "a jurisprudence of doubt."[109]

Yet, in the midst of all this confusion, the Court of late has shown some signs of developing a more integrative law of disestablishment. In *Everson,* as we saw, the Court had read into the disestablishment clause a number of other first principles of the American experiment besides separation of church and state—notably liberty of conscience and the equality of plural faiths before the law. In several recent cases, the Court seems to be importing these principles, alongside separationism, into its disestablishment calculus.

Liberty of Conscience, Equality, and Religious Education

The court's recent cases on the role of government in religious education provide a good example of this new trend. *Lemon v. Kurtzman* (1971) and its immediate progeny, as we saw, had outlawed most forms of government aid to and cooperation with religious schools. The core holdings of these cases have not changed: Government still may not directly fund, endorse, or cooperate in the religious teachings of religious schools. But in four recent cases, the Court has upheld various government programs that grant to religious students or their parents the same general benefits afforded to others. The common rationale of these cases is that students and their parents must be protected in their choices to attend religious schools—even if this results in indirect government funding of religious education. Too zealous an application of separationism intrudes on these parties' liberty of conscience to choose religious education and on equality of treatment in the choices they make.

In *Mueller v. Allen* (1983), the Court upheld a Minnesota law that allowed parents of private school children to claim tax deductions from state income tax for the costs of "tuition, transportation, and textbooks." Ninety-five percent of the private school children in the state attended religious schools. Most of their parents availed themselves of this tax deduction. A taxpayer in the state challenged the law as an establishment of religion.

Using the *Lemon* test, the *Mueller* Court upheld the law. The tax deduction policy had a secular purpose of fostering quality education, Justice Rehnquist wrote for the Court. The motives of the legislature should not be considered: Laws should be upheld against charges of establishment "when a plausible secular purpose for the state's program may be discerned from the face of the statute." The law fostered no entanglement between church and state.

The "more difficult" question for the *Mueller* Court was whether the law had "the primary effect of advancing the sectarian aims of the non-public schools"—the principal ground on which the *Nyquist* Court a decade before had struck down such tax deduction policies. The *Mueller* Court distinguished *Nyquist* rather tendentiously. The saving features of the Minnesota law, Justice Rehnquist argued, were that this was a deduction for educational costs, not religious education; that it allowed deductions for the costs of "private" education, not "nonpublic" education; and that the deductions for religious education allowed by this law were sufficiently diluted by the many other deductions, for medical, charitable, and other causes. The *Nyquist* Court had characterized all such arguments as "ingenious schemes." The *Mueller* Court found that these features sufficiently "reduced the Establishment Clause objections" to the law. The state aid to sectarian schools, Justice Rehnquist concluded, "becomes available only as a result of numerous, private choices of individual parents of school-age children." This saves it from constitutional infirmity.[110]

In *Witters v. Washington Department of Services for the Blind* (1986), the Court upheld a state program that furnished aid to a visually impaired student attending a Christian college. The program provided funds "for special education and/or training in the professions, business or trades" for the visually impaired. Money was to be paid directly to eligible recipients, who were entitled to pursue education in the professional schools of their choice. Mr. Witters's condition qualified him for the funds. His profession of choice was the Christian ministry. He sought funds to attend a Christian college in preparation for the same. The state agency denied funding, on grounds that this was a direct funding of religious education prohibited by *Lemon* and its progeny.

The *Witters* Court disagreed. Applying the *Lemon* test, the Court found the policy, and its application to Mr. Witters, constitutional. The policy served a secular purpose of fostering educational and professional choice for all, including the handicapped. It involved no entanglement of church and state. Its primary purpose was to facilitate this student's professional education, which happened to be religious. This "is not one of 'the ingenious plans for channeling state aid to sectarian schools that periodically reach this Court,'" Justice Marshall wrote. "It creates no financial incentive for students to undertake sectarian education. It does not provide greater or broader benefits for recipients who apply their aid to religious education. . . . In this case, the fact that aid goes to individuals means that the decision to support religious education is made by the individual not by the State."[111]

In *Zobrest v. Catalina Foothills School District* (1993), the Court extended this logic from a college student to a high school student. Both federal and state disability acts required that a hearing-impaired student be furnished with a sign-language interpreter to accompany him or her to classes. The state furnished the interpreters at its own costs. Mr. Zobrest's hearing impairment qualified him for an interpreter's services. But he enrolled at a Catholic high school. The state refused to furnish him with an interpreter, on grounds that this would violate the *Lemon* rule that the state could give no direct aid to a religious school; moreover, the presence of a state-employed interpreter in a Catholic high school would foster an excessive entanglement between church and state.

Following *Mueller* and *Witters*, the *Zobrest* Court upheld the act as "a neutral government program dispensing aid not to schools but to handicapped children." "If a handicapped child chooses to enroll in a sectarian school," Chief Justice Rehnquist wrote for the Court, "we hold that the Establishment Clause does not prevent the school district from furnishing him with a sign-language interpreter."[112]

In *Agostini v. Felton* (1997), the Court extended this logic from the high school to the grade school, overturning the controversial case of *Aguilar v. Felton* (1985).[113] In the earlier *Aguilar* case, the Court had declared unconstitutional New York City's program that sent public school teachers into religious schools to offer remedial services to disadvantaged students. The remedial services in question in *Aguilar* were authorized and funded by Congress in the Elementary and Secondary Education Act (1965), known as the Title I program. The act set detailed standards both for student eligibility and for the education to be offered eligible students. More than 20,000 students in Catholic, Jewish, Protestant, and other religious schools in the city annually availed themselves of these Title I services. Lacking sufficient space in existing public buildings, and lacking sufficient land to build new public buildings adjacent to religious schools, New York City had chosen to offer the remedial services on site to eligible religious school students. State-funded public school teachers with materials were sent into the religious schools to teach the eligible religious school students. Field supervisors were sent out monthly to ensure compliance with the law, in particular to ensure that the Title I funds were directed to remedial, not religious, education in these schools. The program had been in place for nineteen years.

In the early 1980s, six taxpayers challenged the program as a violation of the disestablishment clause. The *Aguilar* Court agreed. Though "well-intentioned," Justice Brennan wrote for the Court in 1985, the program fosters an excessive entanglement of church and state. The religious schools receiving the Title I instructors are "pervasively sectarian," having as a "substantial purpose, the inculcation of religious values." Because of this, "ongoing inspection is required to ensure the absence of a religious message. In short, the scope and duration of New York's Title I program would require a permanent and pervasive State presence in the sectarian schools receiving aid." This, Justice Brennan concluded, is precisely the kind of excessive entanglement between church and state that the disestablishment clause outlaws.[114]

Four justices wrote bitter dissents in *Aguilar*. Justice Rehnquist charged that the Court "takes advantage of the 'Catch 22' paradox of its own creation, whereby aid must be supervised to ensure no entanglement, but the supervision itself is held to cause an entanglement."[115] Justice O'Connor denounced the majority opinion as "wooden," "formalistic," and "lacking in common sense." In the nineteen years of the program, she wrote, quoting the record, "there has never been a single incident in which in a Title I instructor 'subtly or overtly' attempted to 'indoctrinate the students in particular religious tenets at public expense.'" The real losers, she wrote, are disadvantaged children who happen to live "in cities where it is not economically or logistically feasible to provide public facilities for remedial education adjacent to the parochial school. . . . For these children, the Court's decision is tragic."[116]

In 1997, the *Agostini* Court, led by Justice O'Connor, overruled *Aguilar*. The ample procedural subtleties of the case aside,[117] the *Agostini* Court declared that its disestablishment law had changed sufficiently to offset the *Aguilar* holding. Citing *Zobrest*, Justice O'Connor wrote that the mere presence of a state employee in a religious institution is not a per se unconstitutional means of state inculcation of religion or the kind of "symbolic union of church and state" that violates the excessive entanglement prong. Citing *Witters*, she wrote that "we have departed from the rule . . . that all government aid that directly aids the educational functions of religious schools is invalid." The *Aguilar* Court had been "unduly zealous and mechanical" in its application of the *Lemon* test, the Court concluded. In particular, it had used the "excessive entanglement prong" to enforce a form of separationism that could not be squared with other constitutional values. Children in religious schools are just as entitled to Title I benefits as children in public schools. They cannot be denied these benefits simply for the sake of upholding "the abstract principle" of separation of church and state.[118]

Liberty of Conscience and Public Education

One of the Court's common concerns in the foregoing four cases on religious education was to protect liberty of conscience—the right of students and their parents to be free to choose a religious education without discrimination and deprivation by the state and without penalties for the choices they made.

The Court's concern for liberty of conscience is also reflected in the public education case of *Lee v. Weisman* (1992), which we encountered in analyzing the Court's new "coercion" approach (pages 160–161). The *Weisman* Court could easily have outlawed the state sponsorship of a rabbi's public school graduation prayers with a simple recitation of principle and precedent on the separation of church and state. After all, prayer in public schools has been banned since 1962. Though perennially controversial, the ban is one of the few hard and fast rules left in the Court's modern disestablishment law.

The *Weisman* Court's concern, however, was not so much the principle of separation of church and state as the principle of liberty of conscience. Justice Kennedy wrote:

> The undeniable fact is that the school district's supervision and control of a high school graduation ceremony puts public pressure, as well as peer pressure, on attending students to stand as a group, or at least maintain respectful silence during the Invocation and Benediction. The pressure, though subtle and indirect, can be as real as any overt compulsion. . . . *[F]or the dissenter of high school age, who has a reasonable perception that she is being forced by the State to pray in a manner her conscience will not allow, the injury is no less real.* . . . [T]he embarrassment and the intrusion of the religious exercise cannot be refuted by arguing that these prayers, and similar ones said in the future, are of a *de minimis* character. To do so would be an affront to the Rabbi who offered them and to all those for whom the prayers were an essential and profound recognition of divine authority. And for the same reason, we think that the intrusion is greater than the two minutes or so of time consumed for prayers like these. Assuming, as we must, that the prayers were offensive to the student and the parent who now object, the intrusion was both real and, in the context of a secondary school, a violation of the objector's rights.[119]

Equality and Religious Expression

These recent religion and education cases reflect the Court's new concern in disestablishment cases for the principle of liberty of conscience—the right freely to choose or to forgo religious instruction and ceremony. These cases also hint at the Court's new concern for the principle of religious equality—the right of persons of all faiths and of no faiths to receive equal protection and treatment under the law.

The principle of religious equality has long informed the Court's free exercise and free speech cases, as we saw (pages 126–130, 141–146). But this principle has also come to fuller expression in the Court's disestablishment cases respecting religious expression.

In two earlier cases, the Court had already used the principle of religious equality to buffer the principle of separationism. In *McDaniel v. Paty* (1978), the Court outlawed a Tennessee constitutional prohibition on ministers serving in political office. The stated purpose for the prohibition was to "assure" "the separation of church and state." The Court outlawed this prohibition as a violation of a clergy's free exercise rights to participate on equal terms in politics. Tennessee's concern for separation, Chief Justice Burger wrote for the Court, cannot "overbalance legitimate claims to the free exercise of religion." "The essence of the rationale underlying the Tennessee restriction on ministers is that if elected to public office they will necessarily exercise their powers and influence to promote the interests of one sect or thwart the interests of another thus pitting one against the others, contrary to the anti-establishment principle." "However widely that view may have been held in the 18th century," Chief Justice Burger concluded, today, "American experience provides no persuasive support for the fear that clergymen in public office will be less careful of anti-establishment interests or less faithful to their oaths of civil office than their unordained counterparts."[120]

In *Widmar v. Vincent* (1981), the Court declared that granting religious student groups equal access to state university facilities for voluntary meetings is "not incompatible with the Court's Establishment Clause cases." "It is possible—perhaps even foreseeable—that religious groups will benefit from access to University facilities," Justice Powell wrote. "But this Court has explained that a religious organization's enjoyment of merely 'incidental' benefits does not violate" the disestablishment clause.[121] Both religious and nonreligious students alike must be guaranteed equal access to public university forums. The religious speech in question is voluntary and private. In this instance, the principle of separation of church and state must give way to the principle of equality.

The Court has made ample use of this logic of equality in its most recent disestablishment cases. In *Board of Education v. Mergens* (1990), the Court used this principle to uphold the constitutionality of the Equal Access Act. The act mandated that voluntary groups of religious high school students be granted the same access to public high school facilities as is granted to nonreligious groups. "[T]he Act's prohibition of discrimination on the basis of 'political, philosophical, or other' speech," Justice O'Connor wrote for the Court:

is a sufficient basis for meeting the secular purpose prong of the *Lemon* test. Congress' avowed purpose—to prevent discrimination against religious and other types of speech—is undeniably secular. Even if some legislators were motivated by a conviction that religious speech in particular was valuable and worthy of protection, that alone would not invalidate the Act, because what is relevant is the legislative *purpose* of the statute, not the possible religious *motives* of the legislators who enacted the law.

Moreover, the primary effect of the statute is not to endorse religion, but to protect equality.

> [T]here is a crucial difference between *government* speech endorsing religion, which the Establishment Clause forbids, and *private* speech endorsing religion, which the Free Speech and Free Exercise Clauses protect. We think the secondary school students are mature enough and are likely to understand that a school does not endorse or support student speech that it merely permits on a nondiscriminatory basis.[122]

In *Rosenberger v. University of Virginia* (1995), the Court extended this equality principle from public forums to public funds. Voluntary groups of religious students at a state university were just as entitled to funding for its publications as voluntary groups of nonreligious students. To do otherwise, said the Court, would "select for disfavored treatment those student journalistic efforts with religious editorial viewpoints." It would entitle government "to scan the publication to ferret out views that principally manifest a belief in a divine being." This would manifest not equality of treatment but hostility to religion.[123]

In *Capitol Square Review and Advisory Board v. Pinette* (1995) the Court extended this equality principle to protect even the religious expression of a notably unpopular group. The City of Columbus, Ohio, had for more than a century made a ten-acre square surrounding the State House available "for use by the public . . . for free discussion of public questions, or for activities of a broad public purpose." All manner of public and private groups could use the square for meetings, speeches, and displays, so long as they applied for a permit and adhered to stated standards of sanitation, security, and the like. One December, the city put up its own Christmas tree. It granted a rabbi's application to put up a menorah in the square. But it denied the application from the Ku Klux Klan to put up its trademark cross. The Klan leader appealed.

The *Pinette* Court held that the free speech clause protected the Ku Klux Klan's display of the cross and that the disestablishment clause did not prevent it. Citing *Widmar* and its progeny, Justice Scalia wrote that such private expression of religion "is as fully protected under the Free Speech clause as secular private expression." Indeed, "a Free Speech clause without religion would be *Hamlet* without the prince." Moreover, for the state to open its public forum to private religious expression is no establishment of religion. "Religious expression cannot be said to violate the Establishment Clause where it (1) is purely private and (2) occurs in a traditional or designated public forum, publicly announced, and open to all on *equal terms.*"[124]

Conclusions

In 1986, the distinguished American historian Leonard Levy wrote that "the Court has managed to unite those who stand at polar opposites on the results that the Court reaches; a strict separationist and a zealous accommodationist are likely to agree that the Supreme Court would not recognize an establishment of religion if it took life and bit the Justices."[125]

While some of the Court's cases since 1986 have shown hopeful signs of a more integrated law of disestablishment, this description remains largely apt. Few areas of law today are so riven with wild generalizations and hair-splitting distinctions, so given to grand statements of principle and petty applications of precept, so rife with selective readings of history and inventive renderings of precedent. Few areas of law hold such a massive jumble of juxtaposed doctrines and rules. Even a sympathetic reader of the Court's modern disestablishment decisions is tempted to apply to it the definition that Oliver Wendell Holmes Jr. once applied to the common law: "chaos with an index."

It is apt, in this context, to be reminded of the founders' original vision of the disestablishment clause. In the founders' view, the disestablishment clause was designed to complement the free exercise clause in the protection of religious liberty. The free exercise clause outlawed government *proscriptions* of religion—actions that unduly burdened the conscience, restricted religious expression, discriminated against religion, or invaded the autonomy of churches and other religious bodies. The disestablishment clause outlawed government *prescriptions* of religion—actions that unduly coerced the conscience, mandated forms of religious expression, discriminated in favor of religion, or improperly allied the state with churches or other religious bodies. Both the free exercise and the disestablishment clauses thereby provided complementary protections to the first principles of the American experiment—liberty of conscience, freedom of religious expression, equality of plural faiths before the law, and separation of church and state.

In *Everson v. Board of Education* (1947), the Court effectively read each of these first principles into modern disestablishment law. But in most of its cases in the next forty years, the Court focused on the single principle of separation of church and state—yielding secularist dicta and decisions that seemed strangely out of place in a nation so widely devoted to a public religion and a religious public.[126] Since the mid-1980s, the Court has begun to widen its disestablishment calculus, introducing new lines of cases that attempt, albeit awkwardly, to strike new balances among the principles of separation of church and state, equality of plural religions, and liberty of conscience.

This emerging multiprincipled reading of the disestablishment clause holds considerable promise. To be sure, a strong reading of the principle of separation of church and state, evident in some modern First Amendment cases, remains essential.[127] Government officials have no constitutional business interfering in the internal affairs of religious groups. Religious officials have no constitutional business converting the offices of government into instruments of their mission and ministry. Government has no business funding, sponsoring, or actively involving itself in the religious exercises of a particular religious group or religious official. Religious groups have no business drawing on government sponsorship or funding for their core religious exercises. All such conduct violates the principle of separation of church and state and should be outlawed by the disestablishment clause.

But a categorical insistence on the principle of separation of church and state avails us rather little. James Madison warned in 1833 that "it may not be easy, in every possible case, to trace the line of separation between the rights of Religion and the Civil authority, with such distinctness, as to avoid collisions & doubts on *unessential points*."[128] This caveat has become even more salient today. The modern welfare state, for better or worse, reaches deeply into virtually all aspects of modern life—through its network of education, charity, welfare, child care, health care, construction, zoning, workplace, taxation, and sundry other regulations. Madison's solution was "an entire abstinence of the Government from interference [with religion] in any way whatever, beyond the necessity of preserving public order, & protecting each sect against trespasses on its legal rights by others."[129] This traditional understanding of a minimal state role in the life of society in general, and of religious bodies in particular—however alluring it may be in theory—is no longer realistic in practice.

It is thus even more imperative today than in Madison's day that the principle of separation of church and state not be pressed to reach, what Madison called, the "unessentials." It is one thing for the Court to outlaw daily Christian prayers and broadcasted Bible readings from the public school, quite another thing to ban moments of silence and private displays of the Decalogue in the same schools. It is one thing to bar direct tax support for religious education, quite another thing to bar tax deductions for parents who wish to educate their children in the faith. It is one thing to prevent government officials from delegating their core police powers to religious bodies, quite another thing to prevent them from facilitating the charitable services of voluntary religious and nonreligious associations alike. It is one thing to outlaw governmental prescriptions of prayers, ceremonies, and symbols in public forums, quite another thing to outlaw governmental accommodations of private prayers, ceremonies, and symbols in public forums. To press separationist logic too deeply into "unessentials" not only "trivializes" the place of religion in public and private life, as Stephen Carter argues.[130] It also trivializes the power of the Constitution, converting it from a coda of cardinal principles of national law into a codex of petty precepts of local life.

Too zealous an interpretation of the principle of separation of church and state also runs afoul of other constitutive principles of the disestablishment clause—particularly the principles of liberty of conscience and religious equality. The Court must be at least as zealous in protecting religious conscience from secular coercion as protecting secular conscience from religious coercion. The Court should be at least as concerned to ensure the equal treatment of religion as to ensure the equality of religion and nonreligion. It is no violation of the principle of separation of church and state when a legislature or court accommodates judiciously the conscientious scruples of a religious individual or the cardinal callings of a religious body. It is also no violation of this principle when government grants religious individuals and institutions equal access to state benefits, public forums, or tax disbursements that are open to nonreligionists similarly situated. To do otherwise is, indeed, to move toward what Justice Stewart once called "the establishment of a religion of secularism."[131]

9

RELIGIOUS LIBERTY
DOCTRINE IN MINIATURE
Tax Exemption of Religious Property

The foregoing four chapters have provided a bird's-eye view of the development of American constitutional laws touching religion. Chapters 5 and 6 analyzed the two tracks of religious liberty law that prevailed from 1789 to 1940: state constitutional provisions and federal constitutional cases. Chapters 7 and 8 analyzed the Supreme Court's merger of these two tracks of law in its free exercise and disestablishment cases since *Cantwell v. Connecticut* (1940) and *Everson v. Board of Education* (1947).

My principal aim in the foregoing four chapters has been to see a bit of the concreteness and complexity of the American constitutional experiment in religious liberty. My particular concern has been to watch the general plight of the first principles on which this experiment was founded—liberty of conscience, freedom of exercise, religious equality, religious pluralism, separation of church and state, and disestablishment of religion.

The Constitutional Conundrums of Tax Exemption

This chapter takes up one very specific issue that cuts across the foregoing four chapters—whether state tax exemptions of religious property are a valid constitutional practice or a simple historical anomaly.[1] This is by no means the only issue to cut across these four chapters, nor does it have the instant political intrigue of something like prayer in schools or bans on yarmulkes. But what it lacks in political intrigue, this nitty-gritty issue makes up for in constitutional intricacy. Questions of state tax exemption of religious property capture in miniature some of the hardest questions to confront the American experiment in religious liberty throughout its history.

First, property tax exemption questions illustrate the tensions between state and federal laws on religious liberty. Property taxation and exemption have, since the beginning of the republic, been the exclusive prerogative of the states (save in times of war or emergency).[2] By 1940, every state had detailed statutes, and thirty-three states had constitutional guarantees on tax exemption for religious properties.[3] These provisions ranged widely. Some states restricted tax exemptions only to actual worship centers that were regularly used and owned by properly incorporated religious bodies—and in practice made it difficult for Catholics, Jews, and new religious faiths to acquire exemptions. Other states granted exemptions to all religious properties, regardless of their use, ownership, or size—and in practice granted exemptions to any religious group that applied for the same in good faith. Most states fell between these extremes—the exact parameters of each state's law often the product of decades of intense local lobbying, legislation, and litigation.

After *Cantwell* and *Everson* applied the First Amendment religion clauses to the states, the federal courts became an attractive new forum for these disputes, and the First Amendment an attractive new norm to adduce. Those denied tax exemptions for their properties filed actions claiming that the state violated their free exercise rights. Those opposed to such exemptions filed actions claiming that the state had made a law respecting an establishment of religion. Scores of such cases were filed in state and federal courts in the 1940s and thereafter. Three cases were appealed unsuccessfully to the Supreme Court in the 1950s and 1960s.[4] How could or should the Court craft a general constitutional law on this diverse and divisive local issue?

Second, tax exemption questions highlight the tension that has emerged between the religion clauses of the First Amendment under recent judicial interpretation. The disestablishment clause forbids government from imparting special benefits to religious groups. The free exercise clause forbids government from imposing special burdens on religious groups. Neither the exemption nor the taxation of religious property appears to satisfy the mandates of both clauses. To exempt religious property, while taxing that of other nonreligious groups, appears to violate the "no special benefit" mandate of the disestablishment clause. To tax religious property, while exempting that of other nonprofit groups, appears to violate the "no special burden" mandate of the free exercise clause. The controversy thus seems to fall within the *terra incognita* between the First Amendment religion clauses.

Third, tax exemption puts squarely before us the question of how to define religion at law. Under most state laws, tax exemptions are given to *reli-*

gious properties or to properties devoted to *religious* uses and/or owned by *religious* parties. Proof of religion is thus unavoidable under such provisions. Historically, the issue was considered largely a matter of common sense and local consensus; few definitions of religion were offered in statutes, let alone in state constitutions. In practice, the question was whether to set the legal line of religion at Protestantism, Christianity, or theism. That question was resolved almost county by county, commissioner by commissioner when it came to tax exemptions.

The exponential rise of new or newly prominent religious groups in recent decades has tested the edges, and efficacy, of these traditional religion-based tax exemptions. How is the law to decide on the tax exempt status of the properties of Scientologists, Wiccans, the Unification Church, ethical clubs, faith families, communitarian religions, personality cults, nontheistic faiths, and any number of the more than 1,000 religious groups in America—together with their parsonages, monasteries, schools, charities, mission stations, retreat centers, youth camps, recreation centers, publishing houses, and the like. If all such new groups receive tax exemptions for all their properties, does this not place an increasingly disproportionate burden on remaining nonreligious properties? If all such new groups are denied tax exemption for their properties, does this not unduly favor those traditional religions that receive tax exemptions?

The United States Supreme Court has only once addressed these constitutional questions of tax exemption of religious property.[5] In *Walz v. Tax Commission* (1970), the United States Supreme Court charted a "course between the two Religion Clauses" and upheld the constitutionality of such state property tax exemptions. At issue in *Walz* was a New York law, typical of laws in other states, that exempts "real or personal property used exclusively for religious, educational or charitable purposes as defined by law and owned by any [nonprofit] corporation or association organized or conducted exclusively for one or more of such purposes."

In an opinion by Chief Justice Burger, the Court upheld the New York law with arguments from neutrality, separationism, and history. First, the Court declared, such exemptions are accorded in a "neutral manner" not only to religious groups but also to a broad class of charitable, educational, social service, and other nonprofit groups. The exemption affords these groups only "indirect" support, not a direct subsidy.[6] Such neutrally allocated, indirect support neither establishes religious groups nor "converts" them "into arms of the state."

Second, the Court declared, such exemptions foster the separation of church and state. Taxation, by contrast, would "tend to expand" such involvement through tax valuations and assessments of, and government liens and foreclosures on, religious property. The creation of such new channels of cooperation and confrontation would cause too "excessive [an] entanglement" between church and state to be countenanced by the disestablishment clause.

Third, the Court declared, tax exemptions of religious property are the product of an "unbroken" history that "covers our entire national existence and indeed predates it." Such exemptions were customarily accorded by the colonists. They have been sanctioned by Congress and state legislatures for more than two centuries. They have not "led to" an established religion but have "operated affirmatively to help guarantee the free exercise of all forms of religious belief." To disinter a practice so "deeply embedded" in our culture and so widely accepted by "common consent" requires a more compelling case. From these arguments, the Court concluded that tax exemptions of religious property, while neither proscribed by the disestablishment clause nor prescribed by the free exercise clause, are, nonetheless, constitutionally permissible.[7]

The Court has repeated this *Walz* rationale in several subsequent cases involving income and sales tax exemptions.[8] "The collection and payment of [a] generally applicable tax," the Court declared in 1990, "imposes no constitutionally significant burden on [an organization's] religious practices and beliefs. The Free Exercise Clause accordingly does not require the State to grant appellant an exemption from its generally applicable . . . tax."[9] But if a legislature does choose to exempt a religious organization, it must follow the *Walz* course of "benevolent neutrality" to survive disestablishment clause scrutiny. As Justice Brennan put it for the Court in 1989:

> Every tax exemption constitutes a subsidy that affects non-qualifying tax payers, forcing them to become "indirect and vicarious 'donors.'" Insofar as that subsidy is conferred upon a wide array of nonsectarian groups as well as religious organizations in pursuit of some legitimate secular end, the fact that religious groups benefit incidentally does not deprive the subsidy of the secular purpose and primary effect mandated by the Establishment Clause. However when government directs a subsidy exclusively to religious organizations that is not required by the Free Exercise Clause and that either burdens nonbeneficiaries markedly or cannot reasonably be seen as removing a significant state-imposed deterrent to the free exercise of religion, . . . it "provide[s] unjustifiable awards of assistance to religious organizations" and cannot but "convey[y] a message of endorsement" to slighted members of the community.[10]

While the *Walz* Court's conclusion on so tender and tempestuous an issue as such tax exemption of religious property may have been inevitable, its arguments are not ineluctable.

The argument from neutrality does not address the question whether an exemption given for a *religious* use of property is constitutionally permissible. The Court argues that because the state exempts properties devoted to charitable, educational, and other welfare uses, it is constitutionally permissible also to exempt property devoted to religious uses. The Constitution, however, permits government establishments of charity, education, and other forms of social welfare. It forbids government establishments of religion. That exemptions are accorded in a neutral manner for various nonreligious uses of property, therefore, has little bearing on the question of the constitutionality of exemptions for religious uses of property.

The Court's separationism argument is contrived. The Court divines a list of interactions between church and state that taxation of religious property may occasion—tax valuations, foreclosures, and others. But one can devise a list of interactions that tax exemption does occasion—reapplications for exemption, reviews of past uses, reports on present uses, and others. The Court argues that such interactions will result in an unconstitutional "entanglement" between church and state. But the constitutionality of more intrusive and immediate interactions have been consistently upheld against disestablishment clause challenges, when, for example, religious properties are zoned, religious buildings are landmarked, religious societies are incorporated, religious employers are audited, religious broadcasters and publishers are regulated, intrachurch disputes are adjudicated, and many other instances.[11] The expansion of the forms and the functions of the state have made such interactions between the state and religious institutions both inevitable and necessary. The incidental and isolated interaction that would result from the taxation of religious property is trivial by comparison.

The Court's historical argument depends too heavily upon selective presentation of evidence. The Court asserts that tax exemptions of religious property have been adopted by "common consent" for more than two centuries. But a strong vein of criticism has long accompanied the practice in America. The Court asserts that such exemptions have not "led to" an establishment of religion. But historically these exemptions were among the privileges of established religions, whereas dissenting religions were taxed; the issue is whether such exemptions have shed the chrysalis of establishment. The Court adduces numerous examples of earlier tax laws that exempted religious property. But it ignores the variety of *theories* that supported these laws. The Court asserts that such exemption laws "historically reflect the concern of [their] authors" to avoid the "dangers of hostility to religion inherent in the imposition of property taxes." But little evidence from congressional and constitutional debates on tax exemption supports this assertion.

In an attempt to illustrate and integrate some of the general themes of the foregoing four chapters, this chapter traces briefly the history of tax exemption of religious property in America and reconsiders the constitutionality of such exemptions in light of recent First Amendment opinions and commentaries. I conclude that tax exemption of religious properties are consti-

tutionally valid but make a rather different argument for them than that offered by *Walz*.

Tax Exemptions of Religious Property in the Past

Tax exemption of religious property is an ancient privilege. It has roots in
ancient Israel and Sumeria and was accorded to religious properties in the
Greek, Roman, and Christian traditions of the West.[12]

Modern American laws of tax exemption of religious property are rooted
in two more recent traditions: (1) a *common law* tradition, which accorded
such exemptions to established churches that discharged certain state burdens; and (2) an *equity law* tradition, which accorded such exemptions to
all churches that dispensed certain social benefits.[13] These two traditions
have contributed to the widespread development of colonial and then state
laws that exempt religious property from taxation. There are, however,
strong tensions between these two traditions as well, which manifest themselves in both historical and contemporary property tax exemption laws.[14]

Common Law Sources

The English common law that prevailed in most American colonies treated
religion as an affair of law and the church as an agency of the state. In the
course of the sixteenth-century English Reformation, the Tudor monarchs
had consolidated their authority over religion and the church and subjected
them to comprehensive ecclesiastical laws enforceable by both state and
church courts. Many of these laws were adopted or emulated in the American colonies. Tax exemption of religious property was part of this broader
set of ecclesiastical laws.[15]

The common law prescribed orthodox doctrine, liturgy, and morality
and proscribed various forms of heresy, dissent, and nonconformity. Communicant status in the established church was a condition for citizenship
status in the commonwealth. Religious dissenters, if tolerated, were foreclosed from most political and ecclesiastical offices and various social and
economic opportunities.

The common law governed the form and function of the established
church polity. It delineated the boundaries of the parishes and the location
of the churches. It determined the procedures of the vestries and the prerogatives of the consistories. It defined the duties of the clerics and the amount
of their compensation. It dictated the form of the church corporation and
the disposition of its endowments.

The common law regulated the acquisition and maintenance of the established church's properties. Magistrates were authorized to purchase or condemn private properties within their domains and to convey them to the es-

tablished church for meetinghouses, parsonages, cemeteries, and glebe lands. Stern criminal laws sanctioned interference with the enjoyment of these properties. Special property laws prohibited parties from gaining prescriptive or security interests in them. Magistrates levied taxes for the maintenance of the property and the clergy of the established church—the "tithe rates" to meet general ecclesiastical expenses, the "church rates" to pay for the repair or improvement of existing properties, and a host of minor fees. These religious taxes, though paid to the established church alone, were levied on all taxable persons in the commonwealth, regardless of their church affiliation.

The common law also governed the taxation of church and other religious properties. In both England and the colonies, the common law afforded no automatic and unrestricted tax exemption to church properties. All property that lay within the jurisdiction of the Crown and its colonial delegates, including religious property, was considered presumptively taxable at common law, unless it had been specially and specifically exempted by statute. Colonial legislatures readily accorded such privileges to the properties of political officials and to those of immigrants, indigents, and incapacitated persons.

Three restrictions, however, limited the availability of tax exemptions to colonial church properties. First, only certain types of religious property were considered exemptable at common law. The properties of properly incorporated established churches that were devoted to the appropriate "religious uses" prescribed by ecclesiastical law, such as sanctuaries, chapels, parsonages, glebes, and consecrated cemeteries, were generally exemptable. Established church properties, however, that lay vacant, that were devoted to nonreligious uses, or that were held by unincorporated religious bodies were generally taxable. Properties of dissenting religious groups were usually taxed, regardless of their use. Properties held personally by ministers were taxed in some colonies but exempted in others, with exemptions becoming more popular in the later colonial period. These latter colonies also exempted the properties held personally by political magistrates.

Second, these established church properties were given general exemptions only from the religious taxes that were levied for their own maintenance and use. To impose such taxes on established church properties would have been but "an idle ceremony."[16] Other property taxes, however—the quit-rents, poll taxes, land taxes, special assessments, hearth taxes, window taxes, and other occasional rates on realty and personalty—often fell on the properties of the established church as much as on all other properties. A universal exemption for these established church properties from all property taxes was the exception, not the rule, in the colonies.

Third, these tax exemptions could be held in abeyance in times of emergency or abandoned altogether if the tax liability imposed on remaining properties in the community proved too onerous. Thus in times of war, pestilence, poverty, or disaster, established churches and their clergy were expected to contribute to the public coffers regardless of their eligibility for exemption.

This common law pattern of tax exemptions and subsidies could be readily rationalized when the state was responsible to propagate and protect one established religion, to the exclusion of others. Established church corporations were effectively state agencies, their clergy effectively state officials. By devoting their properties to the religious uses prescribed by the common law, church corporations and their clergy were discharging the state's responsibility for the established religion. In return, they received tax support, tax exemptions, and other protections and privileges, like other state agencies. Occasionally the clergy themselves also received such privileges, like other state officials.

These privileges could be accorded, however, only if and to the extent that churches adhered to the established religion and devoted their properties to prescribed religious uses. Thus the properties of dissenting or wayward churches and those devoted to nonreligious uses were taxable. These privileges also could be accorded only in modest proportion, lest the established church grew ostentatious and opulent at the expense of the state and society, as it had prior to the Reformation. Thus the common law limited closely the scope of exemptions once granted.

Equity Sources

The law of equity, applied by English chancery courts and their colonial analogues, accorded tax exemptions to church properties with a different rationale.[17] Consistent with the common law courts, equity courts treated all religious property as presumptively taxable unless specially exempted by statute. Contrary to the common law courts, however, equity courts exempted church properties from taxation not because of the "religious uses" but because of the "charitable uses" to which they were devoted. Church properties could be exempted at equity only if, and to the extent that, they were used "charitably."

A definition of charity was derived from the famous English Statute of Charitable Uses of 1601. The statute regarded as charitable all activities that supported orphans, apprentices, or scholars, that sustained public works (like highways, prisons, and bridges), that subsidized schools and universities, or that succored indigent, ill, incapacitated, elderly, or "decayed" persons.[18] Through interpretation and application of the statute over time, equity courts developed a more general definition of charity as any activity that redounded "to the benefit of an indefinite number of persons, either by bringing their hearts or minds under the influence of education or religion, by relieving their bodies from disease, suffering, or constraint, by assisting them to establish themselves in life, by erecting or maintaining public buildings or works, or by otherwise lessening the burdens of government."[19]

The *effect*, not the intent, of the activity was critical to determining its charitable character. The charitable activity could be motivated by piety or pity; it could be meant to serve religious or secular persons and causes—so long as it yielded a distinctly "public benefit" to a sufficiently "indefinite number of persons." Religion and piety were considered an acceptable species, not a necessary source, of charity and benevolence.

Those institutions that devoted their properties to one or more such charitable uses or that had property entrusted to them for such charitable uses received a variety of equitable privileges. Special trust and testamentary doctrines, like the *cy pres* doctrine that allowed courts to follow the donor's intention so much as possible, enabled them to receive property by deeds and wills that were defective in form and generally unenforceable at common law. Special property rules enabled them to transfer goods and lands to beneficiaries, free from liens, fees, and excises. Special procedural rules allowed them to bring actions that were otherwise barred by the statute of limitations. Special tax rules afforded them both tax subsidies and tax exemptions. They received subsidies from the "poor rates," "education rates," and "charity taxes" that the authorities occasionally levied on the community. They received exemptions from taxes on those portions of their property that were "devoted to charitable uses and other public concernments."[20]

Both the amount of the subsidy and the scope of the exemption received by these charitable institutions were calculated on a case-by-case basis. Overseers, visitors, or commissioners (in later years, attorneys-general), regulated by the equity courts, periodically visited each charitable institution to assess its performance and to determine its needs. Thereafter they recommended to the equity court each charity's entitlement to subsidy and exemption. It was not unusual for the equity court to afford well-established and well-endowed charities only modest subsidies and minimal exemptions in a given year but to afford new and impoverished charities plentiful subsidies and plenary exemptions from tax.

This law of equity provided colonial churches with a second basis for receiving tax exemptions for their properties and tax subsidies for their activities. As religious institutions, they could receive the religious tax exemptions and subsidies afforded by the common law. As charitable institutions, they could receive the charitable tax exemptions and subsidies afforded by equity law. Although the exemptions and subsidies afforded by the common law were restricted by definition to established churches, those afforded by equity were available, at least in theory, to all churches.

Colonial established churches often served as charitable institutions. Church meetinghouses and chapels were used not only to conduct religious services but also to host town assemblies, political rallies, and public auctions, to hold educational and vocational classes, to maintain census rolls and marriage certificates, to house the community library, and to discharge a number of other public functions. Parsonages were used not only to house the minister's family but also to harbor orphans and widows, the sick and the handicapped, and victims of abuse and disaster. Glebe lands were farmed not only to sustain the priest and his family but also to support widows, sojourners, and needy members of the community. Moreover, charitable societies sponsored by the established churches, such as the famous Society for the Propagation of the Gospel in Foreign Parts, helped to found schools, orphanages, hospices, and almshouses throughout the colonies. These acts of public charity were vital parts of the established church's ministry and mission in the colonies. In return, the established churches and the charitable institutions that they founded were entitled to receive charitable tax exemptions and subsidies from the equity courts.

Established churches, however, held no monopoly on charitable activity. Nonconformist churches and private philanthropic groups under their sponsorship were equally active. These nonconformists often used their meetinghouses and parsonages for night shelters, relief stations, and refuge places. Quakers were famous in the seventeenth and eighteenth centuries for their diligence in establishing day schools, hospitals, hospices, almshouses, orphanages, poor farms, and workhouses all along the Atlantic seaboard. Scottish Presbyterians and Irish Catholics helped to form philanthropic groups, like the Scot's Charitable Society and the Charitable Irish Society, which sponsored and subsidized the families of new immigrants and newly emancipated indentured servants. Various religious groups contributed to the founding and later support of some of the great eastern universities and colleges, such as Harvard, William and Mary, Yale, Princeton, and others. In return, these nonconformist churches, and the charitable organizations that they established, received tax exemptions and subsidies from the equity courts.

These twin traditions of religious property exemptions stood sharply juxtaposed on the eve of the American Revolution. Equity courts accorded tax exemptions to any church properties that were devoted to charitable uses. Common law courts accorded tax exemptions only to established church properties that were devoted to prescribed religious uses. In some colonies, the sharp contrasts between these two traditions had begun to soften. Equity courts, following English precedents on "superstitious uses," had occasionally prevented the formation of charities by religious nonconformists. Colonial legislatures, responding to widespread popular agitation, had granted to some Protestant dissenting churches the right to exemption from religious taxes levied for the established church—though formidable administrative obstacles often obstructed the exercise of this right, and the ecclesiastical tax revenues were still generally paid to the established church alone.

State Constitutional Challenges

This colonial law of tax exemption of religious property continued largely uninterrupted in the early decades of the American republic. A number of the early state constitutions provided simply that "all the laws which have heretofore been adopted, used, and approved . . . and usually practised in the courts of law shall still remain and be in full force, until altered or repealed by the legislature."[21] State legislatures and judiciaries were specifically instructed that "all religious bodies or societies of men heretofore united or incorporated for the advancement of religion or learning, or for other pious or charitable purposes, shall be encouraged and protected in the enjoyment of the privileges, immunities, and estates, which they were accustomed to enjoy."[22] Religious bodies that were previously "united or incorporated" thus received the traditional exemptions afforded by the common law and equity law courts.

Three provisions in the new state constitutions and their amendments, however, became grounds for formidable new challenges to this traditional pattern of tax exemption of religious property.

First, all state constitutions eventually outlawed establishments of religion altogether, or at least the state impositions of religious taxes and other forms of compulsory support for religion. These prohibitions undercut the authority of state officials to support one religion over another, to prescribe religious beliefs, to levy religious taxes, and to govern church polities and properties. Religion was no longer an affair of government and law. The cleric was no longer a public official. The church was no longer a subsidized state agency. The meetinghouse was no longer a public property.

These disestablishment provisions rendered the traditional common law exemptions of religious property vulnerable to attack. The establishment rationale on which these exemptions had been based was no longer available. No other consistent rationale had as yet been offered. A small but persistent group of critics from the 1820s onward thus challenged these common law exemptions as vestiges of religious establishment. Their arguments lie at the heart of the anti-exemption case still today.

Such exemptions, critics argued, favor religious groups over nonreligious groups. To exempt owners of religious properties from "their portion of the cost of state services and protections" is not only to subsidize them but also to penalize the owners of nonreligious properties whose tax burdens are proportionately increased.[23] This form of religious subsidy and support, al-

beit indirect, cannot be countenanced under the disestablishment provisions of the state constitutions.

Furthermore, such exemptions favor well-vested, traditional religions
over struggling, newer religions. Since properties are taxed according to
their value, the "humble congregation in a small wooden church" can enjoy
only a fraction of the tax savings enjoyed by "the same-sized congregation
in the beautiful hewn palace, with painted windows, frescoed ceilings, and
silver mounted pews."[24] The disestablishment provisions, if they permit
government benefits to religion at all, mandate uniformity and neutrality in
such treatment. The "inequality and disparity" in the benefits afforded
religious groups under property tax exemption laws, therefore, cannot be
countenanced.[25]

Finally, critics argued, such exemptions encourage the conflation of
church and state. The "silent accumulations of [church] property" occa-
sioned by the laws of tax exemption and religious incorporation, James
Madison warned already in 1817, will inevitably result in "encroachments
by powerful Ecclesiastical Bodies" upon the public square and the political
process.[26] Several decades later, Ulysses Grant portended similarly that tax
exemptions had allowed churches to accumulate such "vast amounts of un-
taxed property" and to aggrandize such "vast political power" that "se-
questration without constitutional authority" and "bloody" confrontation
would eventually ensue. "The separation of Church and the State" required
that all "legal instruments encouraging ecclesiastical aggrandizement of
wealth and power" including tax exemptions, be "expunged."[27]

These criticisms were not just isolated musings. In the middle decades of
the nineteenth century they appeared rather regularly in editorials, pamphlets, and petitions. Beginning in the later 1830s, officials in Virginia,
Pennsylvania, Massachusetts, Ohio, Indiana, Kentucky, and South Carolina
debated proposed constitutional amendments that would severely curtail if
not outlaw such exemptions.

Second, the inherited tax exemption laws were challenged by state
constitutional mandates to revise or to revoke English statutes. State constitutional conventions had initially received and ratified English statutes,
without much amendment or emendation. But as American nationalist
sentiment became more strident in the nineteenth century and judicial
criticisms of English law grew sharper, legislatures began to respond. A
number of states appointed committees to review English statutes and
precedents that had traditionally governed the colonies and states and to
purge those that were found odious or obsolete. Many British statutes
survived such "purges" only in revised form, if at all.

These constitutional purges of English statutes rendered the traditional
equity law of tax exemptions vulnerable to attack. One English statute that
was purged in most states was the English Statute of Charitable Uses of

1601, which traditionally undergirded both the charitable jurisdiction of equity courts and the law of charitable institutions that these courts had helped to devise. Several states thus removed charitable institutions from the jurisdiction of equity courts and relieved them of their traditional equitable privileges. The special testamentary, procedural, and property privileges previously accorded charities were removed. The special tax subsidies and tax exemptions were also withdrawn. Some courts also developed strict rules for the formation and functioning of new charitable institutions. Such institutions were required to procure corporate charters, to provide detailed annual reports of their charitable activities, and to limit severely their property and endowment holdings. In several cases, donations and devises to religious charities were invalidated, religious groups were denied charitable corporate charters, and religious functions were deemed "inappropriate" as charitable uses.[28]

Third, the inherited tax exemption laws were challenged by new state constitutional requirements that property taxes be "universally" applied. In the 1850s and thereafter, many state constitutional conventions thoroughly reformed their property taxation laws. The myriad species of special and sporadic taxes on realty and personalty were consolidated into a general annual tax on real property and a general *ad valorem* tax on various forms of personalty. The multiple layers of tax officials and tax offices were merged into more uniform state and municipal tax commissions. The antiquated tax valuation and tax assessment lists were thoroughly revised. The long lists of tax exemptions and immunities inherited from the colonial period were largely cast aside.

The revised state constitutions now started with the provision that "[t]axation shall be equal and uniform throughout the State, and all property, both real and personal, shall be taxed in proportion to its value."[29] The presumption was that all property was to be universally taxed. Tax exemptions, including those for religious properties, were now clearly an exception to generally applicable levies. They could be granted only if the "public welfare" would be advanced, or if other "good and compelling reasons" could be adduced.

Modern Theory of Tax Exemption

These three challenges prompted proponents of tax exemption of religious property into action. The disestablishment arguments against such exemptions had to be rebuffed. The equitable privileges of churches and their properties had to be restored. The good and compelling reasons for exemption had to be recited.

Later nineteenth-century statesmen and churchmen met these challenges forcefully and developed a theory of tax exemptions of religious property that is at the heart of the pro-exemption case still today. These early proponents did not forsake the common law tradition and equity law tradition of tax exemption in this effort. They fused these two traditions. The basic exemption theory of each tradition was preserved but was cast in more generic form. The basic exemption laws inherited from colonial times remained in place but were given more general application.

The modern theory of tax exemption of religious property was forged in the later nineteenth century in a massive outpouring of judicial opinions, legislative arguments, convention speeches, popular pamphlets, newspaper editorials, printed sermons, and scholarly papers.[30] Although these sources varied widely in quality and clarity, their basic premises and principles admit of rather short summary. "The policy on which the exemption of religious property is granted," declared the Connecticut Supreme Court, "is simply the encouragement of . . . churches."[31] For churches and other religious bodies serve to the advantage of both society in general and the state in particular. They dispense "social benefits" and discharge "state burdens."

Churches dispense intangible, but invaluable, benefits to society through their religious activities, exemption proponents argued. Churches cultivate public spiritedness. They induce citizens to "benevolence, charity, generosity, love of our fellowman, deference to rank, to age and sex, tenderness to the young, active sympathy for those in trouble and distress, beneficence to the destitute." Without such acts and dispositions, a "truly civil society . . . could not long endure."[32] Churches inculcate public morality. They teach chastity and continence, temperance and modesty, obedience and obligation, respect for the person and property of another. They have internal structures of authority to punish parishioners guilty of immorality. Such moral discipline is "probably of as much value to society in keeping the peace and preserving the rights of property as the most elaborate and expensive police system."[33] Churches enhance neighborhood values. Their "immaculate" buildings and grounds are aesthetically pleasing. They attract respected citizens. They promote stability of neighborhood populations.[34] Churches promote democratic principles and practices. They inspire citizens to participate in the political process and to vote for candidates. They instruct officials on moral principles and social needs. They preach against "injustice by the authorities" and "insurrection by the masses."[35] "Churches and religion, therefore," a Massachusetts tax commissioner put it, "make life and property more secure and promote peace, order, and prosperity in the community." Exemptions are thus granted "not that religion may increase . . . but that society may be benefitted."[36]

Churches not only dispense social benefits through their religious activities, exemption proponents argued, but also discharge state burdens through their charitable activities. They discharge the burdens of education through their parochial schools and colleges, educational and vocational programs, literary and literature societies. They discharge burdens of social welfare through their hostels and hospitals, almshouses and night shelters, counseling and crisis centers, youth camps and retirement homes. They discharge burdens of foreign aid through their programs for foreign missions and disaster relief. Churches must be considered, wrote one exuberant pamphleteer, "the most charitable of charities."[37] Through their voluntary social services, the churches save the state enormous costs that would "otherwise be imposed upon the public . . . by general taxation."[38] Tax exemption, proponents concluded, is a suitable *quid pro quo* for such services.

These new "state burden" and "social benefits" arguments in favor of tax exemption skillfully blended traditional arguments. Traditional common law theory taught that religious use exemptions were accorded to properties that discharged state burdens for the established religion. Traditional equity law theory taught that charitable use exemptions were accorded to any properties that dispensed social benefits. These arguments were now reversed and softened. Religious use exemptions, no longer justifiable on establishment grounds, were now justified on the basis of the distinctive social benefits dispensed by all religious groups. Charitable use exemptions, no longer justifiable on unspecified social benefit grounds, were now justified on the basis of the specific state responsibilities discharged by all religious groups. The new theory of tax exemptions thus captured the traditional arguments but recast them to broaden an unduly narrow category of religious use exemptions and to narrow an unduly broad category of charitable use exemptions.

Modern Tax Exemption Law

Not only the modern theory but also the modern law of tax exemption of religious property was forged in the latter half of the nineteenth century and the early part of the twentieth. Such exemptions no longer turned on the isolated statutes and equitable customs inherited from colonial times. Nearly one-half of the states developed new constitutional provisions that guaranteed such exemptions to all religious groups. The remainder of the states developed systematic statutory schemes that were either mandated by or validated under state constitutions.[39]

Consistent with the common law tradition, virtually all states exempted properties "devoted to religious uses" or "used for religious purposes." Most states insisted, however, that such property uses be "actual" and "real." Properties that had been abandoned or sporadically used for religious purposes in the past or that were merely purchased or planned for religious uses in the future were generally taxable. Most states also insisted that such properties be owned by a "religious association"; a few states, particularly in earlier decades, insisted further that such religious associations be incorporated under state law as religious corporations. A few states took no account of the identity of the property owner, so long as the exempt property was devoted to religious uses. This allowed investors to receive property exemptions by leasing them to churches.

The definition and delimitation of the phrase "religious use" was the subject of considerable legislation and litigation. Tax assessors and judges could no longer simply look to the uses prescribed by establishment laws, as they had done in colonial and early republican times. They could no longer simply consider the property uses of the one established church. A more generic and pluralistic definition was required. Over time, a vast spectrum of "religious use" exemptions emerged among the states, ranging from the extremely narrow definitions adopted by such states as Pennsylvania and Illinois to the expansive definitions adopted by such states as Kentucky and California.

All states exempted sanctuaries, synagogues, and other properties devoted to religious worship services, together with the driveways, walkways, parking lots, and other immediate property necessary for their reasonable use. Two conditions, however, were imposed by most states. First, the religious worship that occurred in those buildings had to be "public" in character. Thus secluded cloisters and monasteries, private chapels in orphanages or schools, and the worship facilities of small, exclusive cults, lodges, or those who engaged in private meditation or family worship were often not eligible for religious use exemptions. Second, the property devoted to religious uses had to be "improved." Thus agrarian communal religions, youth retreat groups, or naturalist religions that worshiped in crude temporary shelters or in designated regions of the countryside generally did not receive religious use exemptions.

A few states limited their religious use exemptions to these public worship facilities alone and subjected other religious properties to taxation, even when they were occasionally used for religious services. Most states, however—either by express statutory provision or, more frequently, through judicial interpretation—extended the scope of such exemptions well beyond this narrow core.

First, religious use exemptions were generally accorded to the properties that supported the ministry of the exempted church. Church buildings annexed to or near the church, synagogue, or temple and used for catechization, fellowship, weddings, sanctuary storage, and comparable functions were usually exempted in such states, though acreage and space limitations were sometimes imposed. Separate properties, however, that housed religious printing facilities, mission and evangelism centers, administrative and governmental offices, or religious educational and vocational facilities were often not eligible for religious use exemptions—though sometimes they were eligible for charitable use exemptions.

Second, more than half the states accorded religious use exemptions to parsonages, rectories, and other living quarters of clergy and their families, though strict limitations were often imposed on the size and value of such quarters. A few states insisted further that such quarters be actually occupied by an ordained cleric serving the church that owned the parsonage, not merely a retired minister, church administrator, custodian, or missionary on furlough.

Third, a small minority of states extended religious use exemptions even further to religious properties that provided "auxiliary religious services" to their parishioners. In these states, church-run schools, cemeteries, counseling centers, summer camps, retirement homes, retreat centers, publication and distribution centers, and even wineries, restaurants, and recreation facilities were granted religious use exemptions.

Consistent with the equity law tradition, all states also exempted properties that were devoted to "charitable," "benevolent," or "eleemosynary" uses or purposes. The colonial definition of charity remained in effect: Any use of property that provided distinctive public services to a sufficiently indefinite number of persons was considered charitable. The conditions that were imposed on religious use exemptions were generally also imposed on charitable use exemptions. The charitable use had to be "actual" and "public," and the exempt property usually had to be owned by a charitable association.

Religious associations could readily avail themselves of these charitable use exemptions for their properties. Aside from "purely sacerdotal associations," most religious associations were also considered to be charitable associations. Aside from religious worship services, most religious uses of property were also considered to be charitable uses of property. Although the core "religious uses" and core "charitable uses" of religious property remained distinctive, most religious property uses could be considered at once "religious" and "charitable" under state exemption laws. Thus a variety of uses and improvements of religious property that clearly served the ministry and mission of a religious association were exempted under charitable use categories—the properties occupied and used by church administrative centers, seminaries, Bible societies, missionary societies, religious publishers, church youth camps and retreat centers, parochial schools, Sunday schools, church women's societies, and many others.

Three exemption patterns emerged as a result of these overlapping categories of exempt uses of religious property. First, several states allowed religious associations to mix both religious uses and charitable uses of their properties and to choose either one or both forms of exemption for such uses. Religious use exemptions were often more attractive, since they required only an annual petition for renewal to the local tax assessor. Charitable use exemptions not only required such a petition but also subjected the association to the supervisory jurisdiction of the attorney-general or a charitable commissioner or visitor.

Second, several other states required religious associations to decide whether religious or charitable use of their properties was "primary" or "predominant" and to petition for exemption of their property based on that use alone. If an association could demonstrate that most of the property was devoted to one such exempt use for the majority of the time, an exemption was granted—even if the property was also put to other incidental exempt and nonexempt uses.

Third, a few states required either exclusive religious use or exclusive charitable use of the exempt property. Under such a wooden classification system, religious organizations had to choose either to truncate or to bifurcate their activities. Those organizations that resisted such a choice—for reasons of ideology or economics—on occasion were denied exemption altogether.

The modern law of tax exemption of religious property reflects both the common law tradition and the equity law tradition—as well the tensions between them. It reflects the traditional common law concern to exempt property devoted to religious uses, to predicate such exemptions on explicit statutory authority, to limit the scope of exempt religious uses through strict interpretation of these statutes, to restrict the size and value of properties that fall within this scope, and to restrict the discretion of officials who award exemptions. It also reflects the traditional equity law concern to exempt property devoted to charitable uses, to engage in inventive exegesis of exemption statutes, to expand the scope of exemptions well beyond their original core, and to accord broad discretion to officials to make case-by-case determinations of whether and to what extent a given property can be exempted.

Tax Exemptions of Religious Property at Present

Both the theory and the law of tax exemption of religious property forged in the later nineteenth and early twentieth centuries remain firmly in place among the states today. Judicial opinions continue to recite the "social benefit" and "state burden" arguments that support such exemptions.[40] The inherited constitutional and statutory exemption provisions remain the state law today, although they have been heavily amended and subject to broad judicial interpretation.

The *Walz* case has discouraged, though not foreclosed, First Amendment challenges to these theories and laws.[41] Yet litigation concerning such exemptions has continued apace since 1970 when the *Walz* decision was issued—in part because of the exponential rise of new religious groups that have sought to avail themselves of such exemptions, in part because of the terseness of state exemption provisions and the ambiguity of judicial precedents interpreting them.

Tax Exemptions for New Religious Groups

The exponential rise of new or newly prominent religious groups in America since the 1940s has tested the edges, and the efficacy, of religious use exemptions. Today, there are more than 1,000 religious groups in the United States.[42] Alongside long-standing Christian, Jewish, Muslim, and Native American religious groups, there have now emerged sizeable populations of Hindus, Buddhists, Sikhs, Rastafarians, Unification Church Members, Christian Scientists, Scientologists, and others. In addition, there have emerged hundreds of small, highly selective communitarian religions, faith families, ethical clubs, personality cults, and many other groups.

These new or newly prominent religious groups have sought the same tax exemptions for their properties that have been enjoyed by religious groups with longer tenure in the United States. Courts and commissioners have had few criteria at their disposal to evaluate these petitions for exemption. State property tax laws, unlike federal income tax laws, generally offer no definition of a "religious" association or a "religious" use of property. State and federal constitutional laws offer only rudimentary and inconsistent definitions of "religion."[43] Negotiating the boundary between religion and nonreligion for purposes of deciding the tax status of these groups has thus been the subject of intense litigation in the state courts.

In evaluating new petitions for tax exemption, state courts have developed four alternative tests for "religion." These can be called the (1) common sense; (2) deference; (3) minimal theism; and (4) multifactual analysis tests, respectively. The first two tests make no inquiry into a petitioner's religious beliefs. The other two tests scrutinize the religious beliefs more closely. Application of these tests has produced widely varying results.

Courts in some jurisdictions have adopted a simple *common sense test* to evaluate petitions for tax exemption. They view the "objective facts" of the petitioner's property uses but studiously avoid inquiry into the petitioner's religious inspirations or motivations. They then make a "common sense judgment" regarding whether such uses are religious or secular.

This test is applied primarily in cases raising seemingly spurious petitions for tax exemption. In *Golden Writ of God v. Department of Revenue* (1986), for example, the Supreme Court of Oregon was asked to determine the tax status of some 230 acres of largely untilled farmland, occupied by a large house and a barn. The property was owned by a nonprofit organization consisting of a dozen members who lived in the house and who had recently conveyed their own property to the organization. Members of the organization regarded the property as a "tabernacle," its plants as symbols of divine attributes, and its animals as sacred creatures. They also regarded work on the property as a form of spiritual discipline. The court denied the religious use exemption, arguing that the "objective facts demonstrate non-religious use of the property." "The farmland with a house and a barn were just that," the court reasoned. "The house was primarily used for living quarters, . . . the untilled farmland was otherwise uncultivated and possessed no unusual attributes other than being a nice place to run horses, to study nature and to meditate or pray."[44] Courts in other jurisdictions have used similar common sense arguments to deny exemptions to open lands that are "consecrated" as spiritual havens, farms and ranches that are dedicated to "spiritual catharsis," or private homes that petitioners deem to be "shrines," "cathedrals," or other places of religious worship.[45]

Whereas the common sense test relies heavily on the court's judgment of the good faith of the petitioner's application, the *deference test* relies heavily on the petitioner's self-characterization of its religion. In *Holy Spirit Association for Unification of World Christianity v. Tax Commission* (1982), the New York Court of Appeals formulated the test as follows:

> In determining whether a particular ecclesiastical body has been organized and [uses its property] exclusively for religious purposes the courts may not inquire into or classify the content of the doctrine, dogmas, and teachings held by that body to be integral to its religion but must accept that body's characterization of its own beliefs and activities . . . so long as that characterization is made in good faith and is not sham.[46]

The court applied this test to determine the tax status of the administrative headquarters, missionary residence, and storage facilities owned and operated by the Unification Church, founded by the Reverend Sun Myung Moon. Both the New York tax commissioner and lower courts had denied the exemption because they determined that the Unification doctrine was "so inextricably interwoven with political motives and activities" that it could not be regarded as religious, regardless of the sincerity of the church's members. The New York Court of Appeals reversed. After quoting at length from the religious organization's own description of its beliefs and purposes, the court concluded that "what have been characterized below as political and economic beliefs and activities are in the view of the Church integral aspects of its religious doctrine and program." Because the church's properties are integral to the successful maintenance and dissemination of its religion, the court judged the property had to be exempt from taxation.[47] Other courts have followed this analysis, deferring to a religious organization's good faith self-declarations of both its religion and of what constitutes a religious property and religious property use.[48]

Other courts have adopted a *minimal theism test* to evaluate petitions for exemption submitted by new religious groups. Petitioners must at least "exhibit the minimal requirements of a religion." Such requirements are defined as a "sincere and meaningful belief in God occupying in the life of its possessors a place parallel to that occupied by God in traditional religions and dedicat[ion] to the practice of that belief."[49] Property used in support of such religious beliefs is eligible for exemption.

This minimal theism test has been applied both to affirm and to deny petitions for tax exemption. In *Roberts v. Ravenwood Church of Wicca* (1982), for example, the Supreme Court of Georgia upheld the tax exempt status of a two-story suburban home owned and operated by the Wiccan church. The Wiccan church believed in "a primordial, supernatural force" that created the world and sustained its creatures in a "karmic circle." Members of this religion were seen as divine sparks of this supernatural force with moral responsibilities to themselves and to nature. The church observed eight formal Sabbaths per year and celebrated communion, marriage, and other religious rituals. The two-story home was used both for weekly religious services and for the residence of the church founder, her parishioners, and some nonparishioner tenants. Convinced that the church was sufficiently and sincerely theistic, the court concluded that its property was being used for religious worship and was therefore exempt from taxation.[50]

By contrast, in *Religious Society of Families v. Assessor* (1973), the New York Supreme Court denied tax exemption for the property of the Religious Society of Families, a new cult founded by one "Calvin of the Universe." The society was professedly "this-worldly" in orientation, believing in a variety of ecological and political causes, eugenics, scientific humanism, monogamous relationships, and death by suicide. It was organized as a "neo-monastic community," devoted to agricultural production. Upon rehearsing theistic definitions of religion in dictionaries and earlier cases, the court concluded that the society was "not religious as religion is traditionally defined" and declared its property taxable.[51]

Still other courts have developed a comprehensive *multifactual analysis test* to evaluate petitions for state property tax exemption. In *Ideal Life Church of Lake Elmo v. County of Washington* (1981), the Supreme Court of Minnesota rejected simple litmus tests and dictionary definitions of religion and insisted that each petition for property tax exemption must be subjected to a "multifactual analysis." Under this test, a court or commissioner must consider such factors as the motives for the formation of the religious organization, the presence of a supreme being or something in lieu thereof in the belief system, the presence and sophistication of religious doctrine, the practice and celebration of religious liturgies or rites, the degree of formal religious training required for the religious leaders, the strictures on the ability of members simultaneously to practice other religions, and other factors. Thereafter, the court must make a reasoned decision whether the petitioner is a religious group and whether its property is devoted to religious uses. This approach is modeled, in part, on comparable criteria used by the Internal Revenue Service to determine a group's eligibility for exemption as a "church" under the Internal Revenue Code.[52]

The *Ideal Life* court used this multifactual analysis to reject the exemption petition. The church had been chartered and the minister had been ordained by the Universal Life Church of Modesto, California, upon petitioner's payment by mail of seventy dollars. The church was comprised of some eighteen members, most of whom were also members of one family and each of whom accepted the principles of freedom, fraternity, and choice. Church members professed a general theism but held to no formal religious doctrine, celebrated no religious rituals, and had no restrictions about practicing other faiths. The "church building" was previously a private home, which family members had donated to the church immediately after its organization. It was used both for the family's residence and for the monthly religious meetings, which were apparently open to the public, but neither advertised to nor frequented by the public. Regardless of the petitioner's characterization of itself as a sincere, bona fide religious organization, the court denied the church's petition for tax exemption.[53]

In *Minnesota v. American Fundamentalist Church* (1995), the same Minnesota Supreme Court effectively combined this multifactual approach with the deference approach that considers the petitioner's sincerity. A court should first inquire into the sincerity of a petitioner, the *American Fundamentalist* court argued, and only in doubtful cases turn to these multiple factors to assess their petitioner. Such a combined approach, the court reasoned, "avoid[s] the risk of favoring religious bodies which are similar to mainline churches, and disfavoring others which may be equally sincere, but are non-traditional in their organization, their theology or their methods of worship."

Using this combined approach, the *American Fundamentalist* court denied the petition for tax exemption. The Court noted the petitioner's claim of sincerity and noted its good works—offering religious literature to the public, food to the poor, counseling for the needy, and occasionally hosting a wedding. But using the multiple criteria set out in *Ideal Life,* the Court concluded that this was a "sham" organization seeking tax avoidance. The petitioner's church and parsonage were in reality simply a private home, which was also used as the base for a rather profitable engineering company. The church membership consisted largely of the petitioner's family. The faith lacked any kind of formal training for its ministers and had no specific rituals or sacraments and no liturgy. Much of its literature and most of the communal religious discussions in the home were dominated by concerns for tax avoidance. Contrary to the self-declarations of the petitioner, the Court concluded, this was not a religious organization, and it was not entitled to a tax exemption for its property.[54]

These four tests—common sense, deference, minimal theism, and multifactual analysis—strike different balances between sophistication of analysis, on the one hand, and intrusiveness of inquiry, on the other. The deference test avoids intrusive inquiry into the beliefs of the petitioner but does so at the cost of analytical sophistication. The multifactual analytical test affords close analysis of each petition but does so at the cost of religious intrusion. The common sense test is neither very sophisticated nor very intrusive; the minimal theism test is both more sophisticated and more intrusive, inquiring into the nature of a petitioner's core religious beliefs.

These four tests also produce widely divergent results. The *Golden Writ* petitioners, for example, may not have satisfied the common sense or multifactual analysis tests but may well have satisfied the deference and minimal theism tests. The *Holy Spirit* petitioners may well have satisfied the deference and minimal theism tests but would probably not have survived the commonsense and multifactual analysis tests. The *Ravenwood, Ideal Life,* and *American Fundamentalist* petitioners may have survived the minimal theism test but would probably not survive any of the other three tests.

A sequenced combination of tests seems to strike a better balance than any one of these tests standing alone. Most petitions for tax exemption can and should be accepted using the common sense test or deference test alone. It is only when the reasonableness of the petition or the sincerity of the petitioner are in question that commissioners and courts should look more closely. A test for theism, or some evidence of a transcendent good held by the group, is a useful first step in such closer scrutiny and might well dispose of a case. In particularly doubtful cases, a closer inquiry using the multiple criteria set forth in the *Ideal Life* might be apt, provided these criteria are applied only prudentially, not mechanically.

It must be remembered that in a good number of states, tax exemptions are not constitutional rights but statutory privileges. Although it is not apt for an official to probe a religious petition or petitioner that requests the free exercise right to be left alone, it is apt for some measured inquiry into the petitioner and petition to receive a statutory privilege otherwise not available to it. Too intrusive an inquiry will invite a free exercise challenge. But too little an inquiry will invite all manner of spurious claims. "Charlatanism" might be "a necessary price to pay for religious freedom" in general.[55] But it is not necessary for the state and society to pay a charlatan with particular privileges reserved to the religious alone.

It must also be remembered that the initial determination of tax exemption is usually made not by a court in a public proceeding but by a bureaucrat within the state, county, or municipal tax commissioner's office. Some measure of formality and predictability must thus attend these decisions, or they will become subject to bureaucratic caprice. Too wooden or too generous an application of such tests can still trigger an appeal to the courts, either by the petitioner who is denied an exemption or by a government office that is denied its tax.

New Trends in Tax Exemption Litigation

The tax exemption provisions adopted by most states are cryptic and often devoid of definitions. Judicial precedents interpreting these provisions are copious and often discordant. Churches and other religious organizations that have been denied property tax exemptions have not been hesitant to exploit these ambiguities and seek judicial redress. This has given rise to scores of state court cases on tax exemption of religious property since the 1960s.[56] Although these cases are wide-ranging, several broad trends can be discerned in current laws on tax exemption for religious property.

First, the requirement that the property be "actually" used for exempt purposes has been considerably softened. Traditionally courts did not hesitate to deny exemptions to religious properties whose exempt uses were merely planned for the future or were held in abeyance for financial or other reasons. Today the majority of state courts and legislatures have become less churlish. Most states exempt religious properties as soon as construction of improvements thereon has begun. In a few states, mere acquisition of the property and good faith planning of a religious or charitable use thereon is sufficient to warrant an exemption from property tax.[57] Most states also grant (at least partial) exemptions for properties that religious and charitable groups use only partly or sporadically.[58] Complete abandonment or virtual nonuse of the property, however, still leads to taxation.[59]

Second, the requirement that the religious use of the property be "public" in nature is not so stringently enforced. Traditionally courts struck down exemptions for secluded cloisters, private chapels, religious communes, communal farms, spiritual retreat centers, summer and youth camps, and other religious settings that did not provide a sufficiently "public benefit" to society. Today courts and legislatures in many states have softened the public benefit requirement, often granting exemptions to such properties.[60]

Third, several courts have come to interpret rather liberally the type and amount of contiguous property that is "reasonably necessary" for the religious or charitable use of an exempt property. Traditionally many states limited exemptions to improved properties together with the driveways, walkways, parking lots, and other immediately surrounding lands that facilitated use of the improvement. Today courts in an increasing number of states grant exemptions for large tracts of unimproved land surrounding a worship center or charity on grounds that such lands provide a buffer against residential and industrial encroachment or traffic, enhance the aesthetic appeal of the church, or foster a tranquil, serene setting more conducive to religious worship and spiritual reflection.[61] Courts in other states have exempted convents and communes, residential religious education centers, missionary furlough stations, religious camps, retreats, and parsonages with their surrounding properties on grounds that they are "reasonably necessary for the accomplishment and fulfillment" of a religious or charitable institution.[62] In one case, the "reasonably necessary" rule was extended to allow tax exemption of an unimproved property adjacent to a religious school on the argument that the property was a "nature laboratory" for students who would otherwise have to take expensive field trips outside the city.[63] But in several other recent cases, courts have struck down exemptions for parsonages and other living quarters that are distant from the worship center,[64] or for extensive parking areas surrounding worship centers—particularly if these "parking lots" are in reality vacant land used only on particularly busy days of worship, or if these lots are leased for other uses during the week.[65]

Fourth, virtually all states now grant exemptions based on the primary or predominant use to which the property is devoted.[66] Traditionally some states would allow parties to mix religious and charitable uses and choose freely the category of exemption they deemed most convenient. Today courts have become more inclined to deem either the religious use or the charitable use to be primary and determine the exemption status of the property based on that categorization.[67] Traditionally a few other states forced parties to devote their properties exclusively to religious uses or exclusively to charitable uses; a mixture of uses was fatal to their claim for exemption. Today such a wooden classification system has been sharply criticized and abandoned: If either the religious use or the charitable use is predominant, parties can make other incidental exempt uses of their properties.[68]

Fifth, many states also permit parties to make incidental nonexempt uses of their properties. Traditionally many states denied exemptions to religious properties that in any way mixed exempt and nonexempt uses; even incidental profiteering was fatal to a claim for exemption. Today courts and legislatures have become far less stringent. Some states allow full exemption so long as the primary use is religious or charitable.[69] Even part-time leases of the property to nonexempt entities and purposes does not jeopardize the exemption.[70] Other states allow property devoted to religious or charitable uses to receive partial exemption based on the percentage of space or time devoted to such exempt uses.[71]

Sixth, state courts in the 1990s have become rather generous in defining the ambit of "religious" uses of property.[72] This is, in part, a function of the popularity of the "deference test" of religion—where courts defer to a petitioner's definition of both what is religion and what is a religious property use—and, in part, a function of the courts' increased willingness to accommodate incidental exempt and nonexempt uses without jeopardy to the exemption. As a consequence, religious property has stretched far beyond worship centers and their immediate surrounding land. In the 1990s, state courts have judged the following to be exempt religious (uses of) property: a 146-acre tract of land, only about 25 unimproved acres of which was used for periodic outdoor worship;[73] church camps comprised of agricultural land, recreational areas, and trails;[74] religious education complexes consisting of classrooms, dormitories, recreational facilities, dining facilities, and administrative buildings and surrounding land and roads;[75] a radio station;[76] a vacant lot;[77] a parking lot;[78] a storage building that was once used as sanctuary and parsonage;[79] and a religious education building where no worship occurred.[80]

These trends in recent cases have expanded the ambit and availability of tax exemptions for religious property. The softened definition of an "actual" or "public" exempt use has rendered a number of undeveloped and secluded religious properties eligible for exemption. The broadened definition of what property is considered "reasonably necessary" to support an exempt use has allowed religious organizations to surround their improvements with substantial tracts of unimproved land. The permitted admixture of two or more exempt uses on one property has made exemptions available to the properties of nonprofit organizations that offer multiple services.

These trends have also, however, permitted some abuses of exemption laws. The permitted admixture of predominant exempt uses and incidental nonexempt uses has allowed religious groups to engage in short-term or occasional profiteering on their properties with no adverse tax consequences. The recent relaxation of the category of "religious" uses or properties has served to the ample advantage of at least more traditional religious groups.

Tax Exemptions of Religious Property in the Future

Opponents and proponents of tax exemptions of religious property have thus far found little common ground. Opponents insist that such exemptions are subsidies to religion, which are proscribed by the disestablishment clause and its principle of state separation from religion.[81] Proponents argue that such exemptions are supports for religion, which are prescribed by the free exercise clause and its principle of state accommodation of religion.[82] Opponents look to the future and portend with alarm the further erosion of the state tax base and the further aggrandizement of church wealth and power.[83] Proponents look to the past and portray with approval the long tradition of mutual support and cooperation between church and state in serving society. Enmeshed as it is in this dialectic of separationism and accommodationism, the controversy over the constitutionality of tax exemption of religious property will not admit of swift or easy resolution.

Three decades after the fact, *Walz v. Tax Commission* (1970) still seems like a prudent decision. State tax exemptions of religious property, the *Walz* Court concluded, while neither proscribed by the disestablishment clause nor prescribed by the free exercise clause, are, nonetheless, permissible under the United States Constitution.

Federalism provides one strong argument for this conclusion. Property taxation and exemption have, since the beginning of the republic, been exclusively state affairs. These states have developed wide-ranging forms of tax exemption, which are closely tailored to local norms and habits. There is little compelling argument to subject this diverse and divisive set of legal institutions to a single First Amendment norm enforceable by federal courts. Unduly discriminatory denials of tax exemption for seemingly qualified religious properties should still give rise to federal free exercise cases.[84] Unduly generous extensions of tax exemption for seemingly unqualified nonreligious properties should still give rise to federal disestablishment cases.[85] But mundane and marginal disputes concerning discretionary decisions over tax exemptions of religious properties should be resolved not by federal courts but by local state tribunals, sensitive to the norms and habits of the local communities.

Social theory provides a second strong argument for continuing the practice of tax exemption of religious property. The *Walz* Court explicitly rejected analysis of the traditional "social benefit" and "state burden" theories supporting tax exemption: "We find it unnecessary to justify the tax exemption on the social welfare services or 'good works' that some churches perform for parishioners and others," Chief Justice Burger wrote for the *Walz* Court. "Churches vary substantially in the scope of such services. . . . To give emphasis to so variable an aspect of the work of religious bodies would introduce an element of governmental evaluation and standards as to the worth of particular social welfare programs, thus producing the kind of continuing day-to-day relationships which the policy of neutrality seeks to minimize."[86]

This argument misses the point. Traditional "social benefit" and "state burden" theories for tax exemption were not designed to be litmus tests to determine the eligibility of each individual religious property seeking tax exemption. They were designed to justify the inclusion of a separate category of exemption for "religious properties" or properties devoted to "religious uses." On the whole, the traditional argument goes, religious uses of property dispense a sufficiently unique form of social benefits and discharge a sufficiently large number of state burdens to warrant their inclusion as a separate category of tax exemption. In practice, some religious uses of property are more socially beneficial to a broad public, others less so. The social tasks discharged by one religious property might far outweigh the amount of tax that could have been collected from the property; for other religious properties this might be not be true. But, on the whole, society is better off, the state is more efficiently run, and religious bodies are more free to exercise their ministries if their properties are exempt from taxation.

A number of recent sociology of religion studies on the constructive role of religion in public life underscore this point.[87] Martin Marty summarizes these studies with his typical perspicacity: Religions deal uniquely with the deepest elements of individual and social life. Religions catalyze social, intellectual, and material exchange among citizens. Religions trigger economic, charitable, and educational impulses in citizens. Religions provide healthy checks and counterpoints to social and individual excess. Religions diffuse social and political crises and absolutisms by relativizing everyday life and its institutions. Religions provide prophecy, criticism, and exemplars for society. Religions force others to examine their presuppositions. Religions are unique repositories of tradition, wisdom, and perspective. Religions counsel against apathy. Religions are practiced and durable. Religions provide stamina and leadership, especially in times of individual and social crisis. Religions contribute to the theory and practice of the common good. Religions represent the unrepresented. Religions teach stewardship and preservation. Religions provide fresh starts for the desperate. Religion exalts the dignity and freedom of the individual.[88] No religion lives up to all these claims all the time; some religions never do. But it is these kinds of qualities of religion that give it a unique place in the American polity and warrant a distinct category of tax exemption for their properties.

Tradition provides a third strong argument for the *Walz* Court's conclusion. The *Walz* Court overstated its historical argument by exaggerating the continuity and universality of the tradition of such tax exemptions and by imputing modern concerns to early state legislatures and constitutional conventions that devised these tax exemption policies. But, even granting its occasional interruptions, dissenting voices, and shifting theories, the American tradition of tax exemption of religious property has been long held and widely embraced.

A simple argument from tradition cannot dispose of a constitutional case. But tradition can serve as something of a "null hypothesis"—to be overcome by strong constitutional arguments rather than discarded by simple invocations of principle. As Oliver Wendell Holmes Jr. once put it: "If a thing has been practised for two hundred years by common consent, it will need a strong case for the Fourteenth Amendment to affect it."[89]

No strong principled case can be mustered against tax exemptions of religious property. The strongest argument arises from the principle of liberty of conscience. In essence, the argument goes, all taxpayers are being forced to pay additional taxes to make up for the taxes not collected from religious properties. A simple example illustrates this argument. A small village, consisting of 1,000 plots of property of equal value seeks to collect $10,000 in property taxes. If all properties were taxed, each property holder would have to pay $10 in taxes. But if one plot of property is religious and exempted from taxation, the remaining 999 property holders must each pay $10.01. Why should any one of the remaining 999 taxpayers have to pay an extra penny in taxes to support the religious property—particularly if that party is opposed to religion altogether or opposed to the particular religion of the property that is exempted. Is this not precisely the kind of "continuing and intolerable burden on his pocketbook, his conscience, and his constitutional rights" that the founders sought to outlaw?[90] Is this not a fateful first step down the "slippery slope" that James Madison had identified? "The same authority that can force a citizen to pay three pence only of his property for the support of any one [religious] establishment, may force him to conform to any other establishment in all cases whatsoever."[91]

This argument from liberty of conscience is not convincing. First, because of the social benefits that the exempt property dispenses and the state burdens that it discharges it may well be that the village need not collect $10,000 in taxes, but only $9,990. The village can forgo the additional $10 because the exempted religious property provides that increment of charity, education, or other good works that the village would otherwise need to provide. And the general social benefits afforded by the exempt religious property fall on the conscientiously opposed taxpayer as much as on everyone else.

Second, even if the state still collects the additional $10 or the exempted religious body does not discharge social benefits, a conscientious objection to general taxes collected for the common good avails a party little. Religious pacifists are forced to pay taxes that help to support the military. Fervent Marxists are forced to pay taxes that support a capital economy. Ascetic Amish are forced to pay taxes that support a state social security system that their religious beliefs forbid them to use. Claims of conscience against payments of general taxes, whether based on religion or on antireligion, are ultimately futile. As the Supreme Court once put it: "Because the broad public interest in maintaining a sound tax system is of such a high order, religious belief in conflict with the payment of taxes affords no basis for resisting the tax."[92] This applies as much to antireligious beliefs. Neither religious or antireligious forms of conscientious objection to taxes can be privileged.

A second, weaker argument that is often raised against tax exemptions of religious property arises from the principle of equality. Such tax exemptions give disproportionately large benefits to religions with large property holdings and disproportionately small benefits to religions with no property holdings. Such disparity in treatment, it is argued, violates the principle of equality of all religions before the law.

The easy answer to this argument is that taxation of religious property would be equally disproportionate, but only in reverse. Religions with large properties would face heavy tax burdens; religions with smaller properties would face lighter tax burdens. The purported violation of the principle of equality would be identical. Equal treatment of religion does not require identical treatment; it requires only treating like religious cases alike.

Conclusions

A decade ago, when I was young and naïve, I suggested that a more nuanced understanding of the history of tax exemption of religious property points to a middle way between the wholesale eradication of such exemptions proposed by opponents and the blanket endorsements of exemptions proffered by proponents. Neither group, I argued, has recognized sufficiently that modern tax exemptions of religious property are rooted in both common law and equity law traditions. Neither group has seen that tax exemptions were historically granted on account of both the "religious uses" and the "charitable uses" to which properties were devoted. Thus, besides the all-or-nothing approaches currently debated a third alternative presented itself. Tax exemptions for religious properties could be granted on account not of their religious uses but of their charitable uses. Religious properties would thus be exempted from taxation not because of the internal, cultic, and sacerdotal uses but because of the external, cultural, and social uses to which they are devoted.[93]

In further testimony to my youthful naïveté, I argued that it should be left to the church and not to the state to implement this alternative. Nothing in the First Amendment compelled federal judges to order this reform. Elected state officials had even less incentive to raise this reform, whatever their need for further tax revenues. For tax exemptions have long been regarded as a sign of the state's "benevolent neutrality" toward religion—"a fit recognition by the state of the sanctity of religion," as one official put it.[94] Taxes would be regarded by many as a sign of the state's malevolent adversity toward religion—a reminder of earlier eras of religious persecution and a foretaste of religious repression to come. To give the state the power to tax the church would for many be tantamount to giving it the power to destroy the church.[95]

The catalyst for reform of religious property exemptions, I thus argued, had to come not from the state but from the church and other religious bodies. Churches must consider the costs of exemption—not so much the incremental financial costs to other taxpayers as the important symbolic costs to themselves. For many people, adherents and antagonists alike, tax exemptions and other legal privileges have rendered contemporary churches too mercenary, too opulent, and too self-indulgent—too intent upon building crystal cathedrals, prayer towers, and theme parks than furnishing soup kitchens, youth houses, and night shelters. The church's voluntary renunciation of one of its privileges would do much to allay the anxieties of its adherents and to parry the attacks of its antagonists.

Though a little older and little more cynical, I still stand by this recommendation—but with two qualifications. First, I had argued earlier that a full-scale implementation of this reform should result in the eradication of the "religious use" category of tax exemption altogether. Religious properties would need to qualify for charitable use exemptions or be subject to taxation. The ample sociology of religion literature that has emerged in the past decade persuades me that not all religious uses of property can be reduced to charitable uses—and, indeed, that there is great social and public value in religious uses as such.[96] Moreover, the principle of religious pluralism counsels against so radical a tax reform. Religions take a variety of forms, from the world affirmative and socially active to the world avertive and socially ascetic. To restrict tax exemptions only to the former types of religion stands in considerable tension with this principle of pluralism.

Second, I had earlier put this reform in stark terms: Churches were either charitable or churlish, in this argument, and shame on the latter. This is obviously too strong. There is a place for the sublime sanctuary and the secluded monastery that is not only legally sanctioned but socially salutary. There is a role for the private religious school and the ascetic religious community that is not only socially sanctioned but legally salutary. Not all religious forms, functions, and facilities need to be open and charitable in order to be beneficial to the public; indeed, many would lose their distinctive religious identity and social utility if they were.

That said, a self-imposed ethic of moderation and modesty should still attend a religious body's demands for tax exemption. Not every corner and building on a sweeping church campus is necessarily vital to its ministry. Not every acre of a distant rural summer camp, occasionally occupied by the retired rector or rabbi, can be readily claimed to be religious. Not every storage building, administrative office, and residential center in the city operated by the church, temple, or mosque can be claimed to be equally essential and sacred. When such auxiliary properties and facilities are devoted to charitable uses, a religious body should seize on their exemptions with alacrity. But when such properties and facilities lie largely idle and foreclosed to others, a religious body might do well to render its taxes upon it.

10

TOWARD AN INTEGRATION OF RELIGIOUS LIBERTY

The American Experiment in International Context

Methods and Measures of Integration

The ample vacillations in the Supreme Court's First Amendment cases can be explained, in part, on factual grounds. The application of a sixteen-word guarantee to dozens of diverse and complex issues over the course of a century and more has inevitably led to conflicting decisions. Even a single issue like tax exemption of religious property has drawn to itself an array of juxtaposed rules. "The life of the law has not been logic: it has been experience," Oliver Wendell Holmes reminds us.[1] The American law of religious rights and liberties is no exception.

These vacillations, however, also betray the failure of the Court to develop a coherent framework for interpreting and applying the First Amendment. The Court has tended to rely too heavily on its mechanical tests of free exercise and establishment and to use these tests as substitutes, rather than guides, to legal analysis. The Court has tended to pit the disestablishment and free exercise clauses against each other, rather than treating them as twin guarantees of religious rights and liberties. The Court has been too eager to reduce the religion clauses to one or two principles, thereby often ignoring the range of interlocking first principles of the American experiment. The accumulation of these interpretive shortcomings, particularly in the past two decades, has brought the American experiment to a state of acute crisis—both of law and of faith in the law.[2]

The Court needs to develop a more integrated approach to First Amendment questions that incorporates the first principles of religious rights and liberties on which the American experiment was founded and integrates them into the resolution of specific cases. Such a framework is easy enough to draw up on the blackboard or in the pages of a treatise—and a number of important integrative methodologies and frameworks have been offered of late.[3] In the context of the ongoing constitutional experiment in religious liberty—with the thickly entangled work of federal and state courts and legislatures—deliberate and provisional steps are essential to reaching any type of coherent new framework or methodology.

It might well be necessary, at least as an interim step, that certain clusters of cases simply continue. For example, cases on taxation and labor relations might need to be left for a time to develop their own integrated pockets of principles, precepts, and precedents—without pretending to project them into other areas of religious liberty law.[4] Other subjects, such as property taxation, religious incorporation, or zoning and landmark preservation, that fall mostly within state (not federal) jurisdiction, might properly remain "selectively unincorporated" and thus left to the experimentation of state legislatures and courts.[5] There is ample wisdom in Justice O'Connor's caveat in *Kiryas Joel v. Grumet* (1994):

> It is always appealing to look for a single test, a Grand Unified Theory that would resolve all the cases that might arise under a particular [First Amendment] clause. . . . But the same constitutional principle may operate very differently in different contexts. . . . And setting forth a unitary test for a broad set of cases may do more harm than good. Any test that must deal with widely disparate situations risks being so vague as to be useless. . . . I think a less unitary approach provides a better structure for analysis. If each test covers a narrower and more homogeneous area, the tests may be more precise and therefore easier to apply. . . . Perhaps eventually under this structure we may indeed distill a unified, or at least a more unified [approach].[6]

Whatever interim steps are taken, the Supreme Court—with the help of Congress, the states, and the academy—must strive for this "more unified approach." Such an approach might come in a variety of forms—in another grand synthetic case in the series of *Watson, Cantwell, Everson, Sherbert,* and *Lemon,* or through comprehensive restatements, congressional statutes, or even another constitutional amendment on religious rights and liberties.[7]

Any integrative approach to the First Amendment must certainly embrace "the long-standing traditions of *our people,*" as Justice Scalia urged in response to Justice O'Connor in *Kiryas Joel.*[8] Such traditions are, to my mind, best captured in the roll of "essential rights and liberties" first incorporated into the First Amendment. The task of this volume has been, in part, to lay out some of the rich resources of this American tradition, both in its genesis and its exodus, which can be profitably drawn into a more integrated understanding of religious liberty today.

An integrative approach to the First Amendment must also consider the emerging traditions of other people. The way of integration is not only the way of the past, the original intent of the eighteenth-century founders of the American experiment. It is also the way of the future, the intent of the emerging world system of law and human rights, in which American law has played and must continue to play a vital part.[9]

Resort to international legal and human rights norms might seem a rather unpromising path to developing a more integrated American constitutional law of religious liberty. Not only are Americans better at exporting their constitutional ideas and institutions than importing those of other peoples. But the budding international norms on religious rights and liberties seem, by conventional wisdom, to have rather little that is worth importing. The canon of applicable international human rights norms has developed only slowly and sporadically since World War II. Even as more fully developed in the 1980s and 1990s, these international norms are often seen to affect America's foreign diplomatic relations, not its domestic constitutional law.[10] Very few international cases are at hand, and those that have been reported do not follow the conventional form and format of American constitutional law. International human rights norms would thus seem to be better left outside the ambit of First Amendment inquiry.

To keep this parochial veil drawn shut, however, is to deprive the American experiment of a rich source of instruction and inspiration. Comparative legal analysis is always edifying—if for no other reason than to have confirmation, from a fresh perspective, of the validity and utility of one's own legal norms and practices and to gain an idea or two about reforming them. But especially at this time of transition, if not turmoil, in First Amendment law, comparative legal analysis is particularly necessary and salutary.

Several principles and teachings of international human rights help to confirm, refine, and integrate prevailing First Amendment principles and cases. For example, the prioritizing of the principles of liberty of conscience, free exercise, and religious equality in international human rights instruments suggests a prototype for the integration of American free exercise and disestablishment values. The insistence of international human rights instruments that state abridgments of religious rights and liberties be both "necessary" and "proportionate" confirms the strict scrutiny test of American free exercise jurisprudence—demanding both a "compelling state interest" (necessity) and the "least restrictive alternative" of achieving that interest (proportionality). The heavy emphasis on group religious rights in recent international instruments both confirms the American protection of corporate free exercise rights and encourages greater protection for

minority religious groups in America. The international doctrine of granting "a margin of appreciation" for local religious and political practices
could be put to particularly effective use in our federalist system of government.[11] The international debate over the "universalism versus relativism"
of human rights has profound implications for the American debate concerning federal and state jurisdiction over religious rights.[12]

Moreover, a good deal of what appears in modern international human
rights instruments captures the best of American, and other Western, constitutional learning on religious liberty. Both the Universal Declaration of
1948 and the great Covenants of 1966 encapsulate and elaborate President
Roosevelt's famous "four freedoms"—including religious freedom.[13] More
recent international provisions on religious rights were forged, in no small
measure, by the efforts of American politicians, jurists, and theologians. To
compare First Amendment law with international norms is, in a real sense,
to judge American law by an international standard that it has helped to
shape and by which America often judges other nations.[14]

Religious Rights and Liberties in International Context

Three international instruments contain the most critical protections of
religious rights and liberties: (1) the International Covenant on Civil and
Political Rights (1966) (the 1966 Covenant);[15] (2) the United Nations
Declaration on the Elimination of All Forms of Intolerance and of
Discrimination Based on Religion or Belief (1981) (the 1981 Declaration);[16] and (3) the Concluding Document of the Vienna Follow-up
Meeting of Representatives of the Participating States of the Conference
on Security and Co-operation in Europe, which was promulgated in 1989
(the 1989 Vienna Concluding Document).[17] Viewed collectively, these
three documents confirm most of the "essential rights and liberties" of
religion embodied in the American experiment but prioritize them quite
differently.[18]

1966 Covenant

The 1966 International Covenant on Civil and Political Rights largely re-
peats the capacious guarantee of religious rights and liberties first announced in the 1948 Universal Declaration of Human Rights. Article 18
reads:

1. Everyone shall have the right to freedom of thought, conscience
    and religion. This right shall include freedom to have or to adopt a
    religion or belief of his choice, and freedom, either individually or

in community with others and in public or private, to manifest his religion or belief in worship, observance, practice and teaching.

2. No one shall be subject to coercion which would impair his freedom to have or to adopt a religion or belief of his choice.

3. Freedom to manifest one's religion or beliefs may be subject only to such limitations as are prescribed by law and are necessary to protect public safety, order, health, or morals or the fundamental rights and freedoms of others.

4. The States Parties to the present Covenant undertake to have respect for the liberty of parents and, when applicable, legal guardians to ensure the religious and moral education of their children in conformity with their own convictions.

Article 18 distinguishes between the right to freedom of religion and the freedom to manifest one's religion—what at American law is called liberty of conscience and free exercise of religion, respectively. The right to freedom of religion—the freedom to have, to alter, or to adopt a religion of one's choice—is an absolute right from which no derogation may be made and which may not be restricted or impaired in any manner. Freedom to manifest or exercise one's religion—individually or collectively, publicly or privately—may be subject only to such limitations as are prescribed by law and are necessary to protect public safety, order, health, or morals or the fundamental rights and freedoms of others. The latter provision is an exhaustive list of the grounds allowed to limit the manifestation of religion. Legislatures may not limit the manifestation of religion on any other grounds.

The requirement of necessity implies that any such limitation on the manifestation of religion must be proportionate to its aim to protect any of the listed state interests. Such limitation must not be applied in a manner that would vitiate the rights guaranteed in Article 18. In American law terms, Article 18 upholds the requirement that to pass constitutional muster, a law burdening the exercise of religion must be in service of a compelling state interest and use the least restrictive alternative to achieve that interest.[19]

Articles 2 and 26 of the 1966 Covenant require equal treatment of all persons before the law and prohibit discrimination based, among other grounds, on religion. According to international case law, unequal treatment of equal cases is allowed only if that treatment serves an objective and reasonable purpose and the inequality is proportionate to that purpose.[20]

The Human Rights Committee, established under the 1966 Covenant, has made it explicit in its General Comment No. 22 (48) concerning Article 18 that:

The terms belief and religion are to be broadly construed. Article 18 is not limited in its application to traditional religions or to religions and beliefs with institutional characteristics or practices analogous to those of traditional religions. The Committee therefore views with concern any tendency to discriminate against any religion or belief for any reasons, including the fact that they are newly established, or represent religious minorities that may be the subject of hostility by a predominant religious community.

In this same General Comment, the Human Rights Committee has further clarified that the freedom to manifest one's religion

includes acts integral to the conduct by religious groups of their basic affairs, such as, *inter alia*, the freedom to choose their religious leaders, priests and teachers, the freedom to establish seminaries or religious schools and the freedom to prepare and distribute religious texts or publications.[21]

1981 Declaration

The 1981 Declaration elaborated what the 1966 Covenant adumbrated.[22] The Declaration includes (1) prescriptions of religious rights for individuals and groups; (2) proscriptions on religious discrimination, intolerance, or abuse; (3) provisions specific to the religious rights of parents and children; and (4) explicit principles of implementation. Like the 1966 Covenant, the 1981 Declaration on its face applies to "everyone," whether "individually or in community," "in public or in private."

Articles 1 and 6 of the 1981 Declaration set forth a lengthy illustrative catalogue of rights to "freedom of thought, conscience, and religion"—illustrating more concretely the ambit of what American law calls "liberty of conscience" and "free exercise of religion." Such rights include the right (1) to worship or assemble in connection with a religion or belief and to establish and maintain places for these purposes; (2) to establish and maintain appropriate charitable or humanitarian institutions; (3) to make, to acquire, and to use to an adequate extent the necessary articles and materials related to the rites or customs of a religion or belief; (4) to write, to publish, and to disseminate relevant publications in these areas; (5) to teach a religion or belief in places suitable for these purposes; (6) to solicit and receive voluntary financial and other contributions from individuals and institutions; (7) to train, to appoint, to elect, or to designate by succession appropriate leaders called for by the requirements and standards of any religion or belief; (8) to observe days of rest and to celebrate holy days and ceremonies in accordance with the precepts of one's religion or belief; and (9) to establish and maintain communications with individuals and communities in matters of religion and belief at the national and international levels.

Like the 1966 Covenant, the 1981 Declaration allows the "manifestation of religion" to be subjected to "appropriate" state regulation and adjudication. The 1981 Declaration permits states to enforce against religious individuals and institutions general regulations designed to protect public safety, order, health, or morals, or the fundamental rights and freedoms of others. It is assumed, however, that in all such instances, the grounds for such regulation are enumerated and explicit and that such regulations abide by the international legal principles of proportionality and necessity.

The 1981 Declaration includes more elaborate provisions concerning the religious rights of children and their parents. It guarantees the rights of parents (or guardians) to organize life within the household and to educate their children in accordance with their religion or beliefs. Such parental responsibility, however, must be discharged in accordance with the "best interests of the child." At minimum, the parents' religious upbringing or education "must not be injurious to his physical or mental health or to his full development." Although the drafters debated at length the potential conflicts between the parents' right to rear and educate their children in accordance with their religion and the state's power to protect the best interests of the child, they offered no specific principles to resolve these disputes.

The 1981 Declaration includes suggested principles of implementation and application of these guarantees. It urges states to take all "effective measures to prevent and eliminate discrimination on the grounds of religion or belief in the recognition, exercise and enjoyment of human rights and fundamental freedoms in all fields of civil, economic, political, social and cultural life." It urges states to remove local laws that perpetuate or allow religious discrimination and to enact local criminal and civil laws to combat religious discrimination and intolerance.

The 1981 Declaration, though not a binding legal instrument, provides a principled reference for monitoring a nation's compliance with international standards of religious liberty. It sets a baseline for guiding diplomatic relations and treaties among nation-states. It provides a common ground for nongovernmental and intergovernmental organizations to report and register complaints of religious rights violations. It also provides the United Nations Special Rapporteur, appointed by the United Nations Commission on Human Rights, to provide a general survey and specific on-site evaluations of member states of the United Nations. The United States was among the states under evaluation in 1998.[23]

1989 Vienna Concluding Document

The 1989 Vienna Concluding Document extends these norms and their implementation, particularly for religious groups. Principles 16 and 17 provide a clear distillation of principles that is worth quoting in full:

16. In order to ensure the freedom of the individual to profess and practice religion or belief the participating States will, *inter alia,*

    A. take effective measures to prevent and eliminate discrimination against individuals or communities, on the grounds of religion or belief in the recognition, exercise and enjoyment of human rights and fundamental freedoms in all fields of civil, political, economic, social and cultural life, and ensure the effective equality between believers and non-believers;

    B. foster a climate of mutual tolerance and respect between believers of different communities as well as between believers and non-believers;

    C. grant upon their request to communities of believers, practicing or prepared to practice their faith within the constitutional framework of their states, recognition of the status provided for them in their respective countries;

    D. respect the right of religious communities to establish and maintain freely accessible places of worship or assembly; organize themselves according to their own hierarchical and institutional structure; select, appoint and replace their personnel in accordance with their respective requirements and standards as well as with any freely accepted arrangement between them and their State; solicit and receive voluntary financial and other contributions;

    E. engage in consultations with religious faiths, institutions and organizations in order to achieve a better understanding of the requirements of religious freedom;

    F. respect the right of everyone to give and receive religious education in the language of his choice, individually or in association with others;

    G. in this context respect, *inter alia,* the liberty of parents to ensure the religious and moral education of their children in conformity with their own convictions;

    H. allow the training of religious personnel in appropriate institutions;

    I. respect the right of individual believers and communities of believers to acquire, possess, and use sacred books, religious publications in the language of their choice and other articles and materials related to the practice of religion or belief;

    J. allow religious faiths, institutions and organizations to produce and import and disseminate religious publications and materials;

    K. favorably consider the interest of religious communities in participating in public dialogue, *inter alia,* through mass media.

17. The participating States recognize that the exercise of the above mentioned rights relating to the freedom of religion or belief may be subject only to such limitations as are provided by law and are consistent with their obligations under international law and with their international commitments. They will ensure in their laws and regulations and in their application the full and effective implementation of the freedom of thought, conscience, religion or belief.

These are the basic international provisions on religious rights on the books. Regional instruments—notably the European Charter on Human Rights (1950), the American Convention on Human Rights (1969), and the African Charter on Human and People's Rights (1981)—elaborate some of these guarantees.[24] International treaties involving religious bodies—notably the recent Concordats between the Vatican and Italy, Spain, and Israel as well as the Universal Islamic Declaration of Human Rights (1981) and the Cairo Declaration on Human Rights in Islam (1990)—give particular accent to the religious concerns and constructions of their cosigners.[25] But the foregoing three instruments capture the common lore of current international human rights norms on religious rights and liberties.

International Norms and American Laws Compared

The United States has signed the 1966 Covenant. None of the fourteen reservations, understandings, or declarations that the United States put to the instrument seeks to avoid or evade the standards of strict scrutiny and nondiscrimination on religious grounds set out in Articles 18 and 26 of the document. The 1966 Covenant, however, is not self-executing. It "does not, by itself, create private rights enforceable in U.S. courts."[26] It requires implementing legislation to become effective, and no such legislation to date has been forthcoming.[27] Nonetheless, the 1966 Covenant holds out a high standard of religious liberty, which the United States has pledged to support.[28]

The 1981 Declaration and 1989 Vienna Concluding Document are not binding legal instruments—on the United States or any other nation-state. Nonetheless, as collective expressions of international opinion on the meaning and measure of religious rights and liberties, these two instruments also carry ample moral, intellectual, and diplomatic suasion.

The international human rights norms reflected in these three main instruments both confirm and prioritize several of the "essential rights and liberties of religion" that have long been part of the American experiment. The principles of liberty of conscience, individual and corporate free exercise of religion, and equality of religions before the law form the backbone of the international norms on religious rights and liberties. Liberty of conscience rights, with their inherent protections of voluntarism and prohibitions against coercion, are absolute rights from which no derogation can be made. The exercise of religion can be regulated only to protect either other fundamental rights or public health, safety, and welfare and only when the religious intrusion is "proportionate" to achieving that narrowly stated need. Equality of religions before the law is not only to be protected but to be affirmatively fostered by the state. To achieve the mandated goals of equality and nondiscrimination on grounds of religion, exemptions from generally applicable laws and policies are sometimes necessary, as are affirmative state actions to protect religion or to undo past religious repression.[29]

International human rights norms assume a vast pluralism of confessions and faiths. Multiple forms of religious belief and expression are deserving of special religious rights protection—whether ancient or new, individual or communal, internal or external, private or public, permanent or transient. The special religious functions of parents, teachers, and religious officials are given particular attention and protection in international human rights instruments. The rights of religious minorities and nontraditional religions are given special weight, and states are obligated to be particularly solicitous of their peculiar needs.

The Vienna Concluding Document particularly protects the principle of structural pluralism. It also protects the basic autonomy of various religious organizations, which is assumed in the American principles of corporate free exercise and of separation of the institutions of church and state. Religious associations have rights to function in expression of their founding religious beliefs and values, which the state cannot compromise except on stated grounds that are necessary and proportional. Churches, synagogues, temples, mosques, tribes, and other religious groups thus have rights to organize, assemble, worship, and enforce certain religious laws against their voluntary members (at least up to the limits of endangering the safety of their members in violation of criminal laws). Parents and families have rights to rear, educate, and discipline children in expression of their religious convictions (again with some limitation against endangering the safety of children). Religious publishers and suppliers have rights to produce the particular products needed for their religious cultus. Religious schools have rights to educate and discipline children in accordance with the basic norms and habits of their religious traditions.

Conspicuously absent from international human rights instruments are the more radical demands for separationism, rooted in certain strains of Enlightenment reasoning and reified in the popular American metaphor of a "wall of separation between church and state." *Everson, McCollum, Engel,* and other early disestablishment cases assumed that religious liberty requires the separation of church and state and the cessation of state support for religion. Only the secular state can guarantee religious liberty, it was argued, and only separation can guarantee its neutrality on religious matters.

Such strict separationist logic is not reflected in international human rights instruments nor, indeed, widely shared by nation-states around the world. International norms and many domestic laws regard the material and moral cooperation of religion and state as conducive, and sometimes essential, to the achievement of both religious liberty and national identity. Indeed, today a number of religious groups in the former Soviet bloc and in sub-Saharan Africa regard restitution and affirmative state action toward religion as a necessary feature of any religious rights regime—if nothing else, to undo and overcome past confiscation and repression of religion by the state.[30] Similarly, some Catholic groups in Italy, Iberia, and Latin America urge cooperation of religious and political bodies to preserve the "Catholicization" of public life and culture.[31] Islamic revivalists in various countries urge similar arrangements to enhance the "Islamicization" of the community.[32] Jewish groups argue similarly to protect the Jewish character of the state of Israel.[33] Absolute separationists in this country have fewer allies abroad than is conventionally assumed.

If hypothetically applied in the United States, the international provisions on liberty of conscience would confirm the "strict scrutiny" test for free exercise claims, elaborated in *Sherbert, Yoder,* and the Religious Freedom Restoration Act. It would confirm the "noncoercion" reading of the disestablishment clause reflected most recently in *Lee v. Weisman.* It would confirm the multiple forms of religious accommodation for individual believers upheld under both religion clauses of the First Amendment and in various statutes.

Conversely, the international principle that liberty of conscience is a nonderogable right runs directly counter to the wooden reading of the free exercise clause introduced in the late-nineteenth-century Mormon polygamy cases—*Reynolds, Davis,* and *Late Corporation*—and resurrected this past decade in *Roy, Lyng, Smith,* and their many lower court progeny.

The international norms on equality would applaud the "equal access" and "equal treatment" cases from *Paty* and *Widmar* to *Rosenberger* and *Pinette* as necessary protections of equality. It would confirm the various statutes, regulations, and cases that foster religious equality in the workplace, the school, and in public facilities. It would likewise uphold the application of general taxing, licensing, parading, reporting, and other statutes and regulations to religious groups, finding no ready violation of free exercise rights if such regulations are equally and indiscriminately applied to all like groups.

Conversely, international norms would have little patience with the patently discriminatory treatment of certain religious minorities in America. The United States Supreme Court's failure to accommodate the distinctive theology of polygamous marriage among Mormons, the special sabbatarian needs of Jews, the religious worship patterns of Muslims, and the nontraditional sites and rites of Native Americans would run directly counter to the cardinal principle of equality and nondiscrimination mandated by a number of international human rights instruments. International human rights norms demand not only general toleration of religious minorities but special solicitude for their religious needs that often are not accommodated in majoritarian laws and policies. The Supreme Court's rather cavalier interpretations of both the free exercise and disestablishment clauses under the rubric of neutrality will not do. The kinds of special accommodations and exemptions afforded to Adventist sabbatarianism in *Sherbert* and to Amish communitarianism in *Yoder* come much closer to the solicitude mandated by international human rights norms.

The international principle of structural pluralism would endorse the lines of cases protecting the forms and functions of religious bodies, whether worship centers, religious schools, or religious charities, among others. Cases upholding general regulation of these bodies in furtherance of health, safety, and welfare, and in exercise of taxing and police power would likewise pass muster. Similarly cases upholding generally and generically available governmental support for religion—in the form of tax exemptions or equal access to public facilities or state benefits—would find ample support under international human rights norms.

The principle of structural pluralism, especially as elaborated in the Vienna Concluding Document, would look askance, however, at a case like *Jones v. Wolf,* which permitted government resolution of intrachurch disputes involving "neutral principles" of law. The "deference test" of *Watson, Kedroff,* and *Milivojevich* would find greater favor under international human rights instruments, as would the *Catholic Bishop* and *Amos* holdings that religious employers be allowed to discriminate in favor of their coreligionists in their employment decisions.

This same principle of structural pluralism might also look askance at a case like *Bob Jones University v. United States,* which withheld tax exempt status from a religious university that engaged in racial discrimination on the basis of its religious convictions. The holding of the *Bob Jones* case is intuitively attractive, given the tragic history of slavery and discrimination against African Americans—just as holdings in modern Germany outlawing any private discrimination against Jews are intuitively attractive, given that county's tragic history of anti-Semitism.[34] But international norms of religious rights protect even unpopular and prejudicial policies of a religious body that are firmly grounded and sincerely held—so long as such policies do not threaten or violate the life or limb of its members or impair any party's liberty of exit from the religious body.[35]

The absence of a principle of "disestablishment" in international human rights norms would not call into question the entire line of disestablishment clause cases. Many of these cases, as we have seen, serve to protect the principles of liberty of conscience, equality, and pluralism in a manner consistent with prevailing international norms. But when there is a clash between such principles and the principle of religious establishment, international norms would give preference to the former—as do American cases upholding the principle of accommodation.

According to international human rights norms, the realm of education—where parental religious rights and preferences receive especially strong protection—is not the ideal place for undue zealotry in application of disestablishment values. To be sure, international norms would not countenance any more than American law coerced religious exercises in school classrooms—such as mandatory participation in prayers, pledges, confessions of faith, Bible reading, and the like—however strong the countervailing parental preferences. But the constitutional purging of tax-supported public schools of virtually all religious symbols, texts, and traditions—in favor of purportedly neutral and secular tropes—stands in considerable tension with international principles of religious equality and of parental religious rights.

Finally, the absence of a universal definition, or common method of defining, religion in American law would meet with harsh criticism under international norms. The current system of leaving such definitions to individual states and statutes, courts and agencies has introduced a bewildering array of legal definitions of "religion." As we saw (pages 203–208), some courts and legislatures make a simple "common sense" inquiry as to the existence of religion. Others defer to the good faith self-declarations of religion by the claimant. Others seek to find sufficient analogies between existing religions and new religious claimants. Others insist on evidence of a god or something transcendent that stands in the same position as a god. Others analyze the motives for formation of the religious organization or adoption of a religious belief, the presence and sophistication of a set of doctrines explicating the beliefs, the practice and celebration of religious rites and liturgies, the degree of formal training required for the religious leaders, the strictures on the ability of members to practice other religions, the presence and internal enforcement of a set of ethical rules of conduct, and other factors. All this results in considerable inequality and potentially discriminatory treatment of religious claims and claimants.

It may not be apt to adopt the capacious definition of religion set out in international human rights instruments—particularly given that under the First Amendment one definition of religion must be usefully applied to both religion clauses. But the term "religion" must be assigned some consistent boundaries to be useful, at least for a constitutional rights regime. No universal definition can easily embrace every religious dimension of modern culture. No bright line tests can readily resolve all penumbral cases. Fairness commands as broad a legal definition of religion as possible, so that no legitimate religious claim is excluded. Prudence commends a narrower definition, so that not every claim becomes religious (and thus no claim becomes deserving of special religious rights protection). To define "religion" too closely is to place too much trust in the capacity of the lexicon or the legislature. To leave the term undefined is to place too much faith in the self-declarations of the claimant or the discernment of local judges and administrators.

In my view, the functional and institutional dimensions of religion deserve the strongest emphasis in defining the constitutional realm of religious rights and liberties in America. Of course, religion viewed in its broadest terms embraces all beliefs and actions that concern the ultimate origin, meaning, and purpose of life, of existence. It involves the responses of the human heart, soul, mind, conscience, intuition, and reason to revelation, to transcendent values, to what Rudolf Otto once called the "idea of the holy."[36] But such a definition applied at modern constitutional law would render everything (and thus nothing) deserving of constitutional protection.

Viewed in a narrower institutional sense, religion embraces a creed, a cult, a code of conduct, and a confessional community.[37] A creed defines the accepted cadre of beliefs and values concerning the ultimate origin, meaning, and purpose of life. A cult defines the appropriate rituals, liturgies, and patterns of worship and devotion that give expression to those beliefs. A code of conduct defines the appropriate individual and social habits of those who profess the creed and practice the cult. A confessional community defines the group of individuals who embrace and live out this creed, cult, and code of conduct, both on their own and with fellow believers. By this definition, a religion can be traditional or very new, closely confining or loosely structured, world-avertive or world-affirmative, nontheistic, polytheistic, or monotheistic. Religious claims and claimants that meet this definition, in my view, deserve the closest consideration.[38]

CONCLUDING
REFLECTIONS

Writing in the context of the United States Constitutional Convention of 1787, John Adams, the great Massachusetts jurist and future American president, offered a robust appraisal of the new American experiment:

> The people in America have now the best opportunity and the greatest trust in their hands, that Providence ever committed to so small a number, since the transgression of the first pair [Adam and Eve]; if they betray their trust, their guilt will merit even greater punishment than other nations have suffered, and in the indignation of Heaven. . . . The United States have exhibited, perhaps, the first example of governments erected on the simple principles of nature; and if men are now sufficiently enlightened to disabuse themselves of artifice, imposture, hypocrisy, and superstition, they will consider this event as a [new] era in history. Although the detail of the formation of the American governments is at present little known or regarded either in Europe or in America, it may hereafter become an object of curiosity [for it is] destined to spread over the northern part of . . . the globe. The institutions now made in America will not wholly die out for thousands of years. It is of the last importance, then, that they should begin right. If they set out wrong, they will never be able to return, unless it be by accident to the right path.[1]

More than two centuries later, Adams's sentiments prove remarkably prescient. The eighteenth-century American founders did, indeed, begin on the right path of liberty. And today, we enjoy ample freedom of religion as a consequence. American models of religious liberty have had a profound influence around the globe, and they now figure prominently in a number of national constitutions and international human rights instruments.

To be sure, as Adams predicated, there has always been "a glorious uncertainty in the law" of religious liberty and a noble diversity of understandings of its details.[2] This was as true in Adams's day as in our own. In Adams's day, there were competing models of religious liberty more overtly theological than his—whether Puritan, Evangelical, or Anglican in inspiration. There were also competing models more overtly philosophical than his—whether Classical, Republican, or Enlightenmentarian in inclination.

Today, these and other founding models of religious liberty have born ample progeny, and the great rivalries among them are fought out in the courts, legislatures, and academies throughout the land.

Prone as he was to a dialectical model of religious liberty, Adams would likely approve of our rigorous rivalries of principle—so long as all rivals remain committed to constitutional ideals of democracy, liberty, and rule of law. But Adams would also likely insist that we reconsider his most cardinal insights about the necessary dialectical nature of religious freedom and religious establishment. Too little religious freedom, Adams had insisted, is a recipe for hypocrisy and impiety. But too much religious freedom is an invitation to depravity and license. Too firm a religious establishment breeds coercion and corruption. But too little religious establishment allows secular prejudices to become constitutional prerogatives. Somewhere between these extremes, Adams believed, a society must find its balance.

The balance that Adams and other founders often struck between the freedom of all private religions and the establishment of one public Christian religion can no longer serve in our day. But the balance that the Supreme Court has often struck between the freedom of all private religions and the establishment of one public secular religion also can no longer serve. Somewhere between these extremes, our society must now find a new constitutional balance.

One key to restriking this constitutional balance today lies in the eighteenth-century founders's most elementary and most essential insight—that religion is special and is accorded special protection in the Constitution. "[W]e cannot repudiate that decision," Douglas Laycock writes, "without rejecting an essential feature of constitutionalism, rendering all constitutional rights vulnerable to repudiation if they go out of favor."[3] The founders's vision was that religion is more than simply a peculiar form of speech and assembly, privacy and autonomy. Religion is a unique source of individual and personal identity, involving "duties that we owe to our Creator, and the manner of discharging them," as Madison put it. Religion is also a unique form of public and social identity, involving a vast plurality of sanctuaries, schools, charities, missions, and other forms and forums of faith. Individual and corporate, private and public entities and exercises of religion—in all their self-defined varieties—properly deserve the protection of the First Amendment.

A second key to restriking this constitutional balance today lies in the founders's insight that to be enduring and effective, the constitutional process must involve all voices and values in the community—religious, areligious, and antireligious alike. Constitutionalism ultimately demands ecumenism for its efficacy and credibility. Thus in creating the state and federal constitutions, the founders stretched the roll of delegates and ratifiers to the furthest edges of conscience and credulity. Believers and skeptics, churchmen and statesmen, Protestants and Catholics, Republicans and *Philosophes*, Quakers and Jews—many of whom in decades and centuries past had slandered and slaughtered each other with a vengeance—now came together in a rare moment of solidarity. The founders understood that to create a proper law of religious liberty required that all religions have liberty to participate both in its creation and its unfolding.

A third key to restriking this constitutional balance today lies in repristinating anew the six basic principles of religious liberty that the founders set forth. The founders designed the First Amendment free exercise and disestablishment clauses as twin guarantees of religious liberty for all. The free exercise clause outlawed government *proscriptions* of religion—actions that unduly burdened the conscience, restricted religious expression, discriminated against religion, or invaded the autonomy of churches and other religious bodies. The disestablishment clause outlawed government *prescriptions* of religion—actions that unduly coerced the conscience, mandated forms of religious expression, discriminated in favor of religion, or improperly allied the state with churches or other religious bodies. Both the free exercise and the disestablishment clauses thereby provided complementary protections to the other constitutive principles of the American experiment—liberty of conscience, freedom of religious expression, equality of plural faiths before the law, and separation of church and state.

These three key insights of the American experiment were not only part of the original vision of the eighteenth-century founders. They were also part of the original vision of the Supreme Court justices when they founded a modern national law of religious liberty. All three of these insights recur in *Cantwell v. Connecticut* (1940) and *Everson v. Board of Education* (1947), the two cases that first applied the First Amendment religion clauses to the states.

Cantwell and *Everson* declared anew that religion had a special place in the Constitution and deserved special protection in the nation. In a remarkable countertextual reading, the Court took it upon itself to enforce the First Amendment religion clauses against all levels and branches of government in the nation—whether federal, state, or local, whether executive, legislative, or regulatory. "*Congress* shall make no law" now became, in effect, "*Government* shall make no law respecting an establishment of religion or prohibiting the free exercise thereof."

Cantwell and *Everson* declared anew that all religious voices were welcome in the modern constitutional dialogue about religious liberty. These two cases themselves welcomed hitherto marginal voices: *Cantwell* welcomed a devout Jehovah's Witness who sought protections for his unpopular mission work. *Everson* welcomed a skeptical citizen who sought protection from paying taxes in support of religious schools. Subsequent cases have drawn into the constitutional dialogue a whole host of rival religious and antireligious groups—Catholics, Protestants, and Orthodox, Jews, Muslims, and Native Americans, Mormons, Quakers, and Krishnas, alongside a variety of skeptics, cynics, and secular iconoclasts.

   Cantwell and *Everson* declared anew the efficacy of the six founding principles of the American experiment. The free exercise clause, the *Cantwell* Court declared, protects "freedom of conscience and freedom to adhere to such religious organization or form of worship as the individual may choose." It "safeguards the free exercise of the chosen form of religion," the "freedom to act" on one's beliefs. It protects a "plurality of forms and expressions" of faith, each of which deserves equal protection under the law. "The essential characteristic of these liberties is, that under their shield many types of life, character, opinion and belief can develop unmolested and unobstructed."[4] The disestablishment clause, the *Everson* Court echoed, means that no government "can set up a church"; "can force or influence a person to go or to remain away from church against his will or force him to profess a belief or disbelief in any religion"; can "punish [a person] for entertaining or professing religious beliefs or disbeliefs, for church attendance or non-attendance"; "can, openly or secretly, participate in the affairs of any religious organizations or groups, or vice versa." Government may not exclude "individual Catholics, Lutherans, Mohammedans, Baptists, Jews, Methodists, Nonbelievers, Presbyterians, or the members of any faith, because of their faith, or lack of it, from receiving the benefits of public welfare legislation" or participating in the American public arena.[5] Such was the original vision of the eighteenth-century founders and the original vision of the United States Supreme Court at the start of the modern era of religious liberty.

   A good deal of this volume has been devoted to documenting the Supreme Court's repeated departures from these original insights in both its free exercise and disestablishment cases. Far from being special and specially protected, religion has often become a suspect category at modern constitutional law. The free exercise clause no longer accords religious individuals or groups special exemptions from general laws that burden core claims of conscience or central commandments of the faith. Such religious exemptions now come only from the legislature, and even then the Court has sometimes ignored them or struck them down. The disestablishment clause does not include religious individuals or religious groups among those naturally eligible for government benefits, forums, and programs. Such religious entitlements come only if they are sufficiently buffered by nonreligious entitlements and so long as they are not directed to "sectarian" ends.

   Far from openly engaging and valuing all religious voices and values in modern constitutional dialogue, the Supreme Court has often been notorious in its harsh treatment of some religious groups. No Jew, no Muslim, and no Native American has ever won a free exercise case before the Supreme Court, despite numerous efforts. And when Christians have sought to inject their concerns for equal treatment into neutral legislation, the Supreme Court has struck down these laws as "ingenious and self-serving schemes" that violate the disestablishment clause.

Far from judiciously balancing the multiple principles on which the American religious experiment was founded, the modern Supreme Court has often taken more reductionist approaches. In its early free exercise cases, the Court applied the principles of liberty of conscience, freedom of religious expression, religious pluralism and equality, and separation of church from state. Since the mid-1980s, however, the Court has reduced the free exercise clause to the single principle of neutrality. In its early disestablishment cases, the single principle of separation of church and state dominated the Court's reasoning. Since the mid-1980s, however, individual justices have slowly imported into their analyses new principles of religious equality and liberty of conscience.

Such criticisms, and the ample volumes of others that can be found in the literature, have not been lost on the Supreme Court. In some of its most recent First Amendment cases, the Court seems to be charting something of a new constitutional course to offset some of these criticisms and to return to some of the original vision of the First Amendment. The Court has, in effect, taken up again the challenge of John Adams with which we started these concluding reflections: how to balance the freedom of all religions with the maintenance of a public religion that is neither a newly established secularism nor a traditionally established Christianity. The Court has not yet crafted a coherent new First Amendment logic, let alone a consistent new test, to address this question. But some of these recent cases hold signposts of a new way to define and defend the legal place of religion in America today—not only private religion but also public religion.

Tradition has become one strong vector in the Court's recent First Amendment cases. The Court had used arguments from tradition a few times before, as part of broader rationales for upholding religious tax exemptions and Sabbath Day laws. In *Marsh v. Chambers* (1983), however, this argument from tradition became the exclusive basis for upholding a state legislature's practice of funding a chaplain and opening its sessions with his prayers. Writing for the Court, Chief Justice Burger defended such practices as a noble survival of the traditional public role of religion in American life and law:

In light of the unambiguous and unbroken history of more than 200 years, there can be no doubt that the practice of opening legislative sessions with prayer has become part of the fabric of our society. To invoke Divine guidance on a public body entrusted with making the laws is not, in these circumstances, an "establishment" of religion [but] simply a tolerable acknowledgement of beliefs widely held among the people of this country. . . . "[W]e are a religious people whose institutions presuppose a Supreme Being."[6]

Arguments from tradition, though by themselves rarely convincing, can sometimes bolster a broader rationale for upholding traditional features of a public religion and a religious public. Tradition can sometimes serve effectively as something of a "null hypothesis"—to be overcome by strong constitutional arguments rather than discarded by simple invocations of principle. As Holmes once put it: "If a thing has been practised for two hundred years by common consent, it will need a strong case for the Fourteenth Amendment to affect it."[7] Innocuous long-standing practices, therefore, such as religious tax exemptions, military chaplains, prison prayerbooks, public displays of decalogues and other religious symbols might well be justified.

There are limits and dangers to arguments from tradition, which the Court itself betrayed the following year. In *Lynch v. Donnelly* (1984) the Court upheld a municipality's traditional practice of maintaining a manger scene (a crèche) in a public park as part of a large holiday display in a downtown shopping area. "There is an unbroken history of official acknowledgment by all three branches of government of the role of religion in American life," Chief Justice Burger wrote, repeating his *Marsh* argument and now giving an ample list of illustrations.

There is another reason to uphold this display, however, Burger continued. Crèches, while of undoubted religious significance to Christians, are merely "passive" parts of "purely secular displays extant at Christmas." They "engender a friendly community spirit of good will" that "brings people into the central city and serves commercial interests and benefits merchants."[8] The prayers that are occasionally offered at the crèche, Justice O'Connor wrote in concurrence, merely "solemnize public occasions, express confidence in the future, and encourage the recognition of what is worthy of appreciation in society."[9] Governmental participation in and support of such "ceremonial deism," the Court concluded, cannot be assessed by "mechanical logic" or "absolutist tests" of establishment. "It is far too late in the day to impose a crabbed reading of the [Disestablishment] Clause on the country."[10]

A crabbed reading of establishment would have been better than such a crass rendering of religion. For the Court to suggest that crèches are mere advertisements, prayers mere ceremony, and piety mere nostalgia is to create an empty "American Shinto"—a public religion that is perhaps purged enough of its confessional identity to pass constitutional muster but too bleached and too bland to be religiously efficacious, let alone civilly effective.[11]

Arguments from tradition, while helpful, are thus inherently limited in their ability to define and defend the public place of religion today. Such arguments perforce assume a traditional definition of what a public religion is—namely, a common system of beliefs, values, and practices drawn eclectically from the multiple denominations within a community. In the religiously homogeneous environment of John Adams's day, a public religion of the common denominator and common denomination still had the doctrinal rigor, liturgical specificity, and moral suasion to be effective. In the religiously heterogeneous environment of our day—with more than 1,000 incorporated denominations on the books—no such effective common religion can be readily devised or defended.

More recent cases suggest a budding new way of defining and defending the legal place of public religion. Since the early 1980s, the Court has several times upheld government policies that support the public access and activities of religious groups—so long as these religious groups are voluntarily convened and so long as nonreligious groups also benefit from the same government support. Church-affiliated pregnancy counseling centers, therefore, could be funded as part of a broader federal family counseling program. Religious student groups could have equal access to public school and university classrooms that were open to nonreligious student groups. Religious groups could gain equal access to public facilities that were already opened to other civic groups. Clergy were just as entitled to run for political office as laity. Religious student newspapers were just as entitled to public university funding as those of nonreligious student groups. These holdings were defended on wide-ranging constitutional grounds—as a proper accommodation of religion under the disestablishment clause, as a necessary protection of religion under the free speech or free exercise clauses, as a simple application of the equal protection clause, among other arguments.

One theme common to these cases, however, is that public religion must be as free as private religion. Not because the religious groups in these cases are really nonreligious. Not because their public activities are really nonsectarian. And not because their public expressions are really part of the cultural mainstream. To the contrary, these public groups and activities deserve to be free just because they are religious, just because they engage in sectarian practices, just because they sometimes take their stands above, beyond, and against the mainstream. They provide leaven and leverage for the polity to improve.

A second theme common to these cases is that the freedom of public religion sometimes requires the support of the state. Today's state is not the distant, quiet sovereign of Jefferson's day from which separation was both natural and easy. Today's state, whether for good or ill, is an intensely active sovereign from which complete separation is nearly impossible. Few religious bodies can now avoid contact with the state's pervasive network of education, charity, welfare, child care, health care, family, construction, zoning, workplace, taxation, and other regulations. The modern state, as Harold Berman put it, now "threatens to swallow up the civil society."[12] Both confrontation and cooperation with the modern welfare state are almost inevitable for any religion that seeks to reach out to the public. When a state's regulation imposes too heavy a burden on a particular religion, the free exercise clause should provide a pathway to relief. When a state's appropriation imparts too generous a benefit to particular religions alone, the establishment clause should provide a pathway to dissent. But when a general government scheme provides public religious groups and activities with the same benefits afforded to all other eligible recipients, disestablishment clause objections are not only "crabbed" but corrosive.

A third theme common to these cases is that a public religion cannot be a common religion. If the religious gerrymandering of *Lynch v. Donnelly* and its progeny had not already made this clear, these more recent cases underscore the point. Today, our public religion must be a collection of particular religions, not the combination of religious particulars. It must be a process of open religious discourse, not a product of ecumenical distillation. All religious voices, visions, and values must be heard and deliberated in the public square. All public religious services and activities, unless criminal or tortious, must be given a chance to come forth and compete, in all their denominational particularity.

Some conservative Evangelical and Catholic groups today have seen and seized on this insight better than most.[13] Their rise to prominence in the public square in recent years should not be met with hyperbolic name-calling, glib talk of censorship, or habitual incantation of Jefferson's mythical wall of separation. The rise of the so-called Christian right should be met with the equally strong rise of the Christian left, of the Christian middle, and of many other Jewish, Muslim, and other religious groups who test and contest its premises, prescriptions, and policies. That is how a healthy democracy works. The real challenge of the new "Christian right" is not to the integrity of American politics but to the apathy of American religions. It is a challenge for peoples of all faith and of no faiths to take their place in the marketplace.

A final theme implicit in these cases is that the freedom *of* public religion also requires freedom *from* public religion. In the public religion schemes of nineteenth-century America, it was not so much the courts as the frontier that provided this freedom—a place away from it all, where one could escape with one's conscience and coreligionists. Today, the frontier still provides this freedom—if not physically in small towns and wild mountains, then virtually in our ability to sift out and shut out the public voices of religion that we do not wish to hear.

Both modern technology and modern privacy make escape to the frontier considerably easier than in the days of covered wagons and mule trains. Just turn off CBN. Turn away the missionary at your door. Close your eyes to the city crucifix that offends. Cover your ears to the public prayer that you can't abide. Forgo the military chaplain's pastoral counseling. Skip the legislative chaplain's prayers. Walk by the town hall's menorah and star. Don't read the Decalogue behind the judge. Don't join the religious student group. Don't vote for the collared candidate. Don't browse the Evangelicals's newspapers. Avoid the services of the Catholic counselors. Shun the readings of the Scientologists. Turn down the trinkets of the colporteurs. Turn back the ministries of the hatemongers. All these escapes to the virtual frontier, the law does and will protect—with force if necessary. Such voluntary self-protections from religion will ultimately provide far greater religious freedom for all than pressing yet another tired constitutional case.

DRAFTS OF THE FEDERAL RELIGION CLAUSES, 1787–1789

Drafts in the Constitutional Convention, 1787

1. *"The Legislature of the United States shall pass no Law on the subject of Religion."*—Proposal by Charles Pinckney, May 29, 1787. Proposal died in Committee, without recorded discussion.

2. *"[N]o religious test shall ever be required as a qualification to any office or public trust under the authority of the U[nited] States."*—Motion by Charles Pinckney, August 30, 1787. Motion passed with one dissent.

3. *"The Congress shall have power . . . to establish an University, in which no preferences or distinctions should be allowed on account of religion."*—Motion by James Madison and Charles Pinckney on September 14, 1787. Motion failed 6–4.

Drafts Proposed to the First Congress by the State Ratification Conventions, 1788

1. *"Congress shall make no laws touching religion, or to infringe the rights of conscience."*—New Hampshire Proposal, June 21, 1788.

2. *"That religion, or the duty which we owe to our creator, and the manner of discharging it, can be directed only by reason and conviction, not by force or violence, and therefore all men have an equal, natural and unalienable right to the free exercise of religion according to the dictates of conscience, and that no particular religious sect or society ought to be favored or established by law in preference to others."*—Virginia Proposal, June 26, 1788.

3. *"That the people have an equal, natural, and unalienable right freely and peaceably to exercise their religion, according to the dictates of conscience; and that*

no religious sect or society ought to be favored or established by law in preference to others."—New York Proposal, July 26, 1788.

4. *"That any person religiously scrupulous of bearing arms ought to be exempted, upon payment of an equivalent to employ another to bear arms in his stead. That religion, or the duty which we owe to our Creator, and the manner of discharging it, can be directed only by reason and conviction, not by force or violence; and therefore all men have an equal, natural, and unalienable right to the free exercise of religion according to the dictates of conscience, and that no particular religious sect or society ought to be favored or established by law in preference to others."*—North Carolina Proposal, August 1, 1788; repeated by Rhode Island, June 16, 1790.

Drafts Debated in the First Congress, 1789

5. *"The civil rights of none shall be abridged on account of religious belief or worship, nor shall any national religion be established, nor shall the full and equal rights of conscience be in any manner, or any pretext infringed."*—Draft proposed to the House by James Madison, June 8, 1789.

6. *"No state shall violate the equal rights of conscience, or the freedom of the press, or the trial by jury in criminal cases."*—Draft proposed to the House by James Madison, June 8, 1789.

7. *"[N]o religion shall be established by law, nor shall the equal rights of conscience be infringed."*—Draft proposed to the House by Committee of Eleven, July 28, 1789.

8. *"[N]o person religiously scrupulous shall be compelled to bear arms."*—Draft proposed to the House by Committee of Eleven, July 28, 1789.

9. *"[N]o State shall infringe the equal rights of conscience, nor the freedom of speech or of the press, nor of the right of trial by jury in criminal cases."*—Draft proposed to the House by Committee of Eleven, July 28, 1789.

10. *"Congress shall make no laws touching religion, or infringing the rights of conscience."*—Draft proposed by Charles Livermore on August 15, 1789; passed by the House.

11. *"[T]he equal rights of conscience, the freedom of speech or of the press, and the right of trial by jury in criminal cases, shall not be infringed by any State."*—Draft proposed by Charles Livermore on August 17, 1789; passed by the House.

12. *"Congress shall make no law establishing religion, or to prevent the free exercise thereof, or to infringe the rights of conscience."*—Revised draft proposed by Fisher Ames on August 20, 1789; passed by the House.

13. *"No person religiously scrupulous shall be compelled to bear arms in person."*—Revised draft passed by the House, August 20, 1789.

14. *"Congress shall make no law establishing religion, or prohibiting the free exercise thereof, nor shall the rights of conscience be infringed."*—Final draft pro-

posed by the Style Committee, passed by the House and sent to the Senate, August 25, 1789.

15. *"Congress shall make no law establishing One Religious Sect or Society in preference to others, nor shall the rights of conscience be infringed."*—Draft proposed and defeated in the Senate, September 3, 1789.

16. *"Congress shall not make any law, infringing the rights of conscience, or establishing any Religious Sect or Society."*—Draft proposed and defeated in the Senate, September 3, 1789.

17. *"Congress shall make no law establishing any particular denomination of religion in preference to another, or prohibiting the free exercise thereof, nor shall the rights of conscience be infringed."*—Draft proposed and defeated in the Senate, September 3, 1789.

18. *"Congress shall make no law establishing religion, or prohibiting the free exercise thereof."*—Draft proposed and passed by the Senate, September 3, 1789.

19. *"Congress shall make no law establishing articles of faith or a mode of worship, or prohibiting the free exercise of religion."*—Draft proposed and passed by the Senate, and sent to the House, September 9, 1789.

20. *"Congress shall make no Law respecting an establishment of Religion, or prohibiting the free exercise thereof."*—Draft proposed by Joint House-Senate Committee on September 24, 1789; passed by House and Senate on September 25, 1789.

For detailed discussion of and full citations to these drafts, see Chapter 4.

STATE CONSTITUTIONAL PROVISIONS ON RELIGION

APPENDIX 2
State Constitutional Provisions on Religion as of 1947

State and Year of Constitution	does preamble use "God" or other religious language?	a liberty or right of conscience clause?	a free exercise clause?	a clause against coercion or compulsion to religion or religious support?	a conscientious objection to arms or pacifism clause?	an equality of religion clause?	a clause indicating no state preference for or among religions?	a disestablishment clause?	a clause prohibiting the mandatory payment of money or tithes?	a prohibition on religious test oaths for holding public office?	a prohibition on religious tests or oaths for serving on a jury or as a witness?	a prohibition on religious tests or oaths for voting?	is a tax exemption given to religious property or bodies?	a prohibition against state funding for religious education?	a prohibition against state funding of religion more generally?
Alabama (1901)[1]	yes	yes		yes			yes	yes	yes	yes	—	—	yes	yes	yes
Arizona (1912)	yes	yes						yes		yes	yes	—	yes	yes	yes
Arkansas (1874)	yes	yes		yes			yes		yes	no	no	yes	yes		
California (1879)	yes	yes	yes	yes	yes		yes			—	yes	—		yes	yes
Colorado (1876)	yes	yes	yes	yes			yes		yes	—	—	—		yes	yes
Connecticut (1818)	yes	yes	yes			yes	yes		yes	yes	—	—	yes	yes	
Delaware (1897)	yes	yes	yes	yes			yes		yes	—	—	—	yes		

(continues)

NOTE: These provisions are drawn, in large measure, from Chester James Antieus, Phillip Mark Carroll, and Thomas Carroll Burke, *Religion Under the State Constitutions* (Brooklyn, 1965), 173–239, with some corrections and refinements drawn from the state constitutions in F. Thorpe, ed., *The Federal and State Constitutions*, 7 vols. (Washington, 1909), and *Constitutions of the United States: National and State* (New York, 1962). As this list depicts only the status of the state constitutions in 1947, Alaska and Hawaii are omitted, as they were not yet states.

[1]The year listed for each state constitution is the year of adoption. Some state constitutions were amended between the year of adoption and 1947. This table incorporates such changes and thus provides a statement of the status of religious liberty in the states in the year 1947.

APPENDIX 2 *(continued)*

(continues)

State and Year of Constitution	does preamble use "God" or other religious language?	a liberty or right of conscience clause?	a free exercise clause?	a clause against coercion or compulsion to religion or religious support?	a conscientious objection to arms or pacifism clause?	an equality of religion clause?	a clause indicating no state preference for or among religions?	a disestablishment clause?	a clause prohibiting the mandatory payment of money or tithes?	a prohibition on religious test oaths for holding public office?	a prohibition on religious tests or oaths for serving on a jury or as a witness?	a prohibition on religious tests or oaths for voting?	is a tax exemption given to religious property or bodies?	a prohibition against state funding for religious education?	a prohibition against state funding of religion more generally?
Florida (1887)	yes	yes	yes		yes		yes				yes		yes	yes	yes
Georgia (1945)	yes	yes	yes	yes	yes		yes		yes	yes			yes	yes	yes
Idaho (1890)	yes	yes	yes	yes	yes		yes						yes	yes	yes
Illinois (1870)	yes	yes	yes	yes	yes		yes						yes	yes	yes
Indiana (1851)	yes	yes	yes	yes	yes					yes	yes		yes	yes	
Iowa (1857)	yes	yes	yes	yes	yes			yes		yes	yes				
Kansas (1861)	yes	yes		yes	yes		yes	yes	yes	yes	yes		yes	yes	
Kentucky (1891)	yes	yes	yes	yes			yes						yes	yes	
Louisiana (1921)	yes	yes				yes	yes	yes	yes				yes	yes	
Maine (1820)	yes	yes	yes	yes		yes		yes							
Maryland (1867)	yes	yes	yes	yes	yes	yes	yes		yes	no	no		yes	yes	
Massachusetts (1780)	yes	yes	yes	yes	yes		yes		yes		yes		yes	yes	
Michigan (1890)	yes	yes		yes					yes		yes	yes		yes	yes
Minnesota (1857)	yes	yes		yes					yes	yes	yes	yes	yes	yes	yes

(continues)

APPENDIX 2 (continued)

State and Year of Constitution	does preamble use "God" or other religious language?	a liberty or right of conscience clause?	a free exercise clause?	a clause against coercion or compulsion to religion or religious support?	a conscientious objection to arms or pacifism clause?	an equality of religion clause?	a clause indicating no state preference for or among religions?	a disestablishment clause?	a clause prohibiting the mandatory payment of money or tithes?	a prohibition on religious test oaths for holding public office?	a prohibition on religious tests or oaths for serving on a jury or as a witness?	a prohibition on religious tests or oaths for voting?	is a tax exemption given to religious property or bodies?	a prohibition against state funding for religious education?	a prohibition against state funding of religion more generally?
Mississippi (1890)	yes	yes					yes			no	—	—		yes	yes
Missouri (1945)	yes	yes		yes			yes			yes	yes	—		yes	yes
Montana (1889)	yes	yes	yes	yes			yes			—	—	—	yes	yes	yes
Nebraska (1875)	yes	yes	yes	yes			yes			yes	yes	—	yes	yes	
Nevada (1864)	yes	yes	yes							—	yes	—	yes	yes	
New Hampshire (1784)		yes		yes	yes	yes	yes		yes	—	—	—			yes
New Jersey (1947)	yes	yes	yes	yes			yes	yes	yes	yes	yes	—	yes	yes	yes
New Mexico (1913)	yes	yes	yes							yes	yes	yes	yes	yes	yes
New York (1895)	yes	yes			yes	yes				—	—	—	yes		
North Carolina (1868)	yes	yes			yes		yes			no	yes	—	yes	yes	
North Dakota (1889)	yes	yes	yes	yes			yes			yes	—	—	yes	yes	
Ohio (1851)	yes				yes					yes	yes	—	yes		yes
Oklahoma (1907)	yes									yes	yes	yes	yes	yes	yes
Oregon (1859)	yes	yes	yes							yes	yes	—	yes	yes	yes

APPENDIX 2 *(continued)*

State and Year of Constitution	does preamble use "God" or other religious language?	a liberty or right of conscience clause?	a free exercise clause?	a clause against coercion or compulsion to religion or religious support?	a conscientious objection to arms or pacifism clause?	an equality of religion clause?	a clause indicating no state preference for or among religions?	a disestablishment clause?	a clause prohibiting the mandatory payment of money or tithes?	a prohibition on religious test oaths for holding public office?	a prohibition on religious tests or oaths for serving on a jury or as a witness?	a prohibition on religious tests or oaths for voting?	is a tax exemption given to religious property or bodies?	a prohibition against state funding for religious education?	a prohibition against state funding of religion more generally?
Pennsylvania (1874)	yes	yes		yes	yes		yes		yes	no	—	—	yes	yes	yes
Rhode Island (1843)	yes	yes	yes	yes	yes					yes	—	—	yes	yes	yes
South Carolina (1895)	yes	yes	yes	yes	yes		yes		yes	no	—	—	yes	yes	
South Dakota (1889)	yes	yes		yes	yes		yes		yes		—	—	yes	yes	yes
Tennessee (1870)	yes	yes	yes	yes	yes		yes		yes	yes	yes	—	yes	yes	
Texas (1876)	yes	yes	yes	yes	yes			yes	yes	no	yes	yes	yes	yes	
Utah (1896)		yes	yes			yes	yes			yes	yes	—	yes		
Vermont (1793)				yes	yes			yes	yes			yes	yes	yes	yes
Virginia (1902)	yes	yes		yes			yes		yes	yes	yes	yes	yes	yes	yes
Washington (1889)	yes	yes	yes				yes					yes			
West Virginia (1872)	yes	yes		yes	yes		yes		yes	yes	yes	—		yes	yes
Wisconsin (1848)	yes	yes		yes					yes	yes	yes	—	yes	yes	yes
Wyoming (1890)	yes	yes	yes		yes					yes	yes	—		yes	yes

UNITED STATES SUPREME COURT DECISIONS RELATING TO RELIGIOUS LIBERTY

APPENDIX 3
United States Supreme Court Decisions Relating to Religious Liberty

Issue	Case	Citation	Ratio[1]	Author of Opinion	Holding
Church Property	*Terrett v. Taylor*	13 U.S. (9 Cranch) 43 (1815)	7-0	Story, J.	State may not rescind the property obtained charter of the Episcopal Church and expropriate the church's lands.
Charitable Bequest	*Vidal v. Girard's Executors*	43 U.S. (2 How.) 127 (1844)	7-0	Story, J.	Testamentary bequest for establishment of school for orphans is valid notwithstanding provisions derogatory of Christianity.
Federalism	*Permoli v. First Municipality of New Orleans*	44 U.S. (3 How.) 589 (1844)	8-0	Catron, J.	United States Constitution does not protect citizens' religious liberties in regards to the respective states.
Church Property	*Goesele v. Bimeler*	55 U.S. (14 How.) 589 (1852)	8-0	McLean, J.	Heirs of member of communitarian religious group cannot recover share of property from the religious society.
Church Property: Civil Court Relief	*Smith v. Swormstedt*	57 U.S. (16 How.) 288 (1853)	9-0	Nelson, J.	A court may sit in equity and divide jointly held property to carry out a voluntarily reached agreement of the church.

NOTE: This chart is modeled, in part, after Carl Esbeck's chart, "Table of United States Supreme Court Decisions Relating to Religious Liberty, 1789–1994," *Journal of Law and Religion* 10 (1994): 573–588.

[1] The "ratio" listed below usually includes two numbers only: the majority and the dissenters. If justices concur in the judgment but not in the opinion, they are listed following the number of the majority, designated by a "/". I have not differentiated among dissenting opinions but listed them all together. Similarly, concurring opinions are not listed at all unless they concur in the judgment only. As a shorthand way of denoting the ratio in more complicated cases, I have simply designated the ratio as "Pluralities." In such cases, if the author is listed as "opinion of the Court," then the opinion garnered a majority of votes, and there was disagreement only beyond the majority. If the author is listed as "for the plurality," then there was no clear majority, though there was sufficient consensus for a judgment, and the named author rendered the judgment of the Court.

(continues)

APPENDIX 3 *(continued)*

Issue	Case	Citation	Ratio[1]	Author of Opinion	Holding
Church Property	*Baker v. Nachtrieb*	60 U.S. (19 How.) 126 (1856)	9-0	Campbell, J.	Defecting member of communitarian religious group may not recover share of property from the religious society.
Mandatory Oath	*Cummings v. Missouri*	71 U.S. (4 Wall.) 277 (1866); dissent attached to *Ex parte Garland*, 71 U.S. (4 Wall.) 397 (1866)	5-4	Field, J.	State may not deprive priest of the right to preach for failure to take a mandatory oath disavowing support/sympathy for the cause of the Confederate states.
Church Property	*Watson v. Jones*	80 U.S. (13 Wall.) 679 (1871)	6-2	Miller, J.	Civil courts should defer to the judgment of the highest religious authority in determining which of two internal religious factions is entitled to disputed property.
Church Property: Internal Church Governance	*Bouldin v. Alexander*	82 U.S. (15 Wall.) 131 (1872)	9-0	Strong, J.	Courts have no power to question acts of internal church discipline or excommunication; the rule of the church's highest internal tribunal must govern property disputes dependent on doctrine.
Polygamy; First Application of Free Exercise Clause	*Reynolds v. United States*	98 U.S. 145 (1879)	9-0	Waite, C.J.	Upheld federal criminal law prohibiting polygamy and denied a Mormon's free exercise claim to the practice, stating that beliefs could not be regulated but actions could.
Polygamy	*Murphy v. Ramsey*	114 U.S. 15 (1885)	9-0	Matthews, J.	Upheld laws disenfranchising known and suspected bigamists.

(continues)

APPENDIX 3 *(continued)*

Issue	Case	Citation	Ratio[1]	Author of Opinion	Holding
Tax Exemptions	*Gibbons v. District of Columbia*	116 U.S. 404 (1886)	9-0	Gray, J.	Allowed property tax scheme that exempted "church buildings, and grounds actually occupied by such buildings" but not land owned by but not used for the church.
Church Property	*Speidel v. Henrici*	120 U.S. 377 (1887)	9-0	Gray, J.	Defecting member of communitarian religious group may not recover share of property from the religious group.
Polygamy	*Davis v. Beason*	133 U.S. 333 (1890)	9-0	Field, J.	Upheld a conviction for falsely taking a (mandatory) oath renouncing polygamy.
Polygamy	*The Late Corporation of the Church of Jesus Christ of Latter Day Saints v. United States*	136 U.S. 1 (1890)	6-3	Bradley, J.	Upheld government's dissolution of the Mormon Church's corporate charter and the confiscation of its property for continued advocacy of polygamy.
Church Staff Hiring	*Church of the Holy Trinity v. United States*	143 U.S. 457 (1892)	9-0	Brewer, J.	Refused to apply a new federal law forbidding contracts with foreign aliens to a church seeking to hire a foreign cleric.
Building Grants; First Application of Disestablishment Clause	*Bradfield v. Roberts*	175 U.S. 291 (1899)	9-0	Peckham, J.	Upheld, against disestablishment clause challenge, the allocation and distribution of federal funds to build religious hospital.
Religious School Funding; Indian Trust Disbursement	*Quick Bear v. Leupp*	210 U.S. 50 (1908)	9-0	Fuller, C.J.	Upheld federal distribution of funds (under an Indian treaty) to Catholic schools that offered education to Native Americans.

(continues)

APPENDIX 3 *(continued)*

Issue	Case	Citation	Ratio[1]	Author of Opinion	Holding
Treaty; Church Property	*Ponce v. Roman Catholic Apostolic Church*	210 U.S. 296 (1908)	9-0	Fuller, C.J.	Confirmed church's title to property acquired from Spanish government before the U.S. annexation of Puerto Rico.
Church Property	*Order of St. Benedict v. Steinhauser*	234 U.S. 640 (1914)	9-0	Hughes. J.	Upheld communal ownership of property within monastic order and granted the Order title to the estate of deceased life-long member.
Conscientious Objection	*Selective Draft Law Cases (Arver v. United States)*	245 U.S. 366 (1918)	9-0	White, C.J.	Upheld as constitutional Congress's power to define conscientious objector status and Congress's restriction of the status to ordained ministers, theology students, and members of well-recognized pacifist sects.
Religious School Curriculum	*Meyer v. Nebraska*	262 U.S. 390 (1923); dissent attached to *Bartels v. Iowa,* 262 U.S. 412 (1923)	7-2	McReynolds, J.	State statute mandating English-only instruction in all grade schools held unconstitutional, as applied to private religious school.
Religious School Attendance	*Pierce v. Society of Sisters*	268 U.S. 510 (1925)	9-0	McReynolds, J.	Invalidated state law mandating attendance at public schools as violation of rights of private schools and of parents.
Religious School Regulation	*Farrington v. Tokushige*	273 U.S. 284 (1927)	9-0	McReynolds, J.	States may not impose unduly intrusive and stringent accreditation and regulatory requirements on religious and other private schools.
Naturalization Qualifications; Conscientious Objection	*United States v. Schwimmer*	279 U.S. 644 (1929)	6-3	Butler, J.	Permitted the denial of citizenship to pacifist who refused to swear an oath to take up arms in defense of the country.

(continues)

APPENDIX 3 *(continued)*

Issue	Case	Citation	Ratio[1]	Author of Opinion	Holding
Naturalization Qualifications	United States v. Bland	283 U.S. 636 (1931)	5-4	Sutherland, J.	Refusal to bear arms in defense of the United States is a valid reason to bar a person's naturalization as a U.S. citizen.
Conscientious Objection	Hamilton v. Regents of the University of California	293 U.S. 245 (1934)	9-0	Butler, J.	Due Process Clause of Fourteenth Amendment, though to be construed broadly, confers no right to exemption for pacifists from mandatory R.O.T.C. training at state university.
Federal Jurisdiction; Distribution of Religious Literature	Coleman v. City of Griffin	302 U.S. 421 (1937), letting stand 189 S.E. 427 (Ga. Ct. App. 1936)	9-0	Per curiam	No federal question presented in appeal of city ordinance prohibiting distribution of religious literature on religion grounds; same ordinance addressed substantively in *Lovell v. City of Griffin*, 303 U.S. 444 (1938).
Distribution of Religious Literature	Lovell v. City of Griffin	303 U.S. 444 (1938)	8-0	Hughes, C.J.	Invalidated city ordinance prohibiting distribution of religious literature for violating freedom of the press.
Distribution of Religious Literature	Schneider v. State of New Jersey (Town of Irvington)	308 U.S. 147 (1939)	7-1	Roberts, J.	Invalidated local ordinance prohibiting distribution of religious literature for violating freedom of speech and freedom of the press.
Licensing; Free Exercise Clause Incorporated	Cantwell v. Connecticut	310 U.S. 296 (1940)	9-0	Roberts, J.	Free exercise clause expressly applied to the states through the Fourteenth Amendment; city licensing law, requiring religious groups to procure a license in advance but giving discretion to local administrators to deny such licenses, held unconstitutional.

(continues)

APPENDIX 3 *(continued)*

Issue	Case	Citation	Ratio[1]	Author of Opinion	Holding
Flag Salute	Minersville School District v. Gobitis	310 U.S. 586 (1940)	7/1-1	Frankfurter, J.	Providing no free exercise exemption from public school requirement of saluting and pledging allegiance to the American flag.
Licensing	Cox v. New Hampshire	312 U.S. 569 (1941)	9-0	Hughes, C.J.	City may require all groups to obtain a license/permit and pay a reasonable fee, consonant with the expense incurred by the city to administer the license and maintain public order during and after the parade/procession.
Fighting Words	Chaplinsky v. New Hampshire	315 U.S. 568 (1942)	9-0	Murphy, J.	Cursing a police office is not the exercise of "religion" nor speech protected by the First Amendment.
Distribution of Religious Literature	Jones v. Opelika (I)	316 U.S. 584 (1942)	5-4	Reed, J.	Local ordinance requiring license fee on distribution of all literature, and reserving discretion of revocation, may constitutionally be applied to distributors of religious literature.
Distribution of Religious Literature	Jamison v. Texas	318 U.S. 413 (1943)	8-0	Black, J.	Local ordinance prohibiting distribution of religious pamphlets in the public square and door to door is unconstitutional.
Licensing	Largent v. Texas	318 U.S. 418 (1943)	8-0	Reed, J.	City ordinance that requires permit to solicit orders for books but reserves to city official discretion to deny permits is unconstitutional as applied to religious publications.

(continues)

APPENDIX 3 *(continued)*

Issue	Case	Citation	Ratio[1]	Author of Opinion	Holding
Distribution of Religious Literature	Jones v. Opelika (II)	319 U.S. 103 (1943); dissents attached to *Murdock v. Pennsylvania (City of Jeannette)*, 319 U.S. 117 (1943), and *Douglas v. City of Jeannette*, 319 U.S. 166 (1943)	5-4	Per curiam (relying on Justice Douglas's opinion in *Murdock v. Pennsylvania (City of Jeannette)*, 319 U.S. 105 (1943), and Chief Justice Stone's dissent in *Jones v. Opelika (I)*, 316 U.S. 600 (1942))	Explicitly overruled *Jones v. Opelika (I)*, 316 U.S. 584 (1942); state may not prohibit distribution of religious literature; even if ordinance is "nondiscriminatory" on its face, the liberties guaranteed by the First Amendment are in a preferred position.
Distribution of Religious Literature; Flat License Tax	Murdock v. Pennsylvania (City of Jeannette)	319 U.S. 105 (1943); additional dissent attached to *Douglas v. City of Jeannette*, 319 U.S. 166 (1943)	5-4	Douglas, J.	A flat tax on all persons soliciting or selling goods is a "prior restraint" on those exercising their constitutional right to exercise their religion through distributing tracts and is thus unconstitutional.
Distribution of Religious Literature	Martin v. Struthers	319 U.S. 141 (1943); additional dissent attached to *Douglas v. City of Jeannette*, 319 U.S. 166 (1943)	5-4	Black, J.	Ordinance forbidding door-to-door distribution of religious pamphlets and circulars is unconstitutional because it violates free speech and press.

(continues)

APPENDIX 3   (continued)

Issue	Case	Citation	Ratio[1]	Author of Opinion	Holding
Federal Jurisdiction; Flat License Tax	Douglas v. City of Jeannette	319 U.S. 157 (1943)	7/2–0	Stone, C.J.	Case not properly in federal court; same ordinance addressed substantively in *Murdock v. Pennsylvania (City of Jeannette)*, 319 U.S. 105 (1943).
Flag Salute	West Virginia State Board of Education v. Barnette	319 U.S. 624 (1943)	6–3	Jackson, J.	Overruled *Minersville School District v. Gobitis*, 310 U.S. 586 (1940); First Amendment provides exemption from mandatory participation in rituals that parties conscientiously oppose—including saluting the flag in a public school classroom.
Parent/Guardian Rights	Prince v. Massachusetts	321 U.S. 158 (1944)	5–4	Rutledge, J.	State criminal law regulating child labor, applied to guardian of nine-year-old girl distributing religious tracts on the public streets in the evening, is not a denial or abridgment of free exercise rights.
Flat License Tax; Distribution of Religious Literature	Follett v. Town of McCormick	321 U.S. 573 (1944)	5/1–3	Douglas, J.	City may not impose flat license tax on minister distributing religious literature.
Religious Fraud	United States v. Ballard	322 U.S. 78 (1944)	5–4	Douglas, J.	Truth of religious belief is not subject to the scrutiny of a jury, but jury may be called upon to decide the sincerity of defendant's belief.
Conscientious Objection	In re Summers	325 U.S. 561 (1945)	5–4	Reed, J.	Refusal of bar admission to conscientious objector who refused to swear oath that he would serve in military not a free exercise violation.

(continues)

APPENDIX 3 *(continued)*

Issue	Case	Citation	Ratio[1]	Author of Opinion	Holding
Polygamy	*Chatwin v. United States*	326 U.S. 455 (1946)	7/1-0	Murphy, J.	Defendant who persuaded minor female to join him in "celestial" marriage not guilty of violating Federal Kidnapping Act.
Distribution of Religious Literature	*Marsh v. Alabama*	326 U.S. 501 (1946)	5-3	Black, J.	Statute imposing criminal penalties for distribution of religious literature in company-owned town is unconstitutional, per free exercise and speech clauses.
Distribution of Religious Literature	*Tucker v. Texas*	326 U.S. 517 (1946)	5-3	Black, J.	Statute imposing criminal penalties for distributing religious literature in government-owned town is unconstitutional, per free exercise and speech clauses.
Naturalization Qualifications; First Application of Article VI Test Oath Clause	*Girouard v. United States*	328 U.S. 61 (1946)	5-3	Douglas, J.	Government may not require a party who is conscientiously opposed to swear a military test oath before receiving naturalized citizenship status, per free exercise clause and Article VI ban on religious test oaths.
Polygamy	*Cleveland v. United States*	329 U.S. 14 (1946)	5/1-3	Douglas, J.	Upheld convictions of members of polygamous sect for transporting plural wives across state lines in violation of the Mann "White Slave" Act.
Conscientious Objection	*Eagles v. Samuels*	329 U.S. 304 (1946)	9-0	Douglas, J.	Civilian panel could properly determine that defendant failed to establish right to pre-ministerial deferment under Selective Service Act.

(continues)

APPENDIX 3 (continued)

Issue	Case	Citation	Ratio[1]	Author of Opinion	Holding
School Transportation; Disestablishment Clause Incorporated	Everson v. Board of Education	330 U.S. 1 (1947)	5-4	Black, J.	Expressly applied disestablishment clause to the states through the Fourteenth Amendment; but it is not establishment of religion for states to provide school bus transportation to religious and public school children alike.
Polygamy	Musser v. Utah	333 U.S. 95 (1948)	5/1-3	Jackson, J.	Conviction for polygamy vacated and remanded for consideration of state law questions.
Public School On-Campus Release Time	McCollum v. Board of Education	333 U.S. 203 (1948)	6/1/1-1	Black. J.	Disallowed public school "release time" program, wherein students were released from regular classes once a week to be able to participate in religious classes, which were held on campus.
Religious Speech	Saia v. New York	334 U.S. 558 (1948)	5-4	Douglas, J.	City ordinance prohibiting sound amplification, reserving discretion to police chief but giving no criteria for exercising that discretion, violates free speech because it operates as a prior restraint.
Conscientious Objection	Gara v. United States	340 U.S. 857 (1950), affirming, by an equally divided Court, 178 F.2d 38 (6th Cir. 1949)	4-4	Per ciruam	Upheld conviction for counseling another person conscientiously to object to draft registration and for actively opposing Selective Service Act.
Licensing	Niemotko v. Maryland	340 U.S. 268 (1951)	7/1/1-0	Vinson, C.J.	City may not deny a permit to use a public park for religious purposes when the applicable statute lacks clear criteria for such denials.

(continues)

APPENDIX 3 *(continued)*

Issue	Case	Citation	Ratio[1]	Author of Opinion	Holding
Licensing	*Kunz v. New York*	340 U.S. 290 (1951); concurrence attached to *Niemotko v. Maryland*, 340 U.S. 273 (1951)	6/1/1-1	Vinson, C.J.	City may not deny a license to a Baptist minister to preach in a public park because the licensing regulation improperly gave local officials discretion to deny licenses.
Standing	*Doremus v. Board of Education*	342 U.S. 429 (1952)	6-3	Jackson, J.	Party lacks standing to challenge Bible reading in public school when the student has already graduated.
Release Time from Public Schools	*Zorach v. Clauson*	343 U.S. 306 (1952)	6-3	Douglas, J.	Upheld the constitutionality of granting students release time from public schools to attend religious education or services.
Censorship	*Joseph Burstyn, Inc. v. Wilson*	343 U.S. 495 (1952)	6/2/1-0	Clark, J.	State law requiring permit for commercial showing of films but allowing censorship of films that are "sacrilegious" is a prior restraint and thus an unconstitutional violation of freedoms of speech and press.
Church Property; Regulation of Churches; Internal Church Governance	*Kedroff v. Saint Nicholas Cathedral*	344 U.S. 94 (1952)	8-1	Reed, J.	State religious incorporation law may not prohibit foreign religious authority from selecting church leaders and shift control to local church authorities; internal church law must be allowed to decide who makes such a decision.
Public Forum	*Fowler v. Rhode Island*	345 U.S. 67 (1953)	7/1/1-0	Douglas, J.	Struck down ordinance that prohibited religious speech but allowed for religious services in a public park because it was religiously discriminatory.

(continues)

APPENDIX 3 *(continued)*

Issue	Case	Citation	Ratio[1]	Author of Opinion	Holding
Licensing	*Poulos v. New Hampshire*	345 U.S. 395 (1953)	6/1-2	Reed, J.	Ordinance that leaves officials no discretion in granting permits but nevertheless requires payment of a sliding-scale fee to pay for city expenses incurred because of the permitted activity is constitutional.
Conscientious Objection	*United States v. Nugent*	346 U.S. 1 (1953)	5-3	Vinson, C.J.	Conscientious objector refusing to submit to induction into armed services has not shown the statute to be unconstitutional; Selective Service not required to disclose full FBI file on claimants.
Conscientious Objection	*Sicurella v. United States*	348 U.S. 385 (1955)	7-2	Clark, J.	Willingness to fight in "theocratic" wars does not disqualify a Jehovah's Witness who would otherwise qualify for exemption as a conscientious objector.
Conscientious Objection	*Simmons v. United States*	348 U.S. 397 (1955)	5/2-2	Clark, J.	Reversed conviction of defendant who was denied fair conscientious objection hearing because of government's failure to supply him "fair resume" of materials from his FBI files.
Conscientious Objection	*Gonzales v. United States*	348 U.S. 407 (1955)	6-3	Clark, J.	Reversed conviction of defendant who was denied fair conscientious objection hearing because of government's failure to supply him "fair resume" of materials from his FBI files.

(continues)

APPENDIX 3 *(continued)*

Issue	Case	Citation	Ratio[1]	Author of Opinion	Holding
Loyalty Oath	*First Unitarian Church v. County of Los Angeles*	357 U.S. 545 (1958); concurrence and dissent attached to *Speiser v. Randall,* 357 U.S. 529, 538 (1958)	7/1-1	Brennan, J.	Government may not require a party who is conscientiously opposed to swear a loyalty oath as a prerequisite to receiving a tax exemption.
Sunday Laws	*McGowan v. Maryland*	366 U.S. 420 (1961)	6/2-1	Warren, C.J.	Upheld state law proscribing certain business and commercial activity on Sunday against disestablishment clause challenge.
Sunday Laws	*Two Guys from Harrison Allentown, Inc. v. McGinley*	366 U.S. 582 (1961); concurrence and dissent attached to *McGowan v. Maryland,* 366 U.S. 459, 561 (1961)	6/2-1	Warren, C.J.	Sunday closing law does not violate disestablishment clause.
Sunday Laws	*Braunfeld v. Brown*	366 U.S. 599 (1961); other opinions attached to *McGowan v. Maryland,* 366 U.S. 459, 561 (1961)	Pluralities	Warren, C.J. (for the plurality)	Statute disallowing sales on Sunday does not violate free exercise rights of Jewish appellant, who is a strict Saturday sabbatarian.
Sunday Laws	*Gallagher v. Crown Kosher Super Market of Massachusetts*	366 U.S. 617 (1961); other opinions attached to *McGowan v. Maryland,* 366 U.S. 459, 561 (1961), and to *Braunfeld v. Brown,* 366 U.S. 610, 616 (1961)	Pluralities	Warren, C.J. (for the plurality)	Sunday closing law dows not violate free exercise rights of owner of kosher super-market, Orthodox Jewish customers, or rabbis with a duty to inspect kosher markets per Jewish dietary laws.
Mandatory Public Office Oath	*Torcaso v. Watkins*	367 U.S. 488 (1961)	7/2-0	Black, J.	Requirement of mandatory oath affirming belief in God as a prerequisite for holding public office is unconstitutional.

(continues)

APPENDIX 3 *(continued)*

Issue	Case	Citation	Ratio[1]	Author of Opinion	Holding
Prayer in Public School	*Engel v. Vitale*	370 U.S. 421 (1962)	6-1	Black, J.	Disallowed state program of daily (nondenominational) prayer in public school classrooms.
Federal Jurisdiction; Sunday Laws	*Arlan's Department Store v. Kentucky*	371 U.S. 218 (1962), letting stand 357 S.W.2d 708 (Ky. 1962)	8-1	Per curiam	Dismissed for lack of federal question; state court decision allowed to stand, upholding regulation that provided exemption from Sunday closing law only for those whose religion required rest on another day.
Bible Reading in Public School	*Abington School District v. Schempp*	374 U.S. 203 (1963)	8-1	Clark, J.	Mandatory Bible reading in public school classrooms violates disestablishment clause.
Unemployment Compensation Benefits	*Sherbert v. Verner*	374 U.S. 398 (1963)	6/1-2	Brennan, J.	Free exercise clause forbids state to deny unemployment compensation to claimant discharged from a job that would require her to work on her sabbath.
Bible Reading in Public School	*Chamberlain v. Public Instruction Board*	377 U.S. 402 (1964)	6-3	Per curiam	Reading of Bible and recitation of Lord's Prayer in public school is unconstitutional.
Prisoner's Rights	*Cooper v. Pate*	378 U.S. 546 (1964)	9-0	Per curiam	Muslim prisoner entitled to hearing on the merits that he was denied access to religious publications.

(continues)

APPENDIX 3 *(continued)*

Issue	Case	Citation	Ratio[1]	Author of Opinion	Holding
Conscientious Objection	*United States v. Seeger*	380 U.S. 163 (1965)	9-0	Clark, J.	Section 6(j) of Selective Service Act should be construed broadly, such that claimants may qualify for conscientious objector status if their belief is "sincere and meaningful" and occupies in their life "a place parallel to that filled by the God of those admittedly qualifying for the exemption."
Medical Care; Parent/Guardian Rights	*Jehovah's Witnesses v. King County Hospital*	390 U.S. 598 (1968); affirming 278 F.Supp. 488 (W.D. Wash.)	7-2	Per curiam	Blood transfusions may be administered to children, even if the parents are religiously opposed.
Standing	*Flast v. Cohen*	392 U.S. 83 (1968)	8-1	Warren, C.J.	Federal taxpayer has standing to challenge appropriation of federal funds for religious schools under the disestablishment clause.
Religious School Subsidization: Textbooks	*Board of Education v. Allen*	392 U.S. 236 (1968)	6-3	White, J.	Upheld state law requiring textbooks of "secular subjects" be provided to all students in the state, whether attending public or private (religious or other) schools.
Teaching Evolution in Public School	*Epperson v. Arkansas*	393 U.S. 97 (1968)	8/1-0	Fortas, J.	State criminal law which prohibited the teaching of evolution in a public school or state university violates the disestablishment clause.
Internal Church Governance; Church Property	*Presbyterian Church in the United States v. Mary Elizabeth Blue Hull Memorial Presbyterian Church*	393 U.S. 440 (1969)	9-0	Brennan, J.	Internal church disputes, including property disputes, should be governed by internal church law; civil courts may not use "departure from doctrine" standard, and should defer to the highest internal church authority.

(continues)

APPENDIX 3 *(continued)*

Issue	Case	Citation	Ratio[1]	Author of Opinion	Holding
Church Property	*Maryland and Virginia Churches v. Sharpsburg Church*	396 U.S. 367 (1970)	9-0	Per curiam	Civil courts may resolve church property disputes as long as they do not involve inquiry into church doctrine.
Tax Exemption	*Walz v. Tax Commission*	397 U.S. 664 (1970)	8-1	Burger, C.J.	Upheld state property tax exemption for church property against disestablishment clause challenge.
Conscientious Objection	*Welsh v. United States*	398 U.S. 333 (1970)	4/1-3	Black, J. (for the plurality)	Section 6(j) must be construed broadly; persons whose consciences, "spurred by deeply held moral, ethical, or religious beliefs," do not allow them to be an "instrument of war" are entitled to conscientious objector status.
Conscientious Objection	*Gillette v. United States*	401 U.S. 437 (1971)	7/1-1	Marshall, J.	Congress may exempt persons opposed to participating in all wars, but not those objecting to participation in a particular war, from military service without violating the First Amendment.
Employment	*Dewey v. Reynolds Metals Co.*	402 U.S. 689 (1971); affirming, by an equally divided Court, 429 F.2d 324 (6th Cir. 1970)	4-4	Per curiam	Rejected free exercise claim of a Sabbatarian who claimed he was wrongfully discharged on the basis of his religious beliefs.
Religious School Subsidization	*Lemon v. Kurtzman (I)*	403 U.S. 602 (1971)	6/1/1-0	Burger, C.J.	Disestablishment clause requires laws to have (1) a secular purpose; (2) primary effect that neither advances nor inhibits religion; and (3) no excessive entanglement of church and state; statute that reimbursed religious schools for costs of teaching secular subjects violates (3).

(continues)

APPENDIX 3 *(continued)*

Issue	Case	Citation	Ratio[1]	Author of Opinion	Holding
Construction Grants	Tilton v. Richardson	403 U.S. 672 (1971); additional opinions attached to Lemon v. Kurtzman (I), 403 U.S. 642, 661 (1971)	Pluralities	Burger, C.J.	Upheld federal grants that supported construction of library, science, and arts buildings at religious colleges as well as secular colleges.
Prisoner's Rights	Cruz v. Beto	405 U.S. 319 (1972)	6/1/1-1	Per curiam	Buddhist prisoner must be given "reasonable" opportunities to free exercise of religion.
Compulsory Education	Wisconsin v. Yoder	406 U.S. 205 (1972)	6-1 (but dissenting opinion concurred in part)	Burger, C.J.	Granted free exercise exemption to Amish, which exempted them from full compliance with compulsory school attendance law.
Religious School Subsidization	Lemon v. Kurtzman (II)	411 U.S. 192 (1973)	4/1-3	Burger, C.J. (for the plurality)	*Lemon v. Kurtzman (I)*, 403 U.S. 602 (1971), should not be applied retroactively.
Religious School Subsidization: Textbooks	Norwood v. Harrison	413 U.S. 455 (1973)	7/2-0	Burger, C.J.	State may loan textbooks on secular subjects to religious schools, but not if those schools discriminate on racial grounds.
Religious School Subsidization	Levitt v. Committee for Public Education and Religious Liberty	413 U.S. 472 (1973)	5/3-1	Burger, C.J.	States may not reimburse religious schools for most costs incurred to administer standardized tests and to prepare mandated state records.
Revenue Bonds	Hunt v. McNair	413 U.S. 734 (1973)	6-3	Powell, J.	Upheld issuance of revenue bonds for religious colleges.

(continues)

APPENDIX 3 *(continued)*

Issue	Case	Citation	Ratio[1]	Author of Opinion	Holding
Religious School Subsidization	*Committee for Public Education and Religious Liberty v. Nyquist*	413 U.S. 756 (1973)	Pluralities	Powell, J. (opinion of the Court)	Disallowed state reimbursement for low-income parents for part of religious school tuition; disallowed tax deduction for low-income parents whose children attended religious schools; disallowed direct grants to private schools serving low-income students for maintenance and repair costs.
Religious School Subsidization	*Sloan v. Lemon*	413 U.S. 825 (1973); additional opinions attached to *Committee for Public Education and Religious Liberty v. Nyquist*, 413 U.S. 798, 813 (1973)	6-3	Powell, J.	Disallowed state reimbursement to parents for portion of religious school tuition.
Education Benefits; Conscientious Objection	*Johnson v. Robinson*	415 U.S. 361 (1974)	8-1	Brennan, J.	Statute which grants educational benefits to military draftees but not to draftees who perform civilian alternative service is not unconstitutional.
Education Benefits; Conscientious Objection	*Hernandez v. Veterans' Administration*	415 U.S. 391 (1974)	8/1-0	Brennan, J.	Vacated a Ninth Circuit dismissal, for lack of jurisdiction, of a former conscientious objector's challenge to the statute at issue in *Johnson v. Robinson*, 415 U.S. 361 (1974) and remanded for reconsideration in light of that case.
Title I; Religious School Subsidization	*Wheeler v. Barrera*	417 U.S. 402 (1974)	6/1/1-1	Blackmun, J.	State receiving Title I funds must provide "comparable" but "not identical" services to disadvantaged students in both public and private schools, or forfeit Title I funds.

(continues)

APPENDIX 3 *(continued)*

Issue	Case	Citation	Ratio[1]	Author of Opinion	Holding
Conscientious Objection; Taxes	United States v. American Friends Service Committee	419 U.S. 7 (1974)	8-1	Per curiam	Upheld collection of taxes from those conscientiously opposed to having their taxes support the military.
Religious School Subsidization: Textbooks	Meek v. Pittenger	421 U.S. 349 (1975)	Pluralities	Stewart, J. (for the plurality)	State may loan textbooks, but not other various supplies and film, nor various counseling and other personnel, even if those were mandated by state policy.
Internal Church Governance	Serbian Orthodox Diocese v. Milivojevich	426 U.S. 696 (1976)	6/1-2	Brennan, J.	Internal church law must govern internal church matters, including removal from ecclesiastical posts; civil courts may not give marginal review to ecclesiastical decisions, even if they appear arbitrary, collusive, or fraudulent.
Construction Grants	Roemer v. Maryland Public Works Board	426 U.S. 736 (1976)	3/2-4	Blackmun, J. (for the plurality)	Upheld a state construction grant program that aided religious colleges alongside secular colleges.
Title VII; Employment	Parker Seal Company v. Cummins	429 U.S. 65 (1976), affirming, by an equally divided Court, 516 F.2d 544 (6th Cir. 1975)	4-4	Per curiam	Employer did not make sufficient effort to accommodate Sabbatarian.
State Motto	Wooley v. Maynard	430 U.S. 705 (1977)	Pluralities	Burger, C.J. (opinion of the Court)	State cannot require, upon pain of criminal sanctions, display of state motto upon vehicle license plates that violates religious owner's religious convictions.

(continues)

APPENDIX 3 *(continued)*

Issue	Case	Citation	Ratio[1]	Author of Opinion	Holding
Title VII; Employment Accommodation	*Trans World Airlines, Inc. v. Hardison*	432 U.S. 63 (1977)	7-2	White, J.	Employer's attempted accommodation of employee's religious beliefs was reasonable; no obligation to violate union contracts or incur additional costs without express congressional intent.
Religious School Subsidization	*Wolman v. Walter*	433 U.S. 229 (1977)	Pluralities	Blackmun, J. (for the plurality)	State may provide various personnel, diagnostic services, and standardized testing but may not loan instructional materials to private schools or to parents or provide transportation for field trips by private schools.
Title VII; Employment Accommodation	*Parker Seal Company v. Cummins*	433 U.S. 903 (1977), vacating 429 U.S. 65 (1976)	8-0	Vacated and remanded	Vacated and remanded for consideration in light of *Trans World Airlines, Inc. v. Hardison.* 432 U.S. 63 (1977).
Religious School Subsidization	*New York v. Cathedral Academy*	434 U.S. 125 (1977)	6-3	Stewart, J.	Disallowed reimbursement of religious schools for state-mandated record keeping.
Clergy Disqualified from Public Office	*McDaniel v. Paty*	435 U.S. 618 (1978)	4/2/1/1-0	Burger, J. (for the plurality)	State constitutional prohibition against clergy holding political office is unconstitutional
Labor Law	*National Labor Relations Board v. Catholic Bishop of Chicago*	440 U.S. 490 (1979)	5-4	Burger, C.J.	Denied jurisdiction to the NLRB over a Catholic school's teachers, based on the rights of a religious group to function separately from the state.

(continues)

APPENDIX 3 *(continued)*

Issue	Case	Citation	Ratio[1]	Author of Opinion	Holding
Church Property; Internal Church Governance	*Jones v. Wolf*	443 U.S. 595 (1979)	5-4	Blackmun, J.	Courts may decide intrachurch property disputes using "neutral principles of law," and thus avoid deferring all decisionmaking to internal church authorities.
Religious School Subsidization	*Committee for Public Education and Religious Liberty v. Regan*	444 U.S. 646 (1980)	5-4	White, J.	Upheld reimbursement of religious schools for "actual costs" of state-mandated tests and reporting.
Abortion and Religion	*Harris v. McRae*	448 U.S. 297 (1980)	5-4	Stewart, J.	Upheld congressional restrictions on Medicaid funded abortions.
Ten Commandments in Public School	*Stone v. Graham*	449 U.S. 39 (1980)	5-4	Per curiam	Struck down state statute that required the posting of a plaque bearing the Ten Commandments on the wall of each public school classroom.
Unemployment Compensation Benefits	*Thomas v. Review Board, Indiana Employment Security Division*	450 U.S. 707 (1981)	7/1-1	Burger, C.J.	Government may not deny unemployment benefits to claimant who refused to accept employment, based on individual religious beliefs, at a job that produced parts that would be used in military armaments.
Religious Schools and Unemployment Compensation Taxes	*St. Martin Evangelical Lutheran Church v. South Dakota*	451 U.S. 772 (1981)	8/1-0	Blackmun, J.	The word "church" in the Federal Unemployment Tax Act exempting service performed in the employ of a church applies to schools that have no separate legal existence from a church.

(continues)

APPENDIX 3 *(continued)*

Issue	Case	Citation	Ratio[1]	Author of Opinion	Holding
Distribution of Religious Literature; Charitable Solicitation Law	*Heffron v. International Society for Krishna Consciousness*	452 U.S. 640 (1981)	Pluralities	White, J. (opinion of the Court)	Regulation requiring all persons and groups wishing to sell, exhibit, or distribute materials at a fair do so from a rented booth does not violate First Amendment rights of itinerant religious group.
Equal Access	*Widmar v. Vincent*	454 U.S. 263 (1981)	7/1-1	Powell, J.	When a state university creates a limited public forum open to voluntary student groups, religious groups must be given "equal access" to that forum.
Standing	*Valley Forge Christian College v. Americans United for Separation of Church and State*	454 U.S. 464 (1982)	5-4	Rehnquist, J.	Religious liberty litigant, as federal taxpayer, lacked standing to challenge federal donation of property to religious organizations.
Tax Exemption	*United States v. Lee*	455 U.S. 252 (1982)	8/1-0	Burger, C.J.	Denied free exercise exemption from social security taxes for Amish employer.
Prayer in Public School	*Treen v. Karen B.*	455 U.S. 913 (1982); affirming 653 F.2d 897 (5th Cir. 1981)	9-0	Affirmed on appeal	Affirmed, without comment, a Fifth Circuit opinion which struck down a statute authorizing student volunteers to lead prayer in public school classrooms.
Charitable Solicitation Law	*Larson v. Valente*	456 U.S. 228 (1982)	5-4	Brennan, J.	Disallowed state law requiring only certain religious organizations to make revenue reports.

(continues)

APPENDIX 3 *(continued)*

Issue	Case	Citation	Ratio[1]	Author of Opinion	Holding
Charitable Solicitation Law	*Rusk v. Espinoza*	456 U.S. 951 (1982); affirming 634 F.2d 477 (10th Cir. 1980)	7-2	Affirmed on Appeal	Affirmed, without comment, a Tenth Circuit opinion which struck down ordinance that required officials to distinguish between "religious" and "secular" religious activities of religious bodies for licensing and regulation purposes.
Federal Jurisdiction; Unemployment Tax	*California v. Grace Brethren Church*	457 U.S. 393 (1982)	7-2	O'Connor, J.	Federal District Court did not have jurisdiction to hear case involving state tax.
Zoning; Delegation of Civil Power	*Larkin v. Grendel's Den*	459 U.S. 116 (1982)	8-1	Burger, C.J.	States may not grant veto power to churches over whether a liquor license will be granted to a facility within 500 feet from the church property.
Tax Exempt Status	*Bob Jones University v. United States*	461 U.S. 574 (1983)	7/1-1	Burger, C.J.	Upheld IRS decision to remove federal tax exempt status from religious university that engaged in racial discrimination, on the basis of its religious convictions, in matriculation and employment decisions.
State Income Tax Deduction	*Mueller v. Allen*	463 U.S. 388 (1983)	5-4	Rehnquist, J.	Upheld state law that allowed parents of private school children to claim state income tax deductions for the costs of "tuition, transportation, and textbooks."
Legislative Prayer	*Marsh v. Chambers*	463 U.S. 783 (1983)	6-3	Burger, C.J.	Upheld, against disestablishment clause challenge, the state practice of appointing legislative chaplains to offer prayers at the General Assembly.

(continues)

APPENDIX 3 *(continued)*

Issue	Case	Citation	Ratio[1]	Author of Opinion	Holding
Religious Display	*Lynch v. Donnelly*	465 U.S. 668 (1984)	5-4	Burger, C.J.	Upheld government practice of displaying nativity scene as part of holiday display in city park.
Conscientious Objection	*Wayte v. United States*	470 U.S. 598 (1985)	7-2	Powell, J.	"Passive enforcement policy" and "beg policy" of Selective Service System do not violate First (or Fifth) Amendment.
Religious Display	*Village of Scarsdale v. McCreary*	471 U.S. 83 (1985); affirming, by an equally divided Court, 739 F.2d 716 (2d Cir. 1984)	4-4	Per curiam	Accommodation of displaying a nativity scene, at no expense to city, is not a violation of disestablishment clause.
Fair Labor Standards Act	*Tony and Susan Alamo Foundation v. Secretary of Labor*	471 U.S. 290 (1985)	9-0	White, J.	Application of Fair Labor Standards Act does not obstruct core religious functions of a foundation.
Moment of Silence in Public School	*Wallace v. Jaffree*	472 U.S. 38 (1985)	5/1-3	Stevens, J.	Struck down state law providing for moments of silence (for prayer or meditation) in public schools.
Driver's License Photograph	*Jensen v. Quaring*	472 U.S. 478 (1985), affirming, by an equally divided Court, 728 F.2d 1121 (8th Cir. 1984)	4-4	Per curiam	Struck down requirement that applicant submit to having color photograph taken to affix on driver's license as an unconstitutional burden on applicant's free exercise of her sincerely held religious beliefs.
Sabbath Laws	*Estate of Thornton v. Caldor*	472 U.S. 703 (1985)	8-1	Burger, C.J.	Struck down state law that allowed private sector employees to pick their Sabbath, which employers must accommodate.

(continues)

APPENDIX 3 *(continued)*

Issue	Case	Citation	Ratio[1]	Author of Opinion	Holding
Religious School Subsidization: Shared Time Programs	*Grand Rapids School District v. Ball*	473 U.S. 373 (1985)	Pluralities	Brennan, J. (opinion of the Court)	States may not lend public school personnel to teach remedial and enrichment courses in religious schools.
Title I Remedial Services	*Aguilar v. Felton*	473 U.S. 402 (1985)	5-4	Brennan, J.	States may not use public school teachers to hold remedial educational programs to indigent children in classrooms leased from religious schools.
State Aid for Vocational Education at Religious College	*Witters v. Washington Department of Services for the Blind*	474 U.S. 481 (1986)	8/1-0	Marshall, J.	Upheld state program furnishing aid to a visually impaired student attending a Christian college for vocational education.
Standing	*Bender v. Williamsport Area School District*	475 U.S. 534 (1986)	5-4	Stevens, J.	School board member has no standing, in his capacity as a parent, to appeal a board decision affecting the religious rights of his child in the school.
Military Regulations	*Goldman v. Weinberger*	475 U.S. 503 (1986)	5-4	Rehnquist, J.	Military officer does not have free exercise right to wear his yarmulke on duty.
Social Security Number Requirement	*Bowen v. Roy*	476 U.S. 693 (1986)	Pluralities	Burger, C.J. (for the plurality)	Agency's use of social security number does not violate free exercise rights of native American, who believes such use would impair his child's spirit.

(continues)

APPENDIX 3 *(continued)*

Issue	Case	Citation	Ratio[1]	Author of Opinion	Holding
Federal Jurisdiction	*Ohio Civil Rights Commission v. Dayton Christian Schools*	477 U.S. 619 (1986)	5/4-0	Rehnquist, J.	Federal District Courts should abstain from adjudicating pending state proceedings as long as federal plaintiff has opportunity to litigate his constitutional claim.
Title VII; Employment Accommodation	*Ansonia Board of Education v. Philbrook*	479 U.S. 60 (1986)	Pluralities	Rehnquist, C.J. (opinion of the Court)	Employer not required to accept employee's preferred religious accommodation.
Unemployment Compensation Benefits	*Hobbie v. Unemployment Appeals Commission of Florida*	480 U.S. 136 (1987)	6/1-1	Brennan, J.	Government may not deny unemployment benefits to claimant, a new religious convert, who was discharged for refusal to work on her Sabbath.
Religious Discrimination	*Shaare Tefila Congregation v. Cobb*	481 U.S. 615 (1987)	9-0	White, J.	Jews may rely on racial clause of civil rights statute for cause of action against desecrators of synagogue.
Prisoner's Rights	*O'Lone v. Estate of Shabazz*	482 U.S. 342 (1987)	5-4	Rehnquist, C.J.	Denying free exercise accommodation for Muslim prisoner to engage in collective Friday worship.
Overbreadth Doctrine	*Airport Commissioners of Los Angeles v. Jews for Jesus*	482 U.S. 569 (1987)	9-0	O'Connor, J.	Airport regulation banning all "first amendment activities" within a public (or nonpublic) forum is a violation of the free speech clause.
Creationism in Public School	*Edwards v. Aguillard*	482 U.S. 578 (1987)	6/1-2	Brennan, J.	Struck down state statute that required, in public schools, teaching of both creation and evolution, if a theory of origins was taught at all.

(continues)

APPENDIX 3 *(continued)*

Issue	Case	Citation	Ratio[1]	Author of Opinion	Holding
Employment Discrimination	*Corporation of the Presiding Bishop of the Church of Jesus Christ of Latter-Day Saints v. Amos*	483 U.S. 327 (1987)	5/2/1/1-0	White, J.	Upheld exemption of religious school from Civil Rights prohibition against religious discrimination; religious employer not required to retain employee who has lapsed from its faith.
Standing	*Karcher v. May*	484 U.S. 72 (1987)	8/1-0	O'Connor, J.	State legislators cannot appeal a disestablishment case involving a moment of silence law for which they voted, but which the legislature has chosen not to appeal.
Native American Rights	*Lyng v. Northwest Indian Cemetery Protective Association*	485 U.S. 439 (1988)	5-3	O'Connor, J.	Construction of road through section of national forest regarded as sacred ground by three tribes does not violate free exercise clause; American Indian Religious Freedom Act provides no cause of action.
Unemployment Compensation Benefits	*Employment Division, Oregon v. Smith (I)*	485 U.S. 660 (1988)	5-3	Stevens, J.	State must determine whether religious use of peyote is legal under state law.
Standing	*United States Catholic Conference v. Abortion Rights Mobilization*	487 U.S. 72 (1988)	8-1	Kennedy, J.	A nonparty witness held in contempt had standing to challenge federal court's jurisdiction over case.
Religious Social Agency Subsidization	*Bowen v. Kendrick*	487 U.S. 589 (1988)	5-4	Rehnquist, C.J.	Upheld federal funding of Catholic counseling centers for pregnant teenagers, in implementation of the Adolescent Family Life Act.

(continues)

APPENDIX 3 *(continued)*

Issue	Case	Citation	Ratio[1]	Author of Opinion	Holding
Tax Exemption	*Texas Monthly v. Bullock*	489 U.S. 1 (1989)	3/2/1-3	Brennan, J. (for the plurality)	State sales tax exemption exclusively for religious periodicals violates disestablishment clause.
Unemployment Compensation Benefits	*Frazee v. Illinois Department of Employment Security*	489 U.S. 829 (1989)	9-0	White, J.	State may not deny unemployment benefits to claimant who refused to take a job that might require him to work on Sunday.
Tax Deductions	*Hernandez v. Commissioner of Internal Revenue*	490 U.S. 680 (1989)	5-2	Marshall, J.	Upheld denial of charitable deduction for contributions to the Church of Scientology, given in return for religious services.
Religious Display	*County of Allegheny v. ACLU*	492 U.S. 573 (1989)	Pluralities	Blackmun, J. (for the plurality)	Disallowed county's practice of allowing a privately funded nativity scene in front of its courthouse but upheld the display of a menorah on courthouse grounds.
Tax Exemption	*Jimmy Swaggart Ministries v. Board of Equalization of California*	493 U.S. 378 (1990)	9-0	O'Connor, J.	Levy of state sales and use taxes on religious articles is not a prior restraint.
Unemployment Compensation Benefits	*Employment Division v. Smith (II)*	494 U.S. 872 (1990)	5/1-3	Scalia, J.	Denial of unemployment compensation benefits to Native American who was discharged for sacramental use of peyote, a proscribed narcotic, does not violate free exercise clause.

(continues)

APPENDIX 3 (continued)

Issue	Case	Citation	Ratio[1]	Author of Opinion	Holding
Public Safety Exemption	*Minnesota v. Hershberger*	495 U.S. 901 (1990)	7-2	Vacating and remanding on appeal	Vacated a state supreme court holding that Amish were entitled to free exercise exemption from a law requiring them to place reflective triangles on their buggies for public safety reasons and remanded for reconsideration in light of *Employment Division v. Smith (II)*, 494 U.S. 872 (1990).
Tax Deductions	*Davis v. United States*	495 U.S. 472 (1990)	9-0	O'Connor, J.	Upheld denial of charitable deduction for contribution in return for religious services.
Equal Access	*Board of Education of the Westside Community Schools v. Mergens*	496 U.S. 226 (1990)	4/2/2-1	O'Connor, J. (for the plurality)	Equal Access Act, which applies *Widmar v. Vincent*, 454 U.S. 263 (1981) rule to public high schools, does not violate disestablishment clause.
Title VII; Employment Discrimination	*EEOC v. Arabian American Oil Co.*	499 U.S. 244 (1991)	5/1-3	Rehnquist, C.J.	Nondiscrimination in employment rules of Title VII do not apply outside U.S. to U.S. employers who employ U.S. citizens abroad.
Graduation Prayers in Public School	*Lee v. Weisman*	505 U.S. 577 (1991)	5-4	Kennedy, J.	Ecumenical prayer by Jewish rabbi at a public middle school graduation ceremony violates disestablishment clause.
Forum Analysis; Religious Solicitation	*International Society for Krishna Consciousness v. Lee*	505 U.S. 672 (1992)	Pluralities	Rehnquist, C.J. (opinion of the Court)	An airport terminal operated by a public authority is a nonpublic forum, and therefore a ban on distribution of religious literature and solicitation need only satisfy a reasonableness standard; the ban on solicitation here is reasonable.

(continues)

APPENDIX 3 *(continued)*

Issue	Case	Citation	Ratio[1]	Author of Opinion	Holding
Distribution of Religious Literature	Lee v. International Society for Krishna Consciousness	505 U.S. 830 (1992)	5-4	Per curiam	Ban on distribution of religious materials in airport terminals is invalid under First Amendment, as it does not satisfy a reasonableness standard.
Mootness; IRS Summons	Church of Scientology of California v. United States	506 U.S. 9 (1992)	9-0	Stevens, J.	Compliance with an enforcement order to surrender taped conversations does not render moot an appeal concerning the lawfulness of the search claim.
Equal Access	Lamb's Chapel v. Center Moriches Union Free School District	508 U.S. 384 (1993)	6/2/1-0	White, J.	Public school that opens its school facilities, during nonschool time, to various voluntary community groups may not exclude only those with religious viewpoint; equal access must be given.
Ritual Sacrifice of Animals	Church of the Lukumi Babalu Aye, Inc. v. City of Hialeah	508 U.S. 520 (1993)	9-0, but concurring opinions	Kennedy, J. (opinion of the Court, except as to Part II.A.2)	Local ordinance discriminating against ritual sacrifice of animals violates the free exercise clause.
Religious School Subsidy: Interpreter	Zobrest v. Catalina Foothills School District	509 U.S. 1 (1993)	5-4	Rehnquist, C.J.	State's provision of an interpreter to disabled student at religious high school does not violate disestablishment clause.
Delegation of Civil Power	Board of Education of Kiryas Joel Village School District v. Grumet	512 U.S. 687 (1994)	4/1/1-3	Souter, J. (for the plurality)	State's creation of a single public school district within an exclusively Satmar Hasidic community violates disestablishment clause.

(continues)

APPENDIX 3 *(continued)*

Issue	Case	Citation	Ratio[1]	Author of Opinion	Holding
Religious Display	*Capitol Square Review and Advisory Board v. Pinette*	515 U.S. 753 (1995)	4/3-2	Scalia J. (for the plurality)	City may not ban private display of KKK cross in an otherwise open public forum.
Equal Access	*Rosenberger v. University of Virginia*	515 U.S. 819 (1995)	5-4	Kennedy, J.	State university must grant equal access to funding for voluntary religious student groups as for voluntary nonreligious student groups.
Title 1 Remedial Services	*Agostini v. Felton*	521 U.S. 203 (1997)	5-4	O'Connor, J.	Overturned *Aguilar v. Felton*, 473 U.S. 402 (1985); the mere presence of a state employee in a religious institution is not per se unconstitutional, and thus the state may provide Title I remedial services to students at religious schools.
Free Exercise Standard of Review	*City of Boerne v. Flores*	521 U.S. 507 (1997)	5/1-3	Kennedy, J.	Religious Freedom Restoration Act (1993), which required use of the compelling state interest test for free exercise cases, declared unconstitutional, as applied to the state.

NOTES

Introduction

1. Saul K. Padover, ed., *The Complete Jefferson, Containing His Major Writings* (Freeport, NY, 1943), 538, 673–676, 1147; P. L. Ford, ed., *The Works of Thomas Jefferson*, 12 vols. (New York, 1904–1905), 11:7; Julian Boyd, ed., *The Papers of Thomas Jefferson*, 9 vols. (Princeton, 1950), 1:537–539. See analysis in Sidney E. Mead, *The Lively Experiment: The Shaping of Christianity in America* (New York, 1963), 55–71. The concept of an "experiment" in religious liberty goes back at least to John Locke and was used by American colonists Roger Williams and William Penn in the seventeenth century. See John Locke, "A Second Letter Concerning Toleration (c. 1690)," in *The Works of John Locke*, 12th ed. (London, 1824), 5:59–138, at 63ff., and Chapter 1 herein.

2. 310 U.S. 296 (1940); 330 U.S. 1 (1947).

3. Elhanan Winchester, "A Century Sermon on the Glorious Revolution (London, 1788)," in *Political Sermons of the American Founding Era, 1730–1805*, ed. Ellis Sandoz (Indianapolis, 1991), 969, 988–989.

4. Ezra Stiles, *The United States Elevated to Glory and Honor* (New Haven, 1783), 54–55 (spelling modernized and original italics removed).

5. William W. Bassett, *Religious Organizations and the Law*, rev. ed. (St. Paul, 1998), xi-xvii, with sources listed in xi, n. 1; Martin E. Marty, "Revising the Map of American Religion," *Annals of the American Academy of Political and Social Science* 558 (July 1998): 13–27, at 17.

6. On Jews, see *Goldman v. Weinberger*, 475 U.S. 503 (1986) (rejecting free exercise claim of a military officer to wear his yarmulke on duty); *Board of Education of Kiryas Joel Village School District v. Grumet*, 512 U.S. 687 (1994) (state's creation of a single public school district within an exclusively Satmar Hasidic community violates disestablishment clause). On Native Americans, see *Bowen v. Roy*, 476 U.S. 693 (1986) (administration's use of social security number does not violate free exercise rights of Native American, who believes such use would impair his child's spirit); *Lyng v. Northwest Indian Cemetery Protective Association*, 485 U.S. 439 (1988) (construction of road through section of national forest regarded as sacred ground by three tribes does not violate free exercise clause); *Employment Division, Department of Human Resources of Oregon v. Smith*, 494 U.S. 872 (1990) (denial of unemployment compensation to Native American discharged for sacramental use of peyote, a proscribed narcotic, does not violate free exercise clause). On Muslims,

see *O'Lone v. Estate of Shabazz*, 482 U.S. 342 (1987) (denies free exercise accommodation for Muslim prisoner to engage in collective Friday worship).

7. Mary Ann Glendon and Raul F. Yanes, "Structural Free Exercise," *Michigan Law Review* 90 (1991): 477–550, at 478. See further Angela C. Carmella, "Mary Ann Glendon on Religious Liberty: The Social Nature of the Person and the Public Nature of Religion," *Notre Dame Law Review* 73 (1998): 1191–1216.

8. Religious Freedom Restoration Act (1993), 42 U.S.C. 2000bb-bb4, declared unconstitutional as to state governments in *City of Boerne v. Flores*, 521 U.S. 507 (1997).

9. Steven D. Smith, *Foreordained Failure: The Quest for a Constitutional Principle of Religious Freedom* (New York/Oxford, 1995), vi; Frederick Mark Gedicks, *The Rhetoric of Church and State* (Durham, NC, 1995), 8–24. See analysis in Thomas C. Berg, "Religion Clause Anti-Theories," *Notre Dame Law Review* 72 (1997): 693–751; Christopher L. Eisgruber and Lawrence G. Sager, "Unthinking Religious Freedom," *Texas Law Review* 74 (1996): 577–614.

10. See summary in Rodney K. Smith, "Converting the Religious Equality Amendment into a Statute with a Little 'Conscience,'" *Brigham Young University Law Review* (1996): 644–688; Kent Greenawalt, "Why Now Is Not the Time for Constitutional Amendment: The Limited Reach of *City of Boerne v. Flores*," *William and Mary Law Review* 39 (1998): 689.

11. Francis Bacon, "The Great Instauration (1620)," preface, reprinted in id., *The New Organon and Related Writings*, ed. Fulton H. Anderson (Indianapolis, 1960), 3–30, at 11.

12. Francis Bacon, "The New Organon (1620)," Aphorisms Book One, 70, 82, 103, 104, reprinted in Bacon, *The New Organon and Related Writings*, 31–268, at 67–69, 78–80, 97–98.

13. See generally Barbara Shapiro, "Sir Francis Bacon and the Mid-Seventeenth Century Movement for Law Reform," *American Journal of Legal History* 24 (1980): 331–362; Daniel Coquillette, *Francis Bacon* (Stanford, 1992).

14. Cf. Isaac Kramnick and R. Laurence Moore, *The Godless Constitution: The Case Against Religious Correctness* (New York/London, 1996).

15. See John H. Garvey, *What Are Freedoms For?* (Cambridge, MA, 1996), 42–57.

16. See Mark DeWolfe Howe, *The Garden and the Wilderness: Religion and the Government in American Constitutional History* (Chicago/London, 1965), chap. 1. For modern expositions of this theme, from different perspectives, see Stephen L. Carter, *The Culture of Disbelief: How American Law and Politics Trivializes Religious Devotion* (New York, 1993); Bette Novit Evans, *Interpreting the Free Exercise of Religion: The Constitution and American Pluralism* (Chapel Hill, NC, 1997), 11–45.

17. John T. Noonan Jr., "The Tensions and the Ideals," in *Religious Human Rights in Global Perspective: Legal Perspectives*, ed. Johan D. van der Vyver and John Witte Jr. (The Hague/Boston/London, 1996), 593–606, at 604. See more generally Scott C. Idleman, "The Role of Religious Values in Judicial Decision Making," *Indiana Law Journal* 68 (1993): 433.

18. Cf. Robert M. Cover, "The Supreme Court 1982 Term—Foreword: Nomos and Narrative," *Harvard Law Review* 97 (1983): 4–68. See also Franklin Gamwell,

The Meaning of Religious Freedom: Modern Politics and the Democratic Resolution (Syracuse, NY, 1995).

19. See, e.g., John T. Noonan Jr., *The Lustre of Our Country: The American Experience of Religious Freedom* (Berkeley/Los Angeles/London, 1998); Symposium, "The Relevance of Religion to a Lawyer's Work: An Interfaith Conference," *Fordham Law Review* 66 (1998): 1075–1651; Symposium, "Religion and the Judicial Process: Legal, Ethical, and Empirical Dimensions," *Marquette Law Review* 81 (1998): 177–568.

Chapter One

1. Galatians 5:1,13; 2 Corinthians 3:17; John 8:32,36; Romans 8:21 (RSV). On the prominence and use of the Bible as a political document in eighteenth-century America, see Mark A. Noll, Nathan O. Hatch, and George M. Marsden, *The Search for Christian America*, rev. ed. (Colorado Springs, 1989); Barry Shain, *The Myth of American Individualism: The Protestant Origins of American Political Thought* (Princeton, 1994), 194ff.

2. Donald S. Lutz, *The Origins of American Constitutionalism* (Baton Rouge, LA/London, 1988), 140–141. See the collection in Ellis Sandoz, ed., *Political Sermons of the American Founding Era, 1730–1805* (Indianapolis, 1991); and analysis in Nathan O. Hatch, *The Sacred Cause of Liberty* (New Haven, 1977); Harry S. Stout, *The New England Soul: Preaching and Religious Culture in Colonial New England* (New York/Oxford, 1986).

3. See Lutz, *Origins*, 139–149 (of all citations in these writings, those to the Bible constituted 34 percent, Montesquieu 8.3 percent, Blackstone 7.9 percent, and Locke 2.9 percent).

4. James Madison, "Memorial and Remonstrance Against Religious Assessments (1785)," sec. 9, in *The Papers of James Madison*, ed. W. T. Hutchinson, William M. E. Rachal, and Robert A. Rutland (Chicago, 1962), 8:298.

5. Elhanan Winchester, "A Century Sermon on the Glorious Revolution (1788)," in Sandoz, ed., *Political Sermons*, 969–1000, at 989–990.

6. Thomas Jefferson, "Notes on the State of Virginia (1781–1785)," Query XVII, in *The Complete Jefferson, Containing His Major Writings*, ed. Saul K. Padover (Freeport, NY, 1943), 673–676.

7. Madison, "Memorial and Remonstrance," secs. 8, 11.

8. John Adams, *A Defense of the Constitutions of Government in the United States of America* (1788), in *The Works of John Adams*, ed. C. F. Adams (Boston, 1850–1856), vols. 4–6; see further his "A Dissertation on the Canon and Feudal Law (1774)," in ibid., 3:447–461, esp. 451.

9. See generally Charles N. Cochrane, *Christianity and Classical Culture* (London, 1940); Luke Timothy Johnson, "Religious Rights and Christian Texts," in *Religious Human Rights in Global Perspective: Religious Perspectives*, ed. John Witte Jr. and Johan D. van der Vyver (The Hague/Boston/London, 1996), 65–96.

10. As recounted in Lactantius, *De Mortibus Persecutorum [c. 315]*, 48.2–12, ed. and trans. J. L. Creed (Oxford, 1984), 71–73.

11. Reprinted in Sidney Z. Ehler and John B. Morrall, eds., *Church and State Through the Centuries: A Collection of Historic Documents with Commentaries* (Westminster, MD, 1954), 7.

12. See, e.g., Amnon Linder, *The Jews in Roman Imperial Legislation* (Detroit, 1987).

13. See, e.g., the ample collection in *The Theodosian Code and Novels, and the Sirmondian Constitutions,* trans. Clyde Pharr (Princeton, 1952).

14. Reprinted in Ehler and Morrall, eds., *Church and State,* 10–11.

15. See Harold J. Berman, *Law and Revolution: The Formation of the Western Legal Tradition* (Cambridge, MA, 1983).

16. Reprinted in Ehler and Morrall, eds., *Church and State,* 43–44. See further Brian Tierney, *The Crisis of Church and State,* 1050–1300 (Englewood Cliffs, NJ, 1964), 51ff.

17. On the medieval concept of jurisdiction, see generally Berman, *Law and Revolution,* 221ff., 260ff.

18. See sources and discussion in Brian Tierney, *The Idea of Natural Rights: Studies on Natural Rights, Natural Law, and Church Law, 1150–1625* (Atlanta, 1997); id., *Rights, Law, and Infallibility in Medieval Thought* (Aldershot, UK, 1997); Charles J. Reid Jr., *Rights in Thirteenth-Century Canon Law: A Historical Investigation* (Ph.D. Diss., Cornell University, Ithaca, NY, 1994).

19. See, e.g., James Parkes, *The Jew in the Medieval Community: A Study of His Political and Economic Situation,* 2d ed. (New York, 1976); Solomon Grayzel, *The Church and the Jews in the XIIIth Century* (Philadelphia, 1933).

20. See, e.g., R. H. Helmholz, ed., *Canon Law in Protestant Lands* (Berlin, 1992); id., *Roman Canon Law in Reformation England* (Cambridge/New York, 1990); Udo Wolter, *Ius canonicum in iure civile* (Köln, 1975).

21. Reprinted in Carl Stephenson and Frederick G. Marcham, eds., *Sources of English Constitutional History,* rev. ed. (New York/San Francisco, 1972), 226–228.

22. Reprinted and analyzed in Ehler and Morrall, eds., *Church and State,* 96–144.

23. See my *Law and Protestantism: The Legal Teachings of the Lutheran Reformation* (Cambridge, 2000), chap. 2.

24. See Tierney, *The Idea of Natural Rights,* 288ff.

25. See my *Law and Protestantism,* chaps. 2 and 9.

26. Reprinted in Ehler and Morrall, eds., *Church and State,* 164–173.

27. Reprinted in Stephenson and Marcham, eds., *Sources of English Constitutional History,* 311–312.

28. See generally Joseph Lecler, *Toleration and the Reformation,* 4 vols. (New York, 1960); G. R. Elton, *The Tudor Constitution,* 2d ed. (Cambridge, 1982).

29. See sources and discussion in Walter Klaassen, ed., *Anabaptism in Outline: Selected Primary Sources* (Scottsdale, PA, 1981); Robert Friedmann, *The Theology of Anabaptism* (Scottsdale, PA, 1973); Guy Hershberger, ed., *The Recovery of the Anabaptist Vision* (Scottsdale, PA, 1957). See generally George H. Williams, *The Radical Reformation,* 3d ed. (Kirksville, MO, 1992).

30. See sources and discussion in my "Moderate Religious Liberty in the Theology of John Calvin," *Calvin Theological Journal* 31 (1996): 359–403.

31. For medieval constructions, see Tierney, *The Idea of Natural Rights*, 55ff., 208ff.; and C. Morris, *The Discovery of the Individual, 1050–1200* (London, 1972).

32. *The Book of Common Prayer [1559]*, ed. John E. Booty (Charlottesville, VA, 1976).

33. See sources and discussion in Max L. Stackhouse and Deirdre King Hainsworth, "Deciding for God: The Right to Convert in Protestant Perspectives," in *Sharing the Book: Comparative Religious Perspectives on the Rights and Wrongs of Mission*, ed. John Witte Jr. and Richard C. Martin (Maryknoll, NY, 1999), chap. 8.

34. See sources and discussion in Harold J. Berman and John Witte Jr., "The Transformation of Western Legal Philosophy in Lutheran Germany," *Southern California Law Review* 62 (1989): 1573–1660.

35. See, e.g., Joseph LeCler and Marius-François Valkhoff, *Les premiers défenseurs de la liberté religieuse*, 2 vols. (Paris, 1969); Heinrich Lutz, ed., *Zur Geschichte der Toleranz und Religionsfreiheit* (Darmstadt, 1977); Henry Kamen, *The Rise of Toleration* (New York, 1967).

36. See documents in Wilhelm G. Grewe, *Fontes Historiae Iuris Gentium* (Berlin, 1988), 2:82ff.; and in E. H. Kossmann and A. Mellink, eds., *Texts Concerning the Revolt of the Netherlands* (London/New York, 1974).

37. Quoted in *New England Magazine* (n.s.) 10 (1894): 517, 521. See also James Madison: "It was the belief of all sects at one time that the establishment of Religion by law was right and necessary; that the true religion ought to be established in exclusion of every other; and that the only question to be decided was, which was the true religion. The example of Holland proved that a toleration of sects dissenting from the established sect was safe, and even useful." Quoted by Anson P. Stokes, *Church and State in the United States*, 3 vols. (New York, 1950), 1:120.

38. Reprinted in Ehler and Morrall, eds., *Church and State*, 193–198.

39. Reprinted in ibid., 208–213.

40. Harold J. Berman, *Faith and Order: The Reconciliation of Law and Religion* (Atlanta, 1993), 104.

41. See documents in C. H. Firth and R. S. Rait, eds., *Acts and Ordinances of the Interregnum*, 1642–1660 (London, 1911); Stephenson and Marcham, eds., *Sources of English Constitutional History*. See discussion in Gordon J. Schochet, "The Act of Toleration and the Failure of Comprehension: Persecution, Nonconformity, and Religious Indifference," in *The World of William and Mary*, ed. Dale Hoak and Mordechai Feingold (Stanford, 1996), 165.

42. For a careful demographic study, see Edwin S. Gaustad, *Historical Atlas of Religion in America*, rev. ed. (New York/San Francisco, 1976), 1–36.

43. Ibid. For details of the Anglican establishments, see Thomas J. Curry, *The First Freedoms: Church and State in America to the Passage of the First Amendment* (New York, 1986); Jon Butler, *Awash in a Sea of Faith: Christianizing the American People* (Cambridge, 1990), 1–66, 98–128; and the classic study, Sanford H. Cobb, *The Rise of Religious Liberty in America: A History* (New York, 1902). A comprehensive collection of laws of the day is provided in Nicholas Trott, *The Laws of the British Plantations in America, Relating to the Church and the Clergy, Religion and Learning* (London, 1725).

44. See sources and analysis in my "How to Govern a City on a Hill: The Early Puritan Contribution to American Constitutionalism," *Emory Law Journal* 39 (1990): 41–64.

45. The quoted provisions are from "Plantation Agreement of Providence (1640)" and "Charter of Rhode Island and Providence Plantations (1663)," reprinted in *The Federal and State Constitutions, Colonial Charters, and Other Organic Laws*, ed. F. Thorpe (Washington, DC, 1909), 6:3205–3206, 3211–3213. See analysis in Edwin S. Gaustad, *Liberty of Conscience: Roger Williams in America* (Grand Rapids, MI, 1991); Timothy L. Hall, *Separating Church and State: Roger Williams and Religious Liberty* (Urbana/Chicago, 1998).

46. Reprinted in W. Browne, ed., *Archives of Maryland* (Annapolis, MD, 1883), 1:244, 246.

47. See Curry, *The First Freedoms*, 29–53.

48. J. T. Mitchell and J. Flanders, eds., *Statutes at Large of Pennsylvania* (Philadelphia, 1911), 1:107–109. For discussion of the application and restriction of these legal provisions, see J. William Frost, *A Perfect Freedom: Religious Liberty in Pennsylvania* (Cambridge, 1990).

49. James Madison, Letter to Rev. Adams (1833), in Daniel L. Dreisbach, *Religion and Politics in the Early Republic: Jasper Adams and the Church-State Debate* (Lexington, KY, 1996), 117–121, at 118.

Chapter Two

1. James Madison, Letter from James Madison to Thomas Richie (September 15, 1821), in *Letters and Other Writings of James Madison*, 4 vols. (New York, 1884), 3:228. See also the quote from Madison in *The Debates and Proceedings in the Congress of the United States, March 3, 1789–May 27, 1824* (Washington, DC: Gales and Seaton, 1834–1856), vol. 5, column 776: "As the instrument came from [the drafter] it was nothing more than the draft of a plan, nothing but a dead letter, until life and validity were breathed into it by the voice of the people, speaking through their several State conventions." See discussion in B. N. Ong, "James Madison on Constitutional Interpretation," *Benchmark* 3 (1987): 18; Robert J. Morgan, *James Madison on the Constitution and the Bill of Rights* (New York, 1988).

2. See Jack N. Rakove, *Original Meanings: Politics and Ideas in the Making of the Constitution* (New York, 1996), 3–22, 288–338; and id., "Fidelity Through History (or to It)," *Fordham Law Review* 65 (1997): 1587–1609. Rakove argues for a distinction among the original "meaning," "intention," and "understanding" of the Constitution and urges a use of both "textual" and "contextual" material to comprehend the "original understanding." I am using the generic term "founder" to describe the range of eighteenth-century figures who wrote on questions of religious liberty and/or participated in the formation of state and federal constitutional laws governing the same.

3. For other classifications of the founders' perspectives, see, e.g., Arlin M. Adams and Charles J. Emmerich, *A Nation Dedicated to Religious Liberty* (Philadelphia, 1990), 21–31 (distinguishing Enlightenment separationists, political

centrists, and pietistic separationists); Michael W. McConnell, "The Origins and Historical Understanding of Free Exercise of Religion," *Harvard Law Review* 103 (1990): 1409–1517, at 1430–1455 (contrasting Lockean-Jeffersonian, various evangelical, and Madisonian views); H. Jefferson Powell, *The Moral Tradition of American Constitutionalism: A Theological Interpretation* (Durham, NC, 1993), 52–86 (contrasting Enlightenment, Civic Republican, Protestant, and common law traditions); Thomas J. Curry, *The First Freedoms: Church and State in America to the Passage of the First Amendment* (New York/Oxford, 1986) (dividing views by colonial and state origin).

4. See sources and discussion in my "Moderate Religious Liberty in the Theology of John Calvin," *Calvin Theological Journal* 31 (1996): 359–403.

5. Portions of the following section are drawn from my "Blest Be the Ties That Bind: Covenant and Community in Puritan Thought," *Emory Law Journal* 36 (1987): 579–601; and my "How to Govern a City on a Hill: The Early Puritan Contribution to American Constitutionalism," *Emory Law Journal* 39 (1990): 41–64. For samples of Puritan writings, see Perry Miller and T. Johnson, *The Puritans* (New York, 1938); and Edmund S. Morgan, *Puritan Political Ideas, 1558–1794* (Indianapolis, 1965).

6. Quoted by Timothy Breen, *The Character of the Good Ruler* (New Haven, 1970), 42, n. 24. See provisions in Max Farrand, ed., *The Book of the General Laws and Liberties Concerning the Inhabitants of Massachusetts (1648)* (Cambridge, 1929), 18–20; "The Cambridge Synod and Platform (1648)," in *The Creeds and Platforms of Congregationalism*, ed. Williston Walker (New York, 1960), 234–237.

7. John Cotton, Letter from The Rev. John Cotton to Lord Say and Seal (1636), in Miller and Johnson, eds., *The Puritans*, 209–212.

8. Uriah Oakes, *New England Pleaded with, and Pressed to Consider the Things Which Concern Her* (Boston, 1673), 49 (modern spelling and capitalization).

9. See generally Emil Oberholzer, *Delinquent Saints: Disciplinary Actions in the Early Congregational Churches of Massachusetts* (New York, 1956).

10. See collections in J. W. Thornton, ed., *The Pulpit of the American Revolution* (Boston, 1860); Charles S. Hynemann and Donald S. Lutz, eds., *American Political Writing During the Founding Era, 1760–1805*, 2 vols. (Indianapolis, 1983); W. Plumstead, ed., *The Wall and the Garden: Selected Massachusetts Election Sermons, 1670–1775* (Minneapolis, 1968); Ellis Sandoz, ed., *Political Sermons of the American Founding Era, 1730–1805* (Indianapolis, 1991). See discussion in Harry S. Stout, *The New England Soul: Preaching and Religious Culture in Colonial New England* (New York, 1986); Barry Shain, *The Myth of American Individualism: The Protestant Origins of American Political Thought* (Princeton, 1994).

11. See generally David D. Hall, *The Antinomian Controversy, 1636–1638*, 2d ed. (Durham, NC, 1968); Edmund S. Morgan, *Roger Williams: The Church and the State* (New York, 1967).

12. Nathaniel Ward, *The Simple Cobler of Aggawam in America*, 5th ed. (Boston, 1713), 43.

13. See generally William G. McLoughlin, *New England Dissent, 1630–1833*, 2 vols. (Cambridge, 1971).

14. I have been using this phrase for more than a decade (see my "Blest Be the Ties That Bind," 588, n. 24), without knowing that Jacques Ellul and Paul Ramsey had already used the term in the 1950s. I wish to apologize for this oversight and to thank Robert Tuttle, whose work has brought this to my attention. See Jacques Ellul, *The Theological Foundation of Law*, trans. Marguerite Weiser (Garden City, NY, 1960), 50; Paul Ramsey, *Basic Christian Ethics* (New York, 1950), 371, with discussion in Robert W. Tuttle, "A Treason of the Clerks: Paul Ramsey on Christian Ethics and the Common Law" (Ph.D. Diss., University of Virginia, 1997), 106–107.

15. Samuel Willard, *Covenant-Keeping the Way to Blessedness* (Boston, 1682). See further, id., *Morality Not to Be Relied on for Life* (Boston, 1700); id., *Walking with God* (Boston, 1701).

16. Elisha Williams, *The Essential Rights and Liberties of Protestants: A Seasonable Plea for the Liberty of Conscience, and the Right of Private Judgment in Matters of Religion, Without Any Controul from Human Authority* (Boston, 1744), 7–8.

17. Massachusetts Constitution (1780), Pt. I, Art. II. See comparable provisions in Vermont Constitution (1793), Ch. I, Art. III.

18. Zabdiel Adams, "An Election Sermon (1782)," reprinted in Hynemann and Lutz, eds., *American Political Writing*, 1:539–564, at 556 (capitalization and italics in original removed).

19. See *The Complete Writings of Roger Williams*, 7 vols. (New York, 1963), and analysis in Edwin S. Gaustad, *Liberty of Conscience: Roger Williams in America* (Grand Rapids, MI, 1991). Although he has been lionized in recent histories of religious liberty in America and was embraced by the eighteenth-century Baptist leader Isaac Backus, Roger Williams was not so well known nor so well liked in later-eighteenth-century Evangelical circles. See Gaustad, *Liberty of Conscience*, 19, 207, 220–221; Wallace Coyle, *Roger Williams: A Reference Guide* (Boston, 1977), 1–7.

20. For varying interpretations, see Jon Butler, *Awash in a Sea of Faith: Christianizing the American People* (Cambridge, MA, 1990); Michael J. Crawford, *Seasons of Grace* (New York, 1991); Patricia Bonomi, *Under the Cope of Heaven* (New York, 1986); Edwin S. Gaustad, *The Great Awakening in New England* (Gloucester, MA, 1957).

21. Roger Williams, Letter from Roger Williams to John Cotton (1643), in Williams, *Complete Writings*, 1:392. For careful analysis of the meaning of separatism for Williams, see Timothy L. Hall, *Separating Church and State: Roger Williams and Religious Liberty* (Urbana/Chicago, 1998), 82ff.

22. Jack Nips [John Leland], "The Yankee Spy (1794)," reprinted in Hynemann and Lutz, eds., *American Political Writing*, 2:971–989, at 989.

23. *The Writings of the Late Elder John Leland* (New York, 1845), 118.

24. Isaac Backus, "A Declaration of the Rights, of the Inhabitants of the State of Massachusetts-Bay in New England (1779)," in *Isaac Backus on Church, State, and Calvinism: Pamphlets, 1754–1789*, ed. William G. McLoughlin (Cambridge, 1968), 487.

25. Israel Evans, "A Sermon Delivered at Concord, Before the Hon. General Court of the State of New Hampshire at the Annual Election (1791)," reprinted in Sandoz, ed., *Political Sermons*, 1057–1078, at 1062–1063.

26. *Isaac Backus on Church, State, and Calvinism*, 351, 357–358, 373–375 (emphasis omitted).

27. "Declaration of the Virginia Association of Baptists (December 25, 1776)," in *The Papers of Thomas Jefferson*, ed. Julian P. Boyd (Princeton, 1950), 1:660–661.

28. Backus and a few other Evangelicals who did propound political views tended to agree with Puritans and Republicans that the political office should be restricted to Christians and that the state had a role to play in the cultivation of public morality through laws against blasphemy, theater-going, card-playing, and violations of the Sabbath day of rest. See William G. McLoughlin, *Soul Liberty: The Baptists' Struggle in New England, 1630–1833* (Providence, RI, 1991), 194–195, 267–268.

29. On American Enlightenment views, see generally Henry May, *The Enlightenment in America* (New York, 1976).

30. *Epistola de Tolerantia* (Gouda, 1689), translated by William Popple as *Letter Concerning Toleration* (London, 1689), reprinted in *The Works of John Locke*, 12th ed., 9 vols. (London, 1824), 5:1–58. Locke wrote two subsequent such letters and a had a fragment of a fourth letter underway on his death in 1704. It was the first letter of 1689 that was best known in America.

31. John Locke, *The Reasonableness of Christianity*, in *The Works of John Locke*, 12th ed., 9 vols. (London, 1824), 6:1–158, at 140–143. See discussion in Joshua Mitchell, "John Locke: A Theology of Religious Liberty," in *Religious Liberty in Western Thought*, ed. Noel B. Reynolds and W. Cole Durham Jr. (Atlanta, 1996), 143–160.

32. Jefferson took the lead in this, glossing Locke's *Letter Concerning Toleration* and incorporating a number of its most salient provisions in his famous "Bill for the Establishment of Religious Freedom" (1779). See his "Notes on Locke and Shaftesbury," in *The Papers of Thomas Jefferson*, 1:544–551. See discussion and sources in Sanford Kessler, "Locke's Influence on Jefferson's 'Bill for Establishing Religious Freedom,'" *Journal of Church and State* 25 (1983): 231; S. Gerald Sandler, "Lockean Ideas in Thomas Jefferson's Bill for Establishing Religious Freedom," *Journal of the History of Ideas* 21 (1960): 110.

33. Letter to Edward Livingston (July 10, 1822), in *The Writings of James Madison*, ed. G. Hunt (New York, 1900–1910), 9:98–103, at 102.

34. James Madison, Letter to Rev. Adams (1833), in Daniel L. Dreisbach, *Religion and Politics in the Early Republic: Jasper Adams and the Church-State Debate* (Lexington, KY, 1996), 117–121, at 120. Madison's notion of a wavering "line of separation between the rights of Religion and Civil government" that avails little in "unessentials" is a more telling metaphor to describe the Enlightenment position than Jefferson's more famous metaphor of a "wall of separation between church and state." See Sidney E. Mead, "Neither Church nor State: Reflections on James Madison's 'Line of Separation,'" *Journal of Church and State* 10 (1968): 349. See also Chapter 8, pages 183–184.

35. Thomas Paine, *The Rights of Man* (1791), in *The Complete Writings of Thomas Paine*, ed. P. S. Foner (New York, 1945), 1:243–462, at 292.

36. James Madison, "Memorial and Remonstrance Against Religious Assessments (1785)," in *The Papers of James Madison*, ed. W. T. Hutchinson, William M. E. Rachal, and Robert A. Rutland (Chicago, 1962), 8:298.

37. In his "Detached Memoranda" of c. 1817, Madison highlights his distaste for corporate organized religions by criticizing laws that allowed ecclesiastical bod-

ies to incorporate, to be exempt from taxation, to accumulate property, and to gain political access through legislative chaplains and other means. See Elizabeth Fleet, "Madison's 'Detached Memoranda,'" *William and Mary Quarterly,* 3d ser., 3 (1946): 534–568, at 554.

38. See the classic study of Thomas E. Buckley, *Church and State in Revolutionary Virginia, 1776–1787* (Charlottesville, VA, 1977).

39. *The Papers of James Madison,* ed. W. T. Hutchinson, William M. E. Rachal, and Robert A. Rutland (Chicago, 1962), 1:175.

40. *The Statutes at Large . . . of Virginia,* 12:84–86.

41. See discussion in Paul B. Kauper and Stephen B. Ellis, "Religious Corporations and the Law," *Michigan Law Review* 71 (1973): 1499–1574, at 1529ff.

42. See sources and analysis in Daniel L. Dreisbach, "A New Perspective on Jefferson's Views on Church-State Relations: The Virginia Statute for Establishing Religious Freedom in Its Legislative Context," *American Journal of Legal History* 35 (1991): 172–204; id., "Thomas Jefferson and Bills No. 82–86 of the Revision of the Laws of Virginia, 1776–1786: New Light on the Jeffersonian Model of Church-State Relations," *North Carolina Law Review* 69 (1990): 159–211.

43. The classic expositions are Nathan O. Hatch, *The Sacred Cause of Liberty* (New Haven, 1977); and Gordon S. Wood, *The Creation of the American Republic, 1776–1787* (New York, 1969). For a sampling of more recent historiography, see Barry Shain, *The Myth of American Individualism: The Protestant Origins of American Political Thought* (Princeton, 1994); Paul Rahe, *Republics Ancient and Modern* (Chapel Hill, NC, 1992).

44. Letter to the Clergy of Philadelphia (March 3, 1797), in *The Writings of George Washington from the Original Manuscript Sources, 1745–1799,* ed. J. C. Fitzpatrick (Washington, DC, 1931), 35:416; id., Farewell Address (September 17, 1796), in ibid., 35:214–238, at 229.

45. Letter of John Adams to a Unit of the Massachusetts Militia (1798), in *The Works of John Adams,* ed. J. F. Adams (Boston, 1850–1856), 9:229.

46. Timothy Dwight, "The Duty of Americans at the Present Crisis, Illustrated in a Discourse Preached on the Fourth of July, 1798," in Sandoz, ed., *Political Sermons,* 1380.

47. The phrase is from Benjamin Franklin, "Proposals Relating to the Education of Youth in Pensilvania (1749)," quoted and discussed in Martin E. Marty, "On a Medial Moraine: Religious Dimensions of American Constitutionalism," *Emory Law Journal* 39 (1990): 9–20, at 16–17.

48. See sources in Anson P. Stokes and Leo Pfeffer, *Church and State in the United States,* rev. ed. (Westport, CT, 1975), 83–90; and discussion in Chapter 4, pages 57–60.

49. Article III, 1 Stat. 50, 51–53, ch. 8.

50. Nathan Strong, *Election Sermon* (New Haven, 1790), 15.

51. Oliver Ellsworth, "Report of the Committee to Whom Was Referred the Petition of Simeon Brown and Others. . . . (1802)," in *The Public Records of the State of Connecticut,* ed. Christopher Collier (1967), 11:371, 373. See discussion in William Casto, "Oliver Ellsworth's Calvinism: A Biographical Essay on Religion and Political Psychology in the Early Republic," *Journal of Church and State* 36 (1994): 507–526, at 525. See also Joseph McKeen, *Sermon Preached on the Public*

Fast in the Commonwealth of Massachusetts (Boston, 1793), 15, 17–18: "Though some modern politicians may think religion of no importance to the state, it is clear that the experience of all ages and nations is against them. . . . The more, therefore, that the principles of piety, benevolence, and virtue are diffused among a people, the milder may their government and laws be, and the more liberty are they capable of enjoying because they govern themselves. But if there be little or no regard to religion or virtue among a people, they will not govern themselves, nor willingly submit to any laws, which lay restraint upon their passions; and consequently they must be wretched or be governed by force: they cannot bear freedom, they must be slaves."

52. See Chester J. Antieau, Arthur T. Downey, and Edward C. Roberts, *Freedom from Federal Establishment: Formation and Early History of the First Amendment Religion Clauses* (Milwaukee, 1964), 62–91; John K. Wilson, "Religion Under the State Constitutions, 1776–1800," *Journal of Church and State* 32 (1990): 753.

53. See Adams, *Works*, 8:232; 9:635, 636; and a letter to Abigail Adams (1775), quoted in Edwin S. Gaustad, *A Religious History of America* (New York, 1966), 127.

54. For further analysis, see my "'A Most Mild and Equitable Establishment of Religion': John Adams and the Massachusetts Experiment," *Journal of Church and State* 41 (1999): 213.

55. Massachusetts Constitution (1780), Pt. I, Arts. II and III; this language is retained in Amendment, Art. XI (1833), which replaced Pt. I, Art. III.

56. Ibid., Pt. II, Ch. V.

Chapter Three

1. See Elisha Williams, *The Essential Rights and Liberties of Protestants: A Seasonable Plea for the Liberty of Conscience, and the Right of Private Judgment in Matters of Religion, Without any Controul from Human Authority* (Boston, 1744). The term "essential rights and liberties" was quite common among the founders. The Virginia Ratifying Convention, for example, provided "that, among other essential rights, the liberty of conscience, and of the press, cannot be cancelled abridged, restrained, or modified, by any authority of the United States." Jonathan Elliot, ed., *The Debates in the Several State Conventions, on the Adoption of the Federal Constitution* (Washington, DC, 1854), 1:327 (hereafter cited as *Debates*). James Madison spoke of "essential rights" of religious freedom and rights of conscience. See his speech of August 17, 1789 in *The Debates and Proceedings in the Congress of the United States, March 3, 1789–May 27, 1824* (Washington, DC: Gales and Seaton, 1834–1856), vol. 1, column (col.) 784 (hereafter cited as *Annals*); id., Letter to George Eve, in *The Papers of James Madison*, ed. W. T. Hutchinson, William M. E. Rachal, Robert A. Rutland (Chicago, 1962), 11:404, 405. Likewise, John Adams included religion among "our most essential rights and liberties." "Instructions of the Town of Braintree to their Representative, 1765," in *The Works of John Adams*, ed. C. F. Adams (Boston, 1850–1856), 3:465. The Federal Framer also saw "the free exercise of religion" as one of the "essential rights." Letter IV (October 12, 1787), in *The Anti-Federalist*, ed. Herbert J. Storing (Chicago, 1985), 58.

2. See, e.g., Delaware Declaration of Rights (1776), sec. 3 ("That all men professing the Christian religion ought forever to enjoy equal rights and privileges in this
state"); Constitution of Maryland, Declaration of Rights, XXXIII (1776) ("all persons, professing the Christian religion, are equally entitled to protection in their religious liberty"); Constitution of South Carolina (1778), XXXVIII ("That all denominations of Christian Protestants in this State, demeaning themselves peaceably
and faithfully, shall enjoy equal religious and civil privileges"). See discussion in Edwin S. Gaustad, "Colonial Religion and Liberty of Conscience," in *The Virginia
Statute for Religious Freedom: Its Evolution and Consequences in American History,* ed. Merrill D. Peterson and Robert C. Vaughan (Cambridge, 1988), 23, 39;
Thomas J. Curry, *The First Freedoms: Church and State in America to the Passage
of the First Amendment* (New York/Oxford, 1986), 194–197.

3. See generally Chester J. Antieau, Arthur T. Downey, and Edward C. Roberts,
*Freedom from Federal Establishment: Formation and Early History of the First
Amendment Religion Clauses* (Milwaukee, 1964); Chester J. Antieau, Philip M.
Carroll, and Thomas Carroll Burke, *Religion Under the State Constitutions* (Wash-
ington, DC, 1965).

4. See my "'A Most Mild and Equitable Establishment of Religion': John Adams
and the Massachusetts Experiment," *Journal of Church and State* 41 (1999): 213.

5. See William Lee Miller, *The First Liberty: Religion and the American Republic*
(New York, 1986); Curry, *The First Freedoms;* James E. Wood Jr., *The First Freedom: Religion and the Bill of Rights* (Waco, TX, 1990).

6. Thomas Jefferson, "Freedom of Religion at the University of Virginia (Oct. 7,
1822)," in *The Complete Jefferson, Containing His Major Writings,* ed. Saul K.
Padover, (Freeport, NY, 1943), 958.

7. Jonathan Parsons, *Freedom from Civil and Ecclesiastical Slavery* (Newburyport, RI, 1774), 10.

8. North Carolina Ratification Debates, July 30, 1788, in Elliot, ed., *Debates,*
4:196–197.

9. For a good collection of prevailing sentiments, see *The Palladium of Conscience, or, The Foundation of Religious Liberty Displayed, Asserted and Established, Agreeable to its True and Genuine Principles* (Philadelphia, 1773), a source
frequently reprinted in the young republic.

10. See sources and discussion in Brian Tierney, "Religious Rights: An Historical
Perspective," in *Religious Human Rights in Global Perspective: Religious Perspectives,* ed. John Witte Jr. and Johan D. van der Vyver (The Hague/London/Boston,
1996), 17–45; and James E. Wood Jr., "An Apologia for Religious Human Rights,"
in ibid., 455–483. For conventional meanings of the phrase in early modern European sources, see Karl Schwarz "Der Begriff Exercitium Religionis Privatum,"
Zeitschrift der Savigny-Stiftung (Kan. Ab.) 105 (1988): 495–518.

11. Virginia Bill of Rights (1776), Art. 16.

12. See debate of Virginia Ratifying Convention (June 12, 1788), in Elliot, ed.,
Debates, 3:113–114; see also *The Papers of James Madison,* 11:130–131. See fur-
ther Anson P. Stokes and Leo Pfeffer, *Church and State in the United States,* rev. ed.
(Westport, CT, 1975), 61.

13. For a catalogue of such terms, see, e.g., John Mellen, *The Great and Happy
Doctrine of Liberty* (Boston, 1795), 17–18; Amos Adams, *Religious Liberty an In-*

valuable Blessing (Boston, 1768), 39–40, 45–46; *A Manual of Religious Liberty*, 3d ed. (New York, 1767).

14. Williams, *Essential Rights and Liberties*, 42. See also John Lathorp, *A Discourse on the Peace* (Boston, 1784), 29. The phrase "divine right of private judgment" in matters of religion was commonplace in the eighteenth century. See, e.g., Hugh Fisher, *The Divine Right of Private Judgment, Set in a True Light* (1731), repr. ed. (Boston, 1790).

15. Williams, *Essential Rights and Liberties*, 7–8.

16. Adams, *Works*, 3:452–456; and Massachusetts Constitution (1780), Pt. I, Art. II.

17. James Madison, "Memorial and Remonstrance Against Religious Assessments (1785)," para. 1, in *The Papers of James Madison*, ed. W. T. Hutchinson, William M. E. Rachal, and Robert A. Rutland (Chicago, 1962), 8:298.

18. See esp. John Leland, "The Rights of Conscience Inalienable (1791)," in *Political Sermons of the American Founding Era, 1730–1805*, ed. Ellis Sandoz (Indianapolis, 1991), 1079–1099, at 1085; Israel Evans, "A Sermon Delivered at Concord, Before the Hon. General Court of the State of New Hampshire at the Annual Election (1791)," in Sandoz, ed., *Political Sermons*, 1057–1078, at 1063ff.

19. This theory of "religious voluntarism," though consistently espoused by Enlightenment and Evangelical proponents, was a more recent importation into Puritan theology. Traditionally, Puritans and other Calvinists had emphasized the doctrines of predestination and "birthright" religion, which left less room for voluntary personal choice. For the shifts in late seventeenth- and early eighteenth-century Puritan thought to a voluntarist theory, see E. Brooks Holifield, *The Covenant Sealed: The Development of Puritan Sacramental Theology in Old and New England* (New Haven/London, 1974).

20. Ezra Stiles, *The United States Elevated to Glory and Honor* (New Haven, 1783), 56.

21. "Worcestriensis, Number IV (1776)," in *American Political Writing During the Founding Era, 1760–1805*, ed. Charles S. Hynemann and Donald S. Lutz (Indianapolis, 1983), 1:449–450. The typical caveat follows: "provided it does not issue in overt acts of treason against the state undermining the peace and good order of society." Ibid.

22. Mellen, *The Great and Happy Doctrine of Liberty*, 17 (emphasis added).

23. Ibid., 20.

24. See, e.g., Parsons, *Freedom from Civil and Ecclesiastical Slavery*; Isaac Backus, *Appeal to the Public for Religious Liberty Against the Oppressions of the Present Day* (Boston, 1773).

25. Henry Cumings, *A Sermon Preached at Billerica* (Boston, 1797), 12–13. See also Thomas Jefferson, "Draft of Bill Exempting Dissenters from Contributing to the Support of the Church, 30 Nov. 1776," in *The Founders' Constitution*, ed. Philip B. Kurland and Ralph S. Lerner (Chicago, 1987), 5:74 (arguing that dissenters be "totally free and exempt from all Levies Taxes and Impositions whatever towards supporting and maintaining the [established Anglican] church" as a means of ensuring "equal Liberty as well religious as civil" to all "good People"). These arguments were sometimes extended to claiming "exemptions" and "immunities" from the jurisdiction, discipline, and confessional statements of a local church. See,

e.g., Isaac Foster, *A Defense of Religious Liberty* (Worcester, MA, 1780) (a 192-page tract arguing for exemptions from compliance with the imposition of a new confession, the Saybrook Platform, in a local church).

26. Cumings, *A Sermon Preached at Billerica*, 12–13.

27. See Carol Weisbrod, "Commentary on Curry and Firmage Articles," *Journal of Law and Religion* 7 (1989): 315–321, at 320–321. Locke had made this point in *Letter on Toleration* (1689): "But some may ask: 'What if the magistrate should enjoin anything by his authority that appears unlawful to the conscience of a private person?' I answer that, if government be faithfully administered and the counsels of the government be indeed directed to the public good, this will seldom happen." *The Works of John Locke*, 12th ed., 9 vols. (London, 1824), 5:1–68, at 43, 44–46.

28. Letter to the Religious Society Called Quakers, October, 1789, in *The Writings of George Washington from the Original Manuscript Sources, 1745–1799*, ed. J. C. Fitzpatrick (Washington, 1931), 30:416. See similar sentiments in *George Washington on Religious Liberty and Mutual Understanding: Selections from Washington's Letters*, ed. Edward F. Humphrey (Washington, DC, 1932); and discussion in Paul F. Boller Jr., *George Washington and Religion* (Dallas, 1963).

29. Even early writers who thought exemptions were necessary to protect religious rights and liberties were fully aware that such guarantees could be abused. Thus, on the one hand, they insisted that liberty of conscience could not be used to excuse breaches of the peace or of the public order—a caveat that found its way into almost all state constitutions. On the other hand, they insisted that liberty of conscience not be used to support sham claims to shirk one's civil duties.

In the same passage where he defended the importance of religious exemption, for example, Henry Cumings wrote: "[T]o admit the plea of conscience, when urged, in order to excuse persons from contributing, in any way to the necessary defence, support and well-being of the community to which they belong would evidently be inconsistent with civil union and terminate in the abolition of society; as it would encourage people to sanctify their sordid selfishness and avarice by the sacred name, conscience, in order to free themselves from public expen[s]es." Cumings, *A Sermon Preached at Billerica*, 13–14. It was thus assumed that the conscientious objector would pay for his replacement and the oath-forsaker would provide other guarantees of veracity.

30. See Arlin Adams and Sarah B. Gordon, "The Doctrine of Accommodation in the Jurisprudence of the Religion Clauses," *DePaul Law Review* 37 (1988): 317–345; Frederick Mark Gedicks, "An Unfirm Foundation: The Regrettable Indefensibility of Religious Exemptions," *University of Arkansas Law Journal* 20 (1998): 555–574; Steven G. Gey, "Why Is Religion Special? Reconsidering the Accommodation of Religion Under the Religion Clauses of the First Amendment," *University of Pittsburgh Law Review* 52 (1990): 75–187; Philip A. Hamburger, "A Constitutional Right of Religious Exemption: An Historical Perspective," *George Washington Law Review* 60 (1992): 915–948; Kurt T. Lash, "The Second Adoption of the Free Exercise Clause: Religious Exemptions Under the Fourteenth Amendment," *Northwestern University Law Review* 88 (1994): 1106–1156; Douglas Laycock, "The Last Remnants of Free Exercise," *Supreme Court Review* (1991): 1–68; William P. Marshall, "The Case Against the Constitutionally Compelled Free Exer-

cise Exemption," *Case Western Reserve University Law Review* 40 (1990): 357–412; Michael W. McConnell, "Accommodation of Religion," *Supreme Court Review* (1985): 1–59; id., "Accommodation of Religion: An Update and a Response to the Critics," *George Washington Law Review* 60 (1992): 685–742; Ellis West, "The Right to Religion-Based Exemptions in Early America: The Case of Conscientious Objectors to Conscription," *Journal of Law and Religion* 10 (1994): 367–401.

31. For good summaries of these state developments, see Antieau, Carroll, and Burke, *Religion Under the State Constitutions;* John K. Wilson, "Religion Under the State Constitutions, 1776–1800," *Journal of Church and State* 32 (1990): 753.

32. Delaware Declaration of Rights (1776), sec. 2.

33. Pennsylvania Declaration of Rights (1776), II, VIII.

34. Constitution of New York (1777), art. xxxviii.

35. Constitution of New Jersey, (1776), art. xviii.

36. See, e.g., Joseph Story, *Commentaries on the Constitution* (Boston, 1833), 3:703; and discussion in Arlin M. Adams and Charles J. Emmerich, *A Nation Dedicated to Religious Liberty* (Philadelphia, 1990), 61–62.

37. Virginia Version (June 27, 1788), in Elliot, ed., *Debates*, 1:327, and 3:591, 594.

38. James Madison's First Proposal, introduced in the House on June 8, 1789, in *Annals*, vol. 1, col. 451.

39. Ibid., vol. 1, col. 452.

40. Draft proposed by Fisher Ames of Massachusetts on August 20, 1789. Ibid., vol. 1, col. 796.

41. See Schwarz, "Der Begriff Exercitium Religionis Privatum," 502ff.

42. William Penn, "The Great Case of Liberty of Conscience (1670)," in *The Works of William Penn* (London, 1726), 1:443, 447.

43. Madison, "Memorial and Remonstrance," sec. 1. See also Levi Hart, *Liberty Described and Recommended* (Hartford, 1775), 14–15 (distinguishing religious liberty, ecclesiastical liberty, and spiritual liberty).

44. See, e.g., Williams, *Essential Rights and Liberties*, 46ff.; Isaac Backus, *Isaac Backus on Church, State, and Calvinism: Pamphlets, 1754–1789*, ed. William G. McLoughlin (Cambridge, 1968), 348ff.; Parsons, *Freedom from Civil and Ecclesiastical Slavery*, 14–15; Stiles, *The United States Elevated*, 55ff.; Amos Adams, *Religious Liberty*, 38–46.

45. See respectively, Hart, *Liberty Described and Recommended*, 14; Backus, *Isaac Backus on Church, State, and Calvinism*, 348–349; "A Declaration of Certain Fundamental Rights and Liberties of the Protestant Episcopal Church in Maryland," quoted in Anson P. Stokes, *Church and States in the United States*, 3 vols. (New York, 1950), 1:741.

46. On the significance of these limitations, see Hamburger, "A Constitutional Right," passim.

47. Virginia Declaration of Rights (1776), sec. 16.

48. Constitution of Georgia (1777), art. lvi.

49. Backus, *Isaac Backus on Church, State, and Calvinism*, 317. See also, e.g., *The Freeman's Remonstrance Against an Ecclesiastical Establishment* (Boston, 1777), 13.

50. Isaac Backus, *Truth Is Great and Will Prevail* (Boston, 1781). For comparable sentiments, see John R. Bolles, *A Brief Account of Persecutions, in Boston and Connecticut Governments* (Boston, 1758), 47, 59. See also George Washington, who expressed comparable sentiments to Roman Catholics, Quakers, Jews, and other religious minorities in the young republic. See, e.g., Letter to the Hebrew Congregation of the City of Savannah, May 1790, in Humphrey, ed., *George Washington on Religious Liberty*, 12: "May the same wonder-working Deity, who long since delivered the Hebrews from their Egyptian oppressers, and planted them in the promised land . . . still continue to water them with the dews of Heaven, and to make the inhabitants of every denomination participate in the temporal and spiritual blessings of that people, whose God is Jehovah."

51. Thomas Jefferson, *Notes on the State of Virginia*, in *The Complete Jefferson, Containing His Major Writings*, ed. Saul K. Padover (Freeport, NY, 1943), query 17, 673–676. See also Stiles, *The United States Elevated*, 55–56; Thomas Paine, *Common Sense* (1776), in *Common Sense and the Crisis* (Garden City, NJ, 1960), 50.

52. John Adams, Letter to Thomas Jefferson, June 25, 1813, in *The Adams-Jefferson Letters*, ed. Lester J. Cappon (Chapel Hill, NC, 1959), 333–335, at 334.

53. See "Debates of June 12, 1788," in Elliot, ed., *Debates*, 3:313. See discussion in Christopher L. Eisgruber, "Madison's Wager: Religious Liberty in the Constitutional Order," *Northwestern University Law Review* 89 (1995): 347–410, at 373ff.

54. See Williams, *Essential Rights and Liberties*, 40–42; Stiles, *The United States Elevated*, 55ff.; "Comments of Governor Randolph (June 12, 1788)," in Elliot, ed., *Debates*, 3:207–208; and in Max Farrand, ed., *The Records of the Federal Convention of 1787* (New Haven/London/Oxford, 1911), 3:310.

55. See, e.g., *The Works of James Wilson*, ed. R. G. McCloskey (Cambridge, 1967); and general discussion in W. C. McWilliams, *The Idea of Fraternity in America* (Berkeley, 1973), 112–123; Clinton Rossiter, *The Political Thought of the American Revolution* (New York, 1963), 204.

56. Letter from John Adams to Abigail Adams (October 29, 1775), quoted in John R. Howe Jr., *The Changing Political Thought of John Adams* (Princeton, 1966), 156–157 (capitalization modernized).

57. Letter from Benjamin Rush to John Armstrong (March 19, 1793), in Kurland and Lerner, eds., *The Founders' Constitution*, 5:78.

58. Clinton Rossiter, ed., *The Federalist Papers: Alexander Hamilton, James Madison, John Jay* (New York, 1961), 84.

59. Ibid., 324.

60. Madison, "Memorial and Remonstrance," secs. 4, 8. See discussion in Paul J. Weber, "James Madison and Religious Equality," *Review of Politics* 44 (1982): 163.

61. Letter to Dr. Price, April 8, 1785, in Adams, *Works*, 8:232. Elsewhere, Adams wrote that in Massachusetts, "there is, it is true, a moral and political equality of rights and duties among all the individuals and as yet no appearance of artificial inequalities of conditions." Quoted in Frank Donovan, ed., *The John Adams Papers* (New York, 1965), 181. For comparable sentiments, see, e.g., *The Freeman's Remonstrance*, 5, 10–13 (arguing that "every society of Christians [should be] allowed full, equal, and impartial liberty," and that it is contrary to "scripture, rea-

son, and experience" that "one society of Christians should be raised to domination over all the rest").

62. Backus, *Isaac Backus on Church, State and Calvinism*, 333. See further Timothy L. Hall, "Religion, Equality, and Difference," *Temple Law Review* 65 (1992): 1–89.

63. Phillips Payson, "Election Sermon of 1778," in Hynemann and Lutz, eds., *American Political Writing*, 523, 529. A decade later, Payson apparently changed his mind, arguing in the Massachusetts Ratifying Convention that such religious tests were "attempts to erect human tribunals for the consciences of men, impious encroachments upon the prerogatives of God." "Speech of January 30, 1788," in Elliot, ed., *Debates*, 2:120.

64. Delaware Constitution (1776), Art. XXII. This oath was outlawed by a 1792 amendment to the Delaware Constitution. For quotations and analysis of other original oath provisions, see Daniel L. Dreisbach, "The Constitution's Forgotten Religion Clause: Reflections on the Article VI Religious Test Ban," *Journal of Church and State* 38 (1996): 263–295, at 264–269; Wilson, "Religion Under the State Constitutions," 764–766.

65. "Speech of Isaac Backus (February 4, 1788)," in Elliot, ed., *Debates*, 2:148. See other examples in Kurland and Lerner, eds., *The Founders' Constitution*, 4:633ff.

66. See "Petition of the Philadelphia Synagogue to the Council of Censors of Philadelphia (December 23, 1783)," in Kurland and Lerner, eds., *The Founders' Constitution*, 4:635; and "Jonas Phillips to the President and Members of the Convention (September 7, 1789)," in Farrand, ed., *Records of the Federal Convention*, 3:78–79.

67. "Speech of July 30, 1788," in Farrand, ed., *Records of the Federal Convention*, 3:204. See a comparable defense by Governor Randolph of Virginia that concludes: "It puts all sects on the same footing." Ibid., 3:207.

68. "Speech of July 30, 1788" in Elliot, ed., *Debates*, 4:208.

69. See Wilson, "Religion Under the State Constitutions," 765; Antieau, Carroll, and Burke, *Religion Under the State Constitutions*, 101–107. See further discussion in Chapter 5, pages 89–90.

70. Luther Martin, "The Genuine Information (1787)," in Farrand, ed., *Records of the Federal Convention*, 3:227 (italics in original changed).

71. Madison, "Memorial and Remonstrance," sec. 4 (emphasis added).

72. See further Adams and Emmerich, *A Nation Dedicated to Religious Liberty*, 65–71.

73. House Debates, August 15, 1789, in *Annals*, vol. 1, col. 758 (emphasis added).

74. House Debates, August 20, 1789, in *Annals*, vol. 1, col. 796 (emphasis added).

75. Constitution of New Jersey (1776), Art. XIX.

76. Delaware Declaration of Rights (1776), Sec. 3.

77. Maryland Declaration of Rights (1776), Sec. XXXIII.

78. Virginia Declaration of Rights (1776), Art. 16.

79. Constitution of New York (1777), Art. XXXVIII.

80. Constitution of Massachusetts (1780), Part I, Art. 3, as amended by Art. XI.

81. James Madison's First Proposal, introduced in the House on June 7, 1789, in *Annals*, vol. 1, col. 451.

82. Senate Version (September 3, 1789), in *Journal of the First Session of the United States of America* (New York, 1789), (Evans, First Series, No. 22207), 1:116 (hereafter *Journal of Senate*).

83. Ibid., 1:117.

84. Argument made in support of Amendment to Article I, section 10, in *Annals*, vol. 1, col. 784. Madison argued: "If there was any reason to restrain the Government of the United States from infringing upon these essential rights, it was equally necessary that they should be secured against the State Governments." Ibid. His initial proposed amendment of June 8, 1789 sought to make the protection of equality and liberty of conscience universal, and the disestablishment guarantee binding on the federal government alone: "The civil rights of none shall be abridged on account of religious belief or worship, nor shall any national religion be established, nor shall the full and equal rights of conscience be in any manner, or on any pretext, infringed." Ibid., vol. 1, col. 451. A bit later, he urged: "No State shall violate the equal rights of conscience." Ibid., vol. 1, col. 452. See further Chapter 4, pages 65, 69–70.

85. Martin Luther, *To the Christian Nobility of the German Nation* (1520), in *Three Treatises*, 2d rev. ed. (Philadelphia, 1986), 1–112, at 12, 16. Luther went on to shred this "paper wall" of the Catholics in favor of his own understanding of two kingdoms. See my *Law and Protestantism: The Legal Teachings of the Lutheran Reformation* (Cambridge, 2000), chap. 2.

86. See John Calvin, *Institutes of the Christian Religion* (1559), bk. 3., chap. 19.15; bk. 4., chap. 11.3; bk. 4, chap. 20.1–2. See discussion and other sources in my "Moderate Religious Liberty in the Theology of John Calvin," *Calvin Theological Journal* 31 (1996): 359–403, at 392ff.

87. See references in Daniel L. Dreisbach, "'Sowing Useful Truths and Principles': The Danbury Baptists, Thomas Jefferson, and the 'Wall of Separation,'" *Journal of Church and State* 39 (1997): 455–501, at 481–486.

88. Roger Williams, Letter to John Cotton (1643), in *The Complete Writings of Roger Williams*, 7 vols. (New York, 1963), 1:392. See further references in Chapter 2, notes 19–28.

89. See sources and discussion in Dreisbach, "'Sowing Useful Truths,'" 486–490.

90. James Burgh, *Crito, or Essays on Various Subjects* (London, 1767), 2:117–119 (emphasis removed).

91. Tunis Wortman, "A Solemn Address to Christians and Patriots (New York, 1800)," reprinted in Sandoz, ed., *Political Sermons*, 1477–1528, at 1482, 1487–1488.

92. Ibid., 1488.

93. Williams, *Essential Rights and Liberties*, 46.

94. Madison, "Memorial and Remonstrance," sec. 2.

95. *The Writings of Thomas Jefferson*, ed. H. Washington, (Washington, DC, 1853–1854), 8:113 (emphasis added). The Washington edition of the letter inaccurately transcribes "legitimate" as "legislative." See a more accurate transcription in Dreisbach, "'Sowing Useful Truths,'" 468–469.

96. *The Writings of Thomas Jefferson*, 114. For the original drafts of the letter and the political machinations at work in its drafting and revision, see James Hut-

son, "'A Wall of Separation': FBI Helps Restore Jefferson's Obliterated Draft," *Library of Congress Information Bulletin* 57 (June 1998): 136–139, 163.

97. See Thomas E. Buckley, "The Political Theology of Thomas Jefferson," in Peterson and Vaughan, eds., *The Virginia Statute for Religious Freedom*, 75–108.

98. See entries under "establish" and "establishment" in John Andrews, *A Complete Dictionary of the English Language*, 4th ed. (Philadelphia, 1789); John Ash, *A New and Complete Dictionary of the English Language* (London, 1775); Samuel Johnson, *A Dictionary of the English Language*, 4th ed. (London, 1773); William Perry, *The Royal Standard English Dictionary*, 1st Am. ed. (Worcester, 1788); Thomas Sheridan, *A Complete Dictionary of the English Language*, 2d ed. (London, 1789).

99. See T. Jeremy Gunn, *A Standard for Repair: The Establishment Clause, Equality, and Natural Rights* (New York/London, 1992), 46–47, 71–73.

100. Delaware Declaration of Rights (1776), sect. 3; Pennsylvania Declaration of Rights (1776), II.

101. For Randolph, see Elliot, ed., *Debates*, 3:208; see also ibid., 3:431. For Madison, see ibid., 3:313.

102. Quoted in Antieau, Downey, and Roberts, *Freedom from Federal Establishment*, 106. Cummins went on to say: "It would be impolite for a state to give preference to one religious order over any others in matters of state, and to dictate and prescribe in points of religion, in which men have from different modes of education and circumstances of one kind or other, will and must split in opinion." Ibid.

103. Art. XIX.

104. Elliot, ed., *Debates*, 1:328, 334.

105. *Journal of Senate*, 1:116.

106. Version rejected by the Senate on September 3, 1789. Ibid.

107. Thomas Jefferson, Letter to Rev. Samuel Miller (1808), in Kurland and Lerner, eds., *The Founders' Constitution*, 5:98–99.

108. Madison, "Memorial and Remonstrance," sec. 5.

109. Thomas Paine, *Rights of Man* (1791), pt. 1 in Kurland and Lerner, eds., *The Founders' Constitution*, 5:95–96.

110. For a careful study, see Antieau, Downey, and Roberts, *Freedom from Federal Establishment*, 1–92.

111. See esp. sources and discussion in Leo Pfeffer, *Church, State, and Freedom*, rev. ed. (Boston, 1967); Leonard W. Levy, *The Establishment Clause: Religion and the First Amendment* (New York, 1986).

112. James Madison, Letter to Edward Livingston (1822), in Kurland and Lerner, eds., *The Founders' Constitution*, 5:105–106. See also id., "Memorial and Remonstrance," sec. 9: "Distant as it may be in its present form from the Inquisition, it [i.e., the general assessment for religion] differs from it only in degree. The one is the first step, the other the last step in the career of intolerance."

113. See, e.g., *The Freeman's Remonstrance*, 5–11; Isaac Backus, *The Infinite Importance of the Obedience of Faith, and of a Separation from the World, Opened and Demonstrated* (Boston, 1791), 15–31; id., *Policy as well as Honesty Forbids the Use of Secular Force in Religious Affairs* (Boston, 1779).

114. Declaration of Rights, XXXIII. This was outlawed by amendment, Art. XIII (1810). See Francis Thorpe, ed., *The Federal and State Constitutions, Colonial Charters, and Other Organic Laws*, 7 vols. (Washington, DC, 1909), 3:1189, 1705.

115. For details, see my "A Most Mild and Equitable Establishment of Religion."

Chapter Four

1. See summaries in Anson P. Stokes, *Church and State in the United States* (New York, 1950), 1:447–482; Leo Pfeffer, *Church, State, and Freedom* (Boston, 1953), 106–109, 119–121. For the record, see *Journals of the Continental Congress, 1774–1789*, 34 vols., ed. Worthing C. Ford et al. (Washington, DC, 1904–1937).

2. *Journals of the Continental Congress*, 2:87.

3. Ibid., 9:855 (emphasis in original).

4. 14 Geo. III, c. 83.

5. *Journals of the Continental Congress*, 1:72, 88. See T. Jeremy Gunn, *A Standard for Repair: The Establishment Clause, Equality, and Natural Rights* (New York/London, 1992), 73–78.

6. Quoted by Stokes, *Church and State*, 1:460–461.

7. *Journals of the Continental Congress*, 5:654.

8. Ibid., 18:979.

9. Ibid., 23:574.

10. Ibid., 19:214.

11. Quoted by Stokes, *Church and State*, 1:475.

12. Quoted by ibid., 1:476.

13. Quoted by Pfeffer, *Church, State, and Freedom*, 120.

14. *Journals of the Continental Congress*, 32:340.

15. See Isaac Kramnick and R. Laurence Moore, *The Godless Constitution: The Case Against Religious Correctness* (New York/London, 1996), and the critical review, to which the authors respond, in Daniel L. Dreisbach "The Godless Constitution," *Liberty* (November-December 1996): 11, and elaborated in id., "In Search of a Christian Commonwealth: An Examination of Selected Nineteenth-Century Commentaries on References to God and the Christian Religion in the United States Constitution," *Baylor Law Review* 48 (1996): 927–1000.

16. Jonathan Elliot, ed., *The Debates in the Several State Conventions, on the Adoption of the Federal Constitution, as Recommended by the General Convention at Philadelphia in 1787*, 4 vols. (Washington, DC, 1854), 3:313 (hereafter cited as *Debates*).

17. Ibid., 4:197.

18. Ibid., 3:207–208, 313, 431.

19. Max Farrand, ed., *The Records of the Federal Convention of 1787*, 3 vols. (New Haven/London/Oxford, 1911), vol. 4, rev. ed. (New Haven/London/Oxford, 1937), 3:143–144.

20. See comparable views of James Iredell in Elliot, ed., *Debates*, 4:194–195; and discussion in Catherine Drinker Bowen, *Miracle at Philadelphia: The Story of the Constitutional Convention, May to September, 1787* (Boston/Toronto, 1966), 243–253; Gunn, *A Standard for Repair*, 135–164.

21. Referred to in Farrand, ed., *Records of the Federal Convention*, 1:23; reprinted in ibid., 3:595–609, at 599.

22. Ibid., 2:587–588. The motion makes no express mention of religious liberty, however; when Mason later specified what rights he had in mind, he mentioned only liberty of press, jury trial, and protection against the military in peacetime. Ibid., 2:640.

23. Ibid., 2:616.

24. Ibid., 1:451–452. For recollections of this speech by other convention members, see documents in ibid., 3:471–472, 479, 499, 531. See also Franklin's own reflections on this motion in ibid., 3:296–297.

25. Ibid., 2:342.

26. Ibid., 2:468. A constitutional text proposed by Alexander Hamilton at the conclusion of the 1787 convention, but apparently never considered, had included a more expansive clause: "Nor shall any Religious Sect, or denomination, or religious test for any office or place, be ever established by law." Ibid., 3:617–630, at 628.

27. See, e.g., Elliot, ed., *Debates*, 2:44, 119, 148–149, 199, 215; 3:207–208; 4:195–199. See careful analysis in Chester J. Antieau, Arthur T. Downey, and Edward C. Roberts, *Freedom from Federal Establishment: Formation and Early History of the First Amendment Religion Clauses* (Milwaukee, 1964), 92–110; Daniel L. Dreisbach, "The Constitution's Forgotten Religion Clause: Reflections on the Article VI Religious Test Ban," *Journal of Church and State* 38 (1996): 261–295, at 283–284; Gerard V. Bradley, "The No Religious Test Clause and the Constitution of Religious Liberty: A Machine That Has Gone of Itself," *Case Western Reserve Law Review* 37 (1987): 674–747, 696–697.

28. Elliot, ed., *Debates*, 1:332.

29. I am omitting from analysis the repeated attempt of South Carolina, in the ratification and congressional debates, to have Article VI amended to read "no other religious test shall ever be required." Such an amendment would have allowed for introduction of religious oaths through the prior clause of Article VI binding all federal officials "by Oath or Affirmation to support the Constitution." The proposal received no support each time it was raised. See Elliot, ed., *Debates*, 1:325; *The Debates and Proceedings in the Congress of the United States, March 3, 1789–May 27, 1824*, 42 vols. (Washington, DC: Gales and Seaton, 1834–1856), vol. 1, column (col.) 807 (hereafter *Annals*); *Journal of the First Session of the United States of America* (New York, 1789), (Evans, First Series, No. 22207) (hereafter *Journal of Senate*), 1:122.

30. Elliot, ed., *Debates*, 1:326.

31. Ibid., 1:327 and 3:591, 594.

32. Ibid., 1:328.

33. Ibid., 1:331, 4:244.

34. Ibid., 1:333–335.

35. See Marion Timling, "Thomas Lloyd's Reports of the First Federal Congress," *William and Mary Quarterly*, 3d ser., 18 (1961): 519; James H. Hutson, "The Creation of the Constitution: The Integrity of the Documentary Record," *Texas Law Review* 65 (1986): 1.

36. Among numerous reviews of these debates, see esp. Antieau, Downey, and Roberts, *Freedom from Federal Establishment*, 123–142; Gerard V. Bradley,

Church-State Relationships in America (New York/London/Westport, 1987), 20ff.; Robert L. Cord, *Separation of Church and State: Historical Fact and Current Fiction,* rev. ed. (Grand Rapids, MI, 1988); Gunn, *Standard for Repair,* 39–67; Wilber G. Katz, *Religion and American Constitutions* (Evanston, IL, 1963); Douglas Laycock, "'Nonpreferential' Aid to Religion: A False Claim About Original Intent," *William and Mary Law Review* 27 (1986): 875–923; Michael J. Malbin, *Religion and Politics: The Intentions of the Authors of the First Amendment* (Washington, DC, 1978); Michael McConnell, "The Origins and Historical Understanding of Free Exercise of Religion," *Harvard Law* Review 103 (1990): 1480–1503; Rodney K. Smith, *Public Prayer and the Constitution: A Case Study in Constitutional Interpretation* (Wilmington, DE, 1987), 73–105; Stokes, *Church and State,* 1:518–552.

37. *Annals,* vol. 1, cols. 451, 452.

38. Ibid., vol. 1, col. 468.

39. The committee included John Vining of Delaware, Abraham Baldwin of Georgia, Roger Sherman of Connecticut, Aedanus Burke of South Carolina, Nicholas Gilman of New Hampshire, George Clymer of Pennsylvania, Elias Boudinot of New Jersey, and George Gales of Maryland.

40. Ibid., vol. 1, cols. 757–759.

41. Ibid., vol. 1, cols. 778–780.

42. Ibid., vol. 1, cols. 783–784.

43. Ibid., vol. 1, cols. 795–796.

44. Ibid., vol. 1, col. 796.

45. Ibid., vol. 1, col. 808.

46. Linda DePauw et al., eds., *Documentary History of the First Federal Congress* (Baltimore, 1972–), 3:159, 166.

47. *Journal of Senate,* 1:116–117.

48. Ibid., 1:116.

49. Ibid.

50. Ibid., 1:117.

51. Ibid.

52. Ibid., 1:129.

53. For biographical materials on these and other founders, see, e.g., Stokes, *Church and State,* 1:292ff., 507ff.; Stephen A. Marini, "Religion, Politics, and Ratification," in *Religion in a Revolutionary Age,* ed. Ronald Hoffman and Peter J. Albert (Charlottesville, VA/London, 1994), 184–217; Morton Borden, "Federalists, AntiFederalists, and Religious Freedom," *Journal of Church and State* 21 (1979): 469; M. E. Bradford, *Founding Fathers: Brief Lives of the Framers of the United States Constitution,* 2d rev. ed. (Lawrence, KS, 1994).

54. *Journal of Senate,* 1:145, 148; *Annals,* 1, col. 948.

55. *Annals,* vol. 1, cols. 949–950, 958–959.

56. *Annals,* vol. 1, cols. 18–19. See also *Journal of Senate,* 16 (reporting that the Senate voted for its chaplain on April 25, 1789); *Annals,* vol. 1, col. 233 (recording that the House voted for its chaplain on May 1).

57. *Journal of Senate* (April 27, 1789), as reported in *Annals,* vol. 1, col. 25. A slightly reworded version was passed in the House on April 29, 1789. Ibid., vol. 1, col. 241.

58. *Annals,* vol. 2, col. 2237; 1 Stat. 71.

59. Statutes, 1789, C. VIII, in *Documents of American History*, ed. Henry Steele Commager, 5th ed. (New York, 1949), 130, 131. However, this does not appear in the *Annals* for August 7, 1789. See *Annals*, vol. 1: cols. 59–62, 710–714.

60. See sources and examples in Stokes, *Church and State*, 1:483–517; Ellis Sandoz, "Religious Liberty and Religion in the American Founding Revisited," in *Religious Liberty in Western Thought*, ed. Noel B. Reynolds and W. Cole Durham Jr. (Atlanta, 1996), 245–289; Cord, *Separation of Church and State*, 17–82.

61. See the dictionaries listed in Chapter 3, n. 98 under "respect." See also the early modern sources quoted in *Oxford English Dictionary* (Oxford, 1971) under "respect."

62. For this distinction, see esp. Malbin, *Religion and Politics*, 13–17.

63. See, e.g., *Annals*, vol. 1, col. 948, transcribing the final Senate version of the free exercise clause: "prohibiting *a* free exercise thereof." See also *Annals*, vol. 1, cols. 451, 778–780, variously quoting Madison's call for disestablishment of "*any*" and "*a*" religion. See discussion and sources in McConnell, "Origins and Historical Understanding," 1483, n. 372; Gunn, *Standard for Repair*, 41–44; Leonard W. Levy, *The Establishment Clause: Religion and the First Amendment* (New York, 1986), 94, 188; Walter Berns, *The First Amendment and the Future of Democracy* (New York, 1976), 8ff.

64. See collection of sentiments in Philip B. Kurland and Ralph S. Lerner, eds., *The Founders' Constitution* (Chicago, 1987), 5:111–208.

65. McConnell, "Origins and Historical Understanding," 1486–1488. See entries under "prohibit" in dictionaries listed Chapter 3, n. 98.

66. Report on the Virginia Resolutions (January, 1800), quoted in Kurland and Lerner, eds., *The Founders' Constitution*, 5:141, 146–147, quoted in part and discussed in McConnell, "Origins and Historical Understanding," 1488.

67. The Congressional Record of 1790 includes an instructive anecdote illustrating the Congress's presumption of the free exercise rights of the church and clergy. Medieval canon law had granted to clergy "privilege of forum" or "benefit of clergy"—the right of an ordained cleric to have any criminal case against him heard in a church court, rather than in a civil court. This practice continued after the Reformation, in Catholic and in many Protestant polities alike, and a was a familiar feature of American colonial law. See Richard Burn, *Ecclesiastical Law*, 6th ed., 4 vols. (London, 1797), 1:185–192; and George W. Balzell, *Benefit of Clergy in America and Related Matters* (Winston-Salem, NC, 1955). In an act of 1790, Congress provided: "That the benefit of clergy shall not be used or allowed, upon conviction of any crime, for which, by any statute of the United States, the punishment is or shall be declared to be death." Stokes, *Church and State*, 1:492.

68. See McConnell, "Origins and Historical Understanding," 1500–1503. See also discussion of cases on conscientious objection in Chapter 6, pages 105–107.

69. On the eighteenth-century forms of these faiths, see sources and analysis in Jon Butler, *Awash in a Sea of Faith: Christianizing the American People* (Cambridge, MA, 1990), 67–97, 129–163.

70. Letter to Rev. Adams (1833), in Daniel L. Dreisbach, *Religion and Politics in the Early Republic: Jasper Adams and the Church-State Debate* (Lexington, KY, 1996), 117–121, at 118 (paragraph breaks omitted).

71. See Douglas Laycock, "Religious Liberty as Liberty," *Journal of Contemporary Legal Issues* 7 (1996): 313–356; Michael E. Smith, "The Special Place of Religion in the Constitution," *Supreme Court Review* (1983): 83–123.

Chapter Five

1. The proposed Blaine Amendment read: "No state shall make any law respecting an establishment of religion, or prohibiting the free exercise thereof; no money raised by taxation in any state for the support of public schools, or derived from any public fund therefor nor any public lands devoted thereto, shall ever be under control of any religious sect or denomination; nor shall any money so raised or lands so devoted be divided between religious sects or denominations." The Amendment proposed by Rep. Blaine in 1875 passed the House but was narrowly defeated in the Senate. 4 Congressional Record 5190 (1876). A furious lobbying effort in the 1880s and 1890s sought to resurrect this amendment, but in vain. See Alfred W. Meyer, "The Blaine Amendment and the Bill of Rights," *Harvard Law Review* 64 (1951): 939–945; F. William O'Brien, "The Blaine Amendment, 1875–1876," *University of Detroit Law Journal* 41 (1963): 137–205; id., "The States and 'No Establishment': Proposed Amendments to the Constitution Since 1789," *Washburn Law Journal* 4 (1965): 183–210 (listing 21 failed attempts to introduce such amendments to the United States Constitution).

2. See *The Book of the States* (Chicago, 1972), 21; and Cynthia E. Browne, *State Constitutional Conventions* (Westport/London, 1973), xxviii-xxix, for convenient tables. For multiple editions of these state constitutions, see F. Thorpe, ed., *The Federal and State Constitutions, Colonial Charters, and Other Organic Laws,* 7 vols. (Washington, DC, 1909); see updates in *Constitutions of the United States, National and State* (Dobbs Ferry, NY, 1962–).

3. The provisions here under review are from the following state constitutions: Alabama (1901), I.3, IV.73, XI.217, XII.229, XIV.263; Arizona (1912), II.7, 12, IX.2, 10, XI.7; Arkansas (1874), II.24–26, XVI.5, XIX.1; California (1879), I.4, IV.22, 30, IX.8, 9, XIII.1.5; Colorado (1876), II.4, V.34, IX.7, 8, X.5, XVII.5; Connecticut (1818), I.3, 4, VII.1, 2, VIII.2; Delaware (1897), I.1, 2, VIII.1, IX.4, X.3, 4; Florida (1887), Decl, sec. 5; IX.1, XII.13, XIV.1; Georgia (1945), I.12–14, VII.4; Idaho (1890), I.4, VI.3, IX.5, 6, XIV.1, XXI.19; Illinois (1870), II.3, IX.3, XII.6; Indiana (1851), I.1–8, X.1, XII.6; Iowa (1857), I.3, 4, VI.2; Kansas (1861), Rights, sec. 7; VI.8, VIII.1, XI.1, XII.2, 3; Kentucky (1891), Rights, secs. 1, 5; Revenue, sec. 170; Education, sec. 189; Militia, sec. 220; Louisiana (1921), I.4, IV.8, 16, X.4, 8, XII.13, XIV.15; Maine (1820), I.3, VII.5, IX.1; Maryland (1867), Rights, Arts. 36–39; III.11; Massachusetts (1780), Part I, Arts. II, III, XVIII; Amendment XI (1833), XLVI (1917); Michigan (1890), II.3, 17; V.26, XI.1, XV.1; Minnesota (1857), I.16, 17, VIII.3, IX.1; Mississippi (1890), III.18, IV.66, VIII.208, XIV.265; Missouri (1945), I.5–7, III.38, IX.8, X.6; Montana (1889), III.4, V.35, XI.8, 9, XII.2, XIII.1; Nebraska (1875), I.4, VII.11, VIII.2; Nevada (1864), I.4, II.2, VIII.2; New Hampshire (1784), Part I, 4–6, 13; Part II, 83, 84; New Jersey (1947), I.3, 4, VIII.2; New Mexico (1912), II.11, IV.31, VII.3, VIII.2, IX.14, XII.3, XX.13, XXI.1, 4; New York (1895), I.3, 11, VII.8, VIII.1, XI.4, XVI.1; North Carolina (1868),

I.26, V.5, VII.8, IX.1, XII.1; North Dakota (1889), I.4, VIII.147, 149, 152, IX.159, XI.176, XII.185, XIII.188, XVI.203, XVII.211; Ohio (1851), I.7, VI.1, 2, VII.2; Oklahoma (1907), I.2, 5, II.5, X.6, 15, XI.5; Oregon (1859), I.1–6, X.2; Pennsylvania (1874), I.3, 4, III.17, 18, IX.1, X.2, XI.1; Rhode Island (1843), I.3; South Carolina (1895), I.4, X.1, 4, XI.9, XIII.1, XVII.4; South Dakota (1889), VI.3, VIII.16, XI.6, XV.7, XXII, XXVI.18; Tennessee (1870), I.3, 4, 6, 28; II.28, VIII.3, IX.1, 2, XI.15; Texas (1876), I.4–7, III.51, VII.5, VIII.2, XVI.47; Utah (1896), I.1, 4, III.1, 4, X.1, 12, 13, XIII.2; Vermont (1793), Rights, III, IX; II.64; Virginia (1902), I.16, IV.58, 59, 67, IX.141, XIII.183; Washington (1889), I.11, IX.4, X.6, XXVI.1, 4; West Virginia (1872), III.11, 15, VI.47, X.1; Wisconsin (1848), I.18, 19, X.3, 6; Wyoming (1890), I.18, 19, III.36, VII.8, 12, XV.12, XVI.6, XVII.1, XXI.25, 28. The table in Appendix 2 summarizes these provisions.

Most of these religion clauses are analyzed in the pathbreaking work of Chester J. Antieau, Philip M. Carroll, and Thomas Carroll Burke, *Religion Under the State Constitutions* (Washington, DC, 1965). See also analysis in Carl Zollman, *American Church Law*, repr. ed. (St. Paul, 1933); and further illustrations in Michael S. Ariens and Robert A. Destro, *Religious Liberty in a Pluralistic Society* (Durham, NC, 1996), 99–203; John T. Noonan Jr., *Believers and the Powers That Are* (New York, 1987), 127–232; Mark DeWolfe Howe, *Cases on Church and State in the United States* (Cambridge, MA., 1952).

4. Constitution of Indiana (1851), I.2–7 (deleting section numbers).

5. Constitution of Rhode Island (1843), Art. I.3.

6. Constitution of Oklahoma (1907), Art. I.2.

7. In addition, the Constitution of Florida (1887), Art. XIV.1 explicitly put questions of conscientious objection to the legislature. The rest of the states were silent on the subject.

8. 367 U.S. 488 (1961).

9. See details in Antieau, Carroll, and Burke, *Religion and the State Constitutions*, 100–119.

10. Constitution of Maryland (1867), Rights, Art. 36.

11. Constitution of Arkansas (1874), Art. II.24, 25.

12. Constitution of New Hampshire (1784), Part I, Art. 6, and Constitution of Connecticut (1818), Art. I.4, both repeating Constitution of Massachusetts (1780), Part I, Art. III. By Amendment XI (1833), the Massachusetts Constitution rendered this as "all religious sects and denominations."

13. Constitution of Delaware (1897), Art. IX.4.

14. See generally Paul G. Kauper and Stephen B. Ellis, "Religious Corporations and the Law," *Michigan Law Review* 71 (1973): 1499.

15. Constitution of Virginia (1902), Art. IV.59; Constitution of West Virginia (1872), Art. VI.47. See analysis of the causes and consequences of this restriction in Thomas E. Buckley, "After Disestablishment: Thomas Jefferson's Wall of Separation in Antebellum Virginia," *Journal of Southern History* 61 (1995): 445.

16. 435 U.S. 618 (1978).

17. Constitution of Utah (1896), Art. I.4.

18. See generally, Charles Glenn, *The Myth of the Common School* (Amherst, MA, 1978); Rockne M. McCarthy, James W. Skillen, and William A. Harper, *Dises-*

tablishment a Second Time: Genuine Pluralism for American Schools (Grand Rapids, MI, 1982), 52–72.

19. Constitution of New York (1895), Art. XI.4. See similarly Constitution of New Jersey (1947), Art. VIII. sec. IV.3. Such policies of furnishing transportation to religious school children on public school buses were upheld as constitutional in *Everson v. Board of Education*, 330 U.S. 1 (1947).

20. Constitution of Nevada (1864), Art. XI.10.

21. Constitution of Illinois (1870), Art. VIII.3.

22. Twenty-seven of the thirty-three state constitutions that explicitly outlawed state funding of religion also explicitly authorized such exemptions, and the remaining seven states had strong statutory provisions in effect providing for the same. See further Chapter 9 herein.

23. These western states were Arizona, Idaho, Montana, New Mexico, North Dakota, South Dakota, Washington, and Wyoming. Congress generally included these religious liberty clauses, among others, in the enabling acts that allowed new states into the union. Such clauses were irrevocable without the consent of the Congress and the people of the states, and they remain in place still today, albeit sometimes in new forms. See, e.g., 1953 amendment to the New Mexico compact, consented to by Congress, 67 Stat. 586, chap. 506.3. For other sources and analysis, see Robert F. Williams, *State Constitutional Law*, 2d ed. (Washington, DC, 1993), 76ff.

24. For details, see my "'A Most Mild and Equitable Establishment of Religion': John Adams and the Massachusetts Experiment," *Journal of Church and State* 41 (1999): 213.

25. See, e.g., Jacob C. Meyer, *Church and State in Massachusetts from 1740 to 1833*, repr. ed. (New York, 1968); William G. McLoughlin, *New England Dissent, 1630–1833*, 2 vols. (Cambridge, MA, 1971).

26. See esp. Donald S. Lutz, *The Origins of American Constitutionalism* (Baton Rouge, LA, 1988).

27. Reprinted, with modernized spelling and capitalization in Thorpe, ed., *The Federal and State Constitutions*, 3:1888.

28. Constitution of Virginia (1902), Article I.16 (retained in the 1971 Constitution).

29. See sources and discussion in Morton Borden, *Jews, Turks, and Infidels* (Chapel Hill, NC/London, 1984).

30. *Church of the Holy Trinity v. United States*, 143 U.S. 457, 478 (1892). For overviews of these developments, see, e.g., Harold J. Berman, *Faith and Order: The Reconciliation of Law and Religion* (Atlanta, 1993), 209–238; Isaac A. Cornelison, *The Relation of Religion to Civil Government in the United States of America: A State Without a Church, but Not Without a Religion* (New York, 1895); Philip Schaff, *Church and State in the United States, or the American Idea of Religious Liberty and Its Practical Effects* (New York, 1888); Anson P. Stokes, *Church and State in the United States* (New York, 1950), 1:426ff., 600ff., and vol. 2 passim.

31. The phrase was coined by Sir Matthew Hale in *Taylor's Case*, 1 Vent. 293, 86 English Reports 189 (K.B. 1676), and is repeated in several American tracts and cases. See, e.g., *The Works of James Wilson*, ed. R. G. McCloskey (Cambridge, 1967), 2:671; and *Vidal v. Girard's Executors*, 43 U.S. (2 How.) 127, 198 (1844).

For analysis and other sources, see Stuart Banner, "When Christianity Was Part of the Common Law," *Law and History Review* 16 (1998): 27–62.

32. For an introduction to the vast literature, see Mary Ellen Snodgrass, *Encyclopedia of Frontier Literature* (Santa Barbara/Denver/Oxford, 1997). Classics on religion and the frontier include Peter G. Mode, *The Frontier Spirit in American Christianity* (New York, 1923); James P. Shannon, *Catholic Colonization on the Western Frontier* (New Haven, 1957); William W. Sweet, *Religion in the Development of American Culture, 1765–1840* (New York, 1952). For more recent studies and analysis of the literature, see James R. Rohrer, *Keepers of the Covenant: Frontier Missions and the Decline of Congregationalism* (New York/Oxford, 1995); Laurie F. Maffly-Kipp, *Religion and Society in Frontier California* (New Haven/London, 1994).

33. For demographics, see Edwin S. Gaustad, *Historical Atlas of Religion in America*, rev. ed. (New York, 1976); for a crisp overview, see Martin E. Marty, *Pilgrims in Their Own Land* (Harmondsworth, UK, 1985).

34. See sources and analysis in Nathan O. Hatch, *The Democratization of American Christianity* (New Haven, 1989).

35. Gaustad, *Historical Atlas*, 42.

36. The figures that follow are drawn from the tables in ibid., 4, 42–44, which include actual numbers of churches. In calculating these percentages, I have simply totaled the number of churches in each table and divided the number of churches listed under each category against the total.

Chapter Six

1. 5 U.S. (1 Cranch) 137 (1803).

2. *Fletcher v. Peck* 10 U.S. (6 Cranch) 87 (1810); *Martin v. Hunter's Lessee*, 14 U.S. (1 Wheat) 304 (1816); and *Cohens v. Commonwealth of Virginia*, 19 U.S. (6 Wheat) 264 (1821).

3. *Permoli v. Municipality No. 1 of New Orleans*, 44 U.S. (3 How.) 589, 609 (1845). See also *Barron v. Baltimore*, 32 U.S. (7 Pet.) 243 (1833) (holding that the Bill of Rights in general, and the Fifth Amendment in particular, applied only to the national government). See further Joseph Story, *Commentaries on the Constitution*, 2d ed. (Boston, 1851), 2:597.

4. See Appendix 3.

5. 98 U.S. 145, 164 (1879).

6. See sources and analysis in Leonard J. Arrington and Davis Bitton, *The Mormon Experience: A History of the Latter-Day Saints* (New York, 1979); Klaus J. Hansen, *Mormonism and the American Experience* (Chicago, 1981); Jan Shipps, *Mormonism: The Story of a New Religious Tradition* (Urbana, IL, 1984).

7. 12 Stat. 501–502 (1862).

8. 22 Stat. 30–32 (1882). In *Cannon v. United States*, 116 U.S. 55 (1885), the Court held that proof of sexual intercourse between the man and the multiple women with whom he cohabited was not required for a bigamy conviction.

9. The most pertinent laws, and attendant regulations, are quoted and analyzed in *Murphy v. Ramsey*, 114 U.S. 15 (1885).

10. 18 *Congressional Record* 585–593 (January 1887). For further details, see Frederick Mark Gedicks, "The Integrity of Survival: A Mormon Response to Stanley Hauweras," *DePaul Law Review* 42 (1992): 167.

11. 133 U.S. 333, 341–342 (1890).

12. 136 U.S. 1 (1890) and the companion case *Romney v. United States,* 136 U.S. 1 (1890). *Murphy v. Ramsey,* 114 U.S. 15, 45 (1885) upheld various laws disenfranchising known and suspected bigamists against challenges that the laws violated "constitutional rights and liberties." In defense of the laws, Justice Matthews wrote: "For, certainly, no legislation can be supposed more wholesome and necessary in the founding of a free, self-governing commonwealth . . . than that which seeks to establish it on the basis of the idea of the family, as consisting in and springing from the union for life of one man and one woman in the holy estate of matrimony; the sure foundation of all that is stable and noble in our civilization; the best guarantee of that reverent morality which is the source of all beneficent progress in social and political improvement." See also *Cleveland v. United States,* 329 U.S. 14 (1946).

13. *Reynolds,* 98 U.S. at 164.

14. *Davis,* 133 U.S. at 336–337, 341–342.

15. *Latter Day Corporation,* 136 U.S. at 48–50.

16. Kenneth Driggs, "After the Manifesto: Modern Polygamy and Fundamentalist Mormons," *Journal of Church and State* 32 (1990): 367; Sarah Barringer Gordon, "The Twin Relic of Barbarism: The Legal History of Anti-Polygamy in Nineteenth-Century America" (Ph.D. Diss., Princeton, 1995).

17. Constitution of Utah (1896), Art. I, sec. 4; Art. III.

18. See Dallin H. Oaks and Lance B. Wickman, "The Mission Work of the Church of Jesus Christ of Latter Day Saints," in *Sharing the Book: The Rights and Wrongs of Mission,* ed. John Witte Jr. and Richard C. Martin (Maryknoll, NY, 1999), chap. 12.

19. See Rodney K. Smith, "Getting Off on the Wrong Foot and Back on Again: A Reexamination of the History of the Framing of the First Amendment and a Critique of the *Reynolds* and *Everson* Decisions," *Wake Forest Law Review* 20 (1984): 569–643; Marci A. Hamilton, "The Belief/Conduct Paradigm in the Supreme Court's Free Exercise Jurisprudence: A Theological Account of the Failure to Protect Religious Conduct," *Ohio State Law Journal* 54 (1993): 713–796.

20. *United States v. Macintosh,* 283 U.S. 605, 626 (1931).

21. 40 Stat. 76, 78 (1917).

22. 245 U.S. 366, 389–390 (1918). See similar results in *Eagles v. Samuels,* 329 U.S. 304 (1946); *Eagles v. Horowitz,* 329 U.S. 317 (1946).

23. *United States v. Schwimmer,* 279 U.S. 644, 650–651 (1929).

24. *Macintosh,* 283 U.S. at 624–625 (1931).

25. See *United States v. Bland,* 283 U.S. 636 (1931); *Hamilton v. Regents of the University of California,* 293 U.S. 245 (1934); *In re Summers,* 325 U.S. 561 (1945).

26. 328 U.S. 61 (1946).

27. See *United States v. Seeger,* 380 U.S. 163 (1965); *Welsh v. United States,* 398 U.S. 333 (1970).

28. 175 U.S. 291, 298 (1899).

29. 210 U.S. 50, 81 (1908).

30. 13 U.S. (9 Cranch) 43 (1815).

31. *Goesele v. Bimeler,* 55 U.S. (14 How.) 589 (1852); *Baker v. Nachtrieb,* 60 U.S. (19 How.) 126 (1856); *Speidel v. Henrici,* 120 U.S. 377 (1887) (also holding that the defecting member should not be granted relief because of the doctrine of "laches," a party's undue delay in seeking equity relief). For texts of these cases, and analysis and sources on the Harmony Society, see Robert T. Miller and Ronald B. Flowers, *Toward Benevolent Neutrality: Church, State, and the Supreme Court,* 5th ed. (Waco, TX, 1996), 531–549.

32. 234 U.S. 640 (1914).

33. Ibid., 642, 648.

34. *Watson v. Jones,* 80 U.S. (13 Wall.) 679, 714 (1871).

35. *Smith v. Swormstedt,* 57 U.S. (16 How.) 288 (1853).

36. *Watson v. Jones,* 80 U.S. at 727.

37. Ibid., 728–729.

38. *Bouldin v. Alexander,* 82 U.S. (15 Wall.) 131, 139–140 (1872). Justice Strong elaborated these sentiments in his *Two Lectures upon the Relations of Civil Law to Church Polity, Discipline, and Property* (New York, 1875).

39. See discussion in Chapter 7, pages 133–135; and Douglas Laycock, "Toward a General Theory of the Religion Clauses: The Case of Church Labor Relations and the Right to Church Autonomy," *Columbia Law Review* 81 (1981): 1373–1417; William W. Bassett, *Religious Organizations and the Law,* 2 vols. (St. Paul, 1998).

Among early cases, see *Church of the Holy Trinity v. United States,* 143 U.S. 457 (1892) (court refused to apply a new federal law forbidding contracts with foreign aliens to a church seeking to hire a foreign cleric); *Ponce v. Roman Catholic Apostolic Church,* 210 U.S. 296 (1908) (court confirmed church's title to property acquired from Spanish government before the U.S. annexation of Puerto Rico); *Gonzalez v. Roman Catholic Archbishop of Manila,* 280 U.S. 1 (1929) (court did not intervene in a church decision to withhold an ecclesiastical office to one of its members).

40. 71 U.S. (4 Wall.) 277, 285 (1866).

41. Dissent attached to *Ex parte Garland,* 71 U.S. (4 Wall.) 397 (1866).

42. Amendment XIV (1868), sec. 1. In the vast literature, see sources and analysis in Stuart D. Poppel, "Federalism, Fundamental Fairness, and the Religion Clauses," *Cumberland Law Review* 25 (1995): 247–308, at 254ff.; Jerold H. Israel, "Selective Incorporation: Revisited," *Georgia Law Review* 71 (1982): 253; Michael Kent Curtis, "Conceived in Liberty: The Fourteenth Amendment and the Bill of Rights," *North Carolina Law Review* 65 (1987): 889. See also summary of sources and cases in John E. Nowak and Ronald D. Rotunda, *Constitutional Law,* 5th ed. (St. Paul, 1995), secs. 10.2, 11.6.

43. 262 U.S. 390, 399 (1923).

44. 268 U.S. 510, 535 (1925).

45. *Farrington v. Tokushige,* 273 U.S. 284 (1927) (invalidating a burdensome regulation on private schools); *Cochran v. Louisiana State Board of Education,* 281 U.S. 370 (1930) (upholding state policy of furnishing textbooks to all public and religious schools, over objection of taxpayer that this constituted a taking of his private property in violation of the Fourteenth Amendment due process clause).

46. *Hamilton v. Board of Regents,* 293 U.S. at 262.

47. Ibid., 265 (Cardozo, J. concurring).

48. 302 U.S. 319, 328 (1937).

49. 303 U.S. 444, 450 (1938).

50. 310 U.S. 296, 297, 300 (1940).

51. Ibid., 303.

52. Ibid., 303–304.

53. See Appendix 3.

54. 330 U.S. 1, 14–15 (1947).

55. Ibid., 15–16, 18.

56. Ibid., 8–15, 33–43.

57. See critical reviews in Jo Renee Formicola and Hubert Morken, eds., *Everson Revisited: Religion, Education, and Law at the Crossroads* (Lanham, MD, 1997).

58. See Chapter 5, note 1.

59. See Nowak and Rotunda, *Constitutional Law,* secs. 10.2, 11.6 for discussion of the cases.

Chapter Seven

1. See, e.g., G. Alan Tarr, "Church and States in the States," *Washington Law Review* 64 (1989): 73–110; Angela C. Carmella, "State Constitutional Protection of Religious Exercise: An Emerging Post-*Smith* Jurisprudence," *Brigham Young University Law Review* (1993): 275–325.

2. For other tables, see Carl H. Esbeck, "Table of United States Supreme Court Decisions Relating to Religious Liberty, 1789–1994," *Journal of Law and Religion* 10 (1994): 573–588; Appendix to *E.E.O.C. v. Townley Engineering and Manufacturing Company,* 859 F.2d 610, 625–629 (9th Cir., 1988) (Noonan, J. dissenting).

3. See the comprehensive collection in Robert T. Miller and Ronald B. Flowers, eds., *Toward Benevolent Neutrality: Church, State, and the Supreme Court,* 5th ed., 2 vols. (Waco, TX, 1996) (with supplements). See also selected and edited cases in Robert S. Alley, *The Supreme Court on Church and State* (New York, 1988); Michael S. Ariens and Robert A. Destro, *Religious Liberty in a Pluralistic Society* (Durham, NC, 1996); Terry Eastland, *Religious Liberty in the Supreme Court: The Cases That Define the Debate over Church and State* (Grand Rapids, MI, 1993); Arnold H. Loewy, *Religion and the Constitution: Cases and Materials* (St. Paul, 1999); John T. Noonan Jr., *The Believer and the Powers That Are: Cases, History, and Other Data Bearing on the Relation of Religion and Government* (New York/London, 1987; 2d ed. forthcoming).

4. See Ira Lupu, "Where Rights Begin: The Problem of Burdens on the Free Exercise of Religion," *Harvard Law Review* 102 (1989): 933–990; Michael McConnell and Richard A. Posner, "An Economic Approach to Issues of Religious Freedom," *University of Chicago Law Review* 56 (1989): 1–60, at 38ff.

5. For summaries of these general requirements, see John E. Nowak and Ronald D. Rotunda, *Constitutional Law,* 4th ed. (St. Paul, 1991), secs. 2.12–2.15. For application, see *Bender v. Williamsport Area School District,* 475 U.S. 534 (1986) (school board member has no standing, in his capacity as a parent, to appeal a board decision affecting the religious rights of his child in the school). See also *Cooper v. Pate,* 378 U.S. 546 (1964) (Muslim prisoner entitled to hearing on the

merits that he was denied access to religious publications); *Catholic Conference v. Abortion Rights Mobilization*, 487 U.S. 72 (1988) (a nonparty witness held in contempt given standing to challenge federal court's jurisdiction over case).

6. *Cantwell v. Connecticut*, 310 U.S. 296 (1940).

7. *Torcaso v. Watkins*, 367 U.S. 488 (1961).

8. *Goldman v. Weinberger*, 475 U.S. 503 (1986).

9. *O'Lone v. Estate of Shabazz*, 482 U.S. 342 (1987); see also *Cruz v. Beto*, 405 U.S. 319 (1972) (prisoner must be given "reasonable" opportunities for free exercise of religion).

10. *National Labor Relations Board v. Catholic Bishop of Chicago*, 440 U.S. 490 (1979); see also *Corporation of the Presiding Bishop v. Amos*, 483 U.S. 327 (1987).

11. *Jimmy Swaggart Ministries v. California Board of Equalization*, 493 U.S. 378 (1990).

12. *Kedroff v. St. Nicholas Cathedral*, 344 U.S. 94 (1952).

13. *Frazee v. Illinois Employment Security Department*, 489 U.S. 829 (1989).

14. *Braunfeld v. Brown*, 366 U.S. 599 (1961). See also *McGowan v. Maryland*, 366 U.S. 420 (1961); *Gallagher v. Crown Kosher Super Market of Massachusetts*, 366 U.S. 617 (1961).

15. *Bob Jones University v. United States*, 461 U.S. 574 (1983).

16. *E.E.O.C. v. Townley Engineering* (9th Cir., 1988).

17. See, e.g., *United States v. Seeger*, 380 U.S. 163, 175 (1965); *Thomas v. Review Board of Indiana Employment Security Division*, 450 U.S. 707 (1981); *Hobbie v. Unemployment Appeals Commission of Florida*, 480 U.S. 136 (1987); *Frazee v. Illinois Department of Employment Security*, 489 U.S. 829 (1989). See Stephen Pepper, "Taking the Free Exercise Clause Seriously," *Brigham Young University Law Review* (1986): 299, 325ff.; Lupu, "Where Rights Begin," 953ff. But see criticisms in John T. Noonan Jr., "How Sincere Do You Have to Be to Be Religious?" *University of Illinois Law Review* (1988): 713.

18. Lupu, "Where Rights Begin," 954.

19. See *United States v. Ballard*, 322 U.S. 78 (1944) (allowing for jury instruction questioning the sincerity of claimant's "I Am" religion).

20. See, e.g., *Alamo Foundation v. Secretary of Labor*, 471 U.S. 290 (1985).

21. *Golden Writ of God v. Department of Revenue*, 300 Or. 479 (1986).

22. See Chapter 9, pages 202–210. See further Douglas Laycock, "Towards a General Theory of the Religion Clauses: The Case of Church Labor Relations and the Right to Church Autonomy," *Columbia Law Review* 81 (1981): 1373.

23. On "balancing tests" in constitutional adjudication, see Louis Henkin, "Infallibility Under Law: Constitutional Balancing," *Columbia Law Review* 78 (1978): 1022–1049; Kathleen M. Sullivan, "Categorization, Balancing, and Government Interests," in *Public Values in Constitutional Law*, ed. Stephen E. Gottlieb (Ann Arbor, MI, 1993), 241. For balancing tests in free exercise cases, see Eugene Gressman and Angela C. Carmella, "The RFRA Revision and the Free Exercise Clause," *Ohio State Law Journal* 57 (1996): 65–143.

24. See, e.g., *Swaggart Ministries*, 493 U.S. at 385ff. distinguishing at length *Murdock v. Pennsylvania*, 319 U.S. 105 (1943) and *Follett v. McCormick*, 321 U.S. 573 (1944) to uphold collection of taxes on sales of religious articles. See also *Employment Division v. Smith*, 494 U.S. 872, 879–880 (1990), reaching back to

Reynolds v. United States, 98 U.S. 145 (1879) and *Prince v. Massachusetts,* 321 U.S. 158 (1944) to uphold application of a criminal law against free exercise objection.

25. See, e.g. *Swaggart Ministries* (1990): The free exercise claimant argued that this was a religious group rights case, which would have provided ample protection; the Court characterized it as a tax exemption case. See also *Employment Division v. Smith* (1990): The free exercise claimant argued that this was simply an unemployment compensation case where the Court had consistently found for the discharged employee; the Court characterized it as a case seeking free exercise exemption from criminal laws.

26. 321 U.S. at 171.

27. The cases right before the introduction of the *Sherbert* strict scrutiny test in 1963 were the Court's very cavalier dismissal of Jewish claims to protection from Sunday blue laws. See cases in note 14 above. The case right before the introduction of the *Smith* lower scrutiny standard was the application of the technical *Sherbert* holding to an applicant for a temporary secretarial post, who rejected proffered employment because it might require work on Sunday. *Frazee v. Illinois Department of Employment Security* (1989). The *Smith* case, however, was also a culmination of other cases that had slowly reduced the free exercise clause to a principle of neutrality. See discussion, pages 136–141.

28. See T. Alexander Alekinoff, "Constitutional Law in the Age of Balancing," *Yale Law Journal* 96 (1987): 943–1005, at 948ff.; Gressman and Carmella, "The RFRA Revision," 70ff.

29. See sources and analysis in Nowak and Rotunda, *Constitutional Law,* secs. 11.4–11.7; Stephen E. Gottlieb, "Compelling Governmental Interests: An Essential but Unanalyzed Term in Constitutional Adjudication," *Boston University Law Review* 68 (1988): 917.

30. See, e.g., *City of Cleburne v. Cleburne Living Center,* 473 U.S. 432 (1985). See cases and materials on standards of review under the equal protection clause, in Geoffrey R. Stone et al., *Constitutional Law,* 3d ed. (Boston/New York/London, 1996), 561–595.

31. See esp. Gressman and Carmella, "The RFRA Revision and the Free Exercise Clause"; Douglas Laycock, "The Remnants of Free Exercise," *Supreme Court Review* (1990): 1–68.

32. *Reynolds v. United States,* 98 U.S. 145, 166–167 (1879); *Davis v. Beason,* 133 U.S. 333, 345–348 (1890).

33. 310 U.S. 296, at 303–304.

34. *West Virginia State Board v. Barnette,* 319 U.S. 624, 639 (1943); *Heffron v. International Society for Krishna Consciousness,* 452 U.S. 640, 649 (1981), quoting, in part, *Virginia State Board of Pharmacy v. Virginia Citizens Consumer Council,* 425 U.S. 748 (1976).

35. 374 U.S. 398 (1963).

36. For cases using the strict scrutiny test and finding for the religious claimant, see *Wisconsin v. Yoder* (1972) (exempting Amish from full compliance with compulsory school attendance law); *McDaniel v. Paty,* 435 U.S. 618 (1978) (striking down a state constitutional prohibition against clergy holding political office); *Widmar v. Vincent,* 454 U.S. 263 (1981) (requiring state university to give voluntary re-

ligious student group equal access to facilities). *Thomas v. Review Board* (1981); *Hobbie v. Unemployment Commission* (1987); and *Frazee v. Illinois Department of Employment Security* (1989) each extended the direct holding of *Sherbert* to other unemployment compensation schemes.

For cases using the strict scrutiny test and finding for government, see *Gillette v. United States,* 401 U.S. 437 (1971) (holding that statutory restriction of conscientious objection status to one who, "by religious training or belief, is conscientiously opposed to war in any form" is not a violation of the free exercise or disestablishment clauses); *United States v. Lee* (1982) (holding against an Amish employer seeking to be exempt from paying social security taxes); *Bob Jones University v. United States* (1983) (upholding I.R.S. decision to withdraw federal tax exempt status from a racially discriminatory religious school); *Hernandez v. Commissioner of Internal Revenue,* 490 U.S. 680 (1989) (denial of deductions for costs associated with Church of Scientology training is not a violation of the free exercise clause).

37. *Smith,* 494 U.S. at 879, quoting in part, *United States v. Lee* (Stevens, J. concurring). For prior cases, see *Bowen v. Roy,* 476 U.S. 693, 707–708 (1986) ("Government meets its burden when it demonstrates that a challenged requirement for governmental benefits, *neutral* and *uniform* in its application, is a *reasonable* means of promoting a *legitimate* public interest.") (emphasis added). This language is repeated in *Estate of Shabazz,* 482 U.S. at 349–351; and *Lyng,* 485 U.S. at 448–451.

38. *Smith,* 494 U.S. at 886–887.

39. *Lukumi Babalu Aye v. Hialeah,* 508 U.S. 520 (1993) (local ordinances discriminating against Santerian slaughtering held in violation of free exercise). The *Smith* Court also allowed that a "hybrid claim" combining free exercise rights with other fundamental rights might receive closer scrutiny. For a recent example of this, see, e.g., *Thomas v. Anchorage Equal Rights Commission,* 1999 WL 11337 (9th Cir. Alaska).

40. See esp. Douglas Laycock, "The Remnants of Free Exercise"; Michael W. McConnell, "Free Exercise Revisionism and the *Smith* Decision," *University of Chicago Law Review* 57 (1990): 1109–1153.

41. 42 U.S.C. secs. 2000bb to 2000b–4. For analysis, see Douglas Laycock and Oliver S. Thomas, "Interpreting the Religious Freedom Restoration Act," *Texas Law Review* 73 (1994): 209–245; Thomas C. Berg, "What Hath Congress Wrought: An Interpretive Guide to the Religious Freedom Restoration Act," *Villanova Law Review* 39 (1994): 1–70.

42. Ira C. Lupu, "The Failure of RFRA," *University of Arkansas Law Journal* 20 (1998): 575–617 (showing that, as of June 25, 1997, when RFRA was declared unconstitutional as applied to the states, RFRA claimants had won only 18 of 144 federal cases and 7 of 17 state cases). This winning percentage is somewhat skewed, however, for well over half the litigants were prisoners seeking exemptions from prison regulations and daily decisions. It often proved easy for government to show a compelling interest in prison security and safety, and courts were averse to reviewing the myriad daily administrative decisions that ill-affected prisoners. See ibid.; and Shelly S. Rachanow, "The Effect of *O'Lone v. Estate of Shabazz* on the Free Exercise Rights of Prisoners," *Journal of Church and State* 40 (1998): 125–148.

43. See Symposium, *University of Arkansas Law Journal* 20 (1998): 555–812; "Symposium: Reflections on *City of Boerne v. Flores,*" *William and Mary Law Re-*

view 39 (1998): 601–960; "Symposium: Does Religious Freedom Have a Future? The First Amendment After *Boerne*," *Nexus: A Journal of Opinion* 2 (1997): 1–172; "James R. Browning Symposium for 1994: The Religious Freedom Restoration Act," *Montana Law Review* 56 (1995): 1–324. See also Marci A. Hamilton, "The Religious Freedom Restoration Act: Letting the Fox into the Henhouse Under Cover of Section 5 of the Fourteenth Amendment," *Cardozo Law Review* 16 (1994): 357–398; Christopher L. Eisgruber and Lawrence G. Sager, "Why the Religious Freedom Restoration Act Is Unconstitutional," *New York University Law Review* 69 (1994): 437–476; Scott C. Idleman, "The Religious Freedom Restoration Act: Pushing the Limits of Legislative Power," *Texas Law Review* 73 (1994): 247–334; William van Alstyne, "The Failure of the Religious Freedom Restoration Act Under Section 5 of the Fourteenth Amendment," *Duke Law Journal* 46 (1996): 291–326.

44. 117 S.Ct. 2157, 2164 (1997).

45. Congress now has under discussion a number of more narrowly drawn statutes to blunt the *Smith* test. See Daniel O. Conkle, "Congressional Alternatives in the Wake of *City of Boerne v. Flores:* The (Limited) Role of Congress in Protecting Religious Freedom from State and Local Infringement," *University of Arkansas Law Journal* 20 (1998): 633.

46. See analysis in Thomas C. Berg, "The Constitutional Future of Religious Freedom Legislation," *University of Arkansas Law Journal* 20 (1998): 715, 727ff.

47. For opposing prognoses, see Christopher L. Eisgruber and Lawrence G. Sager, "Congressional Power and Religious Liberty After *City of Boerne v. Flores*," *Supreme Court Review* (1998): 79–139; Michael W. McConnell, "Institutions and Interpretations: A Critique of *City of Boerne v. Flores*," *Harvard Law Review* 111 (1997): 153–195.

48. See *New York v. United States*, 505 U.S. 144 (1992); *United States v. Lopez*, 514 U.S. 549 (1995).

49. *Cantwell*, 310 U.S. at 303–304, 310.

50. Ibid., 304, 308.

51. For a good overview, see W. Glen How and Philip Brumley, "Religious Perspectives on Human Rights, Evangelism, and Proselytism: The Jehovah's Witnesses," in *Sharing the Book: Religious Perspectives on the Rights and Wrongs of Mission*, ed. John Witte Jr. and Richard C. Martin (Maryknoll, NY, 1999), chap. 13.

52. 318 U.S. 413, 414 (1943); 319 U.S. 105, 110 (1943).

53. *Marsh v. Alabama*, 326 U.S. 501 (1946); *Tucker v. Texas*, 326 U.S. 517 (1946).

54. *Murdock v. Pennsylvania*, 319 U.S. 105, 108–109, 111–112 (1943).

55. See *Jones v. Opelika [II]*, 319 U.S. 103 (1943), overruling *Jones v. Opelika [I]*, 316 U.S. 584 (1942); *Largent v. Texas*, 318 U.S. 418 (1943); *Follett v. McCormick*, 321 U.S. 473 (1944).

56. 340 U.S. 290 (1951).

57. 340 U.S. 268 (1951). See similar result in *Saia v. New York*, 334 U.S. 558 (1948) (lack of criteria in ordinance prohibiting amplified religious speech violates free speech clause).

58. 345 U.S. 67 (1953).

59. 345 U.S. 395, 398–408 (1953). The Court relied, in part on *Cox v. New Hampshire*, 312 U.S. 569 (1941), which upheld a general parade permit, offered on a sliding fee scale, for all processions. The *Cox* Court said: "If a municipality has authority to control the use of its public streets for parades or processions, as it undoubtedly has, it cannot be denied authority to give consideration, without unfair discrimination, to time, place and manner in relation to other proper uses of the streets. We find it impossible to say that the limited authority conferred by the licensing provisions of the statute in question . . . contravened any constitutional right." Ibid., 576.

60. See summary of cases in *Heffron v. International Society* (1981).

61. 321 U.S. 158, 165–167 (1944).

62. *Jehovah's Witnesses v. King County Hospital*, 390 U.S. 598 (1968).

63. See Chapter 3, pages 39–42.

64. *Watson v. Jones*, 80 U.S. (13 Wall.) 679, 728 (1871).

65. *Reynolds*, 98 U.S. at 164.

66. *Cantwell*, 310 U.S. at 303.

67. *Gobitis*, 310 U.S. at 594, 597–598 (1940).

68. *Barnette*, 319 U.S. at 642.

69. See *United States v. Ballard* (1944); and *In re Summers*, 325 U.S. 561 (1945) (refusal of bar admission to conscientious objector who refused to serve in military not a free exercise violation).

70. *Girouard v. United States*, 328 U.S. 61 (1946). This case also turned on the test oath clause of Article VI.

71. *First Unitarian Church v. County of Los Angeles*, 357 U.S. 545 (1957).

72. *Torcaso v. Watkins*, 367 U.S. 488 (1961).

73. *McDaniel v. Paty*, 435 U.S. 618, 626 (1978) (citing *Torcaso v. Watkins*).

74. *Sherbert*, 374 U.S at 401, 406.

75. *Thomas v. Review Board* (1981).

76. *Hobbie v. Unemployment Commission* (1987).

77. *Frazee v. Illinois Department* (1989).

78. *Thomas*, 450 U.S. at 717–718. This same principle had earlier been denied to Jewish groups who sought free exercise exemptions from Sunday blue laws. Their argument was that while state law prohibited Sunday work, religious law prohibited Saturday work. This put Jewish merchants and workers at a general commercial disadvantage and required kosher establishments to be closed to Jewish communities for two days instead of one. The Court was not convinced that such regulations burdened "Jewish religion" per se. See cases in note 14 above and analysis in Barbara J. Redman, "Sabbatarian Accommodation in the Supreme Court," *Journal of Church and State* 33 (1991): 495–523; Jerome A. Barron, "Sunday in North America," *Harvard Law Review* 79 (1965): 42–54.

79. *McDaniel v. Paty*, 435 U.S. at 622–626.

80. *Watson*, 80 U.S. at 728–729. See discussion in Chapter 6, pages TK.

81. See this characterization in *Presbyterian Church in the United States v. Mary Elizabeth Blue Hull Presbyterian Church*, 393 U.S. 440, 447 (1969).

82. 344 U.S. 94, 110, 116 (1952).

83. *Presbyterian Church*, 393 U.S. at 449. See further *Maryland & Virginia Churches v. Sharpsburg Church*, 396 U.S. 367 (1970).

84. *Milivojevich*, 426 U.S. at 713–715, 724–725. See generally, Louis Sirico, "Church Property Disputes: Churches as Secular and Alien Institutions," *Fordham Law Review* 55 (1986): 335–362; Frederick Mark Gedicks, "Toward a Constitutional Jurisprudence of Religious Group Rights," *Wisconsin Law Review* (1989): 99–169; Kent Greenawalt, "Hands Off! Civil Court Involvement in Conflicts over Religious Property," *Columbia Law Review* 98 (1998): 1843–1907.

85. 268 U.S. 510 (1925).

86. 440 U.S. 490 (1979).

87. 483 U.S. 327 (1987).

88. 406 U.S. at 216–218.

89. *Cantwell*, 319 U.S. at 310.

90. *Gobitis*, 310 U.S. at 593.

91. *Everson v. Board of Education*, 330 U.S. 1, 16 (1947) (emphasis in original).

92. *Sherbert*, 374 U.S. at 411 (Douglas, J. concurring).

93. 443 U.S. 595, 603, 605 (1979).

94. See sources and analysis in William W. Bassett, *Religious Organizations and the Law*, rev. ed., 2 vols. (St. Paul, 1998), secs. 7.32–36; and case and literature analysis in Nathan Belzer, "Intrachurch Disputes over Property," *St. Thomas Law Review* 11 (1999): 109.

95. 475 U.S. 503 (1986).

96. 476 U.S. 693, 696, 699, 707–708 (1986).

97. 482 U.S. 342, 350, 352 (1987).

98. 485 U.S. 439 (1988).

99. 42 U.S.C. sec. 1996 (1978). See generally Ann E. Beeson, "Dances with Justice: Peyotism in the Courts," *Emory Law Journal* 41 (1992): 1121.

100. *Lyng*, 485 U.S. at 447. See also 451 (recognizing "devastating effects on traditional Indian religious practices").

101. Ibid., 451–452 (citations omitted).

102. 493 U.S. 378, 389, 391 (1990) (emphasis added).

103. 494 U.S. 872 (1990).

104. Ibid., 879.

105. 508 U.S. 520 (1993).

106. For an early defense of this position, see William P. Marshall, "Solving the Free Exercise Dilemma: Free Exercise as Expression," *Minnesota Law Review* 67 (1983): 545.

107. See *Gitlow v. New York*, 268 U.S. 652 (1925).

108. See, e.g., *Lovell v. City of Griffin*, 303 U.S. 444 (1938) (also decided on freedom of press grounds); *Schneider v. State of New Jersey*, 308 U.S. 147 (1939).

109. Equal access principles also were somewhat at work in *Capitol Square Review and Advisory Board v. Pinette*, 115 S.Ct. 2440 (1995), which I treat in Chapter 8, pages 181–182. *McDaniel v. Paty* (1978), holding that the free exercise clause forbids the exclusion of clergy from political participation, can also be read as something of an equal access case—clergy must be given "equal access" to political participation—although the Court does not use that terminology.

110. 454 U.S. 263, 270, 273 (1981).

111. 508 U.S. 384, 387, 394, quoting in part *City Council of Los Angeles v. Taxpayers for Vincent*, 466 U.S. 789 (1984).

112. 115 S.Ct. 2510, 2517–2518, 2520 (1995).

113. Ibid., 2535 (Souter, J. dissenting).

114. See summary in Thomas C. Berg, *The State and Religion in a Nutshell* (St. Paul, 1998), 131–147.

115. See *United States v. Seeger* (1965).

116. 343 U.S. 306, 313–314 (1952).

117. 397 U.S. 664 (1970).

118. 432 U.S. 63 (1977). But cf. *Estate of Thornton v. Caldor, Inc.*, 472 U.S. 703 (1985) (striking down statute that gave employees a categorical right not to work on their sabbath); *Ansonia Board of Education v. Philbrook*, 479 U.S. 60 (1986) (employer is not required to accept the employee's preferred form of religious accommodation).

119. 483 U.S. 327 (1987).

120. *Brandon v. Board of Education of Guilderland School District*, 635 F.2d. 971 (1980), cert. denied, 454 U.S. 1123 (1981), rehearing denied, 455 U.S. 983 (1982).

121. 20 U.S.C. secs. 4071–4074.

122. 496 U.S. 226 (1990).

123. 10 U.S.C. sec. 774.

124. See cases in note 118. See also *Texas Monthly, Inc. v. Bullock*, 489 U.S. 1 (1989) (strikes down special state exemption for religious periodicals); *Board of Education of Kiryas Joel v. Grumet*, 496 U.S. 226 (1990) (creation of public school district that follow boundaries of religious village violates disestablishment clause).

125. 42 U.S.C. sec.. 1996 (1978).

126. *Lyng*, 485 U.S. at 455.

127. Only Justice Stevens touched on this issue in his concurrence, finding that RFRA violated the disestablishment clause. *Boerne*, 117 S.Ct. at 2172 (Stevens, J. concurring).

128. See articles in notes 41, 43, and 47 above. See also Jeb Rubenfeld, "Antidisestablishmentarianism: Why RFRA Was Really Unconstitutional," *Michigan Law Review* 95 (1997): 2347–2384 (arguing that RFRA and RFRA-type legislation constitute an establishment of religion).

129. See Derek H. Davis, "Equal Treatment: A Christian Separationist Perspective," in *Equal Treatment of Religion in a Pluralistic Society*, ed. Stephen V. Monsma and J. Christopher Soper (Grand Rapids, MI, 1998), 136–157; Michael W. McConnell, "Equal Treatment and Religious Discrimination," in Monsma and Soper, eds., *Equal Treatment of Religion*, 30–54.

130. See Douglas Laycock, "Religious Liberty as Liberty," *Journal of Contemporary Legal Studies* 7 (1996): 313–356, esp. at 314–323; Michael E. Smith, "The Special Place of Religion in the Constitution," *Supreme Court Review* (1983): 83–123.

131. 508 U.S. at 559 (Souter, J. concurring) (expressing "doubts about whether the *Smith* rule merits adherence"); 578 (Blackmun, J. and O'Connor, J. concurring) ("*Smith* was wrongly decided").

132. 117 S.Ct. at 2176 (O'Connor, J. dissenting) ("*Smith* was wrongly decided), 2186 (Souter, J. dissenting) (expressing "serious doubts" about *Smith*), 2186 (Breyer, J. dissenting) (calling for briefing and argument on the propriety of *Smith*).

Chapter Eight

1. *Zobrest v. Catalina Foothills School District,* 509 U.S. 1, 24 (1993) (O'Connor, J. dissenting), quoting *Three Affiliated Tribes of Fort Berthold Reservation v. Wold Engineering, P.C.,* 467 U.S. 1. See also *McCollum v. Board of Education,* 333 U.S. 203, 232, 235 (Jackson, J. concurring) (expressing doubt whether the Court had jurisdiction over a local case involving religious instruction in public schools, and urging the Court to devise strict limits to jurisdiction over these cases).

2. 393 U.S. 97, 100 (1968).

3. *Zobrest,* 504 U.S. at 24 (O'Connor, J., dissenting).

4. Ibid., 8.

5. The Court has sometimes inventively interpreted other procedural rules as well. See, e.g., *Agostini v. Felton* (1997), 65 U.S.L.W. 4524 (1997), interpreting Rule 60(b)(5) of the Federal Rules of Civil Procedure. The rule allows a court to lift an injunction if there is a "change in law" that renders inequitable further application of the injunction. In *Agostini,* the Court at once declared a change in prevailing disestablishment law and declared that the disestablishment law had changed sufficiently to warrant a lifting of the injunction. See criticisms of this in ibid., at 4538–4540 (Ginsburg, J. dissenting); and in Jason M. Waite, "*Agostini v. Felton:* Thickening the Establishment Clause Stew," *New England Law Review* 33 (1998): 80.

6. *Frothingham v. Mellon,* 262 U.S. 447 (1923).

7. *Doremus v. Board of Education,* 342 U.S. 429 (1952) (party lacks standing to challenge Bible reading in school since student has already graduated).

8. *Abington School District v. Schempp,* 374 U.S. 203, 224, n. 9 (1963) (emphasis added).

9. *Flast v. Cohen,* 392 U.S. 83 (1968). See also *Larson v. Valente,* 456 U.S. 228, 238–244 (1982), and 264–272 (Rehnquist, J. dissenting) (detailed discussion of Article III standing in disestablishment cases).

10. *Valley Forge Christian College v. American United for Separation of Church and State,* 454 U.S. 464, 487 (1982). See also *Karcher v. May,* 484 U.S. 72 (1987) (state legislators cannot appeal a disestablishment case involving a moment of silence law for which they voted, but which the legislature has chosen not to appeal).

11. See, e.g., *Kiryas Joel Village School District v. Grumet,* 114 S.Ct. 2481 (1994); and broader analysis in Thomas C. Berg, "Slouching Towards Secularism: A Comment on *Kiryas Joel School District v. Grumet,*" *Emory Law Journal* 44 (1995): 433.

12. *Lyng v. Northwest Indian Cemetery Protective Association,* 485 U.S. 439, 451 (1988). See broader analysis in Michael W. McConnell, "Equal Treatment and Religious Discrimination," in *Equal Treatment of Religion in a Pluralistic Society,* ed. Stephen V. Monsma and J. Christopher Soper (Grand Rapids, MI/Cambridge, 1998), 30.

13. *Valley Forge,* 454 U.S. at 509–510 (Brennan, J. dissenting) (references omitted).

14. *Marsh v. Chambers,* 463 U.S. 783 (1983) (upholding state appointment of legislative chaplains exclusively on historical grounds). See also *McGowan v. Maryland,* 366 U.S. 420 (1961) (upholding Sunday blue laws largely on historical

grounds); *Walz v. Tax Commission*, 397 U.S. 664 (1970) (upholding tax exemptions of church property, in part, on historical grounds). See further analysis in Chapter 9, pages 188, 213–214, and in Concluding Reflections, pages 235–237.

15. See examples in Chapter 5, pages 91–93, and detailed discussion in Charles Glenn, *The Myth of the Common School* (Amherst, MA, 1988).

16. *Everson v. Board of Education*, 330 U.S. 1, 15–16 (1947).

17. *Engel v. Vitale*, 370 U.S. 421, 430–432 (1962).

18. *Board of Education v. Allen*, 392 U.S. 236, 251–252 (1968) (Black, J. dissenting).

19. *Everson*, 330 U.S. at 18. For analysis, see Dallin H. Oaks, ed., *The Wall Between Church and State* (Chicago, 1963); Symposium, "Confronting the Wall of Separation," *DePaul Law Review* 42 (1992): 1–397.

20. See *Walz v. Tax Commission* (1970) (using separationist arguments, among others, to uphold a state tax exemptions for churches, charities, schools, and other associations); *Texas Monthly v. Bullock*, 489 U.S. 1 (1989) (using separationist arguments, among others, to outlaw a special state sales tax exemption for religious publications).

21. For detailed analysis, see esp. Leo Pfeffer, *Church, State, and Freedom*, rev. ed. (Boston, 1967); id., *God, Caesar, and the Constitution: The Court as Referee in Church-State Confrontation* (Boston, 1975); Leonard W. Levy, *The Establishment Clause: Religion and the First Amendment* (New York, 1986).

22. 343 U.S. 306, 312–314 (1952).

23. *Engel v. Vitale*, 370 U.S. at 421, 445–446 (Stewart, J. dissenting).

24. *Abington School District v. Schempp*, 374 U.S. 203, 313 (Stewart, J., dissenting). See further Wilber G. Katz, "Freedom of Religion and State Neutrality," *University of Chicago Law Review* 20 (1953): 426.

25. *Wallace v. Jaffree*, 472 U.S. 38, 107, 113 (Rehnquist, J., dissenting).

26. See generally Richard H. Jones, "Accommodationist and Separatist Ideals in Supreme Court Establishment Clause Decisions," *Journal of Church and State* 28 (1986): 193; Arlin M. Adams and Sarah Barringer Gordon, "The Doctrine of Accommodation in the Jurisprudence of the Religion Clauses," *DePaul Law Review* 37 (1988): 317; Michael W. McConnell, "Accommodation of Religion: An Update and a Response to the Critics," *George Washington Law Review* 60 (1992): 685.

27. For analysis see Philip B. Kurland, *Religion and the Law: Of Church, State, and the Supreme Court* (Chicago, 1962).

28. 374 U.S. at 222. See also ibid., 243–244, 299–305 (Brennan, J., concurring) (expounding and illustrating the principle of neutrality).

29. *Lemon v. Kurtzman*, 403 U.S. 602, 612–614 (1973), quoting in part, *Walz*, 397 U.S. at 670, 674–675. See also Burger's comments in *Tilton v. Richardson*, 403 U.S. 672, 677 (1971).

30. Compare, e.g., *Wallace v. Jaffree* (1985) (offering a searching inquiry into legislative history); *Mueller v. Allen*, 463 U.S. 388 (1983) (spurning inquiry into the motives of the legislature or the history of the statute). See also *West Community Schools v. Mergens*, 496 U.S. 226, 238, 248–250 (1990).

31. See analysis in Carl H. Esbeck, "The *Lemon* Test: Should It Be Retained, Reformulated, or Rejected?" *Notre Dame Journal of Law, Ethics and Public Policy* 4

(1990): 513; Gary J. Simson, "The Establishment Clause in the Supreme Court: Rethinking the Court's Approach," *Cornell Law Review* 72 (1987): 905.

32. 397 U.S. at 669–670 (1970) (emphasis added). See further analysis in Chapter 9, pages 187–189.

33. 463 U.S. 388 (1983).

34. 487 U.S. 589 (1988).

35. 403 U.S. at 619–620, 622 (1971), rehearing denied, 404 U.S. 876 (1971).

36. 472 U.S. 38 (1985) and 489 U.S. 1 (1989), respectively.

37. *Allegheny County v. American Civil Liberties Union,* 492 U.S. 573, 627 (O'Connor, J., concurring).

38. *Kiryas Joel,* 114 S.Ct. at 2497 (O'Connor, J., concurring).

39. *Wallace v. Jaffree,* 472 U.S. at 69 (O'Connor, J., concurring), quoting in part *Lynch v. Donnelly* (1984).

40. *Kiryas Joel,* 114 S.Ct. at 2497 (O'Connor, J., concurring).

41. *Board of Education of the Westside Schools v. Mergens,* 496 U.S. 226 (1990) at 248–250.

42. *Allegheny County,* 492 U.S. at 623–637 (O'Connor, J., concurring).

43. *Lynch v. Donnelly,* 465 U.S. 668, 687–694 (O'Connor, J., concurring); see also *Capitol Square v. Pinette,* 115 S.Ct. 2440, 2451–2457 (1995) (O'Connor, J., concurring).

44. *Mergens,* 110 S.Ct. at 2356; *Rosenberger v. University of Virginia,* 115 S.Ct. 2510, 2525–2528 (1995) (O'Connor, J. concurring).

45. *Kiryas Joel,* 114 S.Ct. at 2481, 2497 (O'Connor, J., concurring).

46. See, e.g., Steven D. Smith, "Symbols, Perceptions, and Doctrinal Illusions: Establishment Neutrality and the 'No Endorsement' Test," *Michigan Law Review* 86 (1987): 266; Michael W. McConnell, "Religious Freedom at a Crossroads," *University of Chicago Law Review* 59 (1992): 115, at 147–157.

47. See, e.g., *Rosenberger,* 115 S.Ct. at 2525–2528 (O'Connor, J., concurring) (including only a passing quotation about the "reasonable observer"); *Mergens,* 110 S.Ct. at 2356 (rejecting inquiry into legislative intent, and not referring to the "reasonable observer" standard).

48. See criticisms by Justice Scalia in *Pinette,* 115 S.Ct. at 2447–2449, in which Chief Justice Rehnquist and Justices Scalia and Thomas concurred. But see ibid., at 2458–2461 (Souter, J., concurring with Breyer and O'Connor, JJ.) defending the endorsement test, at least as applied in *Allegheny County v. ACLU* (1989).

49. *Allegheny County,* 492 U.S. at 659, quoting in part, *Lynch v. Donnelly* (1984).

50. *Lee v. Weisman,* 505 U.S. 577, 586–587, 592–594 (1992).

51. *Allegheny County,* 492 U.S. at 657 (Kennedy, J., concurring in judgment in part, dissenting in part).

52. *Kiryas Joel,* 114 S.Ct. 2501–2505 (Kennedy, J., concurring).

53. See further Michael W. McConnell, "Coercion: The Lost Element of Establishment," *William and Mary Law Review* 27 (1986): 933, with (self-)critical updates in id., "Religious Freedom at a Crossroads," 157–165. See also Douglas Laycock, "'Non-Coercive' Support for Religion: Another False Claim About the Establishment Clause," *Valparaiso University Law Review* 26 (1991): 37.

54. 505 U.S. at 587, 589–592.

55. See Souter's illustrations in *Lee v. Weisman*, 112 S.Ct. at 618–619 (Souter, J. concurring); *Kiryas Joel*, 114 S.Ct. at 2491–2492.

56. *Kiryas Joel*, 114 S.Ct. at 2491–2492.

57. *Rosenberger*, 115 S.Ct. at 2539 (Souter, J. dissenting).

58. Ibid. at 2534–2539. See also *Agostini*, 675 U.S.L.W. at 4534–4538 (Souter, J. dissenting). For a nuanced exposition of this doctrine, on which Justice Souter has in part relied, see Douglas Laycock, "Formal, Substantive, and Disaggregated Neutrality Toward Religion," *DePaul Law Review* 39 (1990): 993. See further id., "Religious Liberty as Liberty," *Journal of Contemporary Legal Issues* 7 (1996): 313.

59. *Kiryas Joel*, 114 S.Ct. at 2487–2493.

60. See analysis in Monsma and Soper, eds., *Equal Treatment of Religion in a Pluralistic Society.*

61. See, e.g., Justice O'Connor's explicit concerns for "equal protection of religion" in *Mergens*, 496 U.S. at 235–238, 248–252. See also her comment in *Kiryas Joel*, 114 S.Ct. at 2497: "The emphasis on equal treatment is, I think, an eminently sound approach. In my view, the Religion Clauses—the Free Exercise Clause, the Establishment Clause, Art. VI, cl. 3 [the no religious oath clause], and the Equal Protection Clause as applied to religion—all speak with one voice on this point: Absent the most unusual circumstances, one's religion ought not affect one's legal rights, or duties, or benefits."

62. See esp. the contrast between Justice Kennedy's and Justice Souter's reading of "neutrality" in *Rosenberger v. University of Virginia* (1995).

63. *Bradfield v. Roberts*, 175 U.S. 291 (1899).

64. See, e.g., *Tilton v. Richardson*, 403 U.S. 672 (1971); *Roemer v. Board of Public Works*, 426 U.S. 736 (1976); *Bowen v. Kendrick*, 487 U.S. 589 (1988).

65. *Everson v. Board of Education* (1947); *Board of Education v. Allen*, 392 U.S. 236 (1968).

66. *Walz v. Tax Commission* (1970).

67. See *Sherbert v. Verner*, 374 U.S. 398, 409–410 (1963) (defending the free exercise exemption on grounds of neutrality but explicitly forgoing analysis of the equal protection issue); repeated in *Thomas v. Review Board*, 450 U.S. 707, 719–720 (1981); *Hobbie v. Unemployment Appeals Commission*, 480 U.S. 136, 144–145 (1987).

68. Quoting *Bowen v. Kendrick*, 487 U.S. at 609.

69. *Pinette*, 115 S.Ct. at 2440, 2450 (emphasis added).

70. See Chapter 3, Chapter 4, pages 51–54 and 77–80.

71. See Chapter 5, pages 91–96.

72. *Everson*, 330 U.S. at 15–16.

73. Ibid., 16 (emphasis in original).

74. Ibid., 15–16.

75. See details in Chapter 5, pages 91–93, and Appendix 2.

76. See overviews in Glenn, *The Myth of the Common School*; id., "Secularism and Schooling," (forthcoming).

77. 333 U.S. 203, 209–211 (1948).

78. Ibid., 231 (Frankfurter, J., concurring).

79. 370 U.S. at 421, 430–432 (1962).

80. See also *Treen v. Karen B.*, 455 U.S. 913 (1982) (affd. memo) (striking down statute authorizing student volunteers to lead prayer in public school classroom).

81. 374 U.S. 203 (1963). *Schempp* also involved a companion case, *Murray v. Curlett*. The Court, in a per curiam opinion, extended the *Schempp* holding in *Chamberlain v. Public Instruction Board*, 377 U.S. 402 (1964).

82. 374 U.S. 203, 221, 226 (1963).

83. Ibid., 225.

84. 449 U.S. 39 (1980) (per curiam).

85. 482 U.S. 578, 591–593 (1987).

86. 472 U.S. 38, 59–60 (1985).

87. Except when quoting, I shall use the generic term "religious school." The conventional term "parochial" school not only has a deprecatory tone in common parlance but also when used properly means "parish" school. This term is not inclusive enough, since it does not cover the range of Jewish, Muslim, Protestant, and other schools affiliated with religious groups. The other conventional term, "sectarian" school, is even more deprecatory, even in technical parlance, and I have sought to avoid it herein as well. See Richard A. Baer, "The Supreme Court's Discriminatory Use of the Term, 'Sectarian,'" *Journal of Law and Politics* 6 (1990): 449–468.

88. See further discussion of these cases in Chapter 6, pages 110–112.

89. 330 U.S. at 16, 18.

90. 392 U.S. at 243–244.

91. Respectively, *Tilton v. Richardson*, 403 U.S. 672 (1971); *Hunt v. McNair*, 413 U.S. 734 (1973); *Roemer v. Maryland Public Works Board*, 426 U.S. 736 (1977).

92. 403 U.S. at 679–682.

93. 426 U.S. at 746.

94. *Committee for Public Education v. Nyquist*, 413 U.S. 756, 783, 785 (1973).

95. *Levitt v. Committee for Public Education*, 413 U.S. 472 (1973); *New York v. Cathedral Academy*, 434 U.S. 125 (1977).

96. *Committee for Public Education v. Regan*, 444 U.S. 646 (1980).

97. *Norwood v. Harrison*, 413 U.S. 455 (1973); see also *Wolman v. Walter*, 433 U.S. 229 (1977).

98. *Meek v. Pittinger*, 421 U.S. 349 (1975); for exceptions, see *Wolman v. Walter* (1977).

99. *Aguilar v. Felton*, 473 U.S. 402 (1985), overruled by *Agostini v. Felton*, 65 U.S.L.W. 4524 (1997).

100. *Grand Rapids School District v. Ball*, 473 U.S. (1985).

101. *Wallace v. Jaffree*, 482 U.S. at 110–111 (Rehnquist, J. dissenting).

102. *McCollum*, 333 U.S. at 237–238 (Jackson, J. concurring). See critical analysis in Robert A. Destro, "'By What Right?': The Sources and Limits of Federal Court and Congressional Jurisdiction over Matters 'Touching Religion,'" *Indiana Law Review* 29 (1995): 1–103.

103. See detailed analysis and sources in William W. Bassett, *Religious Organizations and the Law*, rev. ed., 2 vols. (St. Paul, 1998); and representative cases in Michael S. Ariens and Robert A. Destro, *Religious Liberty in a Pluralistic Society* (Durham, NC, 1996).

104. *Larkin v. Grendel's Den*, 459 U.S. 116, 122–123 (1982).

105. Ibid., 127–130 (Rehnquist, J. dissenting).

106. Respectively *Bowen v. Kendrick*, 487 U.S. 589 (1988); and *Texas Monthly, Inc. v. Bullock*, 489 U.S. 1 (1989).

107. Respectively *Corporation of the Presiding Bishop v. Amos*, 483 U.S. 327 (1987); and *Estate of Thornton v. Caldor, Inc.* 472 U.S. 703 (1985).

108. Respectively *Marsh v. Chambers*, 463 U.S. 783 (1983); and *Allegheny County v. ACLU*, 492 U.S. 573 (1989).

109. The phrase is Justice O'Connor's in *Planned Parenthood v. Casey*, 505 U.S. 833 (1992).

110. 463 U.S. 388, 394–399 (1983).

111. 474 U.S. 481, 488 (1986).

112. 509 U.S. 1, 13–14 (1993).

113. 65 U.S.L.W. 4527 (1997).

114. 473 U.S. 402, 411–413 (1985).

115. Ibid., 420–421 (Rehnquist, J., dissenting).

116. Ibid., 424, 430–431 (O'Connor, J., dissenting).

117. On these, see Waite, "Thickening the Establishment Clause Stew."

118. 65 U.S.L.W. at 4530, 4533.

119. 505 U.S. at 593–594 (emphasis added).

120. 435 U.S. 622, 628–629 (1978), quoting in part *Wisconsin v. Yoder*, 406 U.S. 205 (1972).

121. 454 U.S. 263, 271, 273 (1981).

122. 496 U.S. at 248–250.

123. *Rosenberger*, 115 S.Ct. at 2517, 2524.

124. Ibid., 2444, 2446, 2450 (emphasis added).

125. Levy, *The Establishment Clause*, 163, quoted and discussed in McConnell, "Religious Freedom at a Crossroads," 115.

126. See Frederick M. Gedicks, "Public Life and Hostility to Religion," *Virginia Law Review* 78 (1992): 671.

127. See Ira C. Lupu, "The Lingering Death of Separationism," *George Washington Law Review* 62 (1994): 230–279.

128. James Madison, Letter to Rev. Adams (1833), in Daniel L. Dreisbach, *Religion and Politics in the Early Republic: Jasper Adams and the Church-State Debate* (Lexington, KY, 1996), 117–121, at 120 (emphasis added).

129. Ibid.

130. Stephen L. Carter, *The Culture of Disbelief: How American Law and Politics Trivializes Religious Devotion* (New York, 1993).

131. *Abington School District v. Schempp*, 374 U.S. 203, 313 (Stewart, J., dissenting). See McConnell, "Equal Treatment and Religious Discrimination."

Chapter Nine

1. This chapter is, in part, an excerpt and update of my "Tax Exemption of Religious Property: Historical Anomaly or Valid Constitutional Practice?" *Southern California Law Review* 62 (1991): 363–415 (hereafter "Tax Exemption"). I have dropped herein most of the copious citations to the literature that appear in that ar-

ticle. Two major studies of the issue, filled with detailed citations, have appeared since publication of this article: "Symposium on Church Tax Exemptions," *Cumberland Law Review* 22 (1992): 467–680; William W. Bassett, *Religious Organizations and the Law* (St. Paul, 1998), secs. 10.19–10.28. See also related discussion and literature in Carl H. Esbeck, "Government Regulation of Religiously Based Social Services: The First Amendment Considerations," *Hastings Constitutional Law Quarterly* 19 (1992): 343. Summaries of important tax exemption cases appear regularly in the periodicals *Church Law and Tax Report; Religious Freedom Reporter; Church and State;* and *Journal of Church and State.*

2. G. Benson et al., *The American Property Tax: Its History, Administration, and Economic Impact* (Claremont, CA, 1965), 11–12. This is not the case with income taxation, which the Sixteenth Amendment empowers Congress to collect. The Court has addressed five religious liberty cases touching on issues of federal income taxation, in each instance, holding for the federal government. See *United States v. American Friends,* 419 U.S. 7 (1974) (upholding taxation of conscientious objectors to military taxes); *United States v. Lee,* 455 U.S. 252 (1982) (denying free exercise exemption from social security taxes for Amish); *Bob Jones University v. United States,* 461 U.S. 574 (1983) (upholding I.R.S. decision to remove tax exempt status of religious university engaged in racial discrimination); *Hernandez v. Commissioner of Internal Revenue,* 490 U.S. 680 (1989) (upholding denial of charitable deduction for contribution in return for religious services); *Davis v. United States,* 495 U.S. 472 (1990) (same). See also *Gibbons v. District of Columbia,* 116 U.S. 404 (1886) (upholding Congress's property tax on vacant property in D.C. owned by church).

Property taxes or general assessments, which are levied annually, must be distinguished from special assessments, which are levied periodically to fund the maintenance and repair of such public works as roads and bridges. All properties that lie contiguous to such public works are subject to special assessments; no exemptions are generally afforded, even to religious properties. See W. Torpey, *Judicial Doctrines of Religious Rights in America* (Chapel Hill, NC, 1948), 194–197; Bassett, *Religious Organizations,* sec. 10.24. See, e.g., *Sarasota County v. Sarasota Church of Christ,* 667 So.2d 180, 183 (Fla. 1996), upholding the imposition of such a special assessment against the property of a religious organization: "Taxes are levied throughout a particular taxing unit for the general benefit of residents and property. . . . Conversely, special assessments must confer a specific benefit on the land burdened by the assessment."

3. See summaries in Chapter 5, pages 191–192, and Appendix 2 herein.

4. See *Lundberg v. County of Alameda,* 46 Cal. 2d 644 (1956), app. dism. sub nom. *Heisey v. Alameda County,* 352 U.S. 921 (1956); *General Finance Corp. v. Archetto,* 93 R.I. 392, (1961), app. dism. 369 U.S. 423 (1962); *Murray v. Comptroller of the Treasury,* 241 Md. 383 (1966), cert. den. 385 U.S. 816 (1966).

5. In *Camps Newfound/Owatonna v. Town of Harrison,* 117 S. Ct. 1590 (1997), the Court addressed religious property exemptions under the commerce clause of Article I. A camp operated for children of the Christian Science faith was denied a state property tax exemption because the camp served primarily nonresidents of Maine. The Court struck down the law, and its application to this camp, as an unconstitutional violation of the dormant Commerce Clause—an "unjustified discrimination" against interstate commerce.

6. In *Walz v. Tax Commission*, 397 U.S. 664, 675 (1970), the Court wrote: "The grant of a tax exemption is not sponsorship since the government does not transfer part of its revenue to churches but simply abstains from demanding that the church support the state." But in *Regan v. Taxation with Representation*, 461 U.S. 540, 544 (1983), the Court wrote: "A tax exemption has much the same effect as a cash grant to the organization of the amount it would have to pay on its income."

7. 397 U.S. at 674–680 (1970), addressing New York State Constitution (1938), Art. 16.1, and New York Real Property Tax Law, Sect. 420.1

8. See list of cases in note 2. See detailed analysis in Oliver S. Thomas, "The Power to Destroy: The Eroding Constitutional Arguments for Church Tax Exemptions and the Practical Effect on Churches," *Cumberland Law Review* 22 (1991): 605–636; John W. Whitehead, "Tax Exemption for Religious Organizations: A Historical and Constitutional Analysis," *Cumberland Law Review* 22 (1991): 521, 545ff.

9. See *Jimmy Swaggart Ministries v. Board of Equalization of California*, 493 U.S. 378, 392 (1990). The Court confirmed, narrowly, its earlier cases prohibiting flat taxes for licenses that are a prior restraint on the exercise of religion—"the imposing of a condition on the exercise of constitutionally-protected conduct." Ibid., 385–389.

10. *Texas Monthly, Inc. v. Bullock*, 489 U.S. 1, 14–15 (1989) (citations omitted).

11. See sources in "Tax Exemption," n. 8; and further in Carl H. Esbeck, *The Regulation of Religious Organizations as Recipients of Governmental Assistance* (Washington, DC, 1996); Bassett, *Religious Organizations*, passim. See also *Swaggart Ministries*, 493 U.S. at 395–396, where upholding the retroactive imposition of sale and use taxes on a religious ministry, the Court said: "The sorts of government entanglement that we have found to violate the Establishment Clause have been far more invasive than the level of contact created by the administration of neutral tax laws."

12. See P. Adler, *Historical Origin of Tax Exemption of Charitable Property* (Westchester, NY, 1922); L. Grashof, "Die Gesetzgebung der römischen Kaiser über die Güter und Immunitäten der Kirche und Clerus," *Archiv für katholische Kirchenrecht* (n.f.) 36 (1876): 3, 321; Eugen Mack, *Die kirchliche Steuerfreiheit in Deutschland seit der Dekretalengesetzgebung*, repr. ed. (Aalen, 1965); Dean M. Kelley, *Why Churches Should Not Pay Taxes* (New York, 1977).

13. I am using the term "common law" not as an antonym for "statute" but as a generic term to describe the English and the colonial and American customs and statutes enforced by various common law courts. In America, this generally included ecclesiastical laws; there were only very occasional instances of review or enforcement by commissaries or other English officials in the American colonies. I am using the term "equity" not as a synonym for fairness and justice but as a generic term to describe the English and endemic customs and statutes enforced by equity or chancery courts.

14. Two related distinctions that are currently commonplace were not so clear historically. First, the line between property taxation and income taxation was not always sharply drawn. Particularly in rural areas, the income of a person was often so inextricably tied to his or her property that taxation of one was tantamount to taxation of the other. Second, the distinction between taxation of the property itself

(in rem taxation) and of the person or entity occupying the property (in personam taxation) was not always sharply drawn. Tax liability sometimes ran with the land and sometimes followed the prior holder. The following discussion therefore treats certain aspects of personal income taxation as well. See generally, J. Hellerstein and W. Hellerstein, *State and Local Taxation*, 5th ed. (St. Paul, 1988), 115–123; Claude W. Stimson, "The Exemption of Property from Taxation in the United States," *Minnesota Law Review* 18 (1934): 411.

15. For a comprehensive treatment of post-Reformation ecclesiastical law in England and a convenient collection of relevant ecclesiastical statutes, see Richard Burn, *Ecclesiastical Law*, 6th ed., 4 vols. (London, 1797); John Godolphin, *Repertorium canonicum, or, An Abridgement of the Ecclesiastical Laws of This Realm, Consistent with the Temporal*, 3d ed. (London, 1687). A good summary of emerging American and early modern English ecclesiastical law is provided in Nicholas Trott, *The Laws of the British Plantations in American, Relating to the Church and the Clergy, Religion and Learning* (London, 1725); R. Tyler, *American Ecclesiastical Law* (Albany, NY, 1866). For detailed primary sources, see "Tax Exemption," nn. 28–44.

16. Carl F. Zollman, *American Church Law*, repr. ed. (New York, 1933), 239.

17. See generally, C. Crowther, *Religious Trusts: Their Development, Scope, and Meaning* (Oxford, 1954); J. Pomeroy, *A Treatise on Equity Jurisprudence as Administered in the United States of America*, 5th ed. (San Francisco, 1941); G. Duke, *Law of Charitable Uses* (1676), repr. ed., R. W. Bridgman, ed. (London, 1805); M. Chesterman, *Charities, Trusts, and Social Welfare* (London, 1979); G. Jones, *History of the Law and Charity, 1532–1827* (London, 1969); H. Miller, *The Legal Foundations of American Philanthropy* (Madison, WI, 1969). For detailed primary sources, see "Tax Exemption," nn. 45–56.

18. 43 Eliz. I. c. 4, repealed in 51 & 52 Vict. c. 42, 13.

19. *Jackson v. Phillips*, 14 Allen (Mass.) 539, 556 (1867).

20. J. Trumbull and C. Hoadly, eds., *The Public Records of the Colony of Connecticut, 1636–1776* (Hartford, CT, 1890), 3:158.

21. Massachusetts Constitution (1780), Part II, Chap. VI, Art. VI. (1780).

22. Constitution of Pennsylvania (1776), Art. 45.

23. *Orr v. Baker*, 4 Ind. 86, 88 (1853). See further sources in "Tax Exemption," nn. 62–67.

24. *Official Report of the Proceedings and Debates of the Kentucky Constitutional Convention* (1890), 2:2425 (statement of Representative Sachs).

25. See especially J. Quincy, *Tax Exemption: No Excuse for Spoliation* (n.p, n.d.), 8 (pamphlet in Widener Library, Harvard University).

26. W. Fleet, "Madison's 'Detached Memoranda' [c. 1817]," *William and Mary Quarterly*, 3d ser. 3 (1946): 554. Madison manifested similar fears as fourth president of the United States. In a message accompanying his veto of a bill to incorporate the Protestant Episcopal Church in Alexandria, Virginia, Madison wrote: "1. The bill exceeds the rightful authority to which governments are limited by the essential distinction between civil and religious function. . . . 4. Because the bill vests in the said incorporated church an authority to provide for the support of the poor and the education of poor children of the same, an authority which . . . would be a precedent for giving to religious societies as such a legal agency in carrying into ef-

fect a public and civil duty." Reprinted in *The Writings of James Madison*, ed. G. Hunt, 9 vols. (New York, 1900–1910), 8:132–133.

27. F. Israel, ed., *State of the Union Messages of the Presidents, 1790–1966* (New York, 1966), 2:1296. Likewise President Garfield commented: "The divorce between church and state ought to be absolute. It ought to be so absolute that no church property anywhere, in any state, or in the nation, should be exempt from equal taxation; if you exempt the property of any church organization, to that extent you impose a tax upon the whole community." Quoted by J. Morton, *Exempting the Churches: An Argument for the Abolition of This Unjust and Unconstitutional Practice* (New York, 1915), 63.

28. See sources in "Tax Exemption," nn. 72–76.

29. West Virginia Constitution (1861/1863), Art. VIII, sec. 1. See sources in "Tax Exemption," nn. 77–79.

30. Ibid., nn. 80–88. See further Paul G. Kauper, "The Constitutionality of Tax Exemptions for Religious Activities," in *The Wall Between Church and State*, ed. Dallin H. Oaks (Chicago, 1963), 95–116.

31. *First Unitarian Society v. Hartford*, 66 Conn. 368, 375 (1895).

32. *Trustees of the First Methodist Episcopal Church v. City of Atlanta*, 76 Ga. 181, 193 (1886), rev'd. on other grounds, *City of Atlanta v. First Presbyterian Church*, 86 Ga. 730, 13 S.E. 252 (1890).

33. *Commonwealth v. Y.M.C.A.*, 116 Ky. 711, 718 (1903).

34. H. Foote, *The Taxation of Churches* (n.p., c.1870), 27–30 (pamphlet in Library of Congress).

35. See, e.g., *Ward v. New Hampshire*, 56 N.H. 508 (1876); T. Brown, *Some Reasons for the Exemption of Church Property from Taxation* (Rochester, NY, 1881), 12.

36. Quoted by Foote, *The Taxation of Churches*, 19–20. See also A. Bledsoe, *Shall Georgia Tax Church Property?* (Atlanta, c.1897), 5: "It is upon this principle . . . that church property has heretofore been exempted from taxation, viz., that the exemption was worth more to the State than the taxation. Churches are not built for purposes of gain . . . the church is built for the benefit of the public."

37. Ibid.

38. *Y.M.C.A. of Omaha v. Douglas County*, 60 Neb. 642, 646 (1896).

39. For detailed citations, see "Tax Exemption," nn. 89–110. See also Chester J. Antieau, Philip M. Carroll, and Thomas Carroll Burke, *Religion Under the State Constitutions* (Washington, DC, 1965), 120–172; Arvo van Alstyne, "Tax Exemption of Church Property," *Ohio State Law Journal* 20 (1959): 461.

40. For a case citing virtually all the arguments for and against exemptions, see *Murray v. Comptroller of Treasury*, 241 Md. 383 (1966), cert. den. 385 U.S. 816 (1966). Recent courts have not required, however, that "that a church or predominantly religious organization must relieve a burden of government in order to qualify as a charitable institution [since] government is not in the business of religion." *Christian Reformed Church in North America v. City of Grand Rapids*, 104 Mich. App. 10, 19 (1981); see also *General Conference Church of God v. Carper*, 192 Colo. 178, 557 P. 2d 833 (1976).

41. Among federal cases, see *Haring v. Blumenthal*, 471 F. Supp. 1172 (D.D.C. 1979), cert. denied, 452 U.S. 939 (1981) (rejecting charge that tax exemptions for

religious property violate the disestablishment clause); *Diffenderfer v. Central Baptist Church*, 316 F. Supp. 1116 (S.D. Fla. 1970), vacated, 404 U.S. 412 (1972) (same). Among state cases, see *Bexar County Appraisal Review Board v. First Baptist Church*, 846 S.W. 2d (Tx. Ct. App. 1993) (holding that tax exemption of parking lots near a church does not violate state or federal disestablishment clauses); *Appeal of Emissaries of Divine Light*, 140 N.H. 552 (1995) (denying exemption to farm, residence, support buildings and vacant land, and rejecting argument that this discriminates contrary to the First Amendment). But see *In re Springmoor*, 125 N.C. App. 184 (N.C. Ct. App. 1997) (holding that a state statute exempting religiously affiliated homes for the "aged, sick, or infirm" but taxing nonreligiously affiliated such homes violates the disestablishment clause of the U.S. Constitution and the state constitution). See also rejection of free exercise arguments for tax exemption in *Living Faith, Inc. v. Commissioner of Internal Revenue*, 950 F.2d 365 (7th Cir., 1991); *In re Open Door Baptist Church*, 63 Pa. Commw. 292 (1981); *General Association Branch Davidian Seventh Day Adventist v. McLennan County Appraisal District*, 715 S.W.2d 391 (Tex. Ct. App. 1986); *Wisconsin Evangelical Lutheran Synod v. City of Prairie du Chien*, 125 Wis. 2d 541 (1985).

42. Bassett, *Religious Organizations*, xi.

43. See, e.g., Terry L. Slye, "Rendering unto Caesar: Defining 'Religion' for Purposes of Administering Religion-Based Tax Exemptions," *Harvard Journal of Law and Public Policy* 6 (1983): 219; Edward M. Gaffney, "Governmental Definition of Religion: The Rise and Fall of the IRS Regulations of an Integrated Auxiliary of a Church," *Valparaiso University Law Review* 25 (1991): 203.

44. 300 Or. 479, 486–487 (1986).

45. See, e.g., *Appeal of Emissaries of Light* (using common sense analysis to uphold granting a "monastery" an exemption for its chapel but denying it exemption for the surrounding residential building, administrative offices, agricultural and vacant land); *Waushara County v. Graf*, 166 Wisc. 2d 442, cert. den. 113 S.Ct. 269 (1992) (on finding that a group's documents were devoid of religious doctrine but dwelt at length on the tax benefits of contribution and membership, the Court denied tax exemption because "the organization was erected for the sole purpose of cloaking a secular enterprise with the legal protections of religion"). For earlier cases, see "Tax Exemption," n. 137.

46. 55 N.Y.2d 512, 518 (1982).

47. Ibid., 520, 526. See also the related "sincerity of belief" test in *Waushara County v. Graf*.

48. See, e.g., *Institute in Basic Life Principles v. Watersmeet Township*, 217 Mich. App. 7 (1996) (upholding tax exemption for conference retreat center because the party had demonstrated that "the entire property was used in a manner consistent with the [religious] purposes of the owning institution"); *Foundation for a "Course in Miracles," Inc. v. Theodore*, 568 N.Y.S. 2d. 666 (1991) (declaring that "[i]n the absence of any insincerity or deception," tax commissioner must defer to the assertions of the party respecting its religion and religious property use); see similar result in *Good Will Home and Mission v. Garwood Borough*, 281 N.J. Super. 596 (1995).

49. *Roberts v. Ravenwood Church of Wicca*, 249 Ga. 348, 350 (1982).

50. Ibid.

51. 343 N.Y.S.2d 159 (1973). See also, e.g., *Missouri Church of Scientology v. State Tax Commission*, 560 S.W.2d 837, 840 (Mo. 1977) (Scientologist property denied exemption because "while the [petitioner] has some of the trappings and accoutrements of an organized religion, it appears to be more an applied philosophy which has a certain religious connotation, but which falls short of being devoted to the worship of the Supreme Being").

52. Fifteen factors are considered in determining a party's eligibility for federal income tax exemption purposes; these are suggestive and probative, not exhaustive or subject to mechanical application. The features considered are whether the applicant has "(1) a distinctive legal culture; (2) a recognized creed and form of worship; (3) a definite and distinct ecclesiastical government; (4) a formal code of doctrine and discipline; (5) a distinct religious history; (6) a membership not associated with any other church or denomination; (7) a complete organization of ordained ministers ministering to their congregations; (8) ordained ministers selected after completing prescribed courses of study; (9) a literature of its own; (10) established places of worship; (11) regular congregations; (12) regular religious services; (13) Sunday schools for religious instruction of the young; . . . (14) schools for the preparation of its members" and (15) any other facts and circumstances that may bear upon the organization's claim to church status.

These criteria were laid out by then-Commissioner of the Internal Revenue Service, Jerome Kurtz, in "Difficult Definitional Problems in Tax Administration: Religion and Race," *Catholic Lawyer* 23 (1978): 301, 304. These criteria were applied in *American Guidance Foundation v. U.S.*, 490 F.Supp. 304 (D.D.C. 1980). They were confirmed, along with the 15th criterion listed above, in Internal Revenue Manual 7(10)69, *Exempt Organizations Examination Guidelines Handbook* 321.3 (1982) and applied in *Spiritual Outreach Society v. Commissioner*, 927 F.2d. 335 (8th Cir. 1991); *People v. Life Science Church*, 113 Misc. 2d 952 (N.Y., 1982), and numerous subsequent cases. For a recent federal case, using these factors to determine whether a petitioner meets the definition of "religion" for purposes of the Religious Freedom Restoration Act, see *United States v. Meyers*, 906 F.Supp. 1494 (D. Wy. 1995), aff'd 95 F.3d 1475 (10th Cir. 1996), cert. den. 118 S.Ct. 583 (1997).

53. 304 N.W.2d 308 (Minn. 1981).

54. 530 N.W.2d 200 (Minn. 1995).

55. The quote is from *Church of the New Faith v. Pay Roll Tax Commissioners*, 57 AJLR 785, 791 (1983), an Australian case, quoted and discussed in Peter Cumper, "Religious Liberty in the United Kingdom," in *Religious Human Rights in Global Perspective: Legal Perspectives*, ed. Johan D. van der Vyver and John Witte Jr. (The Hague/Boston/London, 1996), 205–242, at 222.

56. For this section, see detailed citations in "Tax Exemption," nn.113–131. Many of these citations and trends are repeated in Bassett, *Religious Organizations*, sec. 10.21.

57. See "Tax Exemption," nn. 113–114. See also *Robbins v. Florida Conference Association of Seventh Day Adventists*, 641 So.2d 893 (Fl. 1997); *Our Saviour Lutheran Church v. Department of Revenue*, 204 Ill. App. 3d (1990). But cf. *Corporation of the Episcopal Church in Utah v. Utah State Tax Commission*, 919 P.2d 556 (Utah, 1996).

58. See, e.g., *Simpson v. International Community of Christ, Church of the Second Advent for the Establishment of the Religion of Cosolargy*, 106 Nev. 458 (1990).

59. See, e.g., *Hausman v. First Baptist Church of Pine Hills*, 513 So.2d (Fl. 1987); *Antioch Missionary Baptist Church v. Rosewell*, 119 Ill. App. 3d 981 (1983); *Saints Memorial Baptist Church v. Delaware County Board of Assessment*, 37 Pa. D. & C. 3d 370 (1985) (denying exemptions where there are no apparent financial impediments to full use).

60. See earlier cases in "Tax Exemption," n. 116. Among recent cases on summer camps, see *Kahal Bnei Emunim v. Town of Fallsburg*, 78 N.Y.2d 194, (1991); *Episcopal Camp Foundation v. Town of Hope*, 666 A.2d 108 (Me. 1995); *In re Mount Shepherd Methodist Camp*, 120 N.C. App. 388 (1995). But cf. *City of Ventnor v. Interdenominational Foreign Mission Society of New Jersey*, 15 N.J. Tax 160 (1994) (denying tax exemption to a missionary furlough station); *Living Springs Retreat Center v. County of Putnam*, 626 N.Y.S. 2d 268 (1995) (denying tax exemption to a "self-described lifestyle/health maintenance facility," even though open to the public, because it is not sufficiently "religious"); *Fellowship International Mission, Inc. v. LeHigh County Board*, 690 A.2d 1271 (Pa. 1997) (denying exemption for residential center used to train foreign missionaries).

61. See "Tax Exemption," nn. 118–119. See more recently, *Pacem In Terris v. County of Isanti*, No. C6–92–472, 1992 WL 382672 (Minn. Tax. Dec. 16, 1992) (in adopting the "buffer zone" justification for upholding an exemption, the Minnesota Tax Court stated that "the law does not require that use of property by an exempt entity be essential—only that it be reasonably necessary").

62. *German Apostolic Christian Church v. Department of Revenue*, 279 Or. 637, 641–42 (1977). For recent cases, see *In re Mount Shepherd Methodist Camp* (land surrounding a church camp "reasonably necessary" for outdoor religious classes, self-discovery, environmental classes, and to buffer the camp from surrounding development); *Hapletah v. Assessor of Town of Fallsburg*, 79 N.Y.2d 244, 250–251 (1992) (finding residential housing for a Jewish educational facility "necessary and reasonably incidental to the primary purpose" of the facility); *Nebraska Annual Conference of the United Methodist Church v. Scotts Bluff County*, 243 Neb. 412 (1993) (upholding exemption for parsonages as "reasonably necessary" to religious use of church).

63. *Moshe Wilhelm/Chabad Lubavitch of Oregon v. Department of Revenue*, No. 3809, 1995 WL 604456, at *2 (Or. T.C. Oct. 12, 1995).

64. *Deal Yeshiva v. Deal Borough*, 16 N.J. 559 (1997) (summarizing several earlier New Jersey cases denying tax exemption for parsonages); *Corporation of the Presiding Bishop of Church of Jesus Christ of Latter-Day Saints; Immanuel Evangelical Lutheran Church of Springfield v. Department of Revenue*, 267 Ill. App. 2d 678 (1994); *Evangelical Lutheran Good Samaritan Society v. Buffalo County*, 243 Neb. 351 (1993); *Holy Spirit Retirement Home, Inc. v. Board of Review of the City of Sioux City, Iowa*, 543 N.W.2d 907 (1995); *Ada County Assessor v. Roman Catholic Diocese of Boise*, 123 Idaho 425 (1993).

65. See, e.g., *Victory Christian Church v. Department of Revenue*, 264 Ill. App. 3d 919 (1994) (denying exemption to parking lot and summarizing earlier cases holding the same). But cf. *Bexar County Appraisal Review Board v. First Baptist*

Church (church-owned parking lots rented for commercial parking during week-days but used primarily as parking for religious activities exempt from property taxes). See also *Agape Church, Inc. v. Pulsaki County,* 307 Ark. 420 (1991) (denying tax exemption to transmission tower and facility used to broadcast religious services).

66. See, e.g., *Phillips v. Mission Fellowship Bible Church,* 59 Ark. App. 242 (1997); *Midwest Presbytery of the Synod of the Reformed Presbyterian Church of North America v. Jefferson County Appraiser,* 17 Kan. App. 2d 676 (Ct. App. 1992); *Nebraska Annual Conference of the United Methodist Church v. Scotts Bluff County Bd. of Equalization,* 243 Neb. 412 (1993); *Central States Christian Endeavors Association v. Nelson,* 898 S.W.2d 547 (Mo. 1995). See earlier cases in "Tax Exemption," nn. 126–128. But see *Victory Christian Church v. Department of Revenue* (property merely leased to church and charity not tax exempt, citing earlier Illinois cases holding similarly).

67. See, e.g., *North Idaho Jurisdiction of Episcopal Churches, Inc. v. Kootenai County,* 94 Idaho 644 (1972); and more recently, *Holy Spirit Retirement Home v. Board of Review of Sioux City,* 543 N.W.2d 907 (Ct. App. Iowa, 1995) (court evaluates both religious and charitable uses of a church retirement home).

68. *St. Ann's; Hapletah v. Assessor of Fallsburg; Lutherans Outdoors in South Dakota v. State Bd. of Equalization,* 475 N.W.2d 140, 143 (S.D. 1991). Ohio had traditionally been the exception to this rule, denying exemption for properties devoted to mixed uses (see cases in "Tax Exemption," n. 128). More recent cases allow for mixed uses, without jeopardy to tax exempt status; see, e.g., *World Evangelistic Enterprise v. Trace,* 96 Ohio App. 3d 78 (1994) and precedents cited therein.

69. *Mars Area School District v. United Presbyterian Women's Association,* 693 A.2d 1002 (Pa. 1997); *Hapletah v. Assessor of Fallsburg; Nebraska Annual Conference of the United Methodist Church v. Scotts Bluff County Bd. of Equalization.*

70. See cases cited in note 69; see further, *Bexar County Appraisal Board; World Evangelistic Enterprise v. Tracy; Central States Christian Endeavors Association v. Nelson,* 898 S.W.2d 547 (Mo. 1995); *First Love Ministries v. Department of Revenue,* No. 3061, 1991 WL 262930 (Or. T.C. Dec. 4, 1991); *Resurrection Lutheran Church v. Department of Revenue,* 212 Ill. App. 3d (1991). But cf. *University Christian Church v. City of Austin,* 789 S.W.2d 361 (1990) (church parking lot leased six days a week no longer tax exempt); *Archdiocese of Philadelphia v. Borough of Darby,* 151 Pa. Cmwlth. 480 (1992) (church property rented out to a charitable organization no longer tax exempt).

71. See *Lutherans Outdoors; In the Matter of Foundation for "A Course in Miracles" Inc.; In re Mount Shepherd Methodist Camp; Appeal of Emissaries of Divine Light; International Community of Christ.*

72. This stands in considerable contrast to the trends before 1990 of restricting "religious uses" and expanding "charitable uses." See citations in "Tax Exemption," nn. 130–131.

73. *International Community of Christ.*

74. *Lutheran Outdoors.*

75. *Hapletah; Mission Fellowship.*

76. *World Evangelistic Enterprise.*

77. *Florida Conference Association of Seventh Day Adventists.*

78. *Bexar County.*

79. *Our Savior Lutheran Church.*

80. *Foundation for "A Course in Miracles" Inc.*

81. See, e.g. the classic argument of Leo Pfeffer, *Church, State, and Freedom,* rev. ed. (Boston, 1967), 210–219; and a more recent statement on classic evangelical grounds in Herbert W. Titus, "No Taxation or Subsidization: Two Indispensable Principles of Religious Freedom," *Cumberland Law Review* 22 (1992): 505–520.

82. See, e.g., the classic argument of Kelley, *Why Churches Should Not Pay Taxes.* See updates in James E. Wood Jr., *Taxation and the Free Exercise of Religion,* 1 ed. (Washington, DC, 1978).

83. A. Balk, *The Free List* (New York, 1971); M. Larson and C. Lowell, *Praise the Lord for Tax Exemption: How the Churches Grow Rich While the Cities and You Grow Poor* (Washington, DC, 1969).

84. See cases listed in note 41 above.

85. Compare *Texas Monthly, Inc. v. Bullock* (1989) (striking down a state sales tax exemption for religious periodicals alone).

86. *Walz,* 397 U.S. at 674.

87. See sources and analysis in A. James Reichley, *Religion in American Public Life* (Washington, DC, 1985); Daniel O. Conkle, "Toward a General Theory of the Establishment Clause," *Northwestern University Law Review* 82 (1988): 1115, 1170ff.

88. See Martin E. Marty, *Advancing the Conversation: Public Religion, Government, and Politics* (forthcoming), chap. 2.

89. *Jackman v. Rosenbaum,* 260 U.S. 22, 31 (1922).

90. *Valley Forge Christian College v. American United for Separation of Church and State,* 454 U.S. 464, 509–510 (1982) (Brennan, J. dissenting) (references omitted).

91. James Madison, "Memorial and Remonstrance Against Religious Assessments (1785)," para. 3, reprinted in *The Papers of James Madison,* ed. W. T. Hutchinson, William M. E. Rachal, and Robert A. Rutland (Chicago, 1962), 8:298.

92. *United States v. Lee,* 455 U.S. 252, 260 (1982).

93. See argument in "Tax Exemption," 395–415; and further in my "Whether Piety or Charity: Classification Issues in the Exemption of Churches and Charities from Property Taxation," in *Religion, the Independent Sector, and American Culture,* ed. Conrad Cherry and Rowland A. Sherrill (Atlanta, 1992), 137–170.

94. *Massachusetts State Tax Commission Report* (1897), quoted by D. Robertson, *Should Churches Be Taxed?* (Philadelphia, 1968), 191. See also J. Bennett, *Christians and the State* (New York, 1958), 234–235 (referring to tax exemptions as "the most remarkable of all forms of aid . . . to religious bodies"); W. Sperry, *Religion in America* (Cambridge, 1963), 60 ("The most important governmental recognition of religion made in America is the exemption of church property from taxation.").

95. Paraphrasing *McCulloch v. Maryland,* 17 U.S. (4 Wheat) 316, 431 (1819).

96. See Bassett, *Religious Organizations,* 10.20, n.1 (criticizing my earlier work for neglecting this point).

Chapter Ten

1. Oliver Wendell Holmes Jr., *The Common Law* (Boston, 1881), 1.

2. See, e.g., Douglas Laycock, "Summary and Synthesis: The Crisis in Religious Liberty," *George Washington Law Review* 60 (1992): 841; Steven D. Smith, "The Rise and Fall of Religious Freedom in Constitutional Discourse," *University of Pennsylvania Law Review* 140 (1991): 149; Stephen L. Carter, "The Resurrection of Religious Freedom?" *Harvard Law Review* 107 (1993): 118.

3. See esp. the integrative efforts of Thomas C. Berg, Christopher L. Eisgruber and Lawrence G. Sager, Carl H. Esbeck, Douglas Laycock, Ira C. Lupu, Michael W. McConnell, and John T. Noonan in works listed in the bibliography herein. See also, among other recent writings, Jesse H. Choper, *Securing Religious Liberty: Principles of Judicial Interpretation of the Religion Clauses* (Chicago, 1995); Kent Greenawalt, *Religious Convictions and Political Choice* (New York/Oxford, 1988); id, *Private Consciences and Public Reasons* (New York/Oxford, 1985); and Michael J. Perry, *Religion and Politics* (Oxford, 1997). A theological critique of some of these theories is set out in Franklin I. Gamwell, *The Meaning of Religious Freedom: Modern Politics and the Democratic Resolution* (Syracuse, 1995). Ample additional bibliographies are included in F. C. DeCoste and Lillian MacPhearson, *Law, Religion, Theology: A Selective Annotated Bibliography* (West Cornwall, CT, 1997); Robert T. Miller and Ronald B. Flowers, *Toward Benevolent Neutrality: Church, State, and the United States Supreme Court,* 5th ed. (Waco, TX, 1996), 843–864.

4. See, e.g., William W. Bassett, *Religious Organizations and the Law* (St. Paul, 1998), chaps. 4–6; David L. Gregory, "The Role of Religion in the Secular Workplace," *Notre Dame Journal of Law, Ethics, and Public Policy* 4 (1990): 749–764; Douglas Laycock, "Toward a General Theory of the Religion Clauses: The Case of Church Labor Relations and the Right to Church Autonomy," *Columbia Law Review* 81 (1981): 1373–1417.

5. See, e.g., Paul G. Kauper and Stephen B. Ellis, "Religious Corporations and the Law," *Michigan Law Review* 71 (1973): 1499; Angela C. Carmella, "Houses of Worship and Religious Liberty: Constitutional Limits to Landmark Preservation and Architectural Review," *Villanova Law Review* 36 (1981): 401; id., "Liberty and Equality: Paradigms for the Protection of Religious Property Use," *Journal of Church and State* 37 (1995): 573; Laurie Reynolds, "Zoning the Church: The Police Power Versus the First Amendment," *Boston University Law Review* 64 (1985): 767.

6. *Kiryas Joel Village School District v. Grumet,* 114 S.Ct. 2481, 2498–2499 (O'Connor, J., concurring). See also *Rosenberger v. University of Virginia,* 115 S.Ct. 2510, 2525–2526 (O'Connor, J., concurring) ("Reliance on categorical platitudes is unavailing. . . . When bedrock principles collide, they test the limits of categorical obstinacy and expose the flaws and dangers of a Grand Unified Theory that may turn out to be neither grand nor unified").

7. For a provocative prototype, see Carl H. Esbeck, "A Restatement of the Supreme Court's Law of Religious Freedom: Coherence, Conflict, or Chaos?" *Notre Dame Law Journal* 70 (1995): 581. For an earlier effort, see *The Williamsburg Charter: A National Celebration of the First Amendment Religious Liberty Clauses*

(1988), reprinted with analysis in *Articles of Faith, Articles of Peace: The Religious Liberty Clauses and the American Public Philosophy,* ed. James D. Hunter and Os Guinness (Washington, DC, 1990), and further discussed in "Symposium on the Williamsburg Charter," *Journal of Law and Religion* 8 (1990): 1–396.

8. *Kiryas Joel,* 114 S.Ct. at 4683 (Scalia, J., dissenting) (emphasis added).

9. See Harold J. Berman, "World Law," *Fordham International Law Journal* 18 (1995): 1617.

10. See, e.g., John H. Mansfield, "The Religion Clauses of the First Amendment and Foreign Relations," *DePaul Law Review* 36 (1986): 1–40. See also the recent International Religious Freedom Act of 1998, 112 Stat. 2787, 22 U.S.C.A. 6401. The act affirms the importance of religious freedom, as reflected in American history and law, and in various international human rights instruments. The act further decries the fresh rise of religious repression and persecution around the world (see sec. 2[a]). The stated policy of the act, in sec. 2(b), reads thus:

(1) To condemn violations of religious freedom, and to promote, and to assist other governments in the promotion of, the fundamental right to freedom of religion.

(2) To seek to channel United States security and development assistance to governments other than those found to be engaged in gross violations of the right to freedom of religion. . . .

(3) To be vigorous and flexible, reflecting both the unwavering commitment of the United States to religious freedom and the desire of the United States for the most effective and principled response, in light of the range of violations of religious freedom by a variety of persecuting regimes, and the status of relations of the United States with different nations.

(4) To work with foreign governments that affirm and protect religious freedom, in order to develop multilateral documents and initiatives to combat violations of religious freedom and promote the right to religious freedom abroad.

(5) Standing for liberty and standing with the persecuted, to use and implement appropriate tools in the United States foreign policy apparatus, including diplomatic, political, commercial, charitable, educational, and cultural channels, to promote respect for religious freedom by all governments and peoples.

11. See generally Clovis C. Morrisson Jr., "Margin of Appreciation in European Human Rights Law," *Revue des droits de l'homme* 6 (1973): 263–286.

12. See sources and discussion in Johan D. van der Vyver, "Universality and Relativism of Human Rights: American Relativism," *Buffalo Human Rights Law Review* 4 (1998): 43–78; Abdullahi Ahmed An-Na'im, Ann Elizabeth Mayer, Sumner B. Twiss, and William Wipfler, "Universality vs. Relativism in Human Rights," in *Religion and Human Rights,* ed. John Kelsay and Sumner B. Twiss (New York, 1994), 31–60. For an interesting prototype that would set certain minimum national standards of religious liberty, while giving an ample margin of appreciation to state and local experimentation, see Stuart D. Poppel, "Federalism, Fundamental Fairness, and the Religion Clauses," *Cumberland Law Review* 25 (1995): 247–308.

13. See "Roosevelt's Eighth Annual Message to Congress (January 6, 1941)," reprinted in *State of the Union Messages of the Presidents, 1790–1966,* ed. F. Israel

(New York, 1966), 3:1, and discussion of its international influence in Louis B. Sohn, *The Human Rights Movement: From Roosevelt's Four Freedoms to the Interdependence of Peace, Development, and Human Rights* (New York, 1982).

14. See generally, Louis Henkin, "Rights, American and Human," *Columbia Law Review* 79 (1979): 405; and International Religious Freedom Act of 1998, quoted in note 10 above. For a good recent example of this, see American official and unofficial judgments of the restrictions of religious liberty in Russia, as recounted in "Symposium—Soul Wars: The Problem of Proselytism in Russia," *Emory International Law Review* 12 (1998): 1–738.

15. International Covenant on Civil and Political Rights, G.A. Res. 2200A, U.N. GAOR, 21st Sess., Supp. No. 16, U.N. Doc. A/6316 (1968), 999 U.N.T.S. 171 (1976) (hereafter cited as ICCPR), reprinted in *Religion and Human Rights: Basic Documents*, ed. Tad Stahnke and J. Paul Martin (New York, 1998), 69–82.

16. Declaration on the Elimination of All Forms of Intolerance and of Discrimination Based on Religion or Belief, adopted November 25, 1981, G.A. Res. 55, 36 U.N. GAOR Supp. (No. 51), U.N. Doc. A/RES/36/55 (1982) (hereafter cited as 1981 Declaration), reprinted in Stahnke and Martin, eds., *Religion and Human Rights*, 102–104.

17. Concluding Document of the Vienna Meeting 1986 of Representatives of the Participating States of the Conference on Security and Co-operation in Europe, Held on the Basis of the Provisions of the Final Act Relating to the Follow-Up to the Conference, January 17, 1989, 28 I.L.M. 527 (hereafter cited as Vienna Concluding Document).

18. For analysis, see Kevin Boyle and Juliet Sheen, *Freedom of Religion and Belief: A World Report* (London/New York, 1997); Malcolm D. Evans, *Religious Liberty and International Law in Europe* (Cambridge, 1997); Bahiyyih G. Tahzib, *Freedom of Religion or Belief: Ensuring Effective International Legal Protection* (The Hague/Boston/London, 1996); John Witte Jr. and Johan D. van der Vyver, eds., *Religious Human Rights in Global Perspective*, vol. 1, *Religious Perspectives*; vol. 2, *Legal Perspectives* (The Hague/Boston/London, 1996) (hereafter cited as *Religious Human Rights*, vol. 1, and *Religious Human Rights*, vol. 2).

19. See Natan Lerner, "Religious Human Rights Under the United Nations," in *Religious Human Rights*, vol. 2, 79–134, at 91–93; Karl Josef Partsch, "Freedom of Conscience and Expression and Political Freedoms," in *The International Bill of Rights: The Covenant on Civil and Political Rights*, ed. Louis Henkin (New York, 1981), 209–245; Alexandre C. Kiss, "Permissible Limitations on Rights," in Henkin, ed., *The International Bill of Rights*, 290–310.

20. See, e.g., the view of the Human Rights Committee in Case 172/1984, *Broeks v. The Netherlands*, Annual Report 1987, at 139.

21. U.N. Doc. CCPR/C/21/Rev.1/Add.4 (1993), reprinted in Stahnke and Martin, eds., *Religion and Human Rights: Basic Documents*, 92–95.

22. The following paragraphs are adapted from W. Cole Durham Jr., Pieter van Dijk, Lauren B. Homer, and John Witte Jr., "The Future of Religious Liberty in Russia: Report of the De Burght Conference on Pending Russian Legislation Restricting Religious Liberty," *Emory International Law Review* 8 (1994): 1–66, at 17–20.

23. See "Report Submitted by Mr. Abdelfattah Amor . . . Addendum: Visit to the United States," E/CN.4/1999/58/Add.1. While Professor Amor's Report is generally very commendatory of American protections of religious freedom for multiple faiths, it includes some useful criticisms and recommendations. At ibid., nos. 70–88, the Special Rapporteur criticizes the reductionism of the "new" free exercise jurisprudence of *Smith* and its progeny; the "absence of a consistent and detailed framework within which the two constitutional clauses on 'non-establishment' and free exercise of religion could be interpreted and applied" (ibid., no. 72); the unduly fragmentary protections of religious freedom in the workplace; and the need for better protection of the religious rights of children, prisoners, and religious minorities (most notably Native Americans). See also Abdelfattah Amor, "The Mandate of the UN Special Rapporteur," *Emory International Law Review* 12 (1998): 945–950. See further Lerner, "Religious Human Rights," 114–127; Evans, *Religious Liberty,* 245–261; Michael Roan, "The Role of Secular Non-Governmental Organizations in the Cultivation and Understanding of Religious Human Rights," in *Religious Human Rights,* vol. 2, 135–159; Donna J. Sullivan, "Advancing the Freedom of Religion or Belief Through the UN Declaration on the Elimination of Religious Intolerance and Discrimination," *American Journal of International Law* 82 (1988): 487.

24. See W. Cole Durham Jr., "Perspectives on Religious Liberty: A Comparative Framework," in *Religious Human Rights,* vol. 2, 1–44; T. Jeremy Gunn, "Adjudicating Rights of Conscience Under the European Convention on Human Rights," in *Religious Human Rights,* vol. 2, 305–330; Evans, *Religious Liberty,* 262ff.

25. See these texts in Stahnke and Martin, eds., *Religion and Human Rights,* 185–189, 221–244. On the religion provisions in the Islamic instruments, see esp. Donna Arzt, "The Treatment of Religious Dissidents Under Classical and Contemporary Islamic Law," in *Religious Human Rights,* vol. 1, 387–454, at 394ff.

26. See sources and analysis in David P. Stewart, "United States Ratification of the Covenant on Civil and Political Rights: The Significance of the Reservations, Understandings, and Declarations," *DePaul Law Review* 42 (1993): 1183, 1202ff; Jeri Nazary Sute, "Reviving RFRA: Congressional Use of Treaty-Implementing Powers to Protect Religious Exercise Rights," *Emory International Law Review* 12 (1999): 1535.

27. See generally Louis Henkin, "U.S. Ratification of Human Rights Conventions: The Ghost of Senator Bricker," *American Journal of International Law* 89 (1995): 341–350; Natalie H. Kaufman and David Whiteman, "Opposition to Human Rights Treaties in the United States Senate: The Legacy of the Bricker Amendment," *Human Rights Quarterly* 10 (1988): 309–337; M. Christian Green, "The 'Matrioshka' Strategy: U.S. Evasion of the Spirit of International Covenant on Civil and Political Rights," *South African Journal of Human Rights* 10 (1994): 357.

28. See Gerald Neumann, "The Global Dimension of RFRA," *Constitutional Commentary* 14 (1997): 33–54.

29. This "affirmative action" for religion by states is especially advocated by Eastern European and African writers. See sources and discussion in Harold J. Berman, "Religious Rights in Russia at a Time of Tumultuous Transition: A Historical Theory," in *Religious Human Rights,* vol. 2, 285–304; Tamas Földesi, "The Main Problems of Religious Freedom in Eastern Europe," in *Religious Human*

Rights, vol. 2, 243–262; Makau wa Mutua, "Limitations on Religious Rights: Problematizing Religious Freedom in the African Context," in *Religious Human Rights*, vol. 2, 417–440.

30. See Berman, "Religious Rights in Russia"; Földesi, "The Main Problems of Religious Freedom in Eastern Europe"; Mutua, "Limitations on Religious Rights." See also, Martin Heckel, "The Impact of Religious Rules on Public Life in Germany," in *Religious Human Rights*, vol. 2, 191–204; Irwin Cotler, "Jewish NGOs and Religious Human Rights: A Case Study," in *Human Rights in Judaism: Cultural, Religious, and Political Perspectives*, ed. Michael J. Broyde and John Witte Jr. (Northvale, NJ/Jerusalem, 1998), 165–271.

31. See, e.g., Paul E. Sigmund, "Religious Human Rights in Latin America," in *Religious Human Rights*, vol. 2, 467–481. See further Paul E. Sigmund, ed., *Religious Freedom and Evangelization in Latin America: The Challenge of Religious Pluralism* (Maryknoll, NY, 1999).

32. See, e.g., Said Arjomand, "Religious Human Rights and the Principle of Legal Pluralism in the Middle East," in *Religious Human Rights*, vol. 2, 331–347.

33. See Cotler, "Jewish NGOs and Religious Human Rights"; Asher Maoz, "Religious Human Rights in the State of Israel," in *Religious Human Rights*, vol. 2, at 349–389.

34. For a summary of the latter, see, e.g., Wolfgang Huber, *Gerechtigkeit und Recht: Grundlinien christlicher Rechtsethik* (Gütersloh, 1996). See also Harold J. Berman, *Faith and Order: The Reconciliation of Law and Religion* (Atlanta, 1996), 300–303, where, in illustrating the importance of historical jurisprudence today, Berman describes the abolition of capital punishment in Germany as a direct consequence of the Nazi experience.

35. See Natan Lerner, *Group Rights and Discrimination in International Law* (Dordrecht, 1991).

36. Rudolf Otto, *The Idea of the Holy: An Inquiry into the Non-Rational Factor of the Idea of the Divine and Its Relation to the Rational*, 2d ed. (New York, 1950).

37. See Leonard Swidler, ed., *Religious Liberty and Human Rights in Nations and Religions* (Philadelphia, 1986), vii. The Special Rapporteur on religious liberty, Elizabeth Odio-Benito, has written similarly that religion is "an explanation of the meaning of life and how to live accordingly. Every religion has at least a creed, a code of action, and a cult." U.N. Doc. E/CN.4/Sub.2/1987/26, at 4.

38. For other efforts, see, e.g., Kent Greenawalt, "Religion as a Concept in Constitutional Law," *California Law Review* 72 (1984): 753; and summary of more recent American approaches in Thomas C. Berg, *Religion and the State in a Nutshell* (St. Paul, 1998), 262–276. On recent international approaches, see Haim H. Cohn, "Religious Human Rights," *Diné Israel: An Annual of Jewish Law Past and Present* 19 (1998): 101–126, at 102–109 (reviewing *Religious Human Rights*, vols. 1 and 2).

Concluding Reflections

1. *The Works of John Adams*, ed. J. F. Adams, 10 vols. (Boston, 1850–1856), 4:290, 292–293, 298. See also James Madison in *Federalist Paper, No. 37*, writing

of the formation of the Constitution: "It is impossible for the man of pious reflection not to perceive in it a finger of the Almighty hand."

2. Adams, *Works,* 9:629–632, at 630.

3. Douglas Laycock, "Religious Liberty as Liberty," *Journal of Contemporary Legal Issues* 7 (1996): 313–356, at 314.

4. *Cantwell v. Connecticut,* 310 U.S. at 303–304, 310 (1940).

5. *Everson v. Board of Education,* 330 U.S. 1, 16 (1947).

6. *Marsh v. Chambers,* 463 U.S. 783 (1983), quoting, in part, *Zorach v. Clauson,* 343 U.S. 306 (1952).

7. *Jackman v. Rosenbaum,* 260 U.S. 22, 31 (1922).

8. *Lynch v. Donnelly,* 465 U.S. 668, 680–686 (1984).

9. Ibid., 693 (O'Connor, J. concurring).

10. Ibid., 687.

11. The phrase is from John T. Noonan Jr., *The Lustre of Our Country: The American Experience of Religious Freedom* (Berkeley/Los Angeles/London, 1998), 230–231. For critical analysis of these cases, see Winnifred Fallers Sullivan, *Paying the Words Extra: Religious Discourse in the Supreme Court of the United States* (Cambridge, 1994); Stephen B. Epstein, "Rethinking the Constitutionality of Ceremonial Deism," *Columbia Law Review* 96 (1996): 2083.

12. Harold J. Berman, "Religious Freedom and the Challenge of the Modern State," in id., *Faith and Order: The Reconciliation of Law and Religion* (Atlanta, 1993), 231.

13. See sources and analysis in Robert Booth Fowler, Allen D. Hertzke, and Laura R. Olson, *Religion and Politics in America: Faith, Culture, and Strategic Choices,* 2d ed. (Boulder/Oxford, 1999).

BIBLIOGRAPHY

Adams, Amos, *Religious Liberty an Invaluable Blessing* (Boston, 1768).

Adams, Arlin M., and Charles J. Emmerich, *A Nation Dedicated to Religious Liberty* (Philadelphia, 1990).

Adams, Arlin M., and Sarah B. Gordon, "The Doctrine of Accommodation in the Jurisprudence of the Religion Clauses," *DePaul Law Review* 37 (1988): 317.

Adams, John, *The Works of John Adams*, ed. C. F. Adams, 10 vols. (Boston, 1850–1856).

Adams, Zabdiel, "An Election Sermon (1782)," in *American Political Writing During the Founding Era, 1760–1805*, 2 vols., ed. Charles S. Hynemann and Donald S. Lutz (Indianapolis, 1983), 1:539.

Adler, P., *Historical Origin of Tax Exemption of Charitable Property* (Westchester, NY, 1922).

Alekinoff, T. Alexander, "Constitutional Law in the Age of Balancing," *Yale Law Journal* 96 (1987): 943.

Alley, Robert S., *The Supreme Court on Church and State* (New York, 1988).

Amor, Abdelfattah, "The Mandate of the UN Special Rapporteur," *Emory International Law Review* 12 (1998): 945.

Andrews, John, *A Complete Dictionary of the English Language*, 4th ed. (Philadelphia, 1789).

An-Na'im, Abdullahi Ahmed, Ann Elizabeth Mayer, Sumner B. Twiss, and William Wipfler, "Universality vs. Relativism in Human Rights," in *Religion and Human Rights*, ed. John Kelsay and Sumner B. Twiss (New York, 1994), 31.

Antieau, Chester J., Arthur T. Downey, and Edward C. Roberts, *Freedom from Federal Establishment: Formation and Early History of the First Amendment Religion Clauses* (Milwaukee, 1964).

Antieau, Chester J., Philip M. Carroll, and Thomas Carroll Burke, *Religion Under the State Constitutions* (Washington, DC, 1965).

Ariens, Michael S., and Robert A. Destro, *Religious Liberty in a Pluralistic Society* (Durham, NC, 1996).

Arjomand, Said, "Religious Human Rights and the Principle of Legal Pluralism in the Middle East," in *Religious Human Rights in Global Perspective: Legal Perspectives*, ed. Johan D. van der Vyver and John Witte Jr. (The Hague/Boston/London, 1996), 331.

Arrington, Leonard J., and Davis Bitton, *The Mormon Experience: A History of the Latter-Day Saints* (New York, 1979).

Arzt, Donna, "The Treatment of Religious Dissidents Under Classical and Contemporary Islamic Law," in *Religious Human Rights in Global Perspective: Religious*

Perspectives, ed. John Witte Jr. and Johan D. van der Vyver (The Hague/Boston/-London, 1996), 387.

Ash, John, *A New and Complete Dictionary of the English Language* (London, 1775).

Backus, Isaac, *Appeal to the Public for Religious Liberty Against the Oppressions of the Present Day* (Boston, 1773).

_____, *The Infinite Importance of the Obedience of Faith, and of a Separation from the World, Opened and Demonstrated* (Boston, 1791).

_____, *Isaac Backus on Church, State, and Calvinism: Pamphlets, 1754–1789*, ed. William G. McLoughlin (Cambridge, 1968).

_____, *Policy as well as Honesty Forbids the Use of Secular Force in Religious Affairs* (Boston, 1779).

_____, *Truth Is Great and Will Prevail* (Boston, 1781).

Bacon, Francis, *The New Organon [1620] and Related Writings*, ed. Fulton H. Anderson (Indianapolis, 1960).

Baer, Richard A., "The Supreme Court's Discriminatory Use of the Term, 'Sectarian,'" *Journal of Law and Politics* 6 (1990): 449.

Balk, A., *The Free List* (New York, 1971).

Balzell, George W., *Benefit of Clergy in America and Related Matters* (Winston-Salem, NC, 1955).

Banner, Stuart, "When Christianity Was Part of the Common Law," *Law and History Review* 16 (1998): 27.

Barron, Jerome A., "Sunday in North America," *Harvard Law Review* 79 (1965): 42.

Bassett, William W., *Religious Organizations and the Law*, rev. ed., 2 vols. (St. Paul, 1998).

Beeson, Ann E., "Dances with Justice: Peyotism in the Courts," *Emory Law Journal* 41 (1992): 1121.

Belzer, Nathan, "Intrachurch Disputes over Property," *St. Thomas Law Review* 11 (1998): 109.

Bennett, J., *Christians and the State* (New York, 1958).

Berg, Thomas C., "The Constitutional Future of Religious Freedom Legislation," *University of Arkansas Law Journal* 20 (1998): 715.

_____, *Religion and the State in a Nutshell* (St. Paul, 1998).

_____, "Religion Clause Anti-Theories," *Notre Dame Law Review* 72 (1997): 693.

_____, "Slouching Towards Secularism: A Comment on *Kiryas Joel School District v. Grumet*," *Emory Law Journal* 44 (1995): 433.

_____, "What Hath Congress Wrought? An Interpretive Guide to the Religious Freedom Restoration Act," *Villanova Law Review* 39 (1994): 1.

Benson, G., et al., *The American Property Tax: Its History, Administration and Economic Impact* (Claremont, CA, 1965).

Berman, Harold J., *Faith and Order: The Reconciliation of Law and Religion* (Atlanta, 1993).

_____, *Law and Revolution: The Formation of the Western Legal Tradition* (Cambridge, 1983).

_____, "Religious Rights in Russia at a Time of Tumultuous Transition: A Historical Theory," in *Religious Human Rights in Global Perspective: Legal Perspec-

tives, ed. Johan D. van der Vyver and John Witte Jr. (The Hague/Boston/London, 1996), 285.

_____, "World Law," *Fordham International Law Journal* 18 (1995): 1617.

Berman, Harold J., and John Witte Jr., "Church and State," in *Encyclopedia of Religion*, ed. Mircea Eliade (New York, 1987), 3:489–505.

_____, "The Transformation of Western Legal Philosophy in Lutheran Germany," *Southern California Law Review* 62 (1989): 1573.

Bledsoe, A., *Shall Georgia Tax Church Property?* (Atlanta, c.1897).

Boller, Paul F., Jr., *George Washington and Religion* (Dallas, 1963).

Bolles, John R., *A Brief Account of Persecutions, in Boston and Connecticut Governments* (Boston, 1758).

Bonomi, Patricia, *Under the Cope of Heaven* (New York, 1986).

Book of Common Prayer [1559], ed. John E. Booty (Charlottesville, VA, 1976).

Book of the General Laws and Liberties of Concerning the Inhabitants of Massachusetts (1648), ed. Max Farrand (Cambridge, MA, 1929).

Book of the States (Chicago, 1972).

Borden, Morton, "Federalists, AntiFederalists, and Religious Freedom," *Journal of Church and State* 21 (1979): 469.

Bowen, Catherine Drinker, *Miracle at Philadelphia: The Story of the Constitutional Convention, May to September, 1787* (Boston/Toronto, 1966).

Boyle, Kevin and Juliet Sheen, *Freedom of Religion and Belief: A World Report* (London/New York, 1997).

Bradford, M. E., *Founding Fathers: Brief Lives of the Framers of the United States Constitution*, 2d rev. ed. (Lawrence, KS, 1994).

Bradley, Gerard V., *Church-State Relationships in America* (New York/London/Westport, 1987).

_____, "The No Religious Test Clause and the Constitution of Religious Liberty: A Machine That Has Gone of Itself," *Case Western Reserve Law Review* 37 (1987): 674.

Breen, Timothy, *The Character of the Good Ruler* (New Haven, 1970).

Browne, Cynthia E., *State Constitutional Conventions* (Westport, CT/London, 1973).

Broyde, Michael J., and John Witte Jr., eds., *Human Rights in Judaism: Cultural, Religious, and Political Perspectives* (Northvale, NJ/Jerusalem, 1998).

Buckley, Thomas E., "After Disestablishment: Thomas Jefferson's Wall of Separation in Antebellum Virginia," *Journal of Southern History* 61 (1995): 445.

_____, *Church and State in Revolutionary Virginia, 1776–1787* (Charlottesville, VA, 1977).

_____, "The Political Theology of Thomas Jefferson," in *The Virginia Statute for Religious Freedom: Its Evolution and Consequences in American History*, ed. Merrill D. Peterson and Robert C. Vaughan (Cambridge, 1988), 75.

Burgh, James, *Crito, or Essays on Various Subjects*, 2 vols. (London, 1767).

Burn, Richard, *Ecclesiastical Law*, 6th ed., 4 vols. (London, 1797).

Butler, Jon, *Awash in a Sea of Faith: Christianizing the American People* (Cambridge, MA, 1990).

Calvin, John, *Institutes of the Christian Religion* (1559), trans. F. L. Battles, ed. John T. McNeill (Philadelphia, 1960).

Cappon, Lester J., ed., *The Adams-Jefferson Letters* (Chapel Hill, NC, 1959).

Carmella, Angela C., "Houses of Worship and Religious Liberty: Constitutional Limits and to Landmark Preservation and Architectural Review," *Villanova Law Review* 36 (1981): 401.

_____, "Liberty and Equality: Paradigms for the Protection of Religious Property Use," *Journal of Church and State* 37 (1995): 573.

_____, "Mary Ann Glendon on Religious Liberty: The Social Nature of the Person and the Public Nature of Religion," *Notre Dame Law Review* 73 (1998): 1191.

_____, "State Constitutional Protection of Religious Exercise: An Emerging Post-*Smith* Jurisprudence," *Brigham Young University Law Review* (1993): 275.

Carter, Stephen L., *The Culture of Disbelief: How American Law and Politics Trivializes Religious Devotion* (New York, 1993).

———, "The Resurrection of Religious Freedom?" *Harvard Law Review* 107 (1993): 118.

Casto, William, "Oliver Ellsworth's Calvinism: A Biographical Essay on Religion and Political Psychology in the Early Republic," *Journal of Church and State* 36 (1994): 507.

Cherry, Conrad, and Rowland A. Sherrill, eds., *Religion, the Independent Sector, and American Culture* (Atlanta, 1992).

Chesterman, M., *Charities, Trusts, and Social Welfare* (London, 1979).

Choper, Jesse H., *Securing Religious Liberty: Principles of Judicial Interpretation of the Religion Clauses* (Chicago, 1995).

Cobb, Sanford H., *The Rise of Religious Liberty in America: A History* (New York, 1902).

Cochrane, Charles N., *Christianity and Classical Culture* (London, 1940).

Cohn, Haim H., "Religious Human Rights," *Diné Israel: An Annual of Jewish Law Past and Present* 19 (1998): 101.

Commager, Henry Steele, ed., *Documents of American History*, 5th ed. (New York, 1949).

Conkle, Daniel O., "Congressional Alternatives in the Wake of *City of Boerne v. Flores:* The (Limited) Role of Congress in Protecting Religious Freedom from State and Local Infringement," *University of Arkansas Law Journal* 20 (1998): 633.

_____, "Toward a General Theory of the Establishment Clause," *Northwestern University Law Review* 82 (1988): 1115.

Constitutions of the United States, National and State (Dobbs Ferry, NY, 1962–).

Coquillette, Daniel, *Francis Bacon* (Stanford, 1992).

Cord, Robert L., *Separation of Church and State: Historical Fact and Current Fiction*, rev. ed. (Grand Rapids, MI, 1988).

Cornelison, Isaac A., *The Relation of Religion to Civil Government in the United States of America: A State Without a Church, but Not Without a Religion* (New York, 1895).

Cotler, Irwin, "Jewish NGOs and Religious Human Rights: A Case Study," in *Human Rights in Judaism: Cultural, Religious, and Political Perspectives*, ed. Michael J. Broyde and John Witte Jr. (Northvale, NJ/Jerusalem, 1998), 165.

Cover, Robert M., "The Supreme Court 1982 Term—Foreword: Nomos and Narrative," *Harvard Law Review* 97 (1983): 4.

Coyle, Wallace, *Roger Williams: A Reference Guide* (Boston, 1977).

Crawford, Michael J., *Seasons of Grace* (New York, 1991).

Crowther, C., *Religious Trusts: Their Development, Scope, and Meaning* (Oxford, 1954).

Cumings, Henry, *A Sermon Preached at Billerica* (Boston, 1797).

Cumper, Peter, "Religious Liberty in the United Kingdom," in *Religious Human Rights in Global Perspective: Legal Perspectives*, ed. Johan D. van der Vyver and John Witte Jr. (The Hague/Boston/London, 1996), 205.

Curry, Thomas J., *The First Freedoms: Church and State in America to the Passage of the First Amendment* (New York, 1986).

Curtis, Michael Kent, "Conceived in Liberty: The Fourteenth Amendment and the Bill of Rights," *North Carolina Law Review* 65 (1987): 889.

Davis, Derek H., "Equal Treatment: A Christian Separationist Perspective," in *Equal Treatment of Religion in a Pluralistic Society*, ed. Stephen V. Monsma and J. Christopher Soper (Grand Rapids, MI, 1998), 136.

Debates and Proceedings in the Congress of the United States, March 3, 1789–May 27, 1824, 42 vols. (Washington, DC: Gales and Seaton, 1834–1856).

DeCoste, F. C., and Lillian MacPhearson, *Law, Religion, Theology: A Selective Annotated Bibliography* (West Cornwall, CT, 1997).

DePauw, Linda, et al., eds., *Documentary History of the First Federal Congress* (Baltimore, 1972–).

Destro, Robert A., "'By What Right?': The Sources and Limits of Federal Court and Congressional Jurisdiction over Matters 'Touching Religion,'" *Indiana Law Review* 29 (1995): 1.

Donovan, Frank, ed., *The John Adams Papers* (New York, 1965).

Dreisbach, Daniel L., "The Constitution's Forgotten Religion Clause: Reflections on the Article VI Religious Test Ban," *Journal of Church and State* 38 (1996): 263.

_____, "In Search of a Christian Commonwealth: An Examination of Selected Nineteenth-Century Commentaries on References to God and the Christian Religion in the United States Constitution," *Baylor Law Review* 48 (1996): 927.

_____, "A New Perspective on Jefferson's Views on Church-State Relations: The Virginia Statute for Establishing Religious Freedom in Its Legislative Context," *American Journal of Legal History* 35 (1991): 172.

_____, *Religion and Politics in the Early Republic: Jasper Adams and the Church-State Debate* (Lexington, KY, 1996).

_____, "'Sowing Useful Truths and Principles': The Danbury Baptists, Thomas Jefferson, and the 'Wall of Separation,'" *Journal of Church and State* 39 (1997): 455.

_____, "Thomas Jefferson and Bills No. 82–86 of the Revision of the Laws of Virginia, 1776–1786: New Light on the Jeffersonian Model of Church-State Relations," *North Carolina Law Review* 69 (1990): 159.

Driggs, Kenneth, "After the Manifesto: Modern Polygamy and Fundamentalist Mormons," *Journal of Church and State* 32 (1990): 367.

Duke, G., *Law of Charitable Uses* (1676), repr. ed., R. W. Bridgman ed. (London, 1805).

Durham, W. Cole, Jr., "Perspectives on Religious Liberty: A Comparative Framework," in *Religious Human Rights in Global Perspective: Legal Perspectives*, ed. Johan D. van der Vyver and John Witte Jr. (The Hague/Boston/London, 1996), 1.

Durham, W. Cole, Jr., Pieter van Dijk, Lauren B. Homer, and John Witte Jr., "The Future of Religious Liberty in Russia: Report of the De Burght Conference on Pending Russian Legislation Restricting Religious Liberty," *Emory International Law Review* 8 (1994): 1.

Dwight, Timothy, "The Duty of Americans at the Present Crisis, Illustrated in a Discourse Preached on the Fourth of July, 1798 (1798)," in *Political Sermons of the American Founding Era, 1730–1805*, ed. Ellis Sandoz (Indianapolis, 1991), 1380.

Eastland, Terry, *Religious Liberty in the Supreme Court: The Cases That Define the Debate over Church and State* (Grand Rapids, MI, 1993).

Ehler, Sidney Z., and John B. Morrall, eds., *Church and State Through the Centuries: A Collection of Historic Documents with Commentaries* (Westminster, MD, 1954).

Eisgruber, Christopher L., "Madison's Wager: Religious Liberty in the Constitutional Order," *Northwestern University Law Review* 89 (1995): 347.

_____, "Unthinking Religious Freedom," *Texas Law Review* 74 (1996): 577.

_____, "Why the Religious Freedom Restoration Act Is Unconstitutional," *New York University Law Review* 69 (1994): 437.

Eisgruber, Christopher L., and Lawrence G. Sager, "Congressional Power and Religious Liberty After *City of Boerne v. Flores*," *Supreme Court Review* (1998): 79.

Elliot, Jonathan, ed., *The Debates in the Several State Conventions, on the Adoption of the Federal Constitution, as Recommended by the General Convention at Philadelphia in 1787*, 4 vols. (Washington, DC, 1854).

Ellul, Jacques, *The Theological Foundation of Law*, trans. Marguerite Weiser (Garden City, NJ, 1960).

Elton, G. R., *The Tudor Constitution*, 2d ed. (Cambridge, 1982).

Epstein, Stephen B., "Rethinking the Constitutionality of Ceremonial Deism," *Columbia Law Review* 96 (1996): 2083.

Esbeck, Carl H., "Government Regulation of Religiously Based Social Services: The First Amendment Considerations," *Hastings Constitutional Law Quarterly* 19 (1992): 343.

_____, "The *Lemon* Test: Should It Be Retained, Reformulated, or Rejected?" *Notre Dame Journal of Law, Ethics, and Public Policy* 4 (1990): 513.

_____, *The Regulation of Religious Organizations as Recipients of Governmental Assistance* (Washington, DC, 1996).

_____, "A Restatement of the Supreme Court's Law of Religious Freedom: Coherence, Conflict, or Chaos?" *Notre Dame Law Journal* 70 (1995): 581.

_____, "Table of United States Supreme Court Decisions Relating to Religious Liberty, 1789–1994," *Journal of Law and Religion* 10 (1994): 573.

Evans, Bette Novit, *Interpreting the Free Exercise of Religion: The Constitution and American Pluralism* (Chapel Hill, NC, 1997).

Evans, Israel, "A Sermon Delivered at Concord, Before the Hon. General Court of the State of New Hampshire at the Annual Election (1791)," in *Political Sermons of the American Founding Era, 1730–1805*, ed. Ellis Sandoz (Indianapolis, 1991), 1057.

Evans, Malcolm D., *Religious Liberty and International Law in Europe* (Cambridge, 1997).

Farrand, Max, ed., *The Records of the Federal Convention of 1787*, 3 vols. (New Haven/London/Oxford, 1911), vol. 4, rev. ed. (New Haven/London/Oxford, 1937).

Fisher, Hugh, *The Divine Right of Private Judgment, Set in a True Light* (1731), repr. ed. (Boston, 1790).

Fleet, Elizabeth, "Madison's 'Detached Memoranda,'" *William and Mary Quarterly*, 3d ser., 3 (1946): 534.

Földesi, Tamas, "The Main Problems of Religious Freedom in Eastern Europe," in *Religious Human Rights in Global Perspective: Legal Perspectives*, ed. Johan D. van der Vyver and John Witte Jr. (The Hague/Boston/London, 1996), 243.

Formicola, Jo Renee, and Hubert Morken, eds., *Everson Revisited: Religion, Education, and Law at the Crossroads* (Lanham, MD, 1997).

Foster, Isaac, *A Defense of Religious Liberty* (Worcester, MA, 1780).

Fowler, Robert Booth, Allen D. Hertzke, and Laura R. Olson, *Religion and Politics in America: Faith, Culture, and Strategic Choices*, 2d ed. (Boulder/Oxford, 1999).

Freeman's Remonstrance Against an Ecclesiastical Establishment (Boston, 1777).

Friedmann, Robert, *The Theology of Anabaptism* (Scottsdale, PA, 1973).

Frost, J. William, *A Perfect Freedom: Religious Liberty in Pennsylvania* (Cambridge, 1990).

Gaffney, Edward M., "Governmental Definition of Religion: The Rise and Fall of the IRS Regulations of an Integrated Auxiliary of a Church," *Valparaiso University Law Review* 25 (1991): 203.

Gamwell, Franklin I., *The Meaning of Religious Freedom: Modern Politics and the Democratic Resolution* (Syracuse, NY, 1995).

Garvey, John H., *What Are Freedoms For?* (Cambridge, MA, 1996).

Gaustad, Edwin S., "Colonial Religion and Liberty of Conscience," in *The Virginia Statute for Religious Freedom: Its Evolution and Consequences in American History*, ed. Merrill D. Peterson and Robert C. Vaughan (Cambridge, 1988), 23.

_____, *The Great Awakening in New England* (Gloucester, MA, 1957).

_____, *Historical Atlas of Religion in America*, rev. ed. (New York/San Francisco, 1976).

———, *Liberty of Conscience: Roger Williams in America* (Grand Rapids, MI, 1991).

_____, *A Religious History of America* (New York, 1966).

Gedicks, Frederick Mark, "The Integrity of Survival: A Mormon Response to Stanley Hauweras," *DePaul Law Review* 42 (1992): 167.

_____, "Public Life and Hostility to Religion," *Virginia Law Review* 78 (1992): 671.

_____, *The Rhetoric of Church and State* (Durham, NC, 1995).

_____, "Toward A Constitutional Jurisprudence of Religious Group Rights," *Wisconsin Law Review* (1989): 99.

_____, "An Unfirm Foundation: The Regrettable Indefensibility of Religious Exemptions," *University of Arkansas Law Journal* 20 (1998): 555.

Gey, Steven G., "Why Is Religion Special: Reconsidering the Accommodation of Religion Under the Religion Clauses of the First Amendment," *University of Pittsburgh Law Review* 52 (1990): 75.

Glendon, Mary Ann, and Raul F. Yanes, "Structural Free Exercise," *Michigan Law Review* 90 (1991): 477.

Glenn, Charles, *The Myth of the Common School* (Amherst, MA, 1978).

Godolphin, John, *Repertorium canonicum, or, An Abridgement of the Ecclesiastical Laws of This Realm, Consistent with the Temporal*, 3d ed. (London, 1687).

Gordon, Sarah Barringer, "The Twin Relic of Barbarism: The Legal History of Anti-Polygamy in Nineteenth-Century America" (Ph.D. Diss., Princeton, 1995).

Gottlieb, Stephen E., "Compelling Governmental Interests: An Essential but Unanalyzed Term in Constitutional Adjudication," *Boston University Law Review* 68 (1988): 917.

_____, ed., *Public Values in Constitutional Law* (Ann Arbor, MI, 1993).

Grashof, L., "Die Gesetzgebung der römischen Kaiser über die Güter und Immunitäten der Kirche und Clerus," in *Archiv für katholische Kirchenrecht* (n.f.) 36 (1876): 3, 321.

Grayzel, Solomon, *The Church and the Jews in the XIIIth Century* (Philadelphia, 1933).

Green, M. Christian, "The 'Matrioshka' Strategy: U.S. Evasion of the Spirit of International Covenant on Civil and Political Rights," *South African Journal of Human Rights* 10 (1994): 357.

Greenawalt, Kent, "Hands Off! Civil Court Involvement in Conflicts over Religious Property," *Columbia Law Review* 98 (1998): 1843–1907.

_____, *Private Consciences and Public Reasons* (New York/Oxford, 1985).

_____, "Religion as a Concept in Constitutional Law," *California Law Review* 72 (1984): 753.

_____, *Religious Convictions and Political Choice* (New York/Oxford, 1988).

_____, "Why Now Is Not the Time for Constitutional Amendment: The Limited Reach of *City of Boerne v. Flores*," *William and Mary Law Review* 39 (1998): 689.

Gregory, David L., "The Role of Religion in the Secular Workplace," *Notre Dame Journal of Law, Ethics, and Public Policy* 4 (1990): 749.

Gressman, Eugene, and Angela C. Carmella, "The RFRA Revision and the Free Exercise Clause," *Ohio State Law Journal* 57 (1996): 65.

Grewe, Wilhelm G., *Fontes Historiae Iuris Gentium* (Berlin, 1988).

Gunn, T. Jeremy, "Adjudicating Rights of Conscience Under the European Convention on Human Rights," in *Religious Human Rights in Global Perspective: Legal Perspectives*, ed. Johan D. van der Vyver and John Witte Jr. (The Hague/Boston/London, 1996), 305.

_____, *A Standard for Repair: The Establishment Clause, Equality, and Natural Rights* (New York/London, 1992).

Hall, David D., *The Antinomian Controversy, 1636–1638*, 2d ed. (Durham, NC, 1968).

Hall, Timothy L., "Religion, Equality, and Difference," *Temple Law Review* 65 (1992): 1.

_____, *Separating Church and State: Roger Williams and Religious Liberty* (Urbana, IL/Chicago, 1998).

Hamburger, Philip A., "A Constitutional Right of Religious Exemption: An Historical Perspective," *George Washington Law Review* 60 (1992): 915.

Hamilton, Marci A., "The Belief/Conduct Paradigm in the Supreme Court's Free Exercise Jurisprudence: A Theological Account of the Failure to Protect Religious Conduct," *Ohio State Law Journal* 54 (1993): 713.

_____, "The Religious Freedom Restoration Act: Letting the Fox into the Henhouse Under Cover of Section 5 of the Fourteenth Amendment," *Cardozo Law Review* 16 (1994): 357.

Hansen, Klaus J., *Mormonism and the American Experience* (Chicago, 1981).

Hatch, Nathan O., *The Democratization of American Christianity* (New Haven, 1989).

_____, *The Sacred Cause of Liberty* (New Haven, 1977).

Heckel, Martin, "The Impact of Religious Rules on Public Life in Germany," in *Religious Human Rights in Global Perspective: Legal Perspectives*, ed. Johan D. van der Vyver and John Witte Jr. (The Hague/Boston/London, 1996), 191.

Hellerstein, J. and W. Hellerstein, *State and Local Taxation*, 5th ed. (St. Paul, 1988).

Helmholz, R. H., *Roman Canon Law in Reformation England* (Cambridge/New York, 1990).

_____, ed., *Canon Law in Protestant Lands* (Berlin, 1992).

Henkin, Louis, "Infallibility Under Law: Constitutional Balancing," *Columbia Law Review* 78 (1978): 1022.

_____, *The International Bill of Rights: The Covenant on Civil and Political Rights* (New York, 1981).

_____, "Rights, American and Human," *Columbia Law Review* 79 (1979): 405.

_____, "U.S. Ratification of Human Rights Conventions: The Ghost of Senator Bricker," *American Journal of International Law* 89 (1995): 341.

Hershberger, Guy, ed., *The Recovery of the Anabaptist Vision* (Scottsdale, PA, 1957).

Hoffman, Ronald, and Peter J. Albert, eds., *Religion in a Revolutionary Age* (Charlottesville, NC/London, 1994).

Holifield, E. Brooks, *The Covenant Sealed: The Development of Puritan Sacramental Theology in Old and New England* (New Haven/London, 1974).

Holmes, Oliver Wendell, Jr., *The Common Law* (Boston, 1881).

How, W. Glen, and Philip Brumley, "Religious Perspectives on Human Rights, Evangelism, and Proselytism: The Jehovah's Witnesses," in *Sharing the Book: Religious Perspectives on the Rights and Wrongs of Mission*, ed. John Witte Jr. and Richard C. Martin (Maryknoll, NY, 1999), chap. 13.

Howe, John R., Jr., *The Changing Political Thought of John Adams* (Princeton, 1966).

Howe, Mark DeWolfe, *Cases on Church and State in the United States* (Cambridge, MA, 1952).

_____, *The Garden and the Wilderness: Religion and the Government in American Constitutional History* (Chicago/London, 1965).

Huber, Wolfgang, *Gerechtigkeit und Recht: Grundlinien christlicher Rechtsethik* (Gütersloh, 1996).

Hunter, James D., and Os Guinness, eds., *Articles of Faith, Articles of Peace: The Religious Liberty Clauses and the American Public Philosophy* (Washington, DC, 1990).

Hutson, James H., "The Creation of the Constitution: The Integrity of the Documentary Record," *Texas Law Review* 65 (1986): 1.

_____, "'A Wall of Separation': FBI Helps Restore Jefferson's Obliterated Draft," in *Library of Congress Information Bulletin* 57 (June 1998): 136.

Hynemann, Charles S., and Donald S. Lutz, eds., *American Political Writing During the Founding Era, 1760–1805*, 2 vols. (Indianapolis, 1983).

Idleman, Scott C., "The Religious Freedom Restoration Act: Pushing the Limits of Legislative Power," *Texas Law Review* 73 (1994): 247.

_____, "The Role of Religious Values in Judicial Decision Making," *Indiana Law Journal* 68 (1993): 433.

Israel, F., ed., *State of the Union Messages of the Presidents, 1790–1966* (New York, 1966).

Israel, Jerold H., "Selective Incorporation Revisited," *Georgia Law Review* 71 (1982): 253.

"James R. Browning Symposium for 1994: The Religious Freedom Restoration Act," *Montana Law Review* 56 (1995): 1–324.

Jefferson, Thomas, *The Complete Jefferson, Containing His Major Writings*, ed. Saul K. Padover (Freeport, NY, 1943).

_____, *The Papers of Thomas Jefferson*, 9 vols., ed. Julian Boyd (Princeton, 1950).

_____, *The Works of Thomas Jefferson*, 12 vols., ed. P. L. Ford (New York, 1904–1905).

Johnson, Luke Timothy, "Religious Rights and Christian Texts," in *Religious Human Rights in Global Perspective: Religious Perspectives*, ed. John Witte Jr. and Johan D. van der Vyver (The Hague/Boston/London, 1996), 65.

Johnson, Samuel, *A Dictionary of the English Language*, 4th ed. (London, 1773).

Jones, G., *History of the Law of Charity, 1532–1827* (London, 1969).

Jones, Richard H., "Accommodationist and Separatist Ideals in Supreme Court Establishment Clause Decisions," *Journal of Church and State* 28 (1986): 193.

Journal of the First Session of the United States of America (New York, 1789) (Evans, First Series, No. 22207).

Journals of the Continental Congress, 1774–1789, 34 vols., ed. Worthing C. Ford et al. (Washington, DC, 1904–1937).

Kamen, Henry, *The Rise of Toleration* (New York, 1967).

Katz, Wilber G., "Freedom of Religion and State Neutrality," *University of Chicago Law Review* 20 (1953): 426.

_____, *Religion and American Constitutions* (Evanston, IL, 1963).

Kaufman, Natalie H., and David Whiteman, "Opposition to Human Rights Treaties in the United States Senate: The Legacy of the Bricker Amendment," *Human Rights Quarterly* 10 (1988): 309.

Kauper, Paul G., "The Constitutionality of Tax Exemptions for Religious Activities," in *The Wall Between Church and State*, ed. Dallin H. Oaks (Chicago, 1963), 95.

Kauper, Paul G., and Stephen B. Ellis, "Religious Corporations and the Law," *Michigan Law Review* 71 (1973): 1499.

Kelley, Dean M., *Why Churches Should Not Pay Taxes* (New York, 1977).

Kelsay, John, and Sumner B. Twiss, eds., *Religion and Human Rights* (New York, 1994).

Kessler, Sanford, "Locke's Influence on Jefferson's 'Bill for Establishing Religious Freedom,'" *Journal of Church and State* 25 (1983): 231.

Kiss, Alexandre C., "Permissible Limitations on Rights," in *The International Bill of Rights: The Covenant on Civil and Political Rights*, ed. Louis Henkin (New York, 1981), 290.

Klaassen, Walter, ed., *Anabaptism in Outline: Selected Primary Sources* (Scottsdale, PA, 1981).

Kossmann, E. H., and A. Mellink, eds. *Texts Concerning the Revolt of the Netherlands* (London/New York, 1974).

Kramnick, Isaac, and R. Laurence Moore, *The Godless Constitution: The Case Against Religious Correctness* (New York/London, 1996).

Kurland, Philip B., *Religion and the Law: Of Church, State and the Supreme Court* (Chicago, 1962).

Kurland, Philip B., and Ralph S. Lerner, eds., *The Founders' Constitution*, 5 vols. (Chicago, 1987).

Kurtz, Jerome, "Difficult Definitional Problems in Tax Administration: Religion and Race," *Catholic Lawyer* 23 (1978): 301.

Lactantius, *De Mortibus Persecutorum* [c. 315], J. L. Creed, ed. and trans. (Oxford, 1984).

Larson, M., and C. Lowell, *Praise the Lord for Tax Exemption: How the Churches Grow Rich While the Cities and You Grow Poor* (Washington, DC, 1969).

Lash, Kurt T., "The Second Adoption of the Free Exercise Clause: Religious Exemptions Under the Fourteenth Amendment," *Northwestern University Law Review* 88 (1994): 1106.

Lathorp, John, A *Discourse on the Peace* (Boston, 1784).

Laycock, Douglas, "The Benefits of the Establishment Clause," *DePaul Law Review* 42 (1992): 373.

_____, "Formal, Substantive, and Disaggregated Neutrality Toward Religion," *DePaul Law Review* 39 (1990): 993.

_____, "'Non-Coercive' Support for Religion: Another False Claim About the Establishment Clause," *Valparaiso University Law Review* 26 (1991): 37.

_____, "'Nonpreferential' Aid to Religion: A False Claim About Original Intent," *William and Mary Law Review* 27 (1986): 875.

_____, "Religious Liberty as Liberty," *Journal of Contemporary Legal Studies* 7 (1996): 313–356.

_____, "The Remnants of Free Exercise," *Supreme Court Review* (1991): 1.

_____, "Summary and Synthesis: The Crisis in Religious Liberty," *George Washington Law Review* 60 (1992): 841.

———, "Toward a General Theory of the Religion Clauses: The Case of Church Labor Relations and the Right to Church Autonomy," *Columbia Law Review* 81 (1981): 1373.

Laycock, Douglas, and Oliver S. Thomas, "Interpreting the Religious Freedom Restoration Act," *Texas Law Review* 73 (1994): 209.

Lecler, Joseph, *Toleration and the Reformation*, 4 vols. (New York, 1960).

Lecler, Joseph, and Marius-François Valkhoff, *Les premiers défenseurs de la liberté religieuse*, 2 vols. (Paris, 1969).

Leland, John, *The Writings of the Late Elder John Leland* (New York, 1845).

———, "The Yankee Spy (1794)," in *American Political Writing During the Founding Era, 1760–1805*, 2 vols., ed. Charles S. Hynemann and Donald S. Lutz (Indianapolis, 1983), 2:971.

Lerner, Natan, *Group Rights and Discrimination in International Law* (Dordrecht, 1991).

———, "Religious Human Rights Under the United Nations," in *Religious Human Rights in Global Perspective: Legal Perspectives*, ed. Johan D. van der Vyver and John Witte Jr. (The Hague/Boston/London, 1996), 79.

Levy, Leonard W., *The Establishment Clause: Religion and the First Amendment* (New York, 1986).

Linder, Amnon, *The Jews in Roman Imperial Legislation* (Detroit, 1987).

Locke, John, *Epistola de Tolerantia* (Gouda, 1689).

———, *The Works of John Locke*, 12th ed., 9 vols. (London, 1824).

Loewy, Arnold H., *Religion and the Constitution: Cases and Materials* (St. Paul, 1999).

Lupu, Ira C., "The Failure of RFRA," *University of Arkansas Law Journal* 20 (1998): 575.

———, "The Lingering Death of Separationism," *George Washington Law Review* 62 (1994): 230–279.

———, "Where Rights Begin: The Problem of Burdens on the Free Exercise of Religion," *Harvard Law Review* 102 (1989): 933.

Luther, Martin, *Three Treatises*, 2d rev. ed. (Philadelphia, 1986).

Lutz, Donald S., *The Origins of American Constitutionalism* (Baton Rouge, LA/London, 1988).

Lutz, Heinrich, ed., *Zur Geschichte der Toleranz und Religionsfreiheit* (Darmstadt, 1977).

Mack, Eugen, *Die kirchliche Steuerfreiheit in Deutschland seit der Dekretalengesetzgebung*, repr. ed. (Aalen, 1965).

Madison, James, *Letters and Other Writings of James Madison*, 4 vols. (New York, 1884).

———, *The Papers of James Madison*, ed. W. T. Hutchinson, William M. E. Rachal, and Robert A. Rutland (Chicago, 1962).

———, *The Papers of James Madison: The Presidential Series*, ed. Robert A. Rutland (Charlottesville, VA, 1984).

———, *The Papers of James Madison: Secretary of State Series*, ed. Robert J. Brugger et al. (Charlottesville, VA, 1984).

———, *The Writings of James Madison*, 9 vols., ed. G. Hunt (New York, 1900–1910).

Maffly-Kipp, Laurie F., *Religion and Society in Frontier California* (New Haven/London, 1994).

Malbin, Michael J., *Religion and Politics: The Intentions of the Authors of the First Amendment* (Washington, DC, 1978).

Manual of Religious Liberty, 3d ed. (New York, 1767).

Marini, Stephen A., "Religion, Politics, and Ratification," in *Religion in a Revolutionary Age*, ed. Ronald Hoffman and Peter J. Albert (Charlottesville, NC/London, 1994), 184.

Marshall, William P., "The Case Against the Constitutionally Compelled Free Exercise Exemption," *Case Western Reserve University Law Review* 40 (1990): 357.

_____, "Solving the Free Exercise Dilemma: Free Exercise as Expression," *Minnesota Law Review* 67 (1983): 545.

Marty, Martin E., *Advancing the Conversation: Public Religion, Government, and Politics* (Chicago, 1999).

_____, "On a Medial Moraine: Religious Dimensions of American Constitutionalism," *Emory Law Journal* 39 (1990): 9.

_____, *Pilgrims in Their Own Land* (Harmondsworth, UK, 1985).

_____, "Revising the Map of American Religion," *Annals of the American Academy of Political and Social Science* 558 (July 1998): 13.

May, Henry, *The Enlightenment in America* (New York, 1976).

McCarthy, Rockne M., James W. Skillen, and William A. Harper, *Disestablishment a Second Time: Genuine Pluralism for American Schools* (Grand Rapids, MI, 1982).

McConnell, Michael W., "Accommodation of Religion," *Supreme Court Review* (1985): 1.

_____, "Accommodation of Religion: An Update and a Response to the Critics," *George Washington Law Review* 60 (1992): 685.

_____, "Coercion: The Lost Element of Establishment," *William and Mary Law Review* 27 (1986): 933.

_____, "Equal Treatment and Religious Discrimination," in *Equal Treatment of Religion in a Pluralistic Society*, ed. Stephen V. Monsma and J. Christopher Soper (Grand Rapids, MI, 1998), 30.

_____, "Free Exercise Revisionism and the *Smith* Decision," *University of Chicago Law Review* 57 (1990): 1109.

_____, "Institutions and Interpretations: A Critique of *City of Boerne v. Flores*," *Harvard Law Review* 111 (1997): 153.

_____, "The Origins and Historical Understanding of Free Exercise of Religion," *Harvard Law Review* 103 (1990): 1409.

_____, "Religious Freedom at a Crossroads," *University of Chicago Law Review* 59 (1992): 115.

McConnell, Michael W., and Richard A. Posner, "An Economic Approach to Issues of Religious Freedom," *University of Chicago Law Review* 56 (1989): 1.

McKeen, Joseph, *Sermon Preached on the Public Fast in the Commonwealth of Massachusetts* (Boston, 1793).

McLoughlin, William G., *New England Dissent, 1630–1833*, 2 vols. (Cambridge, MA, 1971).

_____, *Soul Liberty: The Baptists' Struggle in New England, 1630–1833* (Providence, RI, 1991).

McWilliams, W. C., *The Idea of Fraternity in America* (Berkeley, 1973).

Mead, Sidney E., *The Lively Experiment: The Shaping of Christianity in America* (New York, 1963).

_____, "Neither Church nor State: Reflections on James Madison's 'Line of Separation,'" *Journal of Church and State* 10 (1968): 349.

Mellen, John, *The Great and Happy Doctrine of Liberty* (Boston, 1795).

Meyer, Alfred W., "The Blaine Amendment and the Bill of Rights," *Harvard Law Review* 64 (1951): 939.

Meyer, Jacob C., *Church and State in Massachusetts from 1740–1833*, repr. ed. (New York, 1968).

Miller, H., *The Legal Foundations of American Philanthropy* (Madison, WI, 1969).

Miller, Perry, and Thomas Johnson, *The Puritans* (New York, 1938).

Miller, Robert T., and Ronald B. Flowers, eds., *Toward Benevolent Neutrality: Church, State, and the Supreme Court*, 5th ed., 2 vols. (Waco, TX, 1996).

Miller, William Lee, *The First Liberty: Religion and the American Republic* (New York, 1986).

Mitchell, Joshua, "John Locke: A Theology of Religious Liberty," in *Religious Liberty in Western Thought*, ed. Noel B. Reynolds and W. Cole Durham Jr. (Atlanta, 1996), 143.

Mode, Peter G., *The Frontier Spirit in American Christianity* (New York, 1923).

Monsma, Stephen V., and J. Christopher Soper, eds., *Equal Treatment of Religion in a Pluralistic Society* (Grand Rapids, MI, 1998).

Morgan, Edmund S., *Puritan Political Ideas, 1558–1794* (Indianapolis, 1965).

_____, *Roger Williams: The Church and the State* (New York, 1967).

Morgan, Robert J., *James Madison on the Constitution and the Bill of Rights* (New York, 1988).

Morris, C., *The Discovery of the Individual, 1050–1200* (London, 1972).

Morrisson, Clovis C., Jr., "Margin of Appreciation in European Human Rights Law," *Revue des droits de l'Homme* 6 (1973): 263.

Morton, J., *Exempting the Churches: An Argument for the Abolition of this Unjust and Unconstitutional Practice* (New York, 1915).

Mutua, Makau wa, "Limitations on Religious Rights: Problematizing Religious Freedom in the African Context," in *Religious Human Rights in Global Perspective: Legal Perspectives*, ed. Johan D. van der Vyver and John Witte Jr. (The Hague/Boston/London, 1996), 417.

Neumann, Gerald, "The Global Dimension of RFRA," *Constitutional Commentary* 14 (1997): 33.

Noll, Mark A., Nathan O. Hatch, and George M. Marsden, *The Search for Christian America*, rev. ed. (Colorado Springs, 1989).

Noonan, John T., Jr., *The Believer and the Powers That Are: Cases, History, and Other Data Bearing on the Relation of Religion and Government* (New York/London, 1987).

———, "How Sincere Do You Have to Be to Be Religious?" *University of Illinois Law Review* (1988): 713.

———, *The Lustre of Our Country: The American Experience of Religious Freedom* (Berkeley/Los Angeles/London, 1998).

———, "The Tensions and the Ideals," in *Religious Human Rights in Global Perspective: Legal Perspectives*, ed. Johan D. van der Vyver and John Witte Jr. (The Hague/Boston/London, 1996), 593.

Nowak, John E., and Ronald D. Rotunda, *Constitutional Law*, 5th ed. (St. Paul, 1995).

Oakes, Uriah, *New England Pleaded with, and Pressed to Consider the Things Which Concern Her* (Boston, 1673).

Oaks, Dallin H., ed., *The Wall Between Church and State* (Chicago, 1963).

Oaks, Dallin H., and Lance B. Wickman, "The Mission Work of the Church of Jesus Christ of Latter Day Saints," in *Sharing the Book: Religious Perspectives on the Rights and Wrongs of Mission*, ed. John Witte Jr. and Richard C. Martin (Maryknoll, NY, 1999), chap. 12.

Oberholzer, Emil, *Delinquent Saints: Disciplinary Actions in the Early Congregational Churches of Massachusetts* (New York, 1956).

O'Brien, F. William, "The Blaine Amendment, 1875–1876," *University of Detroit Law Journal* 41 (1963): 137–205.

———, "The States and 'No Establishment': Proposed Amendments to the Constitution Since 1789," *Washburn Law Journal* 4 (1965): 183.

Ong, B. N., "James Madison on Constitutional Interpretation," *Benchmark* 3 (1987): 18.

Otto, Rudolf, *The Idea of the Holy: An Inquiry into the Non-Rational Factor of the Idea of the Divine and Its Relation to the Rational*, 2d ed. (New York, 1950).

Paine, Thomas, *The Complete Writings of Thomas Paine*, ed. P. S. Foner (New York, 1945).

Palladium of Conscience, or, The Foundation of Religious Liberty Displayed, Asserted and Established, Agreeable to its True and Genuine Principles (Philadelphia, 1773).

Parkes, James, *The Jew in the Medieval Community: A Study of His Political and Economic Situation*, 2d ed. (New York, 1976).

Parsons, Jonathan, *Freedom from Civil and Ecclesiastical Slavery* (Newburyport, RI, 1774).

Partsch, Karl Josef, "Freedom of Conscience and Expression and Political Freedoms," in *The International Bill of Rights: The Covenant on Civil and Political Rights*, ed. Louis Henkin (New York, 1981), 209.

Payson, Phillips, "Election Sermon of 1778," in *American Political Writing During the Founding Era, 1760–1805*, 2 vols., ed. Charles S. Hynemann and Donald S. Lutz (Indianapolis, 1983), 523.

Perry, William, *The Royal Standard English Dictionary*, 1st Am. ed. (Worcester, MA, 1788).

Penn, William, *The Works of William Penn*, 2 vols. (London, 1726).

Pepper, Stephen, "Taking the Free Exercise Clause Seriously," *Brigham Young University Law Review* (1986): 299.

Perry, Michael J., *Religion and Politics* (Oxford, 1997).

Peterson, Merrill D., and Robert C. Vaughan, eds., *The Virginia Statute for Religious Freedom: Its Evolution and Consequences in American History* (Cambridge, 1988).

Pfeffer, Leo, *Church, State, and Freedom* (Boston, 1953), rev. ed. (Boston, 1967).

_____, *God, Caesar, and the Constitution: The Court as Referee in Church-State Confrontation* (Boston, 1975).

Plumstead, W., ed., *The Wall and the Garden: Selected Massachusetts Election Sermons, 1670–1775* (Minneapolis, 1968).

Pomeroy, J., *A Treatise on Equity Jurisprudence as Administered in the United States of America*, 5th ed. (San Francisco, 1941).

Poppel, Stuart D., "Federalism, Fundamental Fairness, and the Religion Clauses," *Cumberland Law Review* 25 (1995): 247.

Powell, H. Jefferson, *The Moral Tradition of American Constitutionalism: A Theological Interpretation* (Durham, NC, 1993).

Quincy, J., *Tax Exemption: No Excuse for Spoliation* (n.p, n.d.) (pamphlet in Widener Library, Harvard University).

Rachanow, Shelly S., "The Effect of *O'Lone v. Estate of Shabazz* on the Free Exercise Rights of Prisoners," *Journal of Church and State* 40 (1998): 125.

Rahe, Paul, *Republics Ancient and Modern* (Chapel Hill, NC, 1992).

Rakove, Jack N., "Fidelity Through History (or to It)," *Fordham Law Review* 65 (1997): 1587–1609.

_____, *Original Meanings: Politics and Ideas in the Making of the Constitution* (New York, 1996).

Ramsey, Paul, *Basic Christian Ethics* (New York, 1950).

Redman, Barbara J., "Sabbatarian Accommodation in the Supreme Court," *Journal of Church and State* 33 (1991): 495.

Reichley, A. James, *Religion in American Public Life* (Washington, DC, 1985).

Reid, Charles J., "Rights in Thirteenth-Century Canon Law: A Historical Investigation" (Ph.D. Diss. Cornell, 1994).

Reynolds, Laurie, "Zoning the Church: The Police Power Versus the First Amendment," *Boston University Law Review* 64 (1985): 767.

Reynolds, Noel B., and W. Cole Durham Jr., eds., *Religious Liberty in Western Thought* (Atlanta, 1996).

Roan, Michael, "The Role of Secular Non-Governmental Organizations in the Cultivation and Understanding of Religious Human Rights," in *Religious Human Rights in Global Perspective: Legal Perspectives,* ed. Johan D. van der Vyver and John Witte Jr. (The Hague/Boston/London, 1996), 135.

Robertson, D., *Should Churches be Taxed?* (Philadelphia, 1968).

Rohrer, James R., *Keepers of the Covenant: Frontier Missions and the Decline of Congregationalism* (New York/Oxford, 1995).

Rossiter, Clinton, *The Political Thought of the American Revolution* (New York, 1963).

Rossiter, Clinton, ed., *Federalist Papers: Alexander Hamilton, James Madison, John Jay* (New York, 1961).

Rubenfeld, Jeb, "Antidisestablishmentarianism: Why RFRA Was Really Unconstitutional," *Michigan Law Review* 95 (1997): 2347.

Sandler, S. Gerald, "Lockean Ideas in Thomas Jefferson's Bill for Establishing Religious Freedom," *Journal of the History of Ideas* 21 (1960): 110.

Sandoz, Ellis, ed., *Political Sermons of the American Founding Era, 1730–1805* (Indianapolis, 1991).

_____, "Religious Liberty and Religion in the American Founding Revisited," in *Religious Liberty in Western Thought*, ed. Noel B. Reynolds and W. Cole Durham Jr. (Atlanta, 1996).

Schaff, Philip, *Church and State in the United States, or the American Idea of Religious Liberty and Its Practical Effects* (New York, 1888).

Schochet, Gordon J., "The Act of Toleration and the Failure of Comprehension: Persecution, Nonconformity, and Religious Indifference," in *The World of William and Mary*, ed. Dale Hoak and Mordechai Feingold (Stanford, 1996).

Schwarz, Karl, "Der Begriff Exercitium Religionis Privatum," *Zeitschrift der Savigny-Stiftung (Kan. Ab.)* 105 (1988): 495.

Shain, Barry, *The Myth of American Individualism: The Protestant Origins of American Political Thought* (Princeton, 1994).

Shannon, James P., *Catholic Colonization on the Western Frontier* (New Haven, 1957).

Shapiro, Barbara, "Sir Francis Bacon and the Mid-Seventeenth Century Movement for Law Reform," *American Journal of Legal History* 24 (1980): 331.

Sheridan, Thomas, *A Complete Dictionary of the English Language*, 2d ed. (London, 1789).

Shipps, Jan, *Mormonism: The Story of a New Religious Tradition* (Urbana, IL, 1984).

Sigmund, Paul E., *Religious Freedom and Evangelization in Latin America: The Challenge of Religious Pluralism* (Maryknoll, NY, 1999).

_____, "Religious Human Rights in Latin America," in *Religious Human Rights in Global Perspective: Legal Perspectives*, ed. Johan D. van der Vyver and John Witte Jr. (The Hague/Boston/London, 1996), 467.

Simson, Gary J., "The Establishment Clause in the Supreme Court: Rethinking the Court's Approach," *Cornell Law Review* 72 (1987): 905.

Sirico, Louis, "Church Property Disputes: Churches as Secular and Alien Institutions," *Fordham Law Review* 55 (1986): 335.

Slye, Terry L., "Rendering Unto Caesar: Defining 'Religion' for Purposes of Administering Religion-Based Tax Exemptions," *Harvard Journal of Law and Public Policy* 6 (1983): 219.

Smith, Michael E., "The Special Place of Religion in the Constitution," *Supreme Court Review* (1983): 83.

Smith, Rodney K., "Converting the Religious Equality Amendment into a Statute with a Little 'Conscience,'" *Brigham Young University Law Review* (1996): 644.

_____, "Getting Off on the Wrong Foot and Back on Again: A Reexamination of the History of the Framing of the First Amendment and a Critique of the *Reynolds* and *Everson* Decisions," *Wake Forest Law Review* 20 (1984): 569.

_____, *Public Prayer and the Constitution: A Case Study in Constitutional Interpretation* (Wilmington, DE, 1987).

Smith, Steven D., *Foreordained Failure: The Quest for a Constitutional Principle of Religious Freedom* (New York/Oxford, 1995).

———, "The Rise and Fall of Religious Freedom in Constitutional Discourse," *University of Pennsylvania Law Review* 140 (1991): 149.

———, "Symbols, Perceptions, and Doctrinal Illusions: Establishment Neutrality and the 'No Endorsement' Test," *Michigan Law Review* 86 (1987): 266.

Snodgrass, Mary Ellen, *Encyclopedia of Frontier Literature* (Santa Barbara/Denver/Oxford, 1997).

Sohn, Louis B., *The Human Rights Movement: From Roosevelt's Four Freedoms to the Interdependence of Peace, Development, and Human Rights* (New York, 1982).

Sperry, W., *Religion in America* (Cambridge, 1963).

Stackhouse, Max L., and Deirdre King Hainsworth, "Deciding for God: The Right to Convert in Protestant Perspectives," in *Sharing the Book: Religious Perspectives on the Rights and Wrongs of Mission*, ed. John Witte Jr. and Richard C. Martin (Maryknoll, NY, 1999), chap. 8.

Stephenson, Carl, and Frederick G. Marcham, eds., *Sources of English Constitutional History*, rev. ed. (New York/San Francisco, 1972).

Stewart, David P., "United States Ratification of the Covenant on Civil and Political Rights: The Significance of the Reservations, Understandings, and Declarations," *DePaul Law Review* 42 (1993): 1183.

Stiles, Ezra, *The United States Elevated to Glory and Honor* (New Haven, 1783).

Stimson, Claude W., "The Exemption of Property from Taxation in the United States," *Minnesota Law Review* 18 (1934): 411.

Stokes, Anson P., *Church and State in the United States*, 3 vols. (New York, 1950).

Stokes, Anson P., and Leo Pfeffer, *Church and State in the United States*, rev. ed. (Westport, CT, 1975).

Stone, Geoffrey R., et al., *Constitutional Law*, 3d ed. (Boston/New York/London, 1996).

Storing, Herbert J., ed., *The Anti-Federalist* (Chicago, 1985).

Story, Joseph, *Commentaries on the Constitution*, 3 vols. (Boston, 1833), 2d ed. (Boston, 1851).

Stout, Harry S., *The New England Soul: Preaching and Religious Culture in Colonial New England* (New York/Oxford, 1986).

Strong, Nathan, *Election Sermon* (New Haven, 1790).

Sullivan, Donna J., "Advancing the Freedom of Religion or Belief Through the UN Declaration on the Elimination of Religious Intolerance and Discrimination," *American Journal of International Law* 82 (1988): 487.

Sullivan, Kathleen M., "Categorization, Balancing, and Government Interests," in *Public Values in Constitutional Law*, ed. Stephen E. Gottlieb (Ann Arbor, MI, 1993), 241.

Sullivan, Winnifred Fallers, *Paying the Words Extra: Religious Discourse in the Supreme Court of the United States* (Cambridge, MA, 1994).

Sute, Jeri Nazary, "Reviving RFRA: Congressional Use of Treaty-Implementing Powers to Protect Religious Exercise Rights," *Emory International Law Review* 12 (1999): 1535.

Sweet, William W., *Religion in the Development of American Culture, 1765–1840* (New York, 1952).

Swidler, Leonard, ed., *Religious Liberty and Human Rights in Nations and Religions* (Philadelphia, 1986).

Symposium, "Church Tax Exemptions," *Cumberland Law Review* 22 (1992): 467–680.

Symposium, "Confronting the Wall of Separation," *DePaul Law Review* 42 (1992): 1–397.

Symposium, "Does Religious Freedom Have a Future? The First Amendment After *Boerne*," *Nexus: A Journal of Opinion* 2 (1997): 1–172.

Symposium, "Reflections on *City of Boerne v. Flores*," *William and Mary Law Review* 39 (1998): 601–960.

Symposium, "The Relevance of Religion to a Lawyer's Work: An Interfaith Conference," *Fordham Law Review* 66 (1998): 1075–1651.

Symposium, "Religion and the Judicial Process: Legal, Ethical, and Empirical Dimensions," *Marquette Law Review* 81 (1998): 177–568.

Symposium, "The Religion Clauses of the Constitution," *Notre Dame Journal of Law, Ethics, and Public Policy* 4 (1990): 385–934.

Symposium, "Soul Wars: The Problem of Proselytism in Russia," *Emory International Law Review* 12 (1998): 1–738.

"Symposium on the Williamsburg Charter," *Journal of Law and Religion* 8 (1990): 1–396.

Tahzib, Bahiyyih G., *Freedom of Religion or Belief: Ensuring Effective International Legal Protection* (The Hague/Boston/London, 1996).

Tarr, G. Alan, "Church and States in the States," *Washington Law Review* 64 (1989): 73.

Theodosian Code and Novels, and the Sirmondian Constitutions, trans. Clyde Pharr (Princeton, 1952).

Thomas, Oliver S., "The Power to Destroy: The Eroding Constitutional Arguments for Church Tax Exemptions and the Practical Effect on Churches," *Cumberland Law Review* 22 (1991): 605.

Thornton, J. W., ed., *The Pulpit of the American Revolution* (Boston, 1860).

Thorpe, Francis, ed., *The Federal and State Constitutions, Colonial Charters, and Other Organic Laws*, 7 vols. (Washington, DC, 1909).

Tierney, Brian,, *The Crisis of Church and State, 1050–1300* (Englewood Cliffs, NJ, 1964).

_____, *The Idea of Natural Rights: Studies on Natural Rights, Natural Law, and Church Law, 1150–1625* (Atlanta, 1997).

_____, "Religious Rights: A Historical Perspective," in *Religious Human Rights in Global Perspective: Religious Perspectives*, ed. John Witte Jr. and Johan D. van der Vyver (The Hague/Boston/London, 1996), 17.

_____, *Rights, Law, and Infallibility in Medieval Thought* (Aldershot, UK, 1997).

Timling, Marion, "Thomas Lloyd's Reports of the First Federal Congress," *William and Mary Quarterly*, 3d ser. 18 (1961): 519.

Titus, Herbert W., "No Taxation or Subsidization: Two Indispensable Principles of Religious Freedom," *Cumberland Law Review* 22 (1992): 505.

Trott, Nicholas, *The Laws of the British Plantations in America, Relating to the Church and the Clergy, Religion and Learning* (London, 1725).

Tuttle, Robert W., "A Treason of the Clerks: Paul Ramsey on Christian Ethics and the Common Law" (Ph.D. Diss., University of Virginia, 1997).

Tyler, R., *American Ecclesiastical Law* (Albany, 1866).

van Alstyne, Arvo, "Tax Exemption of Church Property," *Ohio State Law Journal* 20 (1959): 461.

van Alstyne, William, "The Failure of the Religious Freedom Restoration Act Under Section 5 of the Fourteenth Amendment," *Duke Law Journal* 46 (1996): 291.

van der Vyver, Johan D., "Universality and Relativism of Human Rights: American Relativism," *Buffalo Human Rights Law Review* 4 (1998): 43.

van der Vyver, Johan D., and John Witte Jr., eds., *Religious Human Rights in Global Perspective: Legal Perspectives* (The Hague/Boston/London, 1996).

Waite, Jason M., "*Agostini v. Felton:* Thickening the Establishment Clause Stew," *New England Law Review* 33 (1998): 80.

Walker, Williston, ed., *The Creeds and Platforms of Congregationalism* (New York, 1960).

Ward, Nathaniel, *The Simple Cobler of Aggawam in America*, 5th ed. (Boston, 1713).

Washington, George, *George Washington on Religious Liberty and Mutual Understanding: Selections from Washington's Letters,* ed. Edward F. Humphrey (Washington, DC, 1932).

_____, *The Writings of George Washington from the Original Manuscript Sources, 1745–1799,* ed. J. C. Fitzpatrick, 39 vols. (Washington, DC, 1931).

Weber, Paul J., "James Madison and Religious Equality," *Review of Politics* 44 (1982): 163.

Weisbrod, Carol, "Commentary on Curry and Firmage Articles," *Journal of Law and Religion* 7 (1989): 315.

West, Ellis, "The Right to Religion-Based Exemptions in Early America: The Case of Conscientious Objectors to Conscription," *Journal of Law and Religion* 10 (1994): 367.

Whitehead, John W., "Tax Exemption for Religious Organizations, A Historical and Constitutional Analysis," *Cumberland Law Review* 22 (1991): 521.

Willard, Samuel, *Covenant-Keeping the Way to Blessedness* (Boston, 1682).

_____, *Morality Not to Be Relied on for Life* (Boston, 1700).

_____, *Walking with God* (Boston, 1701).

Williams, Elisha, *The Essential Rights and Liberties of Protestants: A Seasonable Plea for the Liberty of Conscience, and the Right of Private Judgment in Matters of Religion, Without Any Controul from Human Authority* (Boston, 1744).

Williams, George H., *The Radical Reformation*, 3d ed. (Kirksville, MO, 1992).

Williams, Robert F., *State Constitutional Law*, 2d ed. (Washington, DC, 1993).

Williams, Roger, *The Complete Writings of Roger Williams*, 7 vols. (New York, 1963).

Williamsburg Charter: A National Celebration of the First Amendment Religious Liberty Clauses (Washington, DC, 1988).

Wilson, James, *The Works of James Wilson*, 2 vols., ed. R. G. McCloskey (Cambridge, 1967).

Wilson, John K., "Religion Under the State Constitutions, 1776–1800," *Journal of Church and State* 32 (1990): 753.

Winchester, Elhanan, "A Century Sermon on the Glorious Revolution (London, 1788)," in *Political Sermons of the American Founding Era, 1730–1805*, ed. Ellis Sandoz (Indianapolis, 1991), 969.

Witte, John, Jr., "Blest Be the Ties That Bind: Covenant and Community in Puritan Thought," *Emory Law Journal* 36 (1987): 579.

———, "The Essential Rights and Liberties of Religion in the American Constitutional Experiment," *Notre Dame Law Review* 71 (1996): 371.

———, "How to Govern a City on the Hill: The Early Puritan Contribution to American Constitutionalism," *Emory Law Journal* 39 (1990): 41.

———, "The Integration of Religious Liberty," *Michigan Law Review* 90 (1992): 1363.

———, *Law and Protestantism: The Legal Teachings of the Lutheran Reformation* (Cambridge, 2000).

———, "Law, Religion, and Human Rights," *Columbia Human Rights Law Review* 28 (1996): 1.

———, "Moderate Religious Liberty in the Theology of John Calvin," *Calvin Theological Journal* 31 (1996): 359.

———, "'A Most Mild and Equitable Establishment of Religion': John Adams and the Massachusetts Experiment," *Journal of Church and State* 41 (1999): 213.

———, "Tax Exemption of Church Property: Historical Anomaly or Valid Constitutional Practice?" *Southern California Law Review* 64 (1991): 363.

———, "Whether Piety or Charity: Classification Issues in the Exemption of Churches and Charities from Property Taxation," in *Religion, the Independent Sector, and American Culture*, ed. Conrad Cherry and Rowland A. Sherrill (Atlanta, 1992), 137.

———, ed., *Christianity and Democracy in Global Context* (Boulder/San Francisco/London, 1993).

Witte, John, Jr., and Johan D. van der Vyver, eds., *Religious Human Rights in Global Perspective: Religious Perspectives* (The Hague/Boston/London, 1996).

Witte, John, Jr., and Richard C. Martin, eds., *Sharing the Book: Religious Perspectives on the Rights and Wrongs of Mission* (Maryknoll, NY, 1999).

Wolter, Udo, *Ius canonicum in iure civile* (Köln, 1975).

Wood, Gordon S., *The Creation of the American Republic, 1776–1787* (New York, 1969).

Wood, James E., Jr., "An Apologia for Religious Human Rights" in *Religious Human Rights in Global Perspective: Religious Perspectives*, , ed. John Witte Jr. and Johan D. van der Vyver (The Hague/Boston/London, 1996), 455.

———, *The First Freedom: Religion and the Bill of Rights* (Waco, TX, 1990).

———, ed., *Taxation and the Free Exercise of Religion* (Washington, DC, 1978).

"Worcestriensis, Number IV (1776)," in *American Political Writing During the Founding Era, 1760–1805*, 2 vols., ed. Charles S. Hynemann and Donald S. Lutz (Indianapolis, 1983), 1:449.

Wortman, Tunis, "A Solemn Address to Christians and Patriots (New York, 1800)," in *Political Sermons of the American Founding Era, 1730–1805*, ed. Ellis Sandoz (Indianapolis, 1991), 1477.

Zollman, Carl, *American Church Law*, repr. ed. (St. Paul, MN, 1933).

INDEX